CONTENTS

THE
DOON VALLEY
DOWN THE AGES

THE
DOON VALLEY
DOWN THE AGES

PREM HARI HAR LAL

INTERPRINT

First Published in 1993 by
INTERPRINT
16-A, Naraina II, New Delhi-110 028, India

ISBN: 81-85017-64-6
Price: Rs. 240/-
© PREM HARI HAR LAL 1993

COVER: SATELLITE IMAGERY OF THE GARHWAL REGION

Printed at Mehta Offset Works, New Delhi, INDIA.

PREFACE

This narrative is the result of my labour of love for the Doon Valley where I was born. My family has been in Dehra Dun since 1867 when my grandfather came, from Landhaura near Roorkee as the "Bakshi" (Tax Superintendent) to the Dehra Dun municipality on its formation in that year. My mother, who was a scholar of sorts of Tulsi's Ramayan, would tell us stories from this great epic before putting us children to bed. One of the stories which I later found intriguing was of Bhagirath taking the waters of the Ganga down to the Bay of Bengal. On one of my shooting trips in the forests, across the Ganga at Haridwar, I chanced to look up towards the Siwaliks. Lo! what did I see - a gap in them with straight sides which appear as if made by some gigantic human effort as opposed to the natural course taken by the Yamuna through the same hills. This picture stayed in my mind for years. On my retirement, from being a corporate executive, in 1982, I started looking around for reference material on the Doon. The result of my researches is this book. I hope it will be of interest to the general reader and to the people of the Doon in particular. It is not a history but is based on the material available and from which I have quoted extensively. Working on the book has given me a lot of pleasure, satisfaction, occupation and a sense of achievement as no one has attempted such a work, on the Doon, before.

One of the reasons for my quoting from old writings on the Valley is that these books are mostly over a hundred years old, and out of print. Unfortunately in 1947 as a result of the influx of refugees from Pakistan and the Europeans leaving the Doon overnight most of the old records were lost. I have had to request some of my English and American friends for providing Xerox copies of written material, on the Doon, in their possession. One such person is Major R.S.W. Bell a descendent of one of the Swetenham daughters. He is now settled in Portugal. He provided the excerpts from Fanny Parks' book.

Frances Susanna Parks was a first cousin of Major Edmund Swetenham who had married the native hill-girl who had captivated his heart by her singing and brought the Cloud End estate in her dowry. The 'my fair friend' referred to by Fanny Parks is Mrs. Swetenham and "my relation" is Major Swetenham. Fanny Parks nee 'Archer arrived in India in 1822 and married C.C. Parks of the Bengal Civil Service. He was District Magistrate, Allahabad and Kanpur before his death in 1854. A marble tablet is embedded in one of the walls of the Kanpur District Magistrate's bungalow on which is inscribed the fact that Fanny Parks stayed in that house. I hope the reader will enjoy reading this book as much as I have in writing it.

Lastly I must thank all my friends and well wishers who have encouraged me in writing this book and given their valuable suggestions and comments. Apart from Major Bell I am specially thankful to the late Peter Versteegh and F.W. Hilwig from Holland, William Hudson from the United States and M.A.R. Skinner, Prof. K.C. Sahni, Mrs. Priyo Kapur, Dr. R.S. Rawat, His Holiness Indresh Charan Das Mahant of Gurudwara of Guru Ram Rai, Pandit Amar Dev Semwal, Major M.C. Sharma I.A.S. Abhai Singh, Chandu Mhatre, Prakash Narula and my two typist friends Sardar Autar Singh and Ravinder Singh who have done all the typing of the manuscript.

My special thanks to Mehta Offset Works, New Delhi, my printers and my nephew Mr. Ashok Jain for their help in bringing out this volume.

Dehra Dun.   PREM HARI HAR LAL
1993.

Dūn, Doon or Dhoon, in the Sanskrit and Hindi languages means a "Valley" which has not been made by river erosion but is formed by Tectonic activity within the earth that causes movements of its crust, as earthquakes, folds, faults or the like. The Oxford Dictionary defines it as "Valley in Shiwalik Hills". There are a number of valleys large and small between the sub-Himalaya and the Shiwalik hills. This is a tale of one of the largest and the best known of them all - the "Valley of the Doon", administratively and commonly known as the District of Dehra Dun in the North-West part of the Indian State of Uttar Pradesh.

The Doon Valley proper is situated between Latitude 30°-30° 32' and Longitude 77°43'-78° 24'. It is nearly 75 kms. long from North-West to South-East and 25 kms. broad from the North-East to South-West. The geographical boundaries are the Himalayas in the North, the Shiwaliks in the South and the rivers Ganga in the East and Yamuna in the West. Since the fortunes of this tract of land have been interlinked with the surrounding areas of Himachal, Haryana and Garhwal regions ever since the Valley has existed, parts of the history of those regions have to be included in this study. The areas to be so included are today's administrative districts of Tehri, Pauri, Bijnor, Saharanpur, Ambala, Sirmur and the Mussoorie and Chakrata Sub-divisions of Dehra Dun district.

In order to appreciate the creation of this Valley a reconciliation has to take place, in the reader's mind between the palaeohistory of the area and Hindu mythology.

According to the sage Ved Vyas, the author of Bhagwat Mahapuraan, the time scale, as calculated before him for human beings is as follows—

He says that one year in the life of a human is equivalent to one day in the life of the gods. In other words their one year is equal to 360 human years. Since the creation of the earth and human life thereon man has passed through 26 different cycles each one consisting of four eras. At present he is passing through the last era of the 27th cycle. The four eras are the *Satyug, Treta, Dwapar* and *Kalyug* which are supposed to be the golden, silver, copper and iron ages of man, when starting from the sublimal he degenerates to the basest man at the end of the last era. The number of human years these eras last are 1,728,000, 1,296,000, 864,000 and 432,000 respectively. So far only 5,000 years of the present *Kalyug* era have passed out of its life of 432 thousand years.

When an era comes to an end human civilisation perishes, and the few survivors start from scratch whether in the same place or in some other part. This has been witnessed at the end of the Ramayan and Mahabharat sagas. The incidents narrated in these two epics are supposed to have taken place at the end of the last *Treta* and *Dwapar* eras. The modern historian has accepted that the Mahabharat took place 5,000 years ago which coincides with the beginning of the present *Kalyug*.

1

The story of Bhagirath's project of taking the Ganga waters to the plains, as a consequence of which dry land appeared in the Doon, should have occurred in the last *Treta Yug* (era), since he was an ancestor of Ram. This would place the time around 1,200 thousand years ago or earlier.

Ramapithicus, the earliest Indian man-like creature whose fossil remnants have been discovered so far, is supposed to have lived in the Shiwaliks 150 million years ago. It can therefore be safely assumed that subsequent to those times a substantial human population existed in the plains of India. These people were subjected to repeated droughts and as a consequence to famines. This led to their quest for a perennial source of water for irrigation. Whether these people were Aryans or not is immaterial.

Water - one of the five essential elements for the survival of animal and plant life on this planet Earth has been deified by the Hindu philosophers, in their scriptures such as "The Ganga". The river Ganga has been deified as it symbolises man's first success in harnessing the waters from the melting snows of the Himalayas.

Valmiki has described the creation of the Himalayas and the descent of the Ganga waters to the plains in his epic *"Ramayan"* in an allegorical form. He says that the Ganga travels in three different directions and is therefore called "Tripathgamini" in the *Puraans*. The three directions are the Celestial, Terrestrial and Subterranean. It also means the three forms of water namely solid, liquid and gas or ice, water and steam. His story is in three parts corresponding to the three directions mentioned above.

The Celestial part of Valmiki's description has been faithfully translated by Mr. Griffith, the Englishman, who translated the four Veds into English in 1889. His translation of the Ganga's story is as follows—

"Thus urged, the sage recounted both
The birth of Ganga and her growth:
The mighty hill with metals stored
Himalaya, is the mountains' Lord:
The father of a lovely pair
Of daughters, fairest of the fair:
Their mother, offspring of the will
Of Meru, everlasting hill,
Mena Himalaya's darling graced
With beauty of her dainty waist.
Ganga was elder born: then came
The fair one known by Uma's name.
Then all the gods of heaven, in need
Of Ganga's help their vows to speed,
To great Himalaya came and prayed
The mountain king to yield the maid.
He, not regardless of the weal
Of the three worlds, with holy zeal
His daughter to the Immortals gave,

2

Ganga whose waters cleanse and save,
Who roams at pleasure, fair and free,
Purging all sinners, to the sea.
The three-pathed Ganga thus obtained,
The gods their heavenly homes regained.
Long time the sister Uma passed
In vows austere and rigid fast,
And the king gave the devotee
Immortal Rudra's bride to be,
Matching with that unequalled Lord
His Uma through the worlds adored.
So now a glorious station fills
Each daughter of the king of hills:
One honoured as the noblest stream,
One mid the goddesses supreme.
Thus Ganga, King Himalaya's child,
The heavenly river, undefiled,
Rose bearing with her to the sky
Her waves that bless and purify.''

The second part of Valmiki's narrative of how the Ganga became terrestrial can be translated as follows—

In the days gone by after the Lord of Lords, Mahadev (another name of Lord Shiv), having married Himalaya's daughter Uma, proceeded to consummate the marriage. A hundred years elapsed in copulation and yet Uma did not conceive. On seeing this Brahma and the other gods started to dissuade the couple from further intercourse. The gods feared that in case, after such a prolonged union between Rudra (Shiv) and Uma a son is born then no one will be able to stand up to him.

The gods therefore beseeched Mahadev to cease his cosmic sex, and keeping the good of all in mind withhold his seminal ejaculation and let the fluid remain within himself.

Shiv agreed to the request and said that Uma and he would try and contain it within themselves. However he asked of the gods, that in case he was unable to do so, on reaching his orgasm then who will accept the discharged fluid?

The gods answered that in that case Earth would accept it. Thereupon Shiv ejaculated and the mountains and trees - nay the whole earth was covered with his sperm.

The gods asked the Fire God to collect the sperm with the aid of the Wind God, and to keep it within the Fire. As fire did so, the whole mountain turned white and a forest of Sarkanda reeds *(Saccharum munja)* grew - the flowers of which are like sperm floating in the air.

The Fire God then asked Ganga to absorb within herself the floating sperm which she did, but was unable to keep her own fertilised ovum resulting from this interpenetration. She asked those present as to how she could relieve herself of this pregnancy. The Fire God told her to deliver the foetus on the leeward side of the Himalaya mountain chain. The boy thus delivered was named Kartikeya, the son of Shiv. The earth where the foetus was delivered turned into burnished gold and its surroundings into silver. The distant geographical areas turned to copper and iron. The placenta etc. of the foetus turned into zinc, lead and other metals.

The above narrative is an allegorical description of the geological formation of the Himalaya - how the union of fire and water in the bowels of the earth results in volcanic and tectonic activity thereby creating mountains, valleys, minerals and metals. The orgasmic release of the male and female union, in other words, the energy released by the union of fire and water inside the earth has given rise to the Himalaya mountain chain with its snows, rivers, valleys and minerals.

The naughty side of this story is that Shiv committed adultery with his sister-in-law Ganga, and kept her hidden in his tresses, away from Uma's sight. When Uma found out he let Ganga go with Bhagirath - the man who brought her to the plains of India.

Another interpretation of the story can be that because Uma could not carry a child for the full period of pregnancy the fertilized ovum was implanted in her sister Ganga. The child so born named Kartikeya is known as the son of Shiv and Parvati (Uma) and not of Shiv and Ganga.

The story of how Shiv assumed the form of the "Linga" to be worshipped by humans runs as follows:

One day the Lord Brahma (Creator) and the Lord Vishnu (Preserver) accompanied by the seven sages (Sapt Rishis, who now reside in the heavens, having become the constellation - the Great Bear), went to Mount Kailash to pay a visit to the third member of their Trinity, the Lord Shiv (Destroyer). Kailash is Shiv's personal abode and the visitors surprised him when he was busy copulating with Durga (Parvati). Neither Shiv nor Durga turned a hair and carried on with their love making. At the sight of them the gods, especially Vishnu, burst out laughing. But the sages, instead of taking it all in good humour, were deeply shocked and angry. They heaped their insults and curses on Shiv: "Thou art a devil and worse than a devil; Be accursed; Let no virtuous person henceforth have any dealings with Thee"; and so on. After pronouncing these curses the sages went off in a huff taking Brahma and Vishnu with them.

Shiv and Durga (Parvati) must have been in such a state of intoxicated abandon that they did not quite realise who their visitors had been, nor that they had been so cursed. But, later, during a lull when they returned to their senses, they questioned their guards and the truth broke upon them like a thunderclap. Thereupon the two died of mortification, in the position that the gods and the sages had seen them.

Shiv saw at once what he must do and set about doing it. First he proclaimed that the act that had so covered them with shame and caused their death should from then on be celebrated throughout mankind. 'My shame has killed me,' he announced, but it has also given me a new life - and a new shape; It is the shape of my Linga; I ordain that humans shall worship it and make sacrifice to it'. Whereupon he listed the benefits that would accrue to those who model it in mud, or stone (the benefits being seven times), or silver (when they would be seven times seven), or gold (seven times cubed). He added, 'Nor shall they ever behold the Prince of Darkness; Embrace the worship

4

of my "Linga". It is white and has three eyes and five faces. It is arrayed in a Tiger's skin....it disperses our terrors and our fears and grants us the object of all our desires'

Thus the worship of the "Linga" (The Phallus) came about as a symbol of procreation since Vedic times.

How Bhagirath brought the River Ganga to the plains of India is told by Vishwamitra to Lord Ram, when he saw the river for the first time and asked about its creation. The tale as told by Vishwamitra according to Valmiki's Ramayan, is as follows—

Once upon a time, an ancestor of Ram named Sagur ruled at Ayodhya. Inspite of having two wives he had no child. Like all humans they were keen on procreating and kept hoping for a son. Raja Sagur's wives were Keshni, who was a princess from Vidharba and Sumati, who was the daughter of the sage Arishtnami Kashyap and sister to Garuda, the mythical bird and aerial transport of Lord Vishnu.

In his attempts to have a child, the Raja and his two Ranis went to Himalaya to pray and meditate at the ashram or monastery of the sage Bhrigu. The sage on seeing their prayers and devotion, prophesied the birth of many sons to them. He told Sagur that one of his wives will give birth to only one son and the other to 60,000 sons. On hearing this the two Ranis asked the sage as to which one of them will have one son and who will have 60,000.

In reply the sage asked them as to who would like one son who would carry on the family name, and who would like 60,000 strong, brave and enterprising sons.

Keshni opted for only one son and Sumati got the blessing of becoming the mother to 60,000 sons.

In the course of time Keshni gave birth to a son, who was named Asumajh. The junior Rani Sumati delivered a gourd like foetus. On opening it 60,000 boys came out. These 60,000 boys were kept in earthen pots filled with Ghee (clarified butter) and were breast fed by wet nurses. (The earthen pots with ghee must have been incubators to keep the weaklings alive.)

On the boys reaching adolescence, the eldest son Asumajh turned out to be a sadist. He would bully and ill-treat the children of the town by throwing them in the river and when they started drowning he would laugh and enjoy himself. When Sagur could no longer control Asumajh's behaviour he banished him from the kingdom.

Asumajh in time had a son named Anshumaan, who was a soft spoken, well behaved lad and a favourite of his grandfather.

Sagur decided to hold an "Ashwamedh Yagya" or horse sacrifice, wherein a specially consecrated horse was set free to roam at will, for a year, followed by a group of the owner's troops. Kings and Chiefs on whose territory the horse roamed were to either pay homage to its owner or fight him by capturing it. If it was not captured by anyone in his wanderings then on returning home it was sacrificed. After all preparations were made towards this end Anshumaan was entrusted with the safe keeping of the horse. The belief went that once a ruler had successfully completed the 'Yagya' he became invincible. This made the other rulers, both in heaven and on earth jealous of such successes. The Yagya was being held in the middle of the plain of Aryavart (the land of the Aryans) or the Indo-Gangetic Plain. The Himalaya and Vindhya mountains had an unobstructed view of each other and in the middle was the plain of Hindustan.

On the final day before the ceremonies could be completed - Indra, the Rain God, disguised as a Demon, stole the sacrificial horse. Without the horse the Yagya and its connected rituals came to a halt. The priests present told Sagur that till the horse was found nothing further could be done. Thereupon Sagur ordered his 60,000 sons to search for the horse by dividing the earth into 60,000 equal parts and each son thoroughly searching one part.

The 60,000 Princes having failed to locate the animal started digging and ploughing every bit of the land. In the process they killed all the creatures that live and thrive underground. On seeing this destruction of the earth's subterranean animal life, the other mortals approached Brahma and beseeched him to stop this wanton destroying of life.

Brahma told them that this earth has been ploughed, dug, drilled and ill used by man in every age. When the human population grows beyond the supporting capacity of this earth the population dies out. Therefore these 60,000 sons who are ill treating the earth will be destroryed by the wrath of Kapil who is none other than the Almighty himself.

The 60,000 having searched, from Vindhyas in the South, Aravallis in the West to Shiwaliks in the North, in vain moved towards the East in search of the horse. This time they saw the sage Kapil in his ashram and spotted their horse grazing nearby. In their anger they ran forward cursing and accusing the sage for stealing their horse. The sage being innocent of the crime got so angry with his accusers that he killed them all by burning them.

A lot of time having elapsed, since the departure of the 60,000, Raja Sagur asked his grandson Anshumaan to go and look for his uncles. He followed the routes taken by them and finally arrived at the spot where he saw them lying as a heap of ashes and the horse grazing nearby. After overcoming his grief on their death, he looked around for water to offer it to their spirits so that they could achieve salvation. He searched for water, far and wide but could not find any. He spotted Garuda, the maternal uncle of the 60,000, who was flying overhead. Garuda came down and told Anshumaan, that in the death of his uncles lies the salvation of mankind. They have died at the hands of Kapil Muni, and it is not fit that their ashes be sprinkled with ordinary water to enable them to achieve salvation. It is only when these ashes are sprinkled with the water of Himalaya's daughter Ganga, will their spirits go to heaven.

Anshumaan was told to go back with the horse and complete his grandfather's "Yagya." Anshumaan on his return informed Sagur of what had transpired. After the ceremonies were over Raja Sagur started contemplating on bringing down the waters of the Ganga to the plain from the land of the gods. Unable to find a solution to the problem of bringing the waters down Raja Sagur eventually passed away after having ruled for 30,000 years.

Raja Sagur was succeeded to the throne by Anshumaan who also unsuccessfully tried to bring down the Ganga for 32,000 years. He abdicated the throne in favour of his son Dalip whose rule lasted another 30,000 years. All of them had failed in their endeavours to bring the Ganga waters to the plain.

6

Bhagirath, Dalip's son on succeeding his father also took up the Ganga water project. Although he could have stayed at home and worked on the problem, yet for the good of his people he left home, leaving the reins of his kingdom to his ministers and devoted himself completely to the project. In order to achieve his goal he went into the Shiwalik and the Himalaya mountains, where after a thousand years of meditation and prayers, he was inspired by Brahma to request Shiv to hold the waters of the Ganga when they fall from the sky and to regulate their flow so that the plains are not flooded by their sudden release.

For a whole year Bhagirath prayed to Shiv to come to his aid and regulate the flow of the Ganga waters. Shiv agreed to the request and said that he would let the waters fall on his forehead and thus break the fall and avoid flooding. When Ganga was told of this arrangement she was thrilled. She thought that by falling on Shiv's head she would be able to drag him, with the momentum of her fall and take him down with her to the sea and thence go underground with him. Shiv on learning of her intentions, decided to make her invisible so that she would lose her identity. When she fell on his head, which looked like the Himalaya, she got entangled in the tresses and could not reach the ground. Having been caught thus in Shiva's matted locks of hair was stuck there for years, and was unable to find a way to flow out. Bhagirath once again had to beseech Shiv to free her. Shiv then placed her in the Bindu Sarover (lake). Once placed in the lake the waters started flowing in seven different channels.

Wahdini, Pavini and Nalini started flowing in the easterly direction, whilst Suchuckshu, Sita and Sindhu went in the westerly direction. The seventh stream - the Ganga started following the path of Bhagirath's chariot. It was in this manner that the Ganga waters fell from the sky, on Shiv's head and then descended on earth. The waters flowing on the ground through the mountain terrain, over ridges and valleys created water falls and streams, at places raging torrents, at places placid, at places meandering, at places striking against boulders and creating sprays and rainbows.

On the route of Ganga's flow to the plain the mighty king Jahnu was performing 'Yagna' when the waters washed away his holy fire. The king thought that Ganga had done this out of pride. He got so enraged that he drank up the waters. The people who were following Ganga's progress to the plain were upset at this action. They beseeched King Jahnu with folded hands and bended knees to free Ganga, and for doing so he would be called her father. The king, thus pacified let the waters flow out of his ear - hence, another name for Ganga is Jahnvi.

Once again the waters followed the path of Bhagirath's chariot and reached the sea, and helped Bhagirath's 60,000 ancestors achieve salvation. Having thus mixed with the waters of the sea Ganga lost her identity and went underground.

Brahma told Bhagirath that since he had brought the Ganga to the plains she would be known as his daughter too. Hence Jahnvi, Tripathga, Divya (Divine) and Bhagirathi are all names of the Ganga whose waters purify all sinners of their sins.

The subterranean flow of the Ganga is represented by the underground streams, flowing under the earth.

According to geologists the Himalaya mountain building activity of the earth's crust started in the late Tertiary era and is still continuing. As per their deductions the rivers of Himalaya are older than the mountains themselves. A system of drainage, in which the main channels flowed, was in existence before the present features of the region were impressed on it. Many great changes have taken place in the Himalaya since the Tertiary times. These changes have, in fact, produced a complete reversal of the direction of the flow of the main rivers.

According to the two geologists, Pilgrim and Pascoe, in prehistoric times a great river flowed from the East to the West, South of the Himalaya chain and North of the Shiwaliks from Assam to the receding Miocene Sea of Sind (Pakistan). This river was named the "Siwalik River" by Pilgrim. Pascoe called it the "Indo-Bramh" because at one time it carried the discharge of the present Brahmaputra, Ganga-Yamuna and Indus. This coincides with the description of the seven channels of the Ganga mentioned by Valmiki in the Ramayan. The creation of the Shiwaliks is now ascribed to the flood plain deposits of this river. After the main uplift of the Himalaya chain this river is supposed to have drained the remnants of the Himalaya Sea sometime between the early Miocene and the end of the Pliocene periods. The Shiwaliks have been built up in three different strata namely lower, middle and upper during the middle Miocene to the end of Pliocene periods. The Shiwalik system which forms the foothills of the Himalaya mountain run from the Indus to the Brahmaputra rivers. These hills are given this name because of the Shiwalik hills near Haridwar where they were first known to modern historians and where the first palaeontological finds were made.

The tectonic movements in N.W. Punjab (now in Pakistan) broke up the course of the "Siwalik River" into three river systems; (1) the present Indus, (2) the five Punjab tributaries of the Indus and (3) the Ganga-Brahmaputra system. As far as the river Yamuna is concerned there is evidence, both physical and historical, that during early times it flowed into the Indus system through the now dried up bed of the "Saraswati" river of the Puraans. Yamuna's course in the South-Easterly direction is recent. (During the Mahabharat period river traffic existed between Mathura, Indraprastha and Dwarka - the kingdom of Krishna). According to the Journal of the Geological Society (IX P 348, 1863), the mythical Saraswati river in Vedic times flowed to the sea through Punjab and Rajasthan, in a channel that is now occupied by an insignificant stream which loses itself in the sands of the Bikaner desert. In the course of time the Yamuna took a more easterly course and ultimately merged into the Ganga at Allahabad.

The following report appeared in the Times of India dated 11th December, 1987 regarding the Saraswati which throws new light on the subject.

BURIED RIVER BASIN TRACED IN RAJASTHAN

"New Delhi, December 10 (UNI).

The ancient Saraswati, which the Vedas refer to as a mighty river of north-west India, still flows through a subterranean channel below the deserts of Rajasthan and could provide a solution for the region's water problem.

A team of scientists of the Central Arid Zone Research Institute in Jodhpur, headed by ICAR emeritus geomorphologist, Mr. Bimal Ghose, which had discovered the course of the Saraswati in 1979, has now mapped the entire Saraswati river basin.

"More than 30 tubewells have been dug in these areas and these are yielding 2,000 to 40,000 litres every hour and these could provide a perennial supply of water for the dry areas of Rajasthan and Gujarat," Mr. Ghose said in a recent report.

"In fact if all these wells were operated simultaneously, the entire area would be flooded in 24 hours"; the report says, "of a dry expanse that has faced repeated droughts in this decade."

"Although this river system is dead in Rajasthan, there are underground links with catchments in Himalayan glaciers and the Soviet-melt water still flows abundantly through these buried channels. This subterraneous flow has never been influenced by drought and climatic extremities typical of arid Rajasthan."

"The Vedic Saraswati could thus be a perennial and a dependable source of fresh water," the report concludes.

"These findings are the culmination of almost a decade of research that in 1979 led to the discovery of the course of the Saraswati. Climatic and terrestrial changes had caused the Saraswati to change course more than five times in the north-western parts of India bordering Pakistan.

The Saraswati had once flowed from the Shiwalik Himalayas to the now dry Kutch district of Gujarat, where it had for centuries met another ancient river - the Luni.

During the course of this research, the team of scientists from CAZRI also established that the Satadru of the Sutlej had once emptied into the Saraswati.

Aerial photographs and landsat imagery were extensively used for correct identification of these channels, which were then verified by field experiments."

The Journal of the Royal Geological Society (Vol. XL, 1870) states that according to the records of 3rd century B.C. the Indus flowed more than 130 kms. to the east of its present course, through the now practically dry bed of a deserted channel, to the Rann of Kutch, which was then a gulf of the Arabian Sea. Maj. C.F. Oldham in his article in the Calcutta Review (1847) states that an old river bed more than 1000 kms. in length is traceable from Ambala, at the foot of the Himalayas, through Bhatinda, Bikaner and Bahawalpur to Sind. This river is known as Hakra, Sotra (Ghaggar) or Wahind and is the channel of a lost river, probably the Saraswati (the Yamuna when it was a tributary of the Indus), at a time when it and the Sutlej flowed independently of the Indus to the Rann of Kutch. This was during the Pliocene period.

From the foregoing references it can be deduced that (a) the Ganga and the Yamuna were originally a part and parcel of the 'Siwalik River' which was flowing from Assam to Sind, (b) their flow was between the Himalayas and the Shiwaliks, and (c) on the breaking-up of the Siwalik River, Ganga was the first one to be diverted from its old course to the present one and the Yamuna changed course much later. However both the rivers have been flowing in their original courses through the Himalayas.

The lithology of the Shiwaliks suggests their origin. They are chiefly the water worn debris of the granitic core of the central Himalaya, deposited in the long and broad valley of the "Siwalik" river. The rounded stones and boulders embedded in their layers point towards this theory.

Valleys are of two types, according to their origin (i) Tectonic or original valleys, and (ii) Erosion valleys.

The valleys of Kashmir, Nepal and the "Duns" of Himachal and Uttar Pradesh including the Doon Valley, are examples of tectonic valleys.

One of the features of the Mussoorie range of the Himalaya, is the extinct volcano popularly known as "Gun Hill". Situated as it is, approximately half way along the length of the Doon Valley, it must have played an important role in the formation of the valley and the subsequent topographical changes in its bed. It is also well known that the Doon is in the earthquake belt. As a result of earthquakes the valley floor has been rising. The last noticeable effect of such a change was after the Kangra earthquake of April 1905.

This earthquake had two linear epicentra namely Kangra-Kulu and Mussoorie-Dehra Dun. The result of it was that the Doon Valley and the surrounding Shiwalik Hills showed a rise of 30 cms. in relation to the height of Mussoorie. There is the possibility that when the original course of the old "Siwalik River" broke up the Ganga continued to flow westwards and emptied out, with the Yamuna, into the Arabian Sea. The other probability is that the Doon Valley may have become a lake, which was being fed by the Ganga and Yamuna and the surplus waters draining through the channel of the latter. It could be that much later, after another tectonic change and because of the geological fault in the Shiwaliks at Haridwar that the Ganga broke through and started flowing in its present course. The watershed of the two rivers, in the Doon, runs roughly from Asarori, base of the Shiwaliks to Rajpur at the base of the Mussoorie range. This is roughly in line with "Gun Hill". This theorisation is further substantiated by the presence of the large clay and silt deposits in Amwala near Dehra Dun town, thickening of sediment in the central part of the valley, and poorly preserved deltaic like sediments at the mouth of the rivers when they reach the basin particularly in the Eastern Doon. The presence of "Jheels" or large ponds at Jogiwala, Gosainwala and Sahaspur as mentioned by Williams, marshy and water-logged areas near Doiwala, Chidarwala and other parts of the Doon are also typical of lake basins.

By going back to the account of the creation of the Ganga as given in the Ramayan it would be worthwhile to correlate the points made therein with the present day knowledge of the scientist. This should be done without getting into any controversies regarding the historical dating of the Epic or the existence of its human characters in point of time. These and other scientific queries are best left to more qualified persons. However, one point that is certain is that the great poet Valmiki either had access to scientific data which was lost and which today's scientist is trying to discover or his imagination was super human to be able to give the various descriptions. Even the Veds do not contain such descriptions or at least they are not known so far.

In the episode of Raja Sagur's sixty thousand and one sons it can be seen how one son is enough to continue the family line whereas 60,000 may not be able to do so. It could be an indirect hint to the people of those times to practice family planning. The perishing of the 60,000 could allude to death by starvation as a result of famine on account of drought. The Indian sub-continent, particularly the plains, are subject to droughts resulting in the failure of crops and thereby creating famine in the land. The 60,000 in search of the horse, ploughed and dug up every inch of the land. This means that the land was so heavily populated that every available inch of it was cultivated and yet in the absence of irrigation the produce was not enough to feed the people.

Raja Sagur on being told by Anshumaan about the plight of his uncles and Garuda's remedy for their salvation, realised that unless a permanent arrangement could be made for irrigating the land for agriculture, his people will continue to die of hunger. To-day's geologist claims that there was no river system between the Himalaya and the

10

Vindhyas on the one hand and the Aravallis and the Assam hills on the other. The "Siwalik River" was flowing above the great plain which was cut off by the Shiwaliks. Therefore agriculture depended mainly on rain water. Thus 'Project Ganga' was born in the mind of man. He strived for it for 92,000 years through successive generations before his efforts bore fruit.

Possibly within this span of 92,000 years the course of the great "Siwalik River" may have broken up into the three river systems mentioned earlier. The Ganga may still have been flowing westward, having been entrapped in the Doon Valley, because of the Shiwaliks.

Bhagirath, perhaps one of the greatest engineers mankind has known, was able to bring the waters of the Ganga to the plains. (In the 19th century A.D., Cautley the Englishman, though on a much smaller scale, repeated Bhagirath's performance by making the Ganga Canal from Haridwar to Kanpur).

The utterance of 'Garuda' to Anshumaan about bringing the waters of the Ganga can be explained as the findings of an aerial survey that may have been carried out. In this survey it may have been noticed that a lake existed in the Doon Valley and the tapping of its waters could be a source of perennial supply of water to the parched plains. It should not be forgotten that 'Garuda' is the mythical bird which is the transport of the Almighty Vishnu himself. The ancestors of Bhagirath were unable to find a way out for draining the waters of this lake. His having gone to the inner Himalayas and having spend 1001 years in trying to obtain the water of the Ganga can well mean that it took a lot of time to survey the land over which Ganga's tributaries flowed and to discover the hydraulics of the system. Having once charted the river system and its flow into the Doon, he was then beset with the problem of cutting through the Shiwaliks without starting a deluge. The various persons, who have been involved in all these efforts represent MAN and his quest for water over different periods in time.

Jahnu who is supposed to have swallowed the waters and let them flow out of his ear could have been the person who collaborated with Bhagirath in making a passage through the Shiwaliks for the waters to flow. Jahnu may have been a ballistics engineer and mining expert who blasted the Shiwaliks at Haridwar. In the Rig Ved Jahnu is mentioned as a great seer who started the family of Kausikas who were the favoured worshippers of the Ashvins the two horsemen—Twin Heralds of Dawn. The river Ganga is also called Jahnvi or daughter of Jahnu, just as she is called Bhagirthi or the daughter of Bhagirath. To-day only the longest tributary of the Ganga upto Devprayag is called the Bhagirathi, which flows from Gaumukh, or the snout of the Gangotri glacier, at the foot of Mount Kailash, the abode of Shiv-Parvati. It is the Alaknanda which has the rivers arising from Kedarnath, Badrinath, Hemkund, Homkund and Pindar glaciers as its affluents. It is only after Devprayag that the river is called the Ganga. This river gets the waters of the largest drainage area of the mid-Himalaya and has a discharge more than the Yamuna.

In order to further elaborate and give credence to the Jahnu episode, in the journey of the Ganga waters to the plains, a bird's eyeview of the Doon shows that the outline of the Valley is like the outer human ear. (See map.).

11

A study of the map shows that while the Yamuna flows out of the Shiwaliks in a serpentine course following their contours, the Ganga, at Haridwar, cuts straight across them. The cut in the Shiwaliks is at their narrowest width between the right bank of the Song river and the mouth of the Ganga going into the plain. The Chandi hill is longitudinal in its situation, and the Motichur range of Shiwalik is laterally placed thus forming a neck of a funnel through which the water flows into the plains. Their maximum height at this point is also comparatively low. The height of Chandi hill is 1900 ft., and that of the Kankhal gorge is 1500 ft. Another feature to be kept in mind is that the Shiwaliks at this point merge with the main Himalayas whereas at the Yamuna end they carry on to form the Paonta/Pinjore or the Kyarda Dun. The height of the Ganga bed at Haridwar is 935 feet above sea level and the two hills come down to 1000 ft. at the points where the river flows through them.

It should not be forgotten that according to the geologists the Yamuna, after the creation of the Ganga, was still flowing westwards as a tributary of the now dried up Saraswati river. It was only after the disappearance of the Saraswati that the Yamuna changed its course and became a tributary of the Ganga.

The mythical ashram of Kapil Muni was supposed to be at what is now called 'Sagar Island'. This is situated in the "Sunder Bans" area of Bengal, below Calcutta, at the mouth of the Hooghly river. A festival is held there annually on January 14, the Makar Sankranti day, to celebrate the salvation of Sagur's sons.

With this background it can be safely assumed that between Bhagirath and Jahnu they were able to bring the snow fed waters of the Ganga to the parched Indo-Gangetic plain.

The fossils obtained from the base of the Shiwaliks at Haridwar in 1839 A.D. were the earliest to be found in this region. They were discovered by Cautley when he was digging the course of his famous Ganga canal. These petrified remains of the vertebrate fauna belong to the species of mammals that lived in the jungles and swamps on the slopes of these hills. They were the immediate ancestors of our modern species of land mammals. The great interest which these discoveries aroused is evident from the following description by Dr. Mantell:—

"Where gullies and fissures expose the section of the beds, abundance of fossil bones appear, lignite and trunks of dicotyledonous trees occur, a few land and fresh water shells of existing species are the only vestiges of mollusca that have been observed. Remains of several species of river-fish have been obtained. The remains of elephants and of mastodontoid animals comprise perfect specimens of skulls and jaws of gigantic size. The tusks of an elephant are 2.895 meters in length and 68 cms. in circumference at the base. This collection is invested with the highest interest not only on account of the number of the variety of the specimens, but also from the extraordinary assemblage of the animals which it represents. In the sub-Himalayas we have, entombed in the same rocky sepulchre, bones of the most ancient extinct species of mammalia with species and genera which still inhabit India : Eleuro-gale, Hyaenodan, Dinotheria, mastodons, elephants, giraffes hippopotami, rhinoceroses, horses, camels, antelopes, monkeys, struthious bird and corocodilian and chelonian reptiles. Among these mammalian relics

12

of the past are the skulls and bones of an animal named Sivatherium that requires a passing notice. This creature forms, as it were, a link between the ruminants and the large pachyderms. It was larger than rhinoceros, had four horns, and was furnished with a proboscis, thus combining the horns of a ruminant with the characters of a pachyderm. Among the reptilian remains are skulls and bones of a gigantic crocodile and of a land turtle which cannot be distinguished from those of species now living in India. But the most extraordinary discovery is that of bones and portions of the carapace of a tortoise of gigantic dimensions, having a length of nearly 20 ft. It has aptly been named the COLOSSOCHELYS ATLAS.''

The existence of earliest Man, in the Shiwaliks, is substantiated by the discovery of fossils of the creature named "Ramapithecus". He is supposed to have inhabited this area during the Miocene era 15,000,000 years ago.

Many factors must have helped in the development of such a rich fauna consisting of herbivores, carnivores, rodents and most important of all the primates - MAN. The presence of abundant food supply by a rich vegetation, which flourished in profusion under genial climate, in a land watered by many rivers and lakes must have been the most prominent of these.

At the Calcutta museum there is a special gallery named the 'Shiwalik Gallery' which houses the representative fossils discovered in the Shiwaliks from Cautley's time onward.

The Archezoic era of geology was 1,500,000,000 to 5,000,000,000 - fifteen hundred million to five thousand million years ago when the earth's crust was formed and unicellular living organisms appeared. So far, scientists have not been able to fix the time of Man's first appearance on earth. The Hindu time scale mentioned earlier gives an idea of human existence on this planet. According to this calendar Man has been inhabiting it for the past 116,640,000 years. During these years he has been almost obliterated due to wars and calamities but has managed to survive 26 times. Till such time as it can be proved otherwise there is no reason to discard this dating of Man's existence on earth.

Once this dating is accepted by the reader there is no reason why it can not also be accepted that Man, during one of the 27 eras was able to create the river Ganga by draining the waters from the Doon Valley. After all existence of the mythical Saraswati river is now scientifically established and historians have started accepting the Mahabharat period as a part of historic reality. Similarly one day they may start treating the Ramayan and all that is mentioned therein a part of ancient Indian history.

Ever since Man started walking upright he has inhabited this area, first on the highlands and then, once it became dry land, on the valley floor itself.

The prehistoric conditions prevailing in the Doon can be gleaned from the Vedic, Puraanic, Smritis, Shrutis, Epics, poems and allied writings as well as local folklore.

From the very beginning the political, cultural, ethnical, economical and administrative conditions in the Doon Valley were governed by the people inhabiting the Ganga and Yamuna valleys and their catchment areas in the mountains.

It is now generally held that the earliest traces of human beings in the Doon Valley and its surroundings belong to the end of the first Inter-glacial period and the beginning of the second Ice Age. This will be about 5,00,000 years ago or the Palaeolithic era. The stone implements found around Haridwar (Bahadarabad on the Ganga Canal) and from the Yamuna valley near Kalsi (in 1960-61 A.D.) point out that this valley had man inhabiting it from the very beginning. These quartzite artifacts are preserved by the Archaeological department of the Government of India. The Scrapers discovered near Haridwar are identical to those discovered in the Soan valley of Punjab and the Narmada and Godavari river basins.

At the same spot copper spears, harpoons, rings and other artifacts have been found pointing out to the existence of man in these areas. Since no records of a direct nature exist with regard to the history of the Doon Valley one has to refer to ancient Indian history in general, and to the history of Uttarakhand and its adjoining regions in particular, to draw inferences with regard to this Valley.

According to Professor D.N. Majumdar there are three main ancient racial strains amongst the inhabitants in the Cis-Himalaya region of the Doon, Garhwal and Himachal Pradesh. The higher altitudes are peopled by Tibetans and other Mongoloid races. The central belt, say Jaunsar-Bawar area and the low lands are composed of a tall, fair race represented by the Khas (Alpinoid) Rajputs, Khas Brahmins, the Kanets and Bhats. The aborigines are the Domes, a generic name used to include all artisan castes including the Kolis, the Koltas, the Bajgirs, the Loadhs and Oadhs who are of Dome origin. This intermixture of different bloods must have occurred over the ages. Amongst the ancient people inhabiting the Doon Valley there must have been Kols and Mundas too.

This is borne out by the fact that in the Kolish dialect village names have the prefix 'KO'. There are a number of villages in the Garhwal hills whose names start with 'KO', for example Kolkhad, Kolkandi, Koladungri and so on. In the Doon two prominent villages are "Kolukhet" and "Kolupani" pointing out the Kol-Munda influence in the Doon. The Kols or Dravidians were a fun loving people. They practised free love before marriage and divorce was available to their men and women. These people were gradually over-run by the Vedic Aryans and other invaders.

Although the Brahmins and Rajputs of Dehra Dun, Garhwal and Himachal do not show any divergence (in the coefficient of racial likeness), the artisan or the Dome elements cannot be taken to be racially of the same stock as that represented by the Brahmins and Rajputs.

The tribes of scavengers (Bhangies), cobblers (Chamars), etc. were all called Domes. These castes and their sub-castes formed a sort of refuge for outcastes of higher races and the notorious immoral character of the women of these tribes or castes must have had some effect in modifying the physique and appearance of the original Dravidians.

Of the earliest inhabitants of the Doon perhaps the only survivors who are still living in the Valley are the 'MIHIRS' of Mehron-ka-gaon (Village of Mihiris) near Sahaspur in the Western Doon.

According to some anthropologists these Mihiris or Mehras are closely allied to the Boksas of Rohilkhand Terai and the Tharus of Oudh-Terai. In the Doon they were mostly cultivators and claim to be of Rajput descent. They are supposed to be the

14

descendants of the 'KIRATS'. The other race which lasted as such after the advent of the Vedic-Aryans were the 'KINARS'. They are now restricted to the Himachal district of Kinnaur. The Kinnar women were considered to be beauties and, according to folk tales, a number of kings are reported to have lost their hearts to them. Basically the Kinnars lived in small groups in the forests and moved to higher altitudes in the summer and came down in the winter. According to a Jatak (folk tale) story a king from Varanasi (Banaras) fell in love with a Kinnar woman whom he saw when he was out hunting, and in order to cohabit with her he killed her husband, calling it an accident. Such accidents have occurred in the Doon in the 20th century also.

The Kirat rulers of Himachal and Uttarakhand region were so powerful that the Vedic Aryans, inspite of their cavalry and arms made of iron, found it difficult to overcome these Kirats of the sub-montane Himalaya. In the Rig Ved the fight between the Kirat king 'Bhed' and the Aryan king 'Sudas' is described in detail. It was only after their battle, on the bank of the river Yamuna, where Bhed was defeated and killed, that the Aryans were able to move eastwards and establish themselves in this region. With the lower areas coming under the Aryans, the Kirats had to withdraw deeper into the higher areas where they lived in small pockets, and their chieftains ruled for centuries. As late as the 10th century A.D. there was a princeling who had his principality in the eastern part of the region. According to the Mahabharat, during Yudhistar's time the Garhwal-Kumaun region was being ruled by the Kirat king Subahu.

A word about the Khas (Alpinoid) inhabitants of this area. This race in its migration from central Europe towards Asia and into North West India preceded the Rig-Vedic Aryans. A line of migration, of the early brachycephalic groups, is found along the Himalayas right from Chitral (in Pakistan), Gilgit and upto Western Nepal, passing through Kashmir, Himachal Pradesh, Garhwal and Kumaun. They were basically pastoral people. To-day Jaunsar-Bawar is one pocket in this area where these people are still living in isolation. This tribe has 'Mahashu' as its main god. In Himachal he is called Mani Mahesh, whereas the Hindus in the rest of the country call him Maheshwar. Apart from Mahashu, each village has its own list of local gods and goddesses who have to be propitiated at all times. Since they did not come under the influence of Vedic Brahmins they do not wear the sacred thread and do not follow the Brahminical rituals in their religious functions. Although the upper or the well to do members of their society claim to be Rajputs and Brahmins, all the others are Domes or Harijans.

These people like the rest of their country-men believe in ghosts and spirits whom they propitiate at every opportunity. They are snake worshippers and are also devotees of the Avtar or incarnation of Vishnu called Narsingh who is half-man and half-lion. Of the innumerable village deities the one known as 'Yaksh' or the 'Spirit' is the most important. A spirit can be either male or female. Till 6th-7th century B.C. the people lived in constant mortal fear of these spirits. They were supposed to haunt the forests and rivers and were always descending on some man or woman. They were exorcised with the help of an exorcist who would sacrifice different animals to propitiate the Spirit. Because of their constant worshipping of 'Yaksh' or 'Jakhs' the Khas people (Alpinoids) came to be called Yakshees, and they, under this name, were employed by Emperor

Ashok not only to build his great chaityas or monasteries but also as mercenaries in his army.

The social fabric of these people is nearly the same today as it may have been when they first came to these areas. One of the social customs still prevalent is polyandry. Another is that a widow or a wife can take a man as a temporary mate called "Tekva" or "Kathala" with whom she can co-habit and procreate in order to keep her husband's name alive. In the Mahabharat the accounts of the births of Dhritrashtra, Pandu, Vidur and the five Pandavas are evidence to the fact that even the Vedic Aryrans were influenced by Khas customs.

Another custom is to give due recognition to the mother's family at the time of a daughter's marriage. A part of the bride-money taken by the girl's people is given to her mother's brother or family. This custom is a remnant from the matriarchal system although to-day they practice the patriarchal way of living. The bridegroom's maternal uncle (mother's brother) is to be treated at par with the father at the wedding. Twice a year, at the time of harvesting of the crops, the married daughters of the family are called to their parental home. When they return to their own homes they are given gifts of new clothes, cash, sweets, other edibles and a minimum of 32 kilograms of food grains. Similarly at various festivals, during the year, the married daughter is given presents, depending on the economic condition of her parents, as also during her pregnancy and after confinement. In this society levirate and other inter-marriages between family members are more liberal than amongst the Vedic Aryans.

By the discovery, in 1951 A.D., of copper artifacts like spears, with and without handles, axes, harpoons, swords etc. from the south face of the Shiwaliks near Haridwar, it is now more or less established that this area was a part of the copper-age civilisation of the Indus valley or as some present day Indian archaeologists would call it, the Saraswati River Valley civilisation. Beyond this discovery there is no other material available from which the conditions prevailing in the Doon can be known.

With the onward march of the Vedic-Aryans from the Punjab region towards the East, this Valley and the surrounding areas must have also come under their influence. After the defeat of the aboriginal hill chief Bhed and his allies on the bank of the Yamuna river, by the Aryan king Sudas, the sub-Himalaya areas became Aryan Territory. According to some of the information available from the Rig-Ved the Himachal-Uttrakhand region was well populated. The people lived in villages and their chief occupations were agricultural and pastoral.

Of the Aryan rulers who were the direct descendants of Manu, the law giver to the Hindus, Raja Baen is a ruler whose capital was at Mayapur (Haridwar). References are made to him in the Rig Ved, Mahabharat and other Puraans. He was supposed to be a tyrant and was assassinated by his subjects. According to Mahabharat, of his two sons, one born of an aboriginal woman and the other of an Alpinoid, the local Brahamins put the latter's son on his father's throne. He was known as Raja Prithu. The next direct reference to the Doon is in the times of Raja Daksha. He was fifth lineal descendant of Prithu. Daksha had his seat at Kankhal, on the Ganga, just below the present town of Haridwar, where there is a temple dedicated to him.

16

According to a legend Daksha was the father-in-law of Lord Shiv who had married Daksha's daughter Sati another incarnation of Parvati and Uma. All the three have appeared in Hindu literature, as the consort of Shiv, at different times. When Daksha performed his first "Yagya" (fire sacrifice) he did not invite Shiv as he was considered socially unfit company, because of his physical deportment. In spite of Sati beseeching her father he did not relent and when Shiv did appear on the scene he was insulted by Daksha. On seeing this Sati jumped into the sacred fire and immolated herself. Shiv was so overcome with grief that he picked up her corpse and with it on his shoulder started wandering aimlessly all over Himalaya. It is on this occasion that Shiv in his anger, is supposed to have performed his famous "Tandava" dance.

The other gods were perturbed on seeing their Lord in this state. They felt that unless the corpse was destroyed Shiv will not be normal again and the world would come to a stand-still. By repeated strikes with bolts of lightning Sati's body was dismembered and wherever her bones fell a 'Devi' sprang from the earth. Devi is considered to be an incarnation of Sati, who is also known as "Shakti". Thus the cult of "Shakti" (Divine Energy) worship was born. This could be the precursor of Tantric thought. The bones are supposed to have fallen all along the Himalaya chain right from Jammu (Vaishno Devi) to Shillong (Kamakhya Devi at Kamrup) and then down to Burma. What is more intriguing is that the form of the idol that is worshipped in the various places, is supposed to be according to that particular part of the body, that fell at that spot. A part of the remains fell at the base of Kasumri pass on the south face of the Shiwaliks in Saharanpur district. At this place is one of the five passes leading from the plains, into the Doon. The other four passes are Timli, Mohand or Mohan, Kansrau and Motichur (Haridwar). The spot where the remains fell in the thickly forested Shiwaliks, the "Shakumbhari Devi" temple was established. Of all the Devis so established this is the only one, at whose temple animal sacrifice is prohibited in her 'Puja' (prayer ritual). When and by whom this temple was established no one knows. However, there are references of Emperor Chandra Gupta Maurya having come and stayed at the town of Behat (known as Brehadvat in those days) and visiting this temple. She is also the family deity of the house of Jasmore, whose founder Rana Jarasar Singh is supposed to have come from Orissa in the 8th century A.D. Since then the Rana of Jasmore is the temporal priest of the temple. The major portion of the offerings, which run into lakhs of rupees now, goes to him and a portion goes to the family of the Brahmin priests who reside at Raipur village in the Doon.

Vegetarianism in the prayer rituals of this temple may have been introduced after Adi Shankaracharya had banned cow slaughter amongst the Hindus. The other possibility being that the Jasmore Rana having come from Orissa, where Buddhism was prevalent at that time, and the people were beef eaters, may have adopted Shankarcharya's dictates and banned animal sacrifice at the temple. As her name implies 'Shak' in Hindi means vegetation and she is considered the goddess of the vegetable kingdom. The people of the Doon are specially devoted to her and she is treated as the local goddess and the protector of the people and of the Doon and Saharanpur districts in particular.

At the time of the "Great Deluge" of Hindu mythology the grandson of Raja Daksha

17

called Vaivasvat Manu played the role of Noah. Unlike Noah, Vaivasvat collected the seeds of all plants, and once the flood waters had receded, planted them to start plant life anew. His lineal descendants were Ram, Lakshman and their family to be followed by the Kaurvas and Pandavas of the Mahabharat.

Since the setting of the Ramayan is in the Eastern and Southern parts of India there is hardly any direct reference to the Doon Valley except with regard to the creation of the Ganga by Ram's ancestor Bhagirath and Ram and Lakshman coming to Rishikesh and Tapoban, to do penance for killing Ravana, as he was a Brahmin. Although modern historians claim that the Mahabharat is the older of the two epics, tradition has it that the Ramayan by Valmiki is older. This is further borne out by the fact that a number of Ramayan's episodes and characters are mentioned in the former. The setting of Mahabharat, the various events occurring in it are in North and Western India.

The earliest historical ruler of the Doon was Bharat whose existence is supported by various mentions in the Vedic and Puraanic literature. He was born out of that famous romantic union of Dushyant and Shakuntla. Their romance has been immortalised in the famous poem "Meghdoot" by Kalidas. Shakuntla is supposed to have been a Garhwali woman. She was the foster daughter of Kanav Rishi who had his ashram on the banks of the Malini river. This river is in the Pauri Garhwal area. Hence it can be presumed that the Doon was a part of the kingdom of Bharat.

In the Mahabharat there is a direct reference to this Valley. The Rishi Bharadwaj had his residence and ashram at Haridwar. It was here, on being seduced by the apsara Ghritachi, that he sired Dron. Dron is supposed to have been born in a bowl or valley which is called "Droni" in Hindi hence was named Dron. From the Mahabharat and the inscription in the Sanskrit script on a coin of Raja Bhadra-mitra (2nd centrury A.D.), found in the Doon, it is clear that this Valley was called "Droni Ghate" (Droni valley). The area around Haridwar was called Bharadwaj.

The story of how Pandu, who was an impotent, because of a curse on him, begot the Pandavas from his wives Kunti & Madri is well known. The Pandav boys were born and brought up at a place in the lower Himalaya somewhere around the Badri-Kedar foothills between the Alaknanda and Bhagirathi watershed. On their way there Pandu and his party came to Nagsidh in the Doon after crossing the Ganga at Haridwar and then went to Shatshring mountain via Kalkoot (Kalsi) and settled there. After Pandu's death it took his family 16 days to reach Hastinapur, a distance of 200 miles. The kingdom of Hastinapur was under the Regency of Dhritrashtra during Pandu's self imposed exile. During this period the 100 Kauravs were also born and Duryodhan was a contemporary of the Pandav Bhim.

The patriarch of the clan Bhishm arranged for the military education of the Pandavas and Kauravas under Acharya (teacher) Dron. He had his Military Academy in the Doon Valley which was referred to as "Dron Doon" also.

When the Pandavs were studying at the Military Academy of Dron Acharya, a local tribal chief's son came to Dron and requested him to take him as a pupil. Dron Acharya refused as he was a tribal and did not belong to the great Kshatriya or Brahmin castes. The boy's name was Eklavya. Disappointed he went away and in a nearby forest set

18

up his abode. Here he made an earthen statue of Dron Acharya and mentally made him his Guru. The boy started practising archery.

During one of their hunting trips the Pandavs came to the area where Eklavya lived. In their retinue there was a servant's dog who strayed to Eklavya's abode. On seeing an ill kempt man dressed in a deer skin the dog started barking at Eklavya, who was practising his archery. Irritated by the dog's continuous barking he shot seven arrows, in quick succession, into the dog's mouth thus causing him to stop barking but without causing any injury. The dog whimpered back to his master where every one was amazed to see him in that condition. On searching, the Pandavs' party came upon Eklavya who was still busy practising. They could not recognise him, because of his dishevelled appearance, till he introduced himself and said that he was a student of the great Guru Dron.

The Pandavs, on their return, narrated the incident to their Guru. Arjun, who had become jealous of Eklavya's achievement taunted the Guru saying that he had announced that there would be no better archer on this earth than Arjun, but that this boy was better than everyone studying at the Academy. After some thought the Guru decided to visit Eklavya. On arriving there he saw that the boy was so engrossed in his archery that he had forgotten all about his personal appearances. On seeing Dron the boy was happy and told him that as his student he was willing to carry out all Guru's wishes. Dron Acharya told him that if the boy really considered him his Guru then he should give "Guru Dakshina" (teacher's wages). The boy replied that he had nothing to give which would be worthy of the teacher. Dron Acharya said that if that be so then he could give him the thumb of his right hand. The boy at once severed it and placed it at the Guru's feet. Thus, the Guru showed his partiality for one of his favourite students at the cost of a deserving and better one by depriving Eklavya of being able to pull the bow string.

Sometimes such stories of favouritism are also heard about the happenings at the present day Military Academy in the Doon. The ceremonial gate of this Academy is named "Dron Dwar" after the great Guru.

After completing their education the Pandavs and Kauravs went back to Hastinapur. Because of Duryodhan's chronic jealousy of the Pandavs a scheme was hatched wherein they were asked to go and live at Varanavat along with Kunti their mother. Here they were accommodated in a palace made of resinous wood, in other words of highly inflammable conifer timbers. The scheme was to set fire to this structure and let the Pandavs perish in the fire. However Vidur, one of their uncles, warned them of the plot. The result was that one night they themselves set fire to the palace and escaped through a tunnel to the bank of the river and adjoining forest. This place is identified as "Lakhamandal" in the Chakrata Sub-division of the Doon. Lakh or Lac in Hindi means Resin and Mandal means region. Walton in his Gazetteer reports a narrow passage at Lakhamandal, leading underground through the rock to the riverside, and which was used, by the people in time of danger from their enemies. For a long time the Pandavs lived incognito in this area. During this period Bhim is supposed to have killed two of the chieftains, of the area, who were tyrants. He even married the sister of one of them and fathered a son called Ghatotkach.

In the course of time the Pandavs married Draupadi as a common wife to all the brothers. To avoid conflict amongst them over cohabiting with her a code of conduct was evolved. The brother who would be with her in the room would leave his shoes outside the door and none of the other brothers dare enter it. On violation of this code the guilty brother had to go into exile for a period of 12 years. Arjun violated this rule and had to undergo this punishment. After division of the kingdom between the Pandavs and the Kauravs, the North-western Himalaya region came under the rule of the Pandavs.

One of the customs from that era which is still in vogue is the practice of polyandry in the Jaunsar-Bawar area of Chakrata Sub-division of the Doon. Even today if a mother-in-law dies leaving an infant son, the daughter-in-law brings him up as one of her husbands. On growing to manhood if the boy wants to cohabit with her, the family and she cannot refuse.

The practice of leaving one's shoes or sandals outside the door of the room is still followed by these people, though the eldest brother has priority over the others.

After having lost Draupadi, their kingdom and their freedom in the great gambling match, Yudhister was given a last chance by Duryodhan. The stakes were that if Yudhister won then everything lost will be returned otherwise he and his brothers would have to go into exile for 13 years. Of these the first 12 years were to be spent away from habitations and the last one year was to be spent living incognito. If they were recognised in the thirteenth year then they would have to again go into exile for another 12 years. However at the end of 13 years they came back to claim the return of their kingdom of Indraprastha. This was refused by Duryodhan and the famous 18 days war was fought at Kurukshetra.

In this war the Kulind ruler of Uttarakhand, his three sons with their war elephants and infantry allied themselves with the Pandavs.

Arjun who had been exiled, because of violating the rule regarding the entry to Draupadi's chamber, arrived in Haridwar (Ganga Dwar) during his wanderings. Here, when he was having a bath in the river, Ulupi, the daughter of the Naga ruler Kauravya saw him and fell in love with him. She took Arjun to her father's palace and married him in a Gandharva wedding. This is a wedding in which a man and woman accept each other as husband and wife, without going through the rituals or taking the vows in the presence of fire and witnesses. It is one of the several forms of marriages which are recognised, as legal, under the Hindu law. A child born of such union, is under the Hindu law, a legitimate child. A son named Iravan was born to Ulupi from her union with Arjun. This Naga Raja's palace could have been on the Nag Sidh hill in the Doon Valley. This was the era of Scythian supremacy and snake worship or Shivaism as opposed to the worship of Vishnu or Vaishnavism. Iravan also fought alongside his father in the great 18 days war.

The land between the catchment areas of the Yamuna, Ganga (with their tributaries) and between the Shiwaliks and the interior Himalaya has been called "Kulinda Region" in the Mahabharat, also by Ptolemy and Varahmihir. The three higher mountain ranges of this region have been called Anantragiri, Bahirigiri and Upgiri. The minor or lower ranges have been mentioned as Ushirbij, Kalshail, Nagshat and Neel Parbat. These minor or lower ones have been identified today as the hillock at the end of the Shiwalik range of Kankhal (Haridwar), the Kalsi hill, Nag Tibba and the hill on the Eastern bank of the Ganga at Rishikesh respectively. These hills more or less conform to the geographical features of the Doon. Among the towns, that were prosperous during the Mahabharat era, was Ekachakra, which has been identified as the present Chakrata town.

The chief of this region lived away from the main town. He was overthrown by a tyrant called Bakasur. Apparently he and his retinue were cannibals and the people under his rule had to provide his food requirements. Every day he had to be given a male human being, two buffaloes and twenty kilograms of rice. Because of the large human population of the area the turn to provide the man from a family came once in two to three years. This cannibal was killed by Bhim when the Pandavs were living in the area.

Another town of that era named Kalind Nagar can be identified as the area around Rishikesh, and Lakshman Jhula where a rope bridge crosses the Ganga on the old pilgrim route to Badrinath. The Raja of the area, Subhahu, played host to the Pandavs when they went to Badrinath. It was with him that they left their vehicles, extra baggage and servants. The reason for leaving them behind was that beyond this point animal drawn vehicles, like chariots and carts could not go because of the lack of roads in the mountainous terrain. Hence from thereon the Pandavs travelled either on foot or on horses or palanquins. On their return they collected their possessions and made their way across the Doon to go to Yamnotri (the source of the Yamuna river).

During the Kaurav-Pandav period the social customs in this area of the Doon were the same as in the rest of the region. The forms of marriages recognised were the same as mentioned in Manu's Hindu Law namely (a) Brahm, (b) Gandharv, (c) Rakshas and (d) Asur. The first is the ritualistic marriage which is usually performed where the families of the boy and girl approve of the match and the wedding takes place with the sacred fire as one of the witnesses. The second form is where the boy and the girl, and this is when they are both majors, take each other as husband and wife because of mutual physical and mental attraction. This can also be termed as a marriage of two minds and the couple cohabit. Arjun married Ulupi - the Naga's daughter, who was a widow, and resided with her father at Haridwar. Similar was the case of Bhim who married Ghatotkacha's mother, Hidambana. She was physically attracted to Bhim and even though he had killed her brother she seduced him, against the tradition of her clan.

Both Ulupi and Hidambana were tribals while Arjun and Bhim were Aryans, yet mutual physical attraction was so great that they did not hesitate in indulging in one night (sex) stands. The third form is when the man abducts the bride from her father's house and the last is when he commits rape. The children born from such unions were recognised as legitimate by society as such and under the law of the land.

Bigamy for the affluent was an accepted social custom as was widow remarriage. A woman having sex with another man, to procreate, in order to keep her husband's name alive, if he was impotent - like Pandu, and the keeping of a slave by a widow, to produce a son to keep the image of her dead husband alive, were accepted social customs. Some of these customs are still alive in certain communities of the area. The

21

custom of celebrating birthdays of sons only was prevalent in those days.

Hunting was popular and there are descriptions of how people hunted and cooked the game, that was killed, over open fires. According to the "Jataks" (folk tales) the rulers of Varanasi would come to the Doon Valley to hunt. Slavery was common. Of the four educational centres in this region Bharadwaj Ashram was situated in the Doon Valley. Bharadwaj was Dron Acharaya's father.

Prof. Jaiswal (author of Hindu Kingdoms) feels that this region administratively was a confederacy of about 100 chieftains whose leader was Kulindraja. Subhahu was one of the Chieftains. This thinking could be based on the fact that in the Garhwal region, at the time of Ajai Pal, taking charge of his domain, there were 52 chieftains, each with his independent fortress and domain. The local administration was probably carried on through village panchayats under the supervision of influential families of the place.

A number of incidents, described in the Mahabharat, are supposed to have taken place in and around the Doon as well as the banks of the Ganga and Yamuna. It appears that the Doon during that period was a well inhabited and prosperous part of the Pandav empire. During the reigns of Parikhshit and his successors it can be assumed that the Doon was under their suzerainty. After the destruction of the Hastinapur kingdom the Doon may have continued to be ruled by the local chieftains. Not much information is available of those times. The last mention of the Valley is when the Pandavs passed through Haridwar and Rishikesh enroute to Himalaya, on the last journey of their lives.

In the Mahabharat the mid-Himalaya is considered holy ground, the well loved home of the gods, where the land is hallowed and there are innumerable places of pilgrimage. Starting from the Kali river in the East to the Yamuna in the West, including the Doon the wanderings of the Pandavs in the area are recalled by some rock or stream commemorating some exploit or some action during their travels. At Bhimgoda or Bhimghora on the outskirt of Haridwar there is a pool of water (fed by an underground spring) and on the rock there is an imprint of what one may call a horse's hoof. This is supposed to have been made by Bhim's horse when he was looking for water and unable to find it struck the rock with his hoof and a spring burst forth.

According to tradition both Ram and Lakshman did penance in the Valley for slaying Ravan who was treated as a Brahmin because of his vast learning and knowledge. Ram performed his austerities at Rishikesh and Lakshman at Tapoban above Muni-ki-Reti near Lakshman Jhoola. The hillock east of Clement Town (Bharuwala Village) is supposed to be the place where Lakshman meditated and obtained super powers (Sidhi). The place is called "Lakshman Sidh" and has a temple.

In the Kedarkhand section of "Skanda Puraan" the following incident is mentioned describing how the river Suswa, in the Doon Valley, came to flow from the foot of the Bharuwala hill. The story runs thus:

Once upon a time, the sage Kashyap gave a great feast to which all the gods were invited Indra, the rain god, was on his way to the feast when he happened to come across 60,000 Brahmins, who were the size of Gulliver's Liliputians. These poor Brahmins were trying, in vain, to cross a cow's hoof-print on the ground, which was filled with rain water - to them a vast lake. Seeing this Indra was unable to restrain his laughter. The Brahmins were so indignant at being made fun of in this manner that they decided to take their revenge on him. They proceeded to create a second Indra who would replace the reigning god. This could only be achieved by means of penance and mortifications, in which they steadily perservered, until the sweat, flowing from their tiny bodies, formed a river. Indra was surprised and greatly alarmed at the initial effect of the Brahmins' efforts. He, therefore, asked Brahma to intercede. Through his good offices they were appeased and Indra was able to retain his throne. The river thus born was at first known as the Sobhan - meaning the pleasant waters, presently it is called the Suswa. How these waters could be called pleasant is beyond comprehension. The terrain through which this river runs is so malarious that any one living by the waters of this and its sister river the Song, during the monsoons is bound to get malaria. Even the birds suffer from malarial fever in this area.

By the time the Puraans were written the legends concerning the mid-Himalaya belt grew with the population and so did the peoples' beliefs and superstitions. The sight of the lofty summits, of the consecutive mountain ranges, crowned with perpetual snow must have inspired the story of Mount Meru, the Olympus of the Indian gods. In the Puraans there are geographical descriptions, as also of the distribution of nations, and peoples then known to the compilers.

In the Skanda Puraan there is a complete section devoted to the geography of Kedar Khand or the mountains and hilly regions between the Yamuna and Kali rivers. The description of the various districts of the region have been given according to the mythological background. Sometimes there are errors in the proper geographical placement of a particular place.

For example the Shakumbhari-Kshetra (or Shakumbhari Sub-division) has been placed in the Bhillang valley whereas it is actually at the base of the south face of the Shiwaliks, in the present day Saharanpur district of Uttar Pradesh. According to the Puraanic description "this area is sacred to Shakumbhari Devi, where the temple exists. She protects the sages in their devotions and there is a grove of Shaka trees. The tiger of the forest and the snake with the jewel pays her worship". This description fits in more accurately with the existing temple in the Shiwaliks rather than placing it in the Himalaya north of the confluence of the Bhillangana and the Bhagirathi rivers. Shakumbhari Devi, as mentioned earlier, is the goddess of vegetation and is one of the forms of Durga who rides a tiger. The temple is deep in the Shiwalik forest where till forty years ago tigers roamed in plenty.

About 1952 or 1953 A.D. an Inspector-General of Forests, who was a Brahmin and a vegetarian and therefore did not shoot for the pot but killed only tigers. He shot two of them in the course of three hours in the Dhaulkhand forest range of the present day Rajaji National Park. The gentleman was coming to Dehra Dun on tour. Having left Delhi by car in the morning he was to have lunch at the Dhaulkhand Forest Rest House as the guest of the Divisional Forest Officer, Saharanpur. The V.I.P. himself had one time been the Forest Officer-in-charge of this division, and it was to this rest house that he would retire, whenever an opportunity arose, with his current girl friend. This was the case even twenty years later in the 1950s. The lady friend, properly chaperoned, was awaiting his arrival at the Rest House. During the party's afternoon rest, after lunch, word came from the Gujars the local pastoral nomads , who were camping in the area with their cattle, that there was a tiger lurking near their camp. The V.I.P., namely the Inspector-General got into his car and had hardly gone any distance when, lo and behold, he found the animal crossing the road a little distance away from the Gujar camp. Of course, the animal fell to the Shikari's bullet and the party returned amidst a lot of jubilation. They had hardly finished tea when another messenger came from the same Gujars saying that the tiger was alive and was near their camp, smacking its lips and waiting for an opportunity to lift one of their cattle. The Inspector-General did not believe him because he had seen the animal, dead as a door nail, lying on the side of the road. Still he went with the informer.

This time he was taken on a different road, but in the same area. After driving a few miles the party was coming back without seeing a tiger or anything resembling one. It was dusk by now and the car's headlights were on. Just as they come around a bend in the road there it stood, right in the middle of the road, looking at the car, probably dazzled by the lights. And, of course, the V.I.P. got his second tiger of the day. It can be well imagined how this event must have been celebrated that night. It may be mentioned here that the Shiwalik tiger, in size, is smaller than his other country cousins.

In such thick jungle snakes are present in abundance. A python 20 feet long was killed in the vicinity of the Devi's temple not very long ago.

By the time the Skanda Puraan came to be written the Uttarakhand region had become one of the major areas of pilgrimage for the Indians. The descriptions and praises of the various holy spots bear the imprint of the influence of the Brahmin clergy. Even the local village deities have been turned into places of pilgrimage. The result is that a traveller could not pass through a village without paying obeisance to the local deity, thereby the local Brahmin clergy.

In the Kedar-Khand section of this Puraan numerous places of pilgrimage are mentioned in and around the Doon Valley. Of the places mentioned therein some can be identified even today.

According to it "the Yamuna flows through the western portion of Uttarakhand and the confluence of the Yamuna with its tributary Hiranya-baku is considered holy. This would be near Kharsali village beyond Barkot in Jaunsar. Still further west is the Tamasa (Tonse river) and where it joins the Yamuna is the Dakseha tirath and north of it the Vishnu tirath (near Kalsi). From the hill above the last mentioned places of pilgrimage flows the Bimuktida stream and at its junction with the Tonse is a temple dedicated to Shiv as Jyoteswar. To the north is the Hem-Sringa peak (the Naga peak) of the Banderpunch range of the Himalaya from which flows the Sidha stream, and at its confluence with the Tonse is the Shiv-Ling to which, at one time, Brahma paid devotion. When Brahma created the world, the Tamasa (Tonse river) was created from the Brahma-kund and there is the Rudra and Vishnu tirath, where there is an image of Vaishnavi Devi, and half a 'kos' beyond the Sakra or Indra tirath.

To the south-east of the Barana tirath at a distance of twelve 'kos' is the Balakhilya peak and river and Balakhilyeswarling. (This is the reference to the Suswa river and the hillock east of Clement Town Bharuwala from where the Suswa rises. It also has reference to the story of the pigmy Brahmins as the Hindi word 'Balak' means a child . To the north-east is the temple dedicated to Shiv as Someswar and from the surrounding hills five rivers originate and afford numerous places of pilgrimage to the devout. One of the streams called Dharam has on its eastern side the Dharamkut peak (Nala Pani hill) where Dharma Raj (Yudhishter of the Pandavs) performed austerities. To the south of this is the Siddhukut peak (the Nagsidh hill) and to the north Apsara giri (mountain).

The area around Ganga-dwar (Haridwar) and Rishikesh is known as Maya-Kshetra. Maya is another name of Sati, the daughter of Daksha who lived at Kankhal, near Ganga-dwar. There is the temple of Daksheswar-ling and the places known as Chandika-tirath (Chandi hill across the Ganga), Dron-tirath and Ram-tirath''.

The description, now given, is of places and tiraths along the Ganga valley northwards of Haridwar.

''To see Rishikesh and Brahm-tirath in itself ensures the fruit of good works. Tapoban (near Lakshman Jhoola on the boundary of Tehri and Dehra Dun districts) is also a place for performing funeral rites of ancestors. It was here that Lord Ram retired to devote himself to religious penance to propitiate for the killing of Ravan. Lakhsmansthan (Lakshman Jhoola—the rope suspension bridge on the Ganga) is a place for achieving good fortune.

In a cave to the left lived the Muni Rishika (after whom Rishikesh is named) and here on the 14th night of the dark half of the month of Shravan (August) a light is seen and voices of people talking are heard.'' (This could be the present day spot called 'Basudhara' at the confluence of the Chandrabhaga and Ganga rivers which is on the boundary of Dehra Dun and Tehri districts, at Muni-ki-Reti. Here people standing on the west bank of the Ganga get an echo of their voices and sounds from the hills across the river. This is what perhaps the author meant when mentioning about hearing people talking.)

Virbhadra is mentioned as a place for doing penance and a temple is dedicated to Shiv as Virbhadreshwar. (This is the site where to-day the Indian Drugs and Pharmaceuticals Antibiotics plant is situated between Raiwala and Rishikesh).

Rishikesh is the area where many Rishis meditated. The establishment of this town goes back to more than 2600 B.C. According to one legend in the 17th ''Satyug'' era two demons, Madhu and Kaitabh, were harassing the people on this earth. These two were Lord Vishnu's children and had been blessed by Brahma himself. Seeing that the two demons were not mending their ways Vishnu killed them. In the fight Vishnu was covered by their blood and to wash his contaminated body he went to various places of pilgrimage to cleanse himself. When he came to Rishikesh he found Rabhaya Rishi in deep meditation. Vishnu was pleased with him and offered him fulfilment of a wish. Rabhaya asked him to be ever present at that place. Vishnu granted his wish adding that he will reside in the place under the name Hrishikesh and the place will be known as Hrishikeshashram, and that in ''Tretayug'', Bharat (Dashrath's son and Ram's brother) will come and meditate here and so will his other three brothers. In Kalyug he (Vishnu) will be known as Bharat and will be worshipped as such, which is done at Bharat Mandir (temple) in the town. To-day the Bharat temple, Raghunath temple, Lakshman temple and Shatrughan temple are dedicated to them.

Rishikesh has been a centre for teaching and meditation from times immemorial. It has been a place of refuge for the Bhrigu Brahmins who came here after being persecuted by Raja Sahastrarjun.

The Jain Tirthankar Rishabhadev's son Bharat married the local Raja Nemi's sister Subhadra. Mahatma Buddha came to this region to preach his philosophy and 170 years after his death a Buddhist monastery was constructed across the Ganga on the Ahogang mountain. Tisus, who took part in the third Buddhist congress, during Emperor Ashoka's reign, lived in this region.

In the Bharat temple, two life size statues of a "Yaksha" and "Yakshi" (angelic demigod and goddess, the contemporary of angels and fairies of the west) were dug up during the renovation of the temple. They are in red sandstone and are carved in the Mathura school probably at the beginning of the 2nd century A.D. Another statue found in the temple complex is that of the Jain sage Mahavir. It is perhaps the oldest so far found in the region and again probably belongs to the time when the Jains and Buddhists were holding sway over this region. There is a statue showing 'Indra' riding an elephant. This is from the Shunga period. A Buddha's head, in red sandstone, from the Gupta period was also found in this area.

The temple of Tapkeshwar Mahadev, situated in the cavern carved out by the Tons river near Garhi, in the cantonment area of Dehra, is also mentioned in the Skanda Puraan. Here in a cavern a Shiv Ling is formed out of the rock and on it water drips from the rock above, which is shaped like the udder of a cow hence Tapkeshwar (Tapak in Hindi means dripping). A mela (fair) is held here annually on the festival of Shivratri.

Another place in the valley is "Sahastradhara"—the "Thousand streams". This refers to the Sulphur Springs situated north of village Raipur beyond the Ordnance Factory. Here there is a Sulphur Spring and a couple of caverns cut out by the Baldi river. In these caves, which are connected by a suspension bridge over the river, are indeed thousands of sprays of dripping water so that an umbrella is useful when entering them.

Water oozes from the hill sides, which are composed of tufaceous limestone, and coats every thing it comes in contact with, twigs of trees and ferns, leaves, rocks and stones all become petrified. Numerous stalactites hang from the roof of the caves, and on the floor are stalagmites formed by the dripping water. One such stalagmite resembles the emblem of Shiv and is worshipped as such. At the beginning of this century an Englishman purchased the land where the Sulphur Spring is situated. He endeavoured to create a trade in bottled Sulphur water but failed.

Many other places of pilgrimage are mentioned in and around the Doon. However not all of them can be identified to-day.

After the Mahabharat era the next mention of the Doon is during the Maurayan period (321-184 B.C.), and at that time again it must have been a well-populated and flourishing region. According to Panini the capital town of the Kulind province, in those

26

days, was Kalkut (Kalsi of today). Emperor Ashok (274-232 B.C.) thought it fit to instal one of his "rock edicts" at Kalsi. It was discovered by an Englishman, Mr. Forest, in the year 1860 A.D. The letters of the inscription were hardly visible, the whole surface of the stone being encrusted with the moss of ages. On removing the black film the surface became nearly as white as marble.

The quartz boulder is about ten feet high, ten feet long and eight feet broad at the base and stands on a ledge overhanging the right bank of the river Yamuna.

The rock has inscribed on it a figure of an elephant with words "Gaj (a) tame" i.e. "Gaj ottama" meaning the most excellent elephant. Ashok had an attachment to various Buddhist symbols. The symbol of the 'White Elephant' recalls the descent of the Buddha, in that form, into the womb of his mother. Thus there is an attempt, on the part of Ashok, to dedicate his edicts, as it were, to the Buddha. The Ashokan pillars have the elephant, the bull, the horse and the lion as their capitals. These were probably chosen by him as symbols of different stages in the life of Buddha. Thus the elephant typifies the Conception, the bull (as presiding over) the Nativity, the horse the great departure—Renunciation and the lion as the Lion (King) among the Sakyas— "Sakyasimha" as the Buddha was known.

The inscription on the rock is in the "Brahmi" script in the eastern dialect of Magadhi, which was the official language of the Court and served as the *lingua franca* for Ashok's empire. In the text of the inscription are mentioned, *inter alia* the names of Ashok's five contemporary kings of the western World namely Antiochus, Ptolemy, Antigonus, Magas and Alexander. According to European history they can be identified with Antiochus Theos of Syria (263-246 B.C.) Ptolemy Philadelphus of Egypt (285-246 B.C.) Antigonus Gonnatus of Macedonia (276-243 B.C.), Magas of Syrene (258 B.C.) and Alexander of Epirus (274-254 B.C.)

The historian's (Indologists) translation of the edict is as follows:—

"Thus saith His Sacred and Gracious Majesty the King:

People perform various ceremonies. In troubles, marriages of sons and daughters, birth of children, departure from home - on these and other occasions people perform many different ceremonies. But in such cases mothers and wives perform numerous and diverse, petty and worthless ceremonies.

Now ceremonies should certainly be performed. But these bear little fruit. That, however, is productive of great fruit which is connected with 'Dharma'. Herein are these:

Proper treatment of slaves and employees, reverence to teachers, restraint of violence towards living creatures and liberality to Brahman and Sramana ascetics. These and such others are called "Dharma-mangalas."

(Kautilya has elaborated on these precepts in his various treatises and laws expounded by him).

Therefore should it be said by a father, or a son, or a brother, or a master, or a friend, a companion and even a neighbour: "This is commendable; this is a ceremony to be performed until the purpose thereof is fulfilled; this shall I perform." For those ceremonies that are other than these - they are all of doubtful effect. It may achieve that purpose or may not. And it is only for this world. But his ceremonial of "Dharma" is not of time. Even if one does not achieve that object in this world, in the world beyond is produced endless merit. But if one achieves that purpose in this world, the gain of both results from it—that object in this world, and endless merit is produced in the other world by this "Dharma—mangala."

His Sacred and Gracious Majesty the King does not regard glory or fame as bringing much gain except that whatever glory or fame he desires, it would be only for this that the people might in the present time and in the future should practice obedience to Dharma and conform to the observances of Dharma. For this purpose does his Sacred and Gracious Majesty the King wish for glory or fame. And what little he exerts himself, that is all for the hereafter, and in order that all may be free from confinement (or bondage). And this is bondage, namely, sin. This is, indeed, difficult of achievement by the lowly or high in rank except by strenuous preliminary effort, renouncing all. But among these two, it is more difficult of achievement by the person of superior rank".

(The above text is more or less the gist of Buddha's Dhammapada.)

In 1912 the Government of Uttar Pradesh (United Provinces of Agra and Oudh as it was then called) built a domed building enclosing the rock thus saving it from vandalism. It is under lock and key of the Department of Archaeology.

The Kulind region or the Central Himalaya and their foothills was divided into six provinces. They were (a) Tamas, consisting of the catchment areas of the Satluj and Tonse rivers, including the two tributaries, Rupi and Supi of the river Yamuna.

(b) Kalkut consisting of the southern catchment area of the river Yamuna, Kalsi, Dehra Dun and the area near Jagadhri in present Haryana. It was named Kalkut or Kalkoot or Kalsheil because of the availability of antimony in abundance which was in great demand as an eye liner (mascara).

(c) Tangan—the Bhotia area of the present day Uttarkashi and Chamoli districts.

(d) Bharadwaj, the area from Haridwar to the upper reaches of Tehri and Garhwal districts of yore.

(e) Randak, the present Pithoragarh district and its northern reaches upto the Tibet border.

(f) Atrey or Govishan is the Almora-Nainital area.

Panini has taken Kulind region as one of the kingdoms established by Kalkootjan and the dynasty was named Kalkoti which ruled between the Mahabharat and the Mauryan period. Their capital town was Kalkoot (Kalsi) on the bank of the Yamuna. On the banks of the Ganga and the hills around Haridwar and Rishikesh there were a number of academies where the gurus taught their pupils and the mendicants meditated on the upper reaches. The Jain monks had their ashrams at Kankhal (Haridwar) and the Buddhists had their Vihars (monastries) around Chandi hill and in Strudhan on the Yamuna.

The inhabitants earned their living by agriculture, trade, animal husbandry and as mercenary soldiers. The hill or Tangan or Gunth ponies, herbs, Shilajit and woollen textiles were in great demand.

The Greek traveller Megasthenes mentions a people, the kirats from the upper Himalaya reaches of the Ganga, who had flat noses and no mouths but a common aperture for breathing and feeding. They were supposed to have been ten feet tall and six feet broad at the shoulders. They were covered with long hair and they subsisted on flowers, fruits and roast meat. They were docile by nature and some of them were brought to the court of Chandragupt Maurya. Because of their being placed in a very different environment death came to them fast. Could they have been the elusive 'YETI'?

Emperor Ashok had arranged for a daily supply of Ganga's water to be brought, from Devprayag, to wherever he may be residing. He would distribute this water amongst the "Sangh" (the Buddhist monks), friends and courtiers, after keeping his requirement.

After the death of Ashok his son Jalok ruled right from Kashmir to Kuru-Panchal.

The next king under whose rule the Doon region may have come was the Indo-Greek ruler Menender or Milinda. This is borne out by the fact that his coins have been found as far north as Subathu in the Simla hills. Otherwise not much is known about the Doon except that the historian Alberuni in his history of India connects the word "Jaun" in Jaunsar-Jaunpur with the Greeks.

There is every possibility that some Greek groups may have settled in the Tonse-Yamuna valleys. The facial features of the Jaunsari people reflect Grecian outlines and they are fair complexioned. The dress of Jaunsari woman is like the Greeks of old. They wear an ankle length skirt and a blouse with puffed half sleeves. It comes down to just above the navel, which is exposed, and tied across below the breasts, thus eliminating the need of a brassiere. These women welcome guests with a kiss. This is sometimes shocking to other native women.

During the Shunga period (184-72 B.C.) the Doon may have been under their rule. This is supported by the fact that a seal of that era was found in Dehra Dun. The inscription on it is "Bhadra—mitrasaya Droni Ghate" in the Shunga script, meaning "Bhadramitra of the Valley of Dron." It appears that this man was the local administrator and as was the practice, in those days, had struck and issued his own coinage.

Later the valley came under the sway of the Kunindas who had their seat either at Behat or at Strudhan, a town 38 miles south of Kalkoot (Kalsi), in Haryana on the banks of the Yamuna. Possibly at that time the river flowed on the course of the present day Western Yamuna canal. Coins of the Kuninda king Amoghbhuti have been found from across the Satluj river to the Ganga and from Srinagar (Garhwal) to Karnal in Haryana.

Patanjali, famous for his grammar, also resided in this area for some time as mentioned in his treatise "Mahabhashya".

With the Shaka invasion of India, the Doon also came under their sway like the rest of the Himalayan foothills from Kashmir to Kumaun. However they merged with the Kushans. The descendants of the Shakas are found in the pastoral people the Gujars who live in the forests of the Shiwaliks in the Doon. The present Shaka calendar of the Government of India was started during the Shaka era.

The Kushans, from their chief Wema Kadphises (64-78 A.D.) onwards, had the lower part of Garhwal, including the Doon under their rule. He had built a strong fort at Mayapur (Haridwar) which was known as Raja Wane's fort. Till the building of the Ganga canal the forts rubble was lying about, where the barrage is today, over an area of 250 acres. During their reign there were a number of townships in and around the

Shiwaliks of the Doon. Some of the towns which are identifiable are Strudhan, Kalkoot (Kalsi) Behat (in Saharanpur district), Virbhadra (the IDPL factory site near Rishikesh), Kankhal and Brahmapur near Haridwar. At Virbhadra when the IDPL (Indian Drugs and Pharmaceuticals Ltd.) complex was built a long wall, probably the remains of a fortress or a palace, was found. It was constructed with 14-15 inch long fire baked red bricks. Unfortunately the people building the complex thought that the best use these bricks could be put to was to use them as soling for the roads in the complex.

At Virbhadra near the main temple on the bank of the Ganga there is a smaller temple. In it is a 'Mukh-ling', or Shiv's emblem with a face engraven on it and made out of red stone. It is sculpted in the Mathura school dating back to the Kushan period. Wema Kadphises was most probably a worshipper of Shiv in his religious faith. Coins of his reign have Shiv, with or without his bull, his trident or his emblem embossed on them.

In Behat (district Saharanpur), Dehra Dun and some places in Garhwal seals and coins of the Yaudheyas' (Yadavas) dynasty have been found. Because of the remarkable resemblance in their coinage some historians support the hypothesis that the Kunindas and Yaudheyas were contemporary powers and worked hand in hand in regaining their independence in the third century A.D. As compared to the Yaudheyas, the Kunindas were a small state and it seems that they eventually merged with the former. This is assumed from the fact that there is no mention of the Kunindas amongst the republics mentioned in Samudragupt's inscription at Allahabad. However it can not be definitely said that whether the Doon was under any of them or there were petty chiefs ruling in the region. The coins may have come to the area in the course of trade and commerce.

From the inscriptions of Shiv Bhawani and Sheelverman found in the Valley, which are in the Brahmi script which was prevalent in the third century A.D., in the Sanskrit language, it is definite that the Valley was under a Raja and not a republic. These two chiefs had performed 'Ashvamedh Yagyas' (Horse sacrifices) in the Valley. Their rule is placed between 290-350 A.D. and before them the rulers were Chatreshwar, Bhanu and Ravan between 243-290 A.D. Shivbhawani's inscription was found in Ambari village (at one time there was a tea garden there) in 1965 A.D. while Sheelverman's sacrificial pits in which the holy flame was burnt were found in Barwala village east of Ambari, in the Western Doon, along the left bank of the Yamuna. These were excavated in 1953-54 A.D. These pits which are shaped like a bird in flight, the only example, so far discovered in the country, of the historical veracity of the Vedic/Puraanic religious rituals of Horse sacrifices.

It may be mentioned here that the British for administrative purpose, had divided the Doon Valley proper into three parts namely Eastern, Central and Western Doons. Jaunsar-Bawar including Chakrata and Mussoorie were separate sub-divisions. The boundaries of the three Doons are, Eastern—the valley east of Rispana river upto the left bank of the Ganga at Rishikesh, Central—between the Rispana and Tons rivers (the town of Dehra and its satellite towns) and from the west of the Tons to the Yamuna in Western Doon. These demarcations are still in force for administrative purposes.

The two inscriptions found on the bricks at the 'Yagya' pits (Fire pits) translated into English, read as under:—

(a) Obeisance to the Almighty: this brick is from the "Ashwamedh Yagya" site of Raja Sheelverman, who was born in Varshney Gotra (Caste) and ruled the land surrounded by two mountains.

(b) Sheelverman who is the sixth descendant of Raja Pone (of the caste Varshney) performed his fourth "Ashwamedh Yagya" at this site.

In between the sentences are motifs which were prevalent in the Kushan period. These bricks are fire baked and red in colour. During that period the bricks used in palaces and temples had motifs on them especially of birds and plants. The bricks dug up at Virbhadra had peacock and leaf motifs on them. Fire baked bricks were in use as is evident from the fact that the temples in Haridwar, Rishikesh, Virbhadra and Lakhamandal, some of which date back to 1st to 3rd century A.D. are built with such bricks.

In the Jaunsar-Bawar area the archaeological finds point out the rulers who lorded it over the Doon after the Sheelverman era. In an ancient temple in the Lakhamandal area, which is situated at the confluence of the Yamuna and Morad rivers, a broken stone with an inscription has been found. This has been dated as belonging to 5th century A.D. According to this inscription this area was ruled by Raja Jai Das and his seven descendants, the last one being Ajeshwar. The size of their kingdom is not mentioned as in the case of Sheelverman.

Lakhamandal was also called Lakshmandal in the old days. It is presumed that this is the spot where the palace made of resinous timbers was built for the destruction of the Pandavs. At one time this was as sanctified a place as the prayags (the various confluences of the tributaries of the Ganga) in the Garhwal mountains. As per Walton's Gazetteer of the Doon there was a tunnel, which went down to the river, probably from an old fortress which is now in ruins. It was perhaps this tunnel which was used by the Pandavs in making good their escape from their burning palace. From the carvings and sculptures strewn about the temples, it is obvious that at one time the area had a prosperous human habitation.

From the information available so far, based on the discoveries of various coins, seals and inscriptions, it appears that after the death of Sheelverman the Doon came under two different rulers. The eastern part namely Haridwar-Rishikesh and their adjoining areas were under a 'Khas' ruler who had his seat at Kartikeynagar (present day Joshimath on the route to Badrinath). In the west the Yamuna valley region was under the rule of the Chaglesh dynasty, as per the Lakhamandal rock-inscription. However till the death of the Gupta king Samudragupt the above mentioned Khas ruler paid him a tribute. May be the other ruler also did the same. According to various sources after Samudragupt's death the Khas ruler declared himself independent of the Guptas.

On ascending the throne Ramgupt (alias Shrumgupt), son of Samudragupt attacked the Khas ruler in order to keep his father's empire intact. His wife and younger brother Chandragupt also went along with him on the expedition. The Khas ruler defeated the

Gupta army which was entrapped in the mountainous terrain. In order to make peace and allow them to withdraw, the Khas demanded that Ramgupt hand over his wife as a peace offering. This was agreed to. The younger brother Chandragupt along with some trusted soliders, went to the enemy's camp dressed as Ramgupt's wife and her maids. Once inside they killed the Khas ruler and won the battle. By this time Chandragupt and his sister-in-law had become enamoured of each other. The result was that the younger brother killed the elder and married his widow. He also occupied the throne as Chandragupt II. This story has a couple of plays and some 9th and 10th century inscriptions of Rastrakutas as its basis. But in all of them the ruler is a Saka ruler and not a Khas.

This Chandragupt II took the additional title of Vikramaditya. He is credited with having a round table of nine exceptional men, well versed in arts and letters at his court, who were like king Arthur's knights of the Round Table. The great poet Kalidas was one of them. Vikramaditya's empire is supposed to have extended upto Bactria in the north. This could mean that the Doon may have again come under his sovereignty and for local administration it was independent. Kalidas in his poem 'Meghdoot' asks "the rain cloud, which is love's messenger, to go to Kankhal via Kurukshetra and from there to go onto that peak of Himalaya from where Ganga rises and where the rocks smell of musk because the musk deer sit on them".

In the Lakhamandal rock inscription the names of nine rulers appear, of which three have been erased with time. There are two Chagleshs mentioned in the list. One of them is credited with having built the Shiv temple at Lakhamandal. From this fact it is deduced that perhaps this town was also the seat of the Government of that area. A branch of the Yadavas was ruling the lower reaches of the Yamuna valley around Kalsi (Singhpur) at that time.

During the post Gupta period this region was being ruled by different chieftains. Of these the Naga and Yadav rulers were prominent. These two communities, in this region have found mention during the Mahabharat times as well. The former were in the Eastern Doon and the latter in the Western Doon.

The inscriptions, on the "Tridents" embedded at Gopeshwar (Garhwal) and Udhampur (Kashmir) Shiv temples, point out that they were placed there by Ganpatinag, who was descendant of Skandnag, Vighunag and Anshunag. These, on the basis of the script used, are supposed to be established in the 6th century A.D. This means that Ganpatinag held sway over the higher Himalaya region from Kedarkhand in the east to Kashmir in the west. There is a possibility that Chaglesh of Lakhamandal was Governor of Ganpatinag.

The information about the Yadav rulers of the Yamuna valley region, in the 6th-8th centuries A.D. is extracted from Princess Ishwara's Lakhamandal inscription. There has been mention of the Yadav kingdom of Strudhan (Behat/Singhpur/Kalsi) since 2nd century B.C. This kingdom spread from the Giri/Tonse rivers to the Ganga and from Lakhamandal to Ambala/Saharanpur in the plains. The founder of this dynasty was Seoverman (not to be confused with Sheelverman, who belonged to a different stock and era). Eleven generations of his descendants, continuously ruled in this region.

Divakarverman, the 11th ruler, was succeeded by his younger brother Bhaskerverman. Bhaskerverman was married to Jayavali who was a commoner's daughter. Their daughter Ishwara was married to Chandragupt who was the son of the ruler of Jallandhar (Punjab). She became a widow at a young age. Her husband probably died of a heart attack since it is mentioned in the inscription that he died while trying to climb on to an elephant's back. After becoming a widow she came back to her parental home to pass the rest of her life. While living there (Lakhamandal) she built a Shiv temple in memory of her husband, and for the salvation of his soul. In one of the inscriptions she prays to the Trinity (Brahma, Vishnu and Mahesh) that as long as the Earth, the Mountains, the Sea, the Moon, the Sun and the Stars exist, so should this temple, to the memory of Chandragupt, exist. The 33 Sanskrit stanzas which are inscribed on stone are the work of the poet Basudeo Bhatt and the inscribing on the rock was done by Ishwarnag, son of Nagdatt. It has been incised with skill and precision and is in a good state of preservation.

In the 7th century A.D. the Chinese pilgrim Hiuen Tsang who was in India during Harsh's reign, gives a good description of the Doon region. Harsh, who ruled for 41 years from A.D. 606 onwards, made the rulers of distant lands, like Jallandhar (Punjab), Kashmir, Garhwal-Kumaun and Nepal, his feudatories.

According to Hiuen Tsang, after travelling for 66 miles (400 Li in Chinese measure) in a north-easterly direction from Thaneshwar (in Haryana) he arrived in Strudhan region (Su-lu-kin-na in Chinese). As per his assessment the boundaries of this area measured 6000 Li or 1000 miles. The Ganga flowed on its eastern boundary whilst the Yamuna in the middle and on the northern boundary were the high Himalayas. This area nearly covers the northern portions of to-days Saharanpur, Ambala districts, Nahan in Himachal Pradesh, Dehra Dun, Tehri and Uttarkashi districts of Garhwal. He describes the towns of Strudhan on the Yamuna, Mayapur (Haridwar-Kankhal) on the Ganga and Brahmapur in the north-east. All these towns were well populated and lot of trade and commerce flowed through them. The people, other than those of Brahmapur, were literate, cultured and civilised and they were not Buddhists in their religious belief. Sanskrit was the state language.

After the death of Harsh a number of local chiefs became independent. One such chief would be Adiverman. Rock inscriptions discovered in a village called Paletha, near Devparyag, above Rishikesh, point out towards this theory. From these inscriptions, discovered in 1964-65 A.D., it appears that the above named chief started his rule in 7th century A.D. and was followed by four of his descendants. Their area of influence appears to be the south-western part of Garhwal, which would include the Doon. These rulers were of the Paurav clan as opposed to the Yadavs of the Yamuna valley. Since there is no mention of the Kalsi rock edict in Hiuen Tsang's account of his travels, in the Doon, it seems that by then Kalsi had been destroyed as a habitation and had gone back to the wild, with the local people having forgotten about the edict. Lakhamandal on the other hand continued to thrive and was probably under a chief from Himachal Pradesh, who could be of Sirmur or Tharoch.

In the last couple of decades of the 7th century A.D. the northern belt of the Garhwal mountains, was being controlled by the founder of the Katuri dynasty named Masantan-va-Vasantan. Simultaneously Kanakpal was laying the foundations of his kingdom in the southern mountains. The Pundir rulers of Mayapur (Haridwar) considered the Katuris as coming from an inferior stock, and would take their daughters in marriage but would not give their own to them. Perhaps at this time the western Doon was under the sway of Raja Risalu who was from the Saka clan. He is supposed to have had his capital at Haripur on the banks of the Yamuna. There is still a village bearing this name. Near this village there is a mound known as Raja Risalu-ki-tibri (King Risalu's hillock) under which his town is supposed to be buried.

Very little is known about the conditions prevailing in the Doon during 8th, 9th and 10th centuries. According to the Muslim historians of these times it appears that towards the end of 10th century A.D. one Chand Rai (Raja Chandra) was ruling over modern day Ambala and Saharanpur districts as well as the lower reaches of the Yamuna valley inside the Doon valley. Similarly Haridwar, Rishikesh and the surrounding areas were under an independent Pundir ruler or under a Viceroy or Governor of the Katuri rulers or may be under Chand Rai.

Pilgrimage to Badri-Kedar shrines was a regular feature and people from the rest of the country used to be eager to come on such trips. Persons who for some reason or the other, mostly because of physical disability, could not come on pilgrimage personally would depute another in their stead. This person was known as ''Proxy'' and his expenses on the journey were borne by the appointer. The benefit of the Proxy's pilgrimage supposedly did not go to him but was to go to his appointer since he had paid for the trip. It was at the end of the 8th and the beginning of the 9th century A.D. that the great Adi Shankara (Shankracharya) came from Kerala to this part of India. Shankaracharya is said to have been responsible for getting the people of India, including Nepal, to renounce Buddhism and revert to the ancient Vedic religion. In this task he was assisted by Udayan Acharya and local princes who were Shivaits or Vaishnavaits. They were glad to assist him because of political motives, as the Buddhist rulers had usurped the best provinces of India. In Garhwal and Kumaun, as in Nepal, Shankara displaced the Buddhist priests of Kedar, Badri and Pashupati temples. In their place he introduced priests from Kerala whose successors still perform the daily rituals at these temples. The dispersion or absorption of the Buddhists in this area must have been accompanied by considerable political activity as is bound to happen in religious revolutions. When he arrived at Rishikesh he found that the idol at the Vishnu temple had been buried by the local Brahmin priests for fear of the Buddhists. He had it dug up and re-established in the temple.

Another school blames the Turkish invasion in which large number of monastries were looted and the Bhikshu Sanghas were destroyed. Furthermore, the Tantric and Vajraic cults also made people lose faith in Buddhism, which finally disappeared from India four centuries later.

By the 11th century A.D. the Western Doon had come under Chand Rai (Raja Chandra) who had his capital at Sarsawa on the bank of the Yamuna in Saharanpur district. The region west of Sirhind, in the Punjab, was ruled by Trilochan Pal who was a descendant of Jaipal, the Brahmin minister of the Turkish rulers—the Shahiyas, who ruled over the Kabul valley and Kandhar. This Brahmin usurped the throne and founded what has been called the Hindu-Shahiya dynasty. During his descendant Jaipal's time Mahmud of Ghazni started to raid India. Jaipal was defeated twice by Mahmud when he resisted the raids on his territories. After the second defeat Jaipal committed suicide. There were constant border disputes between the two Indian rulers namely Chand Rai of Sarsawa and Jaipal's grandson Trilochan Pal, who was the ruler of the Punjab. However, in order to face Mahmud jointly and save themselves, from ruination at his hands, they decided to patch up their differences. To achieve this Trilochan Pal's son Bhimpal was to wed Chand Rai's daughter. When Bhimpal went to Sarsawa to bring back his bride he was put under detention by Chand Rai. Once again the differences between the two rulers flared up.

In 1019 A.D. Mahmud Ghazni on his return journey, after his raid upto Mathura, went up the Ganga/Yamuna Doab along the Yamuna river. Chand Rai wanted to give him a fight instead of letting him plunder and enslave his people. But Bhimpal who was under detention and whose family had faced Mahmud's might advised against it. He suggested that Chand Rai should instead move his wealth along with his war elephants, cavalry and as many troops as possible, into the Shiwalik hills. Accordingly Chand Rai came up the Yamuna valley in the Shiwaliks to a distance of 15 "Farsaks" (one Farsak is approximately 4½ miles). Hence he must have come 66 miles up the river valley which would place him near about Kalsi.

Mahmud, after ransacking Sarsawa pursued Chand Rai into the Doon and on 6th January 1019 A.D. shortly before midnight, attacked his encampment. In the fight and in the chaos that followed most of Chand Rai's soldiers were either killed or taken prisoner. It took Mahmud's men three days to collect all the loot, including the war elephants and the prisoners. The gold, silver and jewels were valued at 3,000,000 Dirhams. The number of prisoners taken was 7,50,000 including women and children. These prisoners were sold in the slave markets of Asia-minor, Iraq and Khorasan for two to ten Dirhams each. Till his death in 1030 A.D. Mahmud continued to raid this country.

During the 11th-12th century A.D. the Doon was probably under the Tomar rulers, of Shakambhari region in Saharanpur district, followed by the Chauhans. Their reign extended over present day Haryana and the north-west Uttar Pradesh hills. According to the Shiwalik pillar inscription of 1163 A.D. found at the foot of the first range, on the Saharanpur side, of the Shiwaliks, Vigrahraj (Bisaldev), who was the grandson of Ajai Raj, was the most powerful ruler. This Ashokan pillar was used by Vigrahraj to have his own virtues and the limits of his empire engraved on it. According to one of the three inscriptions his rule extended from the Himalaya in the north to the Vindhyas in the south. He is also known as Shakambhari Raja. Silver and copper coins of the Chauhans have been found in the Doon valley proper. On the silver coins, on the obverse side, is the Nandi Bull, facing the viewer with the words "Sri Samant Dev" inscribed on top, while on the reverse side is a rider on a horse with a spear in hand, and the name of the Raja inscribed on the rim. Although these Chauhans belonged to Ajmer in Malwa, yet, perhaps because of their having adopted Shakambhari Devi as their family deity, they were known after her and the hills around Ajmer were also known as "Shiwaliks." In the Garhwal region there are three places which are still called Ajmer. A case of national integration !

Haridwar and its surrounding area was supposed to be under the rule of an independent Pundir ruler called Amardev, though there is no historical evidence to this effect. However according to a folk tale he had to give his seven years old daughter in wedlock to the old Katyuri ruler Pritam Dev who had no son, and hoped to beget one by this union. Although Amardev who was independent of Pritam Dev, did not want this marriage, he had to yield because he was afraid of the Katyuri might. The bride Moladei went to Badri on a pilgrimage and whilst at Joshimath she prayed at Narsingh's temple. In the course of time she delivered a son who was named Dhan Dev. His grandson was such a tyrant ruler that he was murdered by his palanquin bearers. With him seated in it they jumped down a ravine and carried him to his end.

With the Muslim invasions and their plundering raids a number of people fled from the plains and sought refuge in the region north of the Shiwaliks and in the Ganga-Yamuna valleys. Amongst them must have been a number of artisans and craftsmen, because in that era this region became a big centre for making idols in stone and metal as well as other handicrafts and musical instruments. The Chandela ruler Yashoverman, in his Khajurao rock inscription, proudly proclaims that the idol of Vishnu that he has installed in his temple was given to him by Devpal of Kanyakubj. His father had got it after winning a war with the Kangra ruler, who had got it as a mark of friendship from the ruler of Tibet, who in turn had obtained it from one of the stone carving centres around Kedarnath. A large number of such idols made in Uttarakhand are in South Indian style. They were probably made by artisans who may have been taught by crafstmen who came in Shankaracharya's entourage.

At the end of the 12th century and the beginning of 13th century A.D. the political situation in the Doon is not known. It may or may not have come under the rule of the Gorkha chiefs Ashokchal Dev and Rachal Dev, who brought Kumaun and Garhwal under their suzerainty in the last quarter of the 12th and first quarter of the 13th century A.D. After their reigns their vassals split the region into innumerable independent principalities. In the Garhwal region there were as many as 64 Chieftains, each having his own fortress (Garhi) perched on a hill-top or some other vantage point. Of these 64 Garhs as many as 24 were in the Doon. Those still known are Kaulagarh, Nala Pani (Garh), Shergarh, Shahpur (Garh), Santor (Garh), Virbhadra (Garh), Laldhang, Chandi, Barkot, Shargarh, Kanigarh and Nanurgarh.

For the next 200 years or so very little is known about the happenings in the Valley.

However, a certain amount of information is available about the Chakrata region and the Yamuna valley. There is a hand-written manuscript, in the Bhandarkar Research Institute, Pune, which is about the kings of Ekchakra. The description given of this kingdom fits in with the geography of present day Chakrata and the adjoining Yamuna valley and its tributaries. In the Mahabharat also this area has been referred to as "Ekchakra", eulogising it as, "where there was no fear of any illness...the climate is salubrious and health giving''. Seven Rulers of Ekchakra are mentioned in the Bhandarkar Library manuscript. Since there is mention of one of these rulers fighting the Muslim rulers of Delhi it is possible that their respective kingdoms adjoined one another. The period of the Ekchakra rulers was probably from 1280 to 1390 A.D.

One of the rulers of Western Doon, during the above period or thereabout, was Rana Dev Pal or Ran Pal with his seat at Santor. Balban of Delhi invaded Dev Pal's kingdom in 1257 A.D., because he had given refuge to Kutgul Khan, who had married Sultan Naseeruddin's widow. On being defeated in battle the Rana fled and Balban's forces occupied the town of Sirmur, west of the Yamuna, in the Kyarda Dun.

The next Delhi ruler to come to the Doon was Sultan Feroze Tughluq. He entered the Doon valley via Ambala and Saharanpur districts and then up along the Yamuna valley. All the way he was accorded a right royal reception by the local chieftains, who had accepted his overlordship. After collecting tribute from them he returned to Delhi. When Feroze Tughluq was 80 years old he handed over the reins of government to his son Mohammed Khan. He was very fond of hunting and at one time he camped in the Western Doon for two months. Because of his weak rule and lust for a life of debauchery he was deposed in an armed coup, by his courtiers. He took refuge with the Raja of Sirmur and his nephew took the throne under the name and style of Ghiasuddin Tughluq II.

Prince Mohammed Khan, with the help of the Raja of Sirmur started making plans to reconquer his throne. His nephew Ghiasuddin sent an army, into the Doon and they were successful in defeating Prince Mohammed Khan and his allies.

In the 14th century the Muslim rulers had brought the districts of Ambala and Saharanpur under their regime. They may have wanted to expand their territories across the Shiwaliks but their attempts were unsuccessful because of the inhospitable terrain and climate. However, this did not stop them from making periodic forays into the Doon Valley and its adjoining areas. The first major ransacking, pillaging and murdering in the Valley, from the Ganga to the Yamuna and beyond was by the Turk Timur or Tamerlane - the Lame, so called because of his limp.

Timur has left a vivid account of his pillaging through the Doon in his autobiography titled "Malfuzat-I-Timuri". It was in the last week of December 1399 A.D. after the capture of Mirat (Meerut) that he turned northwards along the Ganga and Yamuna rivers. Given below is the English translation, by Eliot and Dowson, of a relevant portion of his autobiography.

BATTLES OF THE GANGES

"On the 1st Jumada-L awwal I placed the left wing of the army under the command of Amir Jahan Shah, with orders to march up the Jamuna, to take every fort and town and village he came to, and to put all the infidels of the country to the sword. The Amir led off his army to execute my commands. I ordered Amir Shaikh Nuru-d-din to take charge of the heavy baggage and convey it to the banks of the river Kara-su. (The local name is "Black river" or "Kali Nadi" in Hindi.) I, myself determined upon directing my arms against the infidels on the Ganges. I accordingly marched towards the river, which is fourteen kos from Mirat. Amir Sulaiman Shah whom I had left with the baggage, came up according to order, and joined me on the march with his division. The first day I marched 6 kos, and halted for the night at the village of Mansura. Next day, the 2nd of the month, I arrived early in the morning at Piroz-pur, and then I proceeded for two to three kos along the bank of river in search of a ford. At breakfast time I reached the place of transit, but found no ford. A party of my men entered the river on their horses and crossed by swimming. I also was about to guide my horse into the water to cross in the same way, when the Amirs and Nuyans cast themselves upon their knees, and represented that Prince Pir Muhammad and Amir Jahan Shah, with the right wing of the army, had crossed the river near Piroz-pur, and that it was advisable for me not to cross over that day. I assented to their representation and encamped on the bank of the river, but I ordered Amir Jahan Malik, and others belonging to the division of Prince Shah Rukh, to cross over and pass the night there. On the following day, the 3rd of the month, I marched up the river for a distance of fifteen kos, towards

Tughlikpur, and that place was five kos distant, when I heard that a large body of infidel Hindus had collected at the fords of the river. I immediately ordered Mubashar Bahadur and Ali Sultan Tawachi to proceed with 5,000 horses to chastise these infidels, and I proceeded on my way to Tughlikpur. As I went on, the air and the wind affected me, and I felt a pain in my right arm, which every moment increased. It caused me much suffering, and sundry hot applications were applied. (Timur was probably suffering from rheumatism). I was now informed that there was a force of Hindus coming down the river in forty eight boats with the intention of fighting. This intelligence acted as a cure for my pain, and eagerness for the fight made me forget my suffering. I mounted my horse, and taking with me 1,000 troopers, who were at hand, we struck our heels into the flanks of our horses and hastened to the side of the river. As soon as my braves saw the boats, some of them rode their horses into the river and swam to the vessels; then, seizing fast hold of the sides, they defeated all the efforts of the Hindus to shake them off. They forced their way into some of the boats, put infidels to the sword, and threw their bodies into the river; thus sending them through water to the fires of hell. Some of my men dismounted, and, proceeding to the ford, assailed the enemy with arrows. The occupants of the boats returned the arrows, but the vessels were at length wrested from their possession, and brought with their contents to my presence. The enemy had lashed ten of their boats together with chains and strong ropes, and these vessels maintained the fight. My men plied them with arrows till they slew many of them; they then swam off, and, boarding the boats, put every living soul to the sword, sending them through water to the fires of hell.

When I was at leisure, after this affair with the boats I, on the same day, marched on to Tughlikpur, and there encamped. I sent an Amir Allah-dad, Bayazid Kuchin and Altun Bakshi with a force as an advance-guard to cross the river and to obtain the information for me of the whereabouts of the enemy. After their departure, when three watches of the night had passed, two horsemen came in from Allah-dad to report that the reconnoitring party had discovered a ford by which they had passed the river, and had found on the other side a large body of infidel Hindus, with a great amount of property and goods under the command of a man named Mubarak Khan. Confident in their numbers, they were ready to fight. As soon as I learned this, I ordered my forces to be drawn out, and I mounted my horse and started off greatly incensed. Before morning broke I passed the Ganges with 1,000 horsemen fully equipped for service. After proceeding a kos, the time for morning prayer arrived, so I alighted from my horse in the plain, paid my devotions, and offered my praises. I then again mounted, in full assurance of the favour of Almighty, and went on towards the enemy. Mubarak Khan was informed of my approach, and stood, with 10,000 fighting men, in battle array prepared to fight.

THREE GREAT VICTORIES IN ONE DAY

Attended by my escort, I was carefully examining and scrutinising the enemy, and the whole of my 1,000 horsemen had not come up. The great bulk of the army was engaged in plundering expeditions at a distance. I had but, 1,000 men and the enemy numbered 10,000, still I put my trust in God and prayed to Him for victory. By a wonderful coincidence, just at this juncture, Saiyid Khawaja and Jahan Malik with 5,000 horse whom I had sent on a plundering excursion, having made a sweep, came up in my rear just in the nick of time. If it had not been so I might here have said farewell, for I could hardly have escaped. I deemed their arrival a most fortunate omen, offered my thanks to God and faced the foe. I ordered Amir Allah-dad and Amir Shah Malik to make a charge upon the enemy with the thousand horsemen of my escort and not to be dismayed by the numbers of their antagonists. When, in obedience to my command, they dashed forward, the enemy did not await their charge, but wavered and turned and fled. My brave fellows pursued and killed many of them, made their wives and children prisoners, plundered their property and goods, and secured a vast number of cows and buffaloes. When, by the favour of God, I had secured this victory, I got off my horse and prostrated myself on the ground to pay my thanks.

While the soldiers were occupied in securing the spoil I sat down to take a little rest, but some of the reconnoitring party came in with the information that there was a large number of Hindus assembled in the valley of Kutila, on the side of the Ganges, having made that valley a place of refuge. (In the Zafar Nama the word is "Kupila" which is an old name of Haridwar. Perhaps he made a mistake in the script. His later description of the place also fits in with that of Haridwar.) I instantly mounted, and leaving the greater part (tamami) of my force to secure the spoil, I started off for the valley of Kutila with only five hundred horsemen. When, I reached the place I found an immense number of Gabrs assembled in the darra. (Timur in his Memoirs has called certain infidels who were fire worshippers, "Gabrs". He has even described their tenets. One such "Gabr" named in the autobiography is "Safi" or "Sapi" who was at the siege of Meerut.) Instantly I ordered Amir Shah Malik and Ali Sultan Twachi to charge the enemy without paying the slightest heed to their numbers, although they were twenty to one. Spurring their horses, shouting their war cry, and brandishing their swords, they fell upon the forces (fawaj) of the enemy like hungry lions upon a flock of sheep. At the first charge the ranks of the enemy were broken, and many of their men fell under the blows of the sword. God thus gave me victory with such a small band of followers over such a numerous host of the enemy. After many of them had been slain, those who escaped kept in the thickets and defiles (darra), skulking like foxes and jackals. An immense booty was left, and my braves were busy in securing it. Only one hundred men remained with me as a guard, the other four hundred were engaged in collecting the plunder. At this conjuncture Malik Shaikha, commander of the infidels, with five hundred horse and a large force of foot, knitting their brows with hatred advanced against me. I perceived this force coming to attack me, and my warlike spirit was roused, so, with the hundred men who supported me, I spurred on to meet the foe. When about the distance of a bow-shot remained between us, one of the horsemen, who was in advance of me, turned round and told me that it was a force belonging to Shaikh Kukar, one of my dependents and servants, who was coming to join my camp. These words, so far from the truth, reached my ears, and I was satisfied and turned back. But Malik Shaikha drew his sword, and came dashing on with his men against my followers, of whom several received wounds. When I ascertained the fact that these men were foes, and not the people of Shaikh Kukar I turned rein, and charging the enemy despatched many of them at the first attack. Malik Shaikha received a spear thrust in his stomach, and a sword cut on the head. He fell from his horse, and my men made him prisoner. They bound his hands to his neck and brought him to my presence. Many of the Gabrs were killed and wounded; and few escaped half dead (with fright). Malik Shaikha a very large and powerful man, was brought before me, wounded as he was. The awe of my presence added to his wounds, took such an effect on him that when I asked him a question, he surrendered his soul to the Lord of Hell before he could answer me. God thus granted me two great victories in one day, and I offered my thanksgiving for his favour.

Again I mounted my steed, and as I did so intelligence was brought to me that in the valley (darra) of Kutila, two kos distant, a large number of infidels and Gabrs had collected with their wives and children, and with property, goods and cattle beyond all estimate. The road thither was arduous, through jungle and thickets. When I heard this my first thought was that I had been awake since midnight, I had travelled a long distance without any halt, and had surmounted many difficulties, I had won two splendid victories with a few brave soldiers, and I was very tired, I would therefore stop and take rest. But then I remembered that I had drawn my sword, and had come to Hind with the resolution of waging a holy war against its infidels, and so long as it was possible to fight with them, rest was unlawful for me. Although I had only a few Amirs and few soldiers with me, I placed my trust in God, and determined to attack the enemy. Spurring my horse, I started, and when I had gone a little way, I remembered how three days before I had sent Prince Pir Muhammad and Amir Sulaiman Shah across the river from the village Pirozpur, and I thought how opportune it would be if they were now to join me. But then I said how can they know that I have crossed the river, or how can they conceive that I am engaged in this distant place in action with the infidels. I was going along with my head bent down, engaged in these reflections, when suddenly a large body of men came to view in the distance and every man had something to say about them. I sent forward some scouts to ascertain what force it was, and as they drew near they discovered that it was the division of Prince Pir Muhammad Jahangir and Amir Sulaiman Shah. The scouts immediately proceeded to the prince and told him the state of affairs, how I had already won two great victories that day, and that for the third time I was marching against a numerous body of Gabrs collected at Kutila. The prince and his men had previously heard nothing of me, and now, on getting this timely information, they were very glad, and turned to wait upon me. The scouts whom I had sent to reconnoitre returned, and told me that the prince with his division in martial array was coming up. They added that the prince knew nothing about me until they informed him of the enterprise I had in hand, and that he was now on the way to meet me. This information, so in accordance with my wishes, rejoiced me greatly. It was quite beyond my expectations, for I had no idea of the prince being near; so I was glad, and prostrated myself on the earth in thanks to God for having granted me what my heart desired. It was now the time of afternoon (asr) prayer, and it was the fourth of the month. The prince and Amir Sulaiman Shah came up with their numerous force, and were honoured with an interview. Pressing on with all haste I passed the jungle and thickets and arrived in front of the infidels. After a slight resistance the enemy took to flight, but many of them fell under the swords of my soldiers. All the wives and children of the infidels were made prisoners, and their property and goods, gold, money and grain, horses, camels (shutur), cows and bufalloes in countless numbers, fell as spoil into the hands of my soldiers. Satisfied with this rout of the enemy, I said the afternoon prayers in public in that desert, and I returned thanks to God that I had fought three times with enemies outnumbering my men by ten and twenty to one, and that in each battle I had gained a signal victory.

The day now drew to a close and night came on, but in that desert there was no place for me to alight and pitch my camp, so I turned back with my enormous booty, and encamped in the field where I had won the second victory. There I passed the night in repose.

At this place information was brought to me that fifteen kos off, up the river, and near the mountains, there was a place in which there was the image of a cow, carved out of stone, and that the river (ab) ran from its mouth. In the belief of the people of Hindustan the source of the river Ganges was in this same mountain. The Hindu infidels worship the Ganges, and once every year they come on pilgrimage to this place, which they consider the source of the river, to bathe and to have their heads and beards shaved. They believe these acts to be the means of obtaining salvation and securing future rewards. They dispense large sums in charity among those who wear the Brahmanical thread, and they throw money into the river. When infidels die in distant parts, their bodies are burned and the ashes are brought to this river and are thrown into it. This they look upon as a means of sanctification. When I learned these facts, I resolved to war against these infidels of this place, so that I might obtain the merit of overthrowing them. (This account can be of no other place but Haridwar.)

Information was also brought to me that all the men whom I had defeated in the valley of Kutila, before coming hither, had not been killed. The day having drawn to a close, many had escaped and were hiding in the thickets and broken ground. Neither had all their property been plundered. So I resolved to go again next day to that valley, and to put all the surviving infidels to death. At dawn on the 5th Jumada-I awwal I said my morning prayer, and started with a suitable force for the valley of Kutila, which lies at the foot of lofty mountains and on the banks of the Ganges. During the night all the Gabrs who had been scattered reassembled under their chiefs, and as they had no place of refuge more secure, they resolved that if the Musalmans returned, they would fight till they died. So they were prepared for battle. When I approached the darra, I made the following disposition of my forces for conquering the infidels. I placed my right wing under Prince Pir Mohammad Jahangir and Amir Sulaiman Shah. The left wing I gave into the charge of several Amirs of Jumans. I gave the command of the advance to Amir Shah Malik, and I kept the centre under my own orders. Upon entering the valley the infidels at first, having drawn up their forces, put on a bold appearance and advanced to the attack. I restrained the braves of my advance guard, and of the right and left wings, and, having massed them together, charged the enemy, shouting aloud our war cry until the hills and valleys resounded. The sounds of the kettledrums and other war like instruments fell upon the battlefield, and at the first and second charge dismay seized upon the enemy, and they took to flight. My brave men displayed great courage and daring; they made their swords their banners, and exerted themselves in slaying the foe. They slaughtered many of the infidels, and pursued those who fled to the mountains. So many of these were killed that their blood ran down the mountains and the plain, and thus (nearly) all were sent to hell. The few who escaped, wounded, weary, and half dead, sought refuge in the defiles of the hills. Their property and goods, which exceeded all computation, and their countless cows and buffaloes, fell as spoil into the hands of my victorious soldiers.

When I was satisfied with the destruction I had dealt out to the infidels, and the land was cleaned from the pollution of their existence, I turned back victorious and triumphant, laden with spoil. On that same day I crossed the Ganges, and said my midday prayers in the congregation, on the bank of that river. I prostrated myself in humble thanks to God, and afterwards again mounting my horse, marched five miles down the river and then encamped. It now occurred to my mind that I had marched as a conqueror from the river Sind to Delhi, the capital of the kings of India. I had put the infidels to the edge of the sword on both sides of my route, and had scoured the land; I had seized upon the throne of the kings of India; I had defeated Sultan Mohammed, the king of Delhi, and triumphed over him; I had crossed the rivers Ganges and Jamuna, and I had sent many of the abominable infidels to hell, and had purified the land from their foul existence. I rendered thanks to Almighty God that I had accomplished my undertaking, and had waged against the infidels that holy war I had resolved upon: then I determined to turn my course towards Samarkand, my capital and paradise. On the fifth of the month I mounted and proceeded towards the heavy baggage, and, having travelled several kos, I encamped and sent some Yurutchis (Quarter masters) to go and bring up the baggage.

VICTORIES IN THE SIWALIK HILLS

On Tuesday I marched six kos, and the heavy baggage was now four kos distant. I now learned that an immense number of infidels had collected in the Siwalik hills. Upon inquiring into the nature of these hills, I was informed that the people of Hindustan compute this mountain region at one lac and the fourth part of a lac. (This meaning was derived from the Hindi word "Savalakh" meaning 1 ¼ lakh or 1,25,000, in other words the mountain range with 1,25,000 peaks. However, "Shiwalik" or "Siwalik" is actually a derivative from the name of Lord Shiv composed of the words "Shiv" + 'Lik" meaning mark or symbol. Thus the word could mean the symbol of Shiv.)

43

It has narrow and strong valleys (darra) in which the infidels had assembled. When I received this information I immediately ordered the troops, with the baggage, to march towards the Shiwalik hills, and I, myself, proceeded in that direction. Marching in the evening and into the night, I accomplished five kos, and then encamped in the hills. At this halt Prince Khalil Sultan and Amir Shaikh Nuru-d-din, who had been with the baggage, and to whom I had issued my orders, came up. When I was seated on my cushion of royalty, with all the princes and Amirs around me, Amir Sulaiman Shah, Amir Shah Malik, Amir Shaikh Nuru-d-din and other Amirs rose from their places and coming forward, bowed their knees before me and said: "So long as we, your servants, are able to move hand and foot, we will execute your orders, but what necessity is there for our great Amir to take all this toil and hardship upon himself, and that he should now order us to march against the infidels of the Siwalik, and to rout and destroy them?" I replied: "My principal object in coming to Hindustan, and in undergoing all this toil and hardship, has been to accomplish two things. The first was to war with the infidels the enemies of the Muhammadan religion; and by this religious warfare to acquire some claim to reward in the life to come. The other was a worldy object; that the army of Islam might gain something by plundering the wealth and valuables of the infidels: plunder in war is as lawful as their mothers' milk to Musalmans who war for their faith, and the consuming of that which is lawful is a means of grace." When the Amirs received this answer, they maintained silence. I now despatched some horsemen with all speed to Amir Jahan Shah, whom I had sent off a week before to plunder the forts and towns on the Jamuna, ordering him to rejoin me with all speed, that he and his men might also share in the merit of fighting against the infidels. The Amir came in directly and joined me. Then, placing my trust in God, I mounted my charger, and, on the 10th of the month, marched towards the Siwalik hills.

In a valley (darra) of these hills there was a Rai named Bahruz, the number of whose forces, and whose lofty, rugged, narrow, and strong position, made him superior to all the chiefs of the hills, and, indeed, of most of Hindustan. At the present time especially, he, having heard of my approach, had done his best to strengthen his position, and all the malignant Rais of the country had gathered round him. Proud of the number of his men and soldiers, the height of his Darra and abode, he stood firm, resolved upon fighting. On the other hand, I resolved upon attacking Bahruz and conquering the Siwalik hills.

CONQUEST OF THE SIWALIK

On the 10th Jumada-I-awwal I mounted my horse and drew my sword, determined on fighting the infidels of the Siwalik. First I attended to the disposition of my forces. I gave the command of the right wing to Prince Pir Muhammad Jahangir and Amir Sulaiman Shah; and I placed the left wing under Prince Sultan Hussain and Amir Jahan Shah. I sent forward Shaikh Nuru-d-din and Amir Shah Malik in command of the advance guard of the centre. When my arrangements were complete, we marched, and on approaching the valley, I ordered the drums to be beaten, the instruments to be sounded and the war-cry to be raised, until the hills and valleys echoed with their sounds. I proceeded to the mouth of the Darra, where I alighted from my horse, and sent forward my Amirs and soldiers. They all dismounted, and, girding up their loins, marched forward to the conflict, full of resolution and courage. The demon-like Hindus were lurking in places of ambush, and attacked my soldiers, but these retaliated with showers of arrows, and falling upon them with the sword forced their way into the valley. There they closed with them, and fighting most bravely they slaughtered the enemy with sword, knife, and dagger. So many fell that blood ran down in streams. The infidel Gabrs were dismayed at the sight, and took to flight. The holy warriors pursued them, and made heaps of slain. A few Hindus, in a wretched plight, wounded and half dead, escaped, and hid themselves in holes and caves. An immense spoil, beyond all compute, in money, goods and articles, cows and buffaloes, fell into the hands of my soldiers. All the Hindu women and children in the valley were made prisoners. When I was fully satisfied with the defeat of the insolent infidels of the Siwalik, and with the victory I had gained, I returned triumphant, and encamped in the same place. This night I passed as a guest in the tents of Prince Pir Muhammad Jahangir.

When morning came I ordered all the plunder that had fallen into the hands of my men to be collected, for I understood that some had obtained much and other little, and I had it all fairly divided. On that day, the 11th of the month, I marched and joined the heavy baggage. I encamped at the village of Bahrah, in the country of Miyapur. Next day I again marched, and accomplishing four kos, halted at the village of Shikk Sar. An enormous quantity of plunder, goods and articles, prisoners and cattle, was now collected together with the heavy baggage, and the people of the army were very heavily laden; consequently it was difficult to march more than four or five kos in a day. On the 13th I encamped at the village of Kandar.

On the following day, the 14th Jumada-I-awwal, I crossed the river Jamuna with the baggage, and encamped in another part of the Siwalik hills. Here I learned that in this part of the Siwalik there was a Rajah of great rank and power, by name of Ratan Sen. His valley (darra) was more lofty and more narrow, and his forces more numerous than those of Raja Bahruz. The mountains around are exceedingly lofty, and the jungles and woods remarkably thick, so that access to the valley was impossible, except by cutting through the jungle. When I understood these facts about Ratan Sen, I felt my responsibilities as a warrior of the Faith, and I was unwilling that the night should pass in ease: so I issued a summon for the attendance of the Amirs and other officers. When they were all present, I directed them to prepare their men for battle, and that they should carry hatchets and bills, etc., for clearing away the jungle. I directed some thousands of torches to be lighted, and the drums of departure to be sounded. So at night I mounted my horse, and when I reached the jungle, I ordered my warriors to cut away the jungle, and make a way through. They proceeded to execute my order, and all night long they were occupied in clearing a passage. I went on to the front, and as morning broke I had traversed twelve kos by the way that had been pierced through the jungle. When I emerged from the jungle, the dawn appeared, and I alighted from my horse and said my morning prayers. Then I again mounted, and on the morning of 15th, I found myself between two mountains, one the Siwalik mountain, the other the Kuka mountain. This was the valley (darra), and it was exceedingly strong. The hills on both sides raised their heads to the clouds. In the front of this valley Raja Ratan Sen had drawn out his forces, as numerous as ants or locusts. There he had taken his stand, prepared for battle with an advance-guard, a right wing and left wing, in regular martial array.

As soon as my eye fell upon the dispositions of Raja Ratan Sen, I ordered my warriors to shout their battle-cry aloud, and the drums and other instruments to be sounded. The noise reverberated through the hills, and filled the hearts of the infidels with dismay and trembling, so that they wavered. At this moment I ordered my forces to make one grand charge upon the infidels. At the first onset, the Hindus broke and fled, and my victorious soldiers pursued, slashing their swords, killing many of the fugitives, and sending them to hell. Only a few of them escaped, wounded and dispirited, and hiding themselves like foxes in the woods, thus saved their lives. When the soldiers gave up killing the infidels, they secured great plunder in goods and valuables, prisoners and cattle. No one of them had less than one or two hundred cows, and ten or twenty slaves-the other plunder exceeded all calculation. On this day Prince Pir Muhammad Jahangir and Amir Sulaiman Shah, with the right wing of the army and Prince Sultan Hussain and Amir Jahan Shah with the left wing, returned and joined me. By my orders they had parted from me, and had penetrated the valleys on my right and left. They had encountered and routed many infidels, and had slain great numbers of them, but they had not gained so much spoil (as my division). I was satisfied with the victory I had won over Ratan Sen and his forces, and all that he possessed had fallen into the hands of my soldiers. Day came to a close, and I encamped between the two mountains. The princes and Amirs of the right and left wing, whose way had lain through other valleys, came in to me in the evening, which was the evening of Friday, the 16th, (it must be borne in mind that the Muhammadan day begins at sunset) and reported to me their engagements with the enemy, and the men who had distinguished themselves by feats of valour. After a night's rest, on the morning of Friday, I arose and after saying my prayers I mounted and rode towards the valley of those two mountains, intent upon the conquest of the Siwalik hills........"

The Mansura and Pirozpur villages where Timur camped are on the right bank of the Ganga in the district of Muzaffarnagar. "Tughlikpur" is situated 17 miles north of present Muzaffarnagar town. "Ghauspur" is in Bijnor district on the left bank of Ganga near the Railway station of Balawali. "Kutil Darra" or pass is identified as the pass in the Siwaliks at Chandi. Kankhal and Haridwar were the towns plundered by him. His main opponent Rai Bahruz was perhaps the most powerful chief in the Doon Valley and he was probably blocking the Mohand or Kasumri pass, most probably the former. Five days after the battle with Bahruz, in the Doon, Timur crossed the Yamuna and entered the territory of Ratan Sen of Sirmur. Like the others the people of Sirmur also fell prey to the looting and killing by the marauder's soldiers.

From the number of prisoners taken and or killed, by the various invaders in the Doon, from Mohammed Ghazni to Timur, it seems that during this period the Doon was well populated in places. The fire-worshippers (Gabrs) referred to by Timur were either a tribe living in the Valley and have since perished or been absorbed by subsequent invaders, or perhaps he mistakenly referred to the Hindus thus because of their Vedic ritual of performing 'Havan' or fire worship at their morning prayers, and performing weddings before a sacred fire. This ritual is still practised by Arya Samajists - the followers of the teachings of the reformist Swami Dayanand, the founder of Arya Samaj in the 19th century A.D. Nothing is known about the successors to Rai Bahruz in the Valley. Probably the petty chiefs came back into their own and ruled over areas commanded by their individual fortresses.

After Rai Bahruz (whose real name could have been Bhag Datt or Bramh Datt or Vatsa Raj) who is supposed to have ruled till 1440 A.D. the next man to make an impact on the Doon was Ajay Pal the founder of the last ruling house of Garhwal and the Doon.

Ajay Pal is supposed to have ruled from 1500 to 1548 A.D. and was descended from the Lunar race of Rajputs, of the Panwar clan. His ancestor Kanak Pal had come from Dhar in Malwa (Rajasthan) and settled in Garhwal in the 9th century A.D.

According to a local folk tale Kanak Pal, on coming from Malwa, first settled in Saharanpur district and established the town of Gangoh. This is deduced from the discovery of coins of the Kanerki or Kanak series found in that area. Later on he is supposed to have gone into Garhwal via Haridwar.

The other traditional folk tale is that Kanak Pal was the younger step brother of the Raja of Dhar. Although Kanak Pal was proficient in all the requirements of a prince and ruler, he came under the influence of a sadhu (hermit) and became an ascetic at a young age. On the death of his guru (the sadhu) he left home, along with a couple of friends, and set off on a pilgrimage. Having arrived at Haridwar he wished to go to Badrinath. His friends tried to dissuade him because of the discomfort and difficulties faced while travelling in the mountainous terrain. Raja Bhanu Pratap of Chandpur-Garh sub-division of Garhwal had a daughter whom he was keen to marry to a man befitting his own station in life. One night the Lord Badri of Badrinath told Bhanu Pratap, in a dream, that a prince from Dhar was coming on a pilgrimage to him and was at present at Haridwar. ''Go forth and bring him to me and thereafter marry him to your daughter. Thus your daughter and her descendants shall rule this land'', he said.

Bhanu Pratap acted accordingly and Kanak Pal, who wanted to continue his ascetic life, on seeing the daughter and hearing of the dream married her and lived in Garhwal happily ever after. In course of time he ruled over his father-in-law's fiefdom.

Ajay Pal was the 36th descendant of Kanak Pal and assumed the reins of government in 1500 A.D. or thereabout. He is credited with having brought the 52 or 64 fiefs of Garhwal under one flag - his flag. The beginning of his reign was a turbulent one for him. The neighbouring ruler of Champawat attacked and defeated him. Having lost his army Ajay Pal fled and hid in one of the Himalaya ranges.

According to a folklore Ajay Pal then went into deep meditation and prayed to Lord Shiv, standing on one foot. Shiv was pleased by his devotion and he appeared in a vision and asked Ajay Pal to climb on his shoulders. Shiv then started increasing in height and became so tall that the Raja could see the tips of the heights of the Shiwalik ranges of the Doon. The Raja was scared and requested to be put down. Shiv put him down and told him that his rule will be, as far as his eyes had beheld. Encouraged by this vision he reorganised the remnants of his army and attacked his enemy who made peace once they were defeated. The defeat of Ajay Pal was the first and last of his career. Thereafter it was a matter of annexing one Garh (fortress) after another. He is also supposed to have built the town of Srinagar (Garhwal) as his capital. This town continued to be the capital of Garhwal Raj for the next 386 years till the Gorkha invasion when Raja Pradyuman Shah fled, abandoning it. The story of the founding of Srinagar town according to tradition is as follows:-

Once Ajay Pal came hunting in the area where Srinagar was later built. Here one of his hunting dogs was killed by a hare. Everyone was surprised by this incident of a harmless hare killing the hound. That night "Devi or Shakti" appeared to Ajay Pal in a dream and told him that he was on hallowed ground. She further said, "In the middle of the river (Alaknanda) carved on a rock is a "Sriyantra" which is my (Devi's) sign thus making it hallowed ground. This is the reason that the hare was able to get the better of your hound. Therefore you should establish your capital here and worship the 'Yantra' daily". Thus Ajay Pal moved his capital from Dewalgarh to Srinagar. Of course the rationale would be that this place is more or less in the middle of Garhwal which is easily accessible by river and road, and being on the pilgrim route to the Badri/Kedar shrines.

Another super-feat attributed to him is that he put up the doors of his palace, single handed. Apparently no timber was used in the building of the palace at Srinagar. It was all built of stone. When hundreds of workers could not put up the gate, Ajay Pal after a lot of fasting and prayer, put it up in the middle of the night. A maid servant saw him performing this feat. She was promptly killed by him because he wanted it kept a secret. Perhaps this could be a case of human sacrifice which was prevalent in those days. Such sacrifices were performed at the building of palaces, forts, tombs and even water channels. Maybe he performed this sacrifice on the completion of the palace. This palace was destroyed in the earthquake of 1803 A.D.

After consolidating his territory he introduced a number of social, economic and religious reforms. During his reign the Afghan General, Khwas Khan, crossed and recrossed the Doon thrice with his troops, in his fight against Islam Shah. He was the son of the Afghan ruler of Hindustan, Sher Shah Suri, the builder of the Grand Trunk Road from Calcutta to Peshawar. Apparently Khwas Khan had been befriended by Ajay Pal and was therefore allowed to pass through his domains.

It was from Ajay Pal's time that the Garhwal rulers were considered the incarnation of Lord Badrinath, and were known as "Bolden Badri" meaning the "Speaking Badri". They were also the temporal priests of the deity. The appointments, dismissals and other connected matters in respect of the ritualistic priests - the "Rawals" were in the hands of the Garhwal rulers. Ajay Pal was succeeded by Sahaj Pal who probably ruled from 1548 to 1581 A.D. His contemporary at that time was the great Mughal Akbar whose empire bordered that of Garhwal - the Shiwaliks being the boundary pillars. Haridwar was under Akbar while Najibabad, Afzalgarh and Chandi, across the Ganga, were in Garhwal. A large area of the Valley proper was under forests.

It is surprising that Akbar with all his might allowed the Garhwal ruler to keep his independent identity. From the findings of the historians it appears that although Garhwal remained independent it maintained diplomatic relations with the Mughal Court.

According to traditional history the Garhwal ruler had accepted the over-lordship of Akbar. This is based on the following story. The Garhwal ruler being, then, at court was summoned before the Emperor and was asked to give an account of his income and a description of his dominion. Whereupon the following day he presented a statement of his finances, and as for the description of his country placed a drawing of an emaciated camel before the king. On being asked its meaning he explained that "my domain is like this camel, full of high mountains and deep valleys and the income is just about enough to keep the body and soul, of my people, together". It is said that the Emperor was so pleased with the Raja's presence of mind that he exempted him from paying anything to the Royal treasury.

Right through the Mughal reign from Akbar onwards the Doon and its forests were their favourite hunting grounds. Again tradition has it that the present site of the Manager's bungalow at Arcadia Tea Estate in the Doon is where they (the Mughals) had one of their hunting lodges. They trapped Cheetahs in the Doon for their sport. Akbar in his life time is supposed to have collected as many as 9000 of them. Of course this is in praise of the Emperor, like a lot of other exaggerations, in the accounts written those days, by the sycophant courtiers.

At Haridwar, which was part of the Mughal empire, Akbar had a mint. Here copper coins were struck. On these coins there was the name of the mint on one side and the year of minting on the other. One of Akbar's items of daily use was Ganga water from Haridwar. Court officers had been appointed at Haridwar whose job it was to send the daily requirement of water by couriers, in sealed containers, to wherever the Emperor was staying.

Inspite of the fact that Akbar was friendly towards the hill Rajas, one of his fanatic and bigoted mansabdars played havoc in the low lands of their domains right from Doti-Kumaun to Sirmur, including the Doon. He was Hussain Khan 'Tukariya', a 3000 horse mansabdar. How he earned the nickname 'Tukariya' is in itself a story of his bigotry.

One day he inadvertently stood up to receive an old Hindu, who had a long white beard, thinking he was a Muslim. When he realised that the visitor was a Hindu Tukariya was very upset for having shown such courtesy to an infidel. Since that day he ordered that every Hindu must have a 'Tukara' (piece) of coloured cloth attached to his garment on the shoulder whenever he came out of his house. This would identify him as a Hindu. The young men of Lahore where he was the Governor, nicknamed him "Tukariya", a name which stuck to him throughout history. He used to get a lot of pleasure and satisfaction in destroying temples and killing Hindus. In deference to the life led by the prophet, Tukariya was very austere in his living habits.

Tukariya's last foray was in the Basantpur village area of Eastern Doon. In those days it was a prosperous region because 80 years later it was again looted by Khalil-ulah-Khan. In this raid Tukariya suffered a severe wound and he had to withdraw. He travelled by boat down the Ganga and was arrested at Garhmukteswar, under the orders of Akbar who thought that Tukariya had become a rebel. He was taken to Fatehpur Sikri where he died of his wounds.

Balbhadra Shah's reign from 1581 to 1591 A.D. which followed that of Sahaj Pal's was uneventful as far as the Doon was concerned. It continued to be a province of Garhwal Raj, barring the trans-Yamuna area which was under Sirmur.

50

The entire area on the right bank of the Yamuna from Paonta northwards was the territory of Sirmur Raj from the time of Raja Rasaloo. Rasaloo was the second son of Sal Bahan I, Rawal of Jaisalmer, who had captured a large area of Himachal Pradesh and ruled over it. The old capital of the state was situated in a corner of the Paonta valley and was named Sirmur. There is still a village in the area by that name. The place was probably named after one of Rasaloo's grandsons or it may have been the other way round, that the grandson was named after the place, having been born there. The custom in those days was, at least in Himachal Pradesh and Garhwal, to name the state after the name of its capital town. Despite subsequent shiftings of the capital the name of the state continued to be Sirmur as was the case with the state of Tehri-Garhwal also after 1815 A.D. The original town of Sirmur was devastated by a flood in the Giri river. There are several legends about the destruction of the town because of the curse of a woman during the reign of Raja Madan Singh. One of them goes like this:-

A woman who was well versed in necromancy and acrobatics came to Madan Singh's court and offered to perform her feats before him. She entertained him with various gymnastics. The Raja challenged her that if she would cross the river Giri, by walking on a rope slung across it, he would give her half his kingdom. She took up the challenge and successfully crossed the river. On seeing this achievement the Raja and some of his courtiers became apprehensive about losing a part of the state. He therefore offered the remaining half of the state to her if she would recross in the same manner. She started back and when she was mid-way he had the rope cut and she plunged to her death. Before drowning she uttered a curse that the State and the Raja would perish. The devastation of the capital Sirmur by a flood in the Giri and the Raja perishing in it without an heir are supposed to be the sequel to this episode. This is the most prevalent and popular of the various tales. But they all have in common the curses of a woman.

After the above mentioned calamities had befallen the people of Sirmur they were without a ruler and chaos prevailed in the State. There are again a number of stories of how they got a new ruler for themselves. The most widely accepted tale is that the elders amongst the surviving populace of Sirmur decided to send a deputation to Jaisalmer and to request the Rawal (Ruler) there to send a prince of his blood to rule over Sirmur once again. The ruler of Jaisalmer at this time was Sal Bahan II who received the deputation from Sirmur and heard their tale of woe, and the request for a ruler. He acceded to the request and told his third son Hasoo to accompany the deputationists to Sirmur and ascend the throne as an independent ruler. The prince and his wife along with their entourage safely reached Sirhind, when Hasoo suddenly died. However, it became known that his widow was pregnant. The party resumed its journey to Sirmur and on the way she gave birth to a boy, under a Dhak or Palas (Flame of the Forest or *Butea frondosa)* tree. This is the tree the flowers of which are boiled in water, on the festival of Holi and the orange coloured liquid thus obtained is sprinkled by the festive revellers. The birth took place at a place called Poka near the Sirmur Tal (lake). The boy was named Plasoo after the Palas (Dhak) tree and his descendants were called ''Plassias''. The Dhak or Palas tree is worshipped by women who wish to bear a son.

The boy Plasoo took the name of Raja Shubh Bans Prakash on ascending the Sirmur throne in 1195 and ruled till 1199 A.D. His son Malhi Prakash (also known as Milay Prakash) succeeded him and shifted the state capital to Rajban (a cement factory has been established there now by the Cement Corporation of India, a Public Sector Undertaking) about 25 kms from Paonta. Malhi Prakash re-conquered and consolidated the old territories which had been occupied by neighbouring chiefs during the chaotic times when the State was without a ruler. He even marched against the neighbouring ruler of Garhwal and wrested the fort of Malda situated along the Bhagirathi river. On Malhi Prakash's death Udit Prakash occupied the throne in 1217 A.D.

The same year, Udit Prakash on finding the climate of Rajban unhealthy moved the seat of his government to Kalsi. In 1227 A.D. he abdicated in favour of his son Kaul Prakash who ruled from Kalsi.

Kaul Prakash extended his territory towards the west by annexing parts of Jubbal, Tharoch and Balson states in Himachal Pradesh. It was during his reign that the Nizam-ul-Mulk Mohammad Khan (or Junaidi) who had rebelled against the Sultana Razia, daughter of Altumash took refuge in the hills of Sirmur-Bordar, where he died. Bordar is identifiable as Bhadraj, the western-most peak of the Mussoorie range, above the Yamuna. Kaul Prakash died in 1239 A.D. and was succeeded by Raja Somer Prakash.

Somer Prakash is said to have invaded and occupied the fort of Ratesh, which at that time was in Keonthal state. Earlier it was a feudatory of Sirmur. He moved his seat from Kalsi to Ratesh and from there ruled for nine years, till his death. Raja Suraj Prakash succeeded him in 1248 A.D. The seat of the government was still at Ratesh when Suraj Prakash got news that the people of Kalsi had rebelled against him, devastated the town of Kalsi, and also attacked the palace. It is said that his daughter checked and drove away the rebels from the palace gates. The Raja came to Kalsi, subdued the rebellion and re-established order. After his campaigns of subjugation of the Thakurs of Jubbal, Balson, Kumharsen, Ghind, Theog, Sahri and Rawain in Garhwal, he returned to Kalsi, and re-established his seat there. After the death of Suraj Prakash in 1259 till 1374 A.D., seven rulers came to the throne. Nothing of great consequence or worth mentioning occurred during their reigns.

Raja Bhagat Prakash who ruled from 1374 to 1386 A.D. became a tributary of the Delhi Court, in 1379, under Firuz Tughlak. He and several of his successors frequently visited the Western Doon during the course of their hunting excursions. In 1382 Sultan Firuz Shah Tughlak came into the Doon and after collecting tribute from the Rais of Sirmur (Kalsi) and the neighbouring Zamindars returned to Delhi.

The two year reign of Jagat Prakash, who succeeded Bhagat Prakash in 1386, A.D. was characterised by disorder and chaos because of his own mismanagement and carelessness; and the Thakurs who had been subjugated by Suraj Prakash declared independence.

Raja Bir Prakash who came to the throne in 1387 A.D., devoted himself to the reorganisation of the state's administration, put down a rebellion, and brought to heel all the Thakurs who had declared independence. He had moved his government to the village of Hat Koti at the junction of the boundaries of Jubbal and Rawain on the bank of the Pabar river. Here he built a temple to Durga along with a fort, in thanks - giving for his victories. The ruins of the fort are still there. He died in 1398 A.D.

Nakat Prakash, who followed Bir Prakash moved his government to the hill village of Neri and his successor Garbh Prakash moved it to Jogri fort in Ratesh. During Nakat Prakash's reign Timur ransacked the area of Kyarda Dun on his way to Jammu after pillaging the Doon. On the other hand Timur in his diary of this campaign mentions one Raja Ratan Sen. The reign of Sirmur's Raja Ratan Prakash commences from 1471 A.D. Hence it appears that during Timur's time the Kyarda Dun was not under the Sirmur ruler but under some other Ratan Sen. Possibly the lower reaches of Sirmur had become independent.

From the time of Bir Prakash till the reign of Dharam Prakash who came to the Gaddi (throne) in 1538 the seat of government remained away from Kalsi although it continued to be an important town of the state. From that year onwards it was back again at Kalsi. His grandson Raja Bakhat Prakash succeeded him in 1585 A.D.

During Bakhat Prakash's reign an incident took place which resulted in his losing some of his territory. Maan Chand who was one of the fourteen Thakurs of Kotaha region of the state, had received his estate as a jagir from the Sirmur ruler. Bakhat Prakash asked for Maan Chand's daughter's hand in marriage. This was refused. Maan Chand was attacked by Bakhat Prakash and being unable to stand upto the attack he fled with his daughter and family to the court of Emperor Jahangir and sought asylum. There he became a Muslim and took the name Raja Moman Murad and gave his daughter in marriage to Jahangir. The Emperor gave him enough troops with whose help he was able to recapture his jagir and became independent of Sirmur. He ruled for twelve years and then one day committed suicide, after poisoning his wife and children.

Bakhat Prakash was succeeded by Budhi Prakash who moved his seat to Rajpur (not to be confused with the town on the Mussoorie road). His grandson Karam Prakash started his rule in 1616 and governed from Kalsi till 1621.

Once, when on a hunting expedition, Karam Prakash came to the site where the town of Nahan now stands. He took a fancy to the place and laid the foundation of his new capital and fort. Originally the place was named Nahar (which means lion). Apparently a sadhu lived at the spot where the palace now stands and he had a pet lion and the town was named after the animal. The name changed to Nahan, over a period of time and became the state capital in 1621 and remained so till the merger of the state in 1947.

This narrative of the house of Sirmur will be picked up at a later stage.

Balbhadra Shah of Garhwal ruled from 1581 to 1591. His original name was Balbhadra Pal and it was only after he was given the title of "Shah" by Akbar that he and his successors were called "Shahs". Legend has it that once he was hunting in the Terai area, adjoining Najibabad, where Akbar was also camping in the vicinity. The two met and hunted together. Balbhadra on one occasion saved Akbar from being attacked by a tiger. A friendship developed between the two and Akbar took him to the Royal court.

While Balbhadra was at Akbar's court word came that some hill people on the frontier were up in arms. On seeing the Emperor upset, Balbhadra offered to take his troops and deal with the insurgents. The offer was accepted and he was able to quell the rebellion. Thereupon he was given a "Khilat", a sword and the family title of "Shah". His name was even changed to "Bahadur Shah". In spite of all these bestowings of titles and khilats it seems that the Garhwal rulers continued to be independent of the Mughals.

The physical prowess of Balbhadra Shah is recounted in a folk tale. There was a heavy door in his palace which had required 30-40 men to place it in its position. Sometime later the door started tilting, and was about to fall when the Raja noticed it and straightened it without any help.

His successor Raja Man Shah came to the throne of Garhwal at the age of thirteen. The name of his Regent is not known. However, during his tenure he was able to subdue the Tibetan raiders who used to come down the Niti and Mana passes and harrassed the people. He severely punished one of the Tibetan chiefs named Kakuwa More. After being defeated the Tibetan agreed to give the Garhwali ruler one kilogram of gold dust and one four-horned ram, annually, with a written promise of good behaviour. Man Shah extended his territorial limits from Haridwar to Manglore beyond Roorkee. There were people of all hues and qualities, each a specialist in his field, at Man Shah's court.

One of his ministers was a poet cum astrologer called Bharat. As an astrologer he was held in great esteem at the royal courts of Akbar and Jahangir. He was a friend of Raja Todar Mal, is mentioned thrice in the Akbar-Nama, and is credited with having made Akbar's and Jahangir's horoscopes. He was given the title of "Jyotik Rai" (astrologer-counsellor). In Tuzuk-I-Jahangiri or The Memoirs of Jahangir, five of the innumerable predictions made by Jyotik Rai are mentioned, and also how he was rewarded by the Emperor.

An English indigo trader and traveller of that period, William Finch, describes the territory of Man Shah as "betwixt Jemini and Ganges lyeth the land of Rajaw Mansa". The most fertile areas of the state were the Doon and the Bhabbar. In 1611 he was succeeded by his son Shyam Shah.

During Shyam Shah's reign his people were faced with the scourge of plague which raged continuously for eight years, from 1616 to 1624, and took a heavy toll of the populace. A large number of villages became desolate. The number of casualties is not known.

According to The Memoirs of Jahangir, "On 15th March 1621 A.D. Raja Shyam Singh; Zamindar of Srinagar (in Garhwal), was given a horse and an elephant". Obviously from this observation it appears that he was at the Mughal court and was bestowed these honours by the Emperor. The Tuzuk-I-Jahangiri further states:

"As the air of Agra, in consequence of the increase of the temperature, did not agree with me, on Monday, the 13th of the Divine month of Aban and 16th year (of my reign April-May 1621) the standards were raised to go towards the hill country of the North, so that if the air of that quarter be equable, I might choose some spot of ground on the bank of river Ganges, and found a city there, to make a permanent place of residence for the hot weather, or else turn the reins of purpose in the direction of Kashmir.

On the 7th of the month of Safar A.H. 1031 the camp was pitched at Haridwar on the bank of the Ganges. It is one of the most famous places of worship of the Hindus, and many Brahmans and recluses have chosen a corner of retirement in this place and worship God according to the rule of their religion. I gave alms in cash and goods to each of them according to his requirements. As the climate of this skirt of hills was not approved by me, and I could not see a spot of ground on which to make a permanent residence, I proceeded towards the skirt of the hill country of Jammu and Kangra".

In 1624 a Jesuit monk, Father Antonio de Andrade, went to the Garhwal court at Srinagar. He was the first European (a Portugese) to enter the Doon. In 1600 he had come to the Jesuit mission at Goa. He started from there for Tibet in order to bring back, to the fold, the lost Tibetan Christians. In those days these missionaries thought that Tibetan Buddhism was in reality a form of Christianity and that the people, because of lack of missionary guidance, had strayed from the true path. Andrade, and his companions Father Manuel Marques and two Indian Christian servants, joined a group of pilgrims, at Delhi, who were going on a pilgrimage to the Garhwal shrines of Badri-Kedar.

On reaching Haridwar the Mughal frontier guards, thinking that the missionaries were Mughal runaways wanted to arrest them, and send them to the Emperor whilst their counterparts - the Garhwal Guards thought they were Mughal spies and did not want them to enter Garhwal. After a few days detention their antecedents were ascertained and they were allowed to proceed northwards via Rishikesh. After assuring the officials of Srinagar that they were going to Tibet to retrieve their lost brethren, Andrade and party were allowed to proceed. A detailed account of his travels to Tibet and back is given in the book 'La Prima Catholica Net Tibet' and the work of Wessels "Early Jesuit Travellers in Central Asia". On 11th April 1626 Andrade laid the foundation of a church at Chaprand in Tibet.

Shyam Shah was a large hearted, and a broad minded ruler. In matters of religious faith every one was free to practice according to one's belief. He had even allowed Father Andrade to build his residence, in Srinagar, next to the royal palace. He, however, did not tolerate disobedience of his orders, even from religious sects. In 1630, after the Kumbh Mela at Haridwar, a large number of Naga sadhus were going to Badrinath. On reaching Srinagar they were asked, under the Raja's orders to deposit their spears, knives, bows and arrows and other arms in the State's armoury, before proceeding further, and to collect them on the way back. On their refusing to do so, he ordered his troops to see the Nagas out of the State. He was one of the few rulers of Garhwal who believed in working hard and playing hard.

After his morning court session he would openly ride his elephant to meet his Muslim mistress who lived in the town. She would entertain him with wine, song and dance till the afternoon when he would come back and sit in court till the evening. At night he would invite his ministers and courtiers to entertainment in the palace. He had a large harem consisting of pretty women of all castes, colours and creeds. In his court were men of learning who were well looked after.

Shyam Shah, during the summer months would go boating in the evenings, with his entourage, on the river Alaknanda. On the evening of 29th July, 1631 his boat capsized and he was drowned. At his cremation sixty of his ranis committed Sati, some of them being forced into the pyre.

Sometime after his death a folk tale started doing the rounds. According to it his spirit, in royal splendour, would move about, in Srinagar town, at night. One night, in a lane, his guru's son, who used to stutter, came upon the royal procession. He walked upto the Raja and blessed him, whereupon he was given a bag of gold coins with the admonition that if he spoke about this incident to any living being he would die.

The next ruler of Garhwal, and hence of the Doon upto the river Yamuna was Dulo Ram Shah or Ram Shah II who ruled for a very short period. His rule did not leave an impact on the history of his state. His successor Mahipat Shah made some significant changes in the social systems and also tried to expand his territories.

One of Mahipat Shah's earliest campaigns was against the ruler of Daba a province of Tibet. This ruler would make frequent raids into adjoining areas of Garhwal and, harass the people with looting and killing. Mahipat Shah, after defeating him, set up his own administration of Daba before withdrawing. Whilst on this campaign he brought about a big social change.

The orthodox Hindu only eats food cooked by himself, or by one of the family members or by a Brahmin who has cooked it according to tradition. Tradition is that the cook, after his ablutions will wear only an unstitched piece of clothing, which usually is a dhoti or a loin cloth, and then enter the kitchen and cook. The people eating have to dress likewise and without having any physical contact with the cook, would be served by him. If any physical contact is made then the cook and the food becomes defiled and the former has to have a bath while the latter is thrown in the garbage.

The cooks had to be without any covering while cooking and feeding the troops over long periods, in the cold of Tibet. As a consequence a lot of them fell ill. This resulted in a shortage of cooks in the Garhwal army. The troops also found it tedious to undress every time they sat down, in the kitchen, to eat. The outcome of this was that the efficiency of the army was going down. Mahipat Shah issued an ordinance that hereafter the people of Garhwal could cook and eat their food fully clothed. This relieved a hardship of the people. If a Garhwali Brahmin cooks, with his clothes on, some of the orthodox plains' Hindus will not eat the food so cooked. Of course, the reason for this tradition is to emphasise the practice of personal hygiene for the persons involved in manning the kitchen.

One of Mahipat Shah's generals called Lodi Rikhola was deputed to bring to book the raiders who would come into the Doon valley proper from the adjoining areas of Sirmur. He subdued the raiders, made boundary pillars and probably built the fortress of Shergarh in the Western Doon. In the process of securing the western boundary with Sirmur, Lodi Rikhola went to the extent of defeating its forces and occupying its forts of Viratgarh and Kalsi. The ruler of Sirmur at this time was Raja Karam Prakash who had shifted his seat from Kalsi to Nahan in 1621. Lodi Rikhola had made such a name for himself amongst the Sirmurians that a number of folk tales were woven around him. One of them was that the people of Sirmur had vowed that until they could produce a 'Brave' like Rikhola, to avenge their defeat, they would not tie the loose straw at the end of their house roofs and the women will not tie their skirts with a string, but after wrapping it around the waist tuck it in at the side like a sarong.

Mahipat Shah was a follower of 'Tantrik' practices and believed in 'Shakti'. For hours on end he would be engrossed in meditation and Tantrik rituals. As a consequence he gradually became an alcoholic and his mind became deranged. Once when he was at Rishikesh he went to visit the Bharat temple. On beholding the idol of Bharat he felt that it was staring at him in anger. Saying that he had come to pay obeisance to the idol, but the idol was staring at him in anger, he ordered the idol's eyes to be pulled out. When he was shown the eyes that had been pulled out he realised that they were nothing but pieces of 'Quartz'. He was full of remorse and ordered them to be re-set.

Another time on his way to the Kumbh Mela at Haridwar he came across a group of about 500 Naga sadhus (the armed wing of the various spiritual centres of the Hindus) who were walking about carrying their various arms. They did not bother about the Raja in whose territory they were. He got so enraged that he ordered his soldiers to kill them. The troops went on a rampage and in the process also killed a number of ordinary pilgrims. One of the persons killed was an old sadhu, from whose wounds flowed milk instead of blood. On seeing this happening the Raja was upset and became scared. In order to atone for his sins, on his return to Srinagar, he called the learned Pandits of the state and asked them for ways of doing so.

The Pandits, apart from the usual recourse to giving of alms, performing 'Pujas', feeding the poor etc. gave him three alternatives to act upon, namely:-
(a) The Raja should commit self-immolation under a Peepal tree; or
(b) drink molten gold; or
(c) die fighting in battle in the face of the enemy.

After completing the giving of alms and distribution of charities etc. he decided upon the third alternative. The first was rejected on the ground that death by burning befitted a woman and not a man. The second amounted to committing suicide, hence the third alternative was to be carried out. With this aim in mind he unnecessarily mounted a campaign against the Raja of Kumaun. In the fight that ensued ten thousand men were killed on both sides because of the foible of the deranged mind of a Raja, who died as he chose to. By his actions Mahipat Shah created unnecessary enmity with Sirmur and Kumaun which would later result in serious repercussions for his successors.

Mahipat Shah was succeeded by his minor son Prithvipati Shah alias Prithvi Shah. It seems that the boy Raja's mother, Rajmata (Dowager) Rani Karnavati, became the Regent and ruled in his name. However the contemporary Muslim historians have called her the "Nak Cutty" Rani. "Nak Cutty" means, Nak=Nose, Cutty=Chopper i.e. "Nose Chopper" Rani. During her reign, if any one did not carry out her orders, she would have the person's nose chopped off, hence earning her the nickname of Nose-Chopper.

However, she is also credited with having carried out a number of development works in the Doon. Among them is the Rajpur canal which still runs right through the centre of the town of Dehra Dun and ends in the water tank in front of Guru Ram Rai's flag staff. The water from this canal is now diverted to the city's main water supply works on Rajpur Road.

Another project was the establishment of a township called Karanpur, which today is a part of Dehra and holds the campus of the D.A.V. College.

In those days the village of Nawada was the administrative headquarters of the Valley. The village is situated about 5 miles south-east of Dehra. Here she built a huge palace and a water tank. The remnants of these structures could be seen till the early part of the present century. Apparently it was abandoned after the Gorkha conquest of the Valley. During that period the present day villages of Ajabpur, Kaulagarh, Kyarkoolee, Bhat Beer, Bhogpur, Sahaspur, Kalyanpur, Nagal, Rajpur, Bhagwantpur, and Thano were all flourishing market towns of the Doon Valley. It was during her rule that the Doon Valley proper was lost to Garhwal and came under Emperor Shah Jahan.

For a long time the Mughal ruler had an ambition to subdue the Raja of Garhwal, who had been independent, into accepting his suzerainty if not becoming a part of the empire. The rulers of Sirmur, Karam Prakash and then his son Mandhata Prakash, had been asking for Mughal help to regain their territory of Kalsi (Kanigarh) and Viratgarh which had been conquered by the Garhwali General Lodi Rikhola. Considering that a woman was ruling Garhwal the Mughal Governor of Kangra, Najabat Khan, volunteered to win the territory for Shah Jahan as he (Najabat Khan) wished to ingratiate himself further with the Emperor. He told the Emperor that either he would conquer Garhwal and make it part of the Mughal empire or else he would obtain a large sum of money from the Rani for the royal treasury. Shah Jahan gave him all the help he wanted in addition to two thousand horse cavalry troopers for the campaign. He also issued a Firman to Mandhata Prakash, of Sirmur, to join Najabat Khan in this venture, along with his army. Thus accompanied by a force of ten thousand infantry, four thousand cavalry, innumerable non-combatants and the troops of Sirmur, Najabat Khan launched his campaign by attacking the fort of Shergarh on the Yamuna river in the Doon. Earlier also it was the wish of the Mughal Governor Karori Mirza of Saharanpur and Meerut to establish a permanent Mughal out-post in the Doon Valley proper. He wanted to establish it at Kaulagarh (Kailagarh in Masir-ul-Umra) Fort in Central Doon. A village

58

behind Forest Research Institute still bears this name and is on the East bank of the Tons river. This is where the first tea plantation in India, was later established. It would have been an ideal location for policing the Valley being in the centre of it.

Najabat Khan and Mandhata Prakash after taking Shergarh went and captured Kalsi (Kanigarh) fort. Then, at the request of the latter, the Mughal forces helped in regaining the fort of Viratgarh from the Garhwali forces. These two forts and their command areas were returned to Sirmur whose territories they had originally been. Marching eastwards Najabat Khan took the fort of Santurgarh. This he entrusted for safe keeping and maintaining, on his behalf, to a local Zamindar of Lakhanpur named Jagtu. A thousand infantry and a hundred cavalry troops were left there to guard the area. Continuing his march eastwards through the present day areas of Doiwala, Majri and Thano villages he arrived at Rishikesh. All along the way he hardly met any resistance from the Garhwali troops. It appears that the Sirmur troops stayed back in their territory and did not accompany the Mughal General. From Rishikesh moving southwards he occupied the fort at the confluence of the Ganga and the Rambha rivulet near Virbhadra (present IDPL Factory area) where the ruins of this fort were existing till 1947. Having arrived at Haridwar he crossed the Ganga at Chandi and entered the hill terrain of Garhwal Bhabhar. Here Najabat Khan faced stiff resistance from the Garhwali soldiers.

The Garhwali general in that region placed his troops at strategic points from where they could stop the enemy from advancing towards Srinagar. In spite of the opposition Najabat Khan advanced to within 60 miles of Srinagar via Chila, Kanaun, Lakshman Jhoola and Mohan Chatti. Fearing that Srinagar would be over-run and Garhwal lost, for ever, to the Mughals, Nak Cutty Rani, the Regent, sent her emissaries to Najabat Khan.

The Rani's proposals were that she was willing to accept the suzerainty of the Emperor and if given fifteen days time she would give rupees ten lakhs as a gift, provided the Mughal forces were withdrawn. These proposals were accepted. After the fifteen days period was over the Rani came up with all kinds of excuses for not making the payments. So much so that six weeks had elapsed by which time only rupees one lakh were paid. The delaying tactics of the Rani paid dividends. During the six weeks period the Mughal forces ran out of their food and the few supplies coming to them were looted on the way, by the Garhwalis. In addition to this problem malaria fever broke out amongst them taking a heavy toll of lives. Najabat Khan, riding to victory after victory, had not thought of these contingencies. His famished and sick army was attacked unceasingly by the enemy. By the time he realised that he had been trapped by a woman it was too late. According to the historian Kanungo:-

"Najabat Khan with a miserable remnant of his army escaped from the territory of the queen with their noses, if not their honour, intact." Najabat Khan returned to the Mughal territories via Kotdwar and Najibabad after suffering a humiliating defeat.

After the withdrawal of Najabat Khan, Garhwali rule was reimposed on the Valley except in the area across the Yamuna which was left with Sirmur.

In or about 1640 A.D. Prithvi Pati or Prithvi Shah assumed his full ruling powers from the Regent.

Initially he had to withstand the Mughal onslaught on his territories as a result of having insulted the Emperor's ambassador. It is said that on the occasion of Prithvi Shah's coronation, when he assumed full ruling powers, Shah Jahan sent an embassy with a "Khilat" (a robe of honour). Instead of receiving the ambassador at the palace gate and escorting him inside, as would have been done had the Emperor come in person, he ordered the ambassador to be brought to his presence as he was only a servant. He was made to salute the Raja as he would his own Emperor and made to sit on the ground with the rest of the courtiers. The "Khilat" was pushed under the bed on which the Raja was sitting. After a time he was allowed to leave and made to withdraw in the same fashion, as he would from his Emperor's presence that is by walking backwards and saluting. At first light he escaped from Srinagar and on arrival at the Royal court narrated his experience. The Emperor was seething with rage at this open insult. He deputed one of his Generals, Khalil-ullah Khan, to bring the Garhwal ruler to book. A campaign was undertaken for this purpose. The following account is given in the "Shah Jahan Nama".

"When the Khan in question set out with the royal forces, the Zamindar of Sirmur, who had never felt disposed to ally himself with the servants of the crown, came under the guidance of good fortune and joined them. He was then rendered conspicuous amongst his compeers by the promulgation of an edict from the threshold of empire and sovereignty, investing him with the title of Raja Sabhak Prakash.

Sirmur is a mountainous tract to the north of the new metropolis (Delhi or Shahjahanabad), measuring 30 kos in length and twenty-five in breadth, in which ice-houses had been established for His Majesty's private use; whence, from the beginning of the month of Isfandiar (February) till the end of Mihr (September), an abundant supply was constantly reaching the metropolis during the time the royal standards were planted. (These were wells, built of stone, in which snow was tightly packed in the winter months and were situated in shady spots where sunlight did not penetrate. Once the well was full it was covered with a thatch roof and sealed with mud and plaster. Such wells were in use in Mussoorie till World War I and the remnants of some of them can still be seen).

From these emporia (stores) porters would carry loads of snow and ice on their backs as far as Dhamras, the name of a place situated on the bank of river Yamuna at a distance of sixteen kos, but the road to which is extremely difficult. (This place can not be identified today). There it was packed in boxes, and sent down the stream on rafts to Daryapur, (this is present day Tajewala where the Yamuna canal head-works are situated) one of the dependencies of pargana Khizrabad, which is also sixteen kos off from Dhamras. From that point it was transported to the metropolis on board of boats in the course of three days and nights. (This is the approximate time taken by the flood waters, in the Yamuna, to reach Delhi from Tajewala). For rendering this service to the Emperor, the Sirmur Raja had earned the nickname of 'Barfi-Raja' at the royal court. (Baraf meaning ice).

Khalilullah Khan, in company with the aforesaid Raja and some other Zamindars of those parts, having reached the Doon, which is a strip of country lying outside of Srinagar, twenty kos long and five broad, one extremity of its length being bounded

60

by the river Yamuna and the other by the Ganges, which possesses many flourishing towns in various quarters, laid the foundation of fieldwork close to Kilagarh (present day Kaulagarh) and completed it in the course of a week. He then deputed one of the mansabdars to keep guard there with 200 matchlock men, and set out in advance with whole of his comrades. On reaching Bahadur Khanpur, (not identifiable today) which is a place belonging to the Doon, and lies between the rivers Yamuna and Ganges, in consequence of the peasantry that dwelt in that neighbourhood having taken refuge in the hills and forests and defiles, and obstinately refusing to return, he despatched the ever triumphant troops from every side to coerce them, who succeeded in inflicting suitable chastisement. A number of the rebels therefore fell by the sword of vengeance, and many more were taken prisoners; after which the remainder tendered their allegiance, and innumerable herds of cattle fell into the hands of the soldiery. Here, likewise, he threw up a fortified post, and left behind a confidential person with some mansabdars and 500 infantry and matchlockmen, to garrison it, so that the passage of travellers to and fro might remain uninterrupted. Having then set out himself from thence he approached the town of Basantpur, which is also a dependency of the Doon, and halted half-way up the hill. Opposite the above town, he constructed another redoubt, in which he posted one of the mansabdars with 250 matchlockmen. From thence he moved to Sahijpur, a place abounding in streams and fountains, and clothed with flowers and verdure, where he erected a fort on top of an embankment, measuring 1000 yards in circumference, and fifteen feet in height, that had in former times been crowned by a stronghold, inasmuch as some traces of the ancient works were still visible, and he deputed a trusty individual to hold the post, backed by 250 musketeers. On reaching the banks of the Ganga, after crossing which one enters the hill country, he sent a detachment with the royal artillery to the other side of the stream, with a view to their taking possession of the thana of Chandi, which is one of the dependencies of Srinagar, but lies outside the Doon of Kilagarh (Kaulagarh).

Meanwhile, Bahadur Chand, Zamindar of Kumaun, under the guidance of a fortunate destiny, espoused the royal cause and came and joined the above mentioned Khan. As soon as this fact was conveyed to the Imperial ear, the respository of all good, through the representations of Khalilullah, a conciliatory Firman and a Khilat set with jewels were forwarded to him. As the season for prosecuting military operations in that region and the fitting period for an invasion of the hill-country had passed away, the rains being now at hand, and the Doon having been taken possession of, a mandate was issued to Khalilullah Khan, to defer the campaign in the hills for the present. After delivering the Doon to Chatur Bhuj, who had expressed an ardent desire for it, and confiding the thana of Chandi to Nagar Das, the chief of Haridwar, to set out for court, the Khan accordingly, having set his mind at rest by fulfilling these instructions, started for the presence''.

Thus once again the Doon Valley came under the Mughals.

After the withdrawal of Khalilullah Khan from the scene the Garhwal troops were successful in recapturing the fort of Santurgarh and its neighbouring area, from Chatur Bhuj's men. At that time the annual revenue income of the Doon Valley was 60 lakhs

61

Dams or 1½ lakh rupees which went to Chatur Bhuj, a Hazari Mansabdar, for services rendered in the campaign. On hearing of this incursion by the Garhwalis, the Emperor ordered Kasim Khan Mir Atish to go to the aid of the Imperial forces in the Valley. On 2nd January, 1656 he entered the Valley with 4000 troops. On his surrounding the fort, the Garhwalis being unable to withstand the siege withdrew, and while doing so set fire to their godowns of foodgrains. Kasim Khan Mir Atish withdrew after razing the fort to the ground.

With the Doon lost to the Mughals and the traditional enemies on his northern (the Tibetans), eastern (the Kumaunies) and western (the Sirmurians) borders waiting for an opportunity to attack, Prithvi Shah was forced to accept the sovereignty of the Mughal court. For this purpose he wrote a number of letters to Shah Jahan's daughter, Jahanara Begum, claiming that he was a faithful ally of the Mughals and that if Prince Dara Shikoh would intercede with the Emperor on his behalf he would accept Mughal sovereignty. Dara Shikoh agreed to help the Garhwal Raja in getting pardon from the Emperor. On getting this information crown prince Medni Shah was sent to Delhi where he was presented to the Emperor on 30th July, 1656. A "Nazar", of 1000 gold asharfis, was made by him to the Emperor, on behalf of his father. Prithvi Shah was forgiven and his son was honoured with a jewelled Khilat, woollen shawl, jewelled armlet and an Arab horse with a silver saddle. An ambassador was sent to Srinagar, who took an elephant, eleven horses, a khilat and a shawl as presents for the Garhwal ruler. From subsequent events it appears that the territories of the Doon and Bhabhar were also restored to Garhwal.

The goodwill so established was short-lived. In 1658 Suleman Shikoh son of Dara Shikoh, had to seek refuge or political asylum with Prithvi Shah because Dara had lost the battle of succession, to the Mughal throne, to his brother Aurangzeb. Suleman was being hunted by his uncle's troops and to evade capture he sought refuge in Srinagar. The story of his flight, the loss of his wealth and retinue, including his harem are well documented by various historians. However the stories of his being handed over to Emperor Aurangzeb's troops and of his stay in the Garhwal capital are many.

According to one contemporary historian the Garhwal Raja was so lavish in his hospitality towards the Mughal prince that he is supposed to have married one of his daughters to him. If this story is true it could have far reaching political overtones. Aurangzeb was still shaky on his throne, Dara had befriended Prithvi Shah, and in time if he (Dara) came to the throne the Garhwali-Mughal inter-marriage would come in handy. The Garhwali historian, poet and painter, Mola Ram, does not mention this episode in his poem "Garh-Rajvansh Kavya". He was the grandson of Suleman Shikoh's Vazir, Diwan Shyam Das.

Mola Ram's father, Kehir Das, and grandfather had stayed back in Srinagar, when their master Suleman Shikoh was taken away, to be handed over to Aurangzeb. The father and son were given permanent asylum in Garhwal and their descendants are still living in Srinagar. The work of Mola Ram referred to above, and discovered a few years ago in Srinagar, throws light on Garhwal history from a Garhwali point of view, though at times he becomes too romantic and poetic in his writings. Some of the episodes, mentioned in his works, are sometimes not found in the works of contemporary historians. Mola Ram is the founder of the Garhwal school of painting. His works have won international acclaim.

During the time Suleman was at Srinagar, Alamgir (Aurangzeb) had sent a Firman to Raja Sobhag Prakash of Sirmur, who had succeeded Mandhata Prakash in 1647, asking him to prevent and intercept all correspondence passing through his territory between Suleman and his father, Dara, who was at Lahore. The guards placed to intercept the correspondence should be carefully supervised. Further, he (Sobhag Prakash) should help Raja Raj Rup; son of Raja Jagat Singh, of Nurpur (Jammu state), who had been deputed to chastise the ruler of Garhwal. Later Aurangzeb, by a Firman, gave Sirmur the area of Kalesar (Now in Haryana on the right bank of the Yamuna, below Paonta) which was then part of Saharanpur in the Delhi province and was managed by two local Zamindars. There is an island in the middle of the river Yamuna opposite Kalesar where the boundaries of the three states of Uttar Pradesh, Himachal and Haryana meet. Kalesar at one time used to be a famous spot for fishing. People still try their luck, but because of indiscriminate netting and bombing 'luck' has become very 'poor' indeed.

Aurangzeb entrusted to Raja Jai Singh, the former adviser cum counsellor of the Prince, the task of getting Suleman to court, from Garhwal, dead or alive. Jai Singh wrote a number of letters to Prithvi Shah, at first offering rewards which were spurned and then threats of military action against him, in case he did not hand over the Mughal prince. According to Bernier, a European traveller in India at that time, Prithvi Shah answered that "the loss of his whole territory would effect him less than the idea that he had been guilty of so base and ungenerous an action". Thereupon the Mughal forces were ordered to march against Garhwal. Although they were able to occupy the Doon and the Bhabhar area with ease, it was a matter of regret for them that they could not make much headway in the mountainous region because of the terrain. At Raiwala, in the Valley, permanent accommodation was built for the Mughal troops.

According to the Sirmur Gazetteer, "the Emperor Alamgir in the third year of his reign (1661) conferred on Sobhag Prakash the area of Kalankhar, by a Firman, on the ground that it was being mismanaged. The Gazetteer further states "This would seem to be the present area of Kolagadh, near Dehra Dun. It was held for long in proprietorship by the ruler of Sirmur state and after merger it was treated as his personal property". This statement is partly wrong since it was Kowlagarh Tea Estate which was the personal property of His Highness after the merger of the State in 1947.

By now it was two years (1660) since Suleman had come to Garhwal. At the orders of Aurangzeb (as mentioned above) Raja Sobhag Prakash of Sirmur along with Raja Raj Rup and the Mughal General Rad Khan attacked Garhwal. The Sirmur troops were able to come to within four miles west of the present town of Tehri, (which is under threat of submersion by the waters of the proposed Tehri Dam), upto the village of Malideval. Here the Garhwal army took a stand and the enemy was pushed back across the Yamuna. With this failure Aurangzeb became desperate. According to one story he was able to persuade a powerful Garhwali minister to have Suleman poisoned, and if he (the minister) was successful he would be made the Raja in place of Prithvi Shah.

The minister was able to send the poison to Suleman, as medicine for some minor ailment, but suspecting foul play Suleman fed some of it to his cat. The cat died at once, thus saving the life of the Prince. When this episode was conveyed by him to Prithvi Shah he had the minister beheaded.

Aurangzeb sent Kunwar Ram Singh, son of Raja Jai Singh to Srinagar to prevail upon the Raja to surrender Suleman and thus save Garhwal from further action by the Mughal court. The Raja was still adamant and he politely told Ram Singh that as long as he was alive he will not hand over Suleman.

Because of the increasing pressure on the Raja, Suleman decided to escape to Tibet. One night accompanied by a couple of trusted servants, he left Srinagar for Tibet. Having lost their way they went round and round in circles around Srinagar. They were hiding in a cave during the day when a cowherd saw them and reported to Raj Kumar Medni Shah. His men caught Suleman and brought him to the Raj Kumar. On account of the pressure from Aurangzeb, who had already occupied part of Garhwal, Medni Shah and his father's ministers had entered into a conspiracy to hand over Suleman to Ram Singh. Another reason why the ministers and Medni Shah had decided on this course was that Suleman or people in his camp had slaughtered a cow on some Muslim festival. They (the Garhwalis) did not take any action against Suleman for fear of the Raja, who on hearing of the incident was also annoyed but overlooked it. Since the ministers were with him, Medni Shah had gradually taken the state's administration in his own hands relegating his father to a secondary position, keeping him virtually under house arrest. Medni Shah had taken a page out of Aurangzeb's book who had incarcerated Shah Jahan a couple of years earlier.

On assuming control, Medni Shah who was more worldly wise than his own father, wrote to the Mughal court that he was willing to hand over Suleman. Kunwar Ram Singh, Tarbiat Khan and other Mansabdars were deputed to receive and bring the Mughal Prince to Delhi. Medni Shah himself escorted Suleman to Kotdwar where he was handed over to the Mughal party on 27th Dec., 1660. Medni Shah, is also reported to have gone with them to the Mughal court. There at the intercession of Raja Jai Singh, the Emperor forgave the Garhwal ruler for his faults of the past. Medni Shah had been accused of treachery for the way he had misled Suleman to accompany him. On discovering it Suleman is reported to have uttered a curse that the kingdom of Garhwal shall perish for this betrayal. It seems that Suleman's Begums and their attendants were also transported to Delhi with him whilst his Diwan, Shyam Das, and his son along with their heavy baggage were kept back in Srinagar. On his return from Delhi Medni Shah gave Shyam Das the option of either staying on in Srinagar or go to Delhi and face possible imprisonment at the hands of Aurangzeb. Medni Shah confiscated the property left behind by Suleman and put the Diwan and his son under house arrest paying them five rupees a day for their maintenance. Once they agreed to make Srinagar their permanent home they were given a Jagir of 60 villages and were appointed as teachers of Persian to the ruler and his family.

In 1664, on the death of Prithvi Shah, Medni Shah celebrated his formal ascendancy to the throne and was honoured by the Emperor with a Khilat on the occasion. Aurangzeb called Medni Shah to Delhi and entrusted him with the job of annexing Butolgarh or Keonthal fort, in Himachal Pradesh, which had been eluding capture by Mughal troops. Medni Shah with his Garhwali troops was able to successfully carry out this campaign. For his services Aurangzeb restored the Doon, by a Firman, to Medni Shah. On getting back the Valley Medni Shah established a fort and seat of administration in the Western Doon, naming the place Prithvipur, in memory of his father. The village is till there and the remnants of the old fort are visible in the area.

This place flourished as the administrative headquarters of the Ruler's local representative. It fell on lean days, according to a folk tale, when one of the Subedars (the local Governor) raped his daughter and she committed suicide to hide her shame.

Bazbahadur Chand of Kumaun, an old time enemy of Garhwal attacked in the beginning of 1665, and with the help of some Garhwali traitors was able to come to Srinagar. After he was monetarily compensated for the expense of his army and payment of a tribute, he signed a treaty and withdrew to his capital. Medni Shah complained to Aurangzeb about this unwarranted attack on his domain (Garhwal). The Emperor who considered Medni Shah his protege immediately ordered the royal troops to go and occupy Kumaun as a punishment to Bazbahadur. They were able to occupy the low lands but were unable to make much progress in the mountainous region. Bazbahadur sought Aurangzeb's forgiveness for having attacked Garhwal and in the course of time through Alivardi Khan's intervention, was forgiven.

A number of folk tales have come down from the times of Prithvi Shah and Medni Shah.

One of them is regarding the payment of "Jizya" (tax) imposed on the Hindus by Aurangzeb. The Garhwal ruler was told to collect and remit this tax to Delhi. To carry the amount so collected one of the courtiers, Puria Naithani, was deputed to take it. He was also told to present before the Emperor a true picture of the poor economic and topographic condition of Garhwal and ask for exemption from the tax. Puria gave Rs. 1.25 lakhs to the Emperor and made his petition for exemption. On being asked to give evidence in support of his contentions he is reported to have produced a bitter gourd (karela) and placed it before Aurangzeb and said "Your Majesty ! my country is like the ridges and depressions on the surface of this gourd (karela) and the people generally poor".

Another tale is that after a State banquet Puria Naithani threw away the silver plate out of which he had eaten. The Emperor was annoyed at this behaviour and threatened him with dire consequences unless he could satisfactorily explain his action. Puria was prepared for this and had purposely acted in this manner. He told the court that in his native land new plates are used at each meal, the used ones being thrown away. They are made from "Saloo and Maloo", which are leaves and twigs for making leaf plates. In the Doon and Garhwal region the "Camel's Foot" climber (Bauhinia vahlii) grows wild and in abundance. Its leaves are large, deeply cleft and resemble the footprint of a camel. It grows as much as 8 metres in one season. The leaves are bound together by twigs the size of a pin, giving it the shape and size of a plate. They are cheap and hygienic and are discarded after each meal. "Malo" is the leaf and "Salo" the twig.

The Emperor was pleased with his ready wit and not only forgave the misdemeanour but gave him a reward. He exempted Garhwal from the "Jizya" and gave orders that no temples be destroyed in the region.

According to tradition the Garhwal ruler is considered the human representative of Lord Badrinath, on earth. As such it is his prerogative to be the first person to have a bath in the Ganga, at Har-ki-Paori, at the appointed time on the day of the "Kumbh". The other potentates who may be from bigger states, take second place. At one such "Kumbh" mela at Haridwar, Medni Shah was camping at Chandi Ghat across the Ganga and a number of Hindu Rajas from the plains were also staying in Haridwar. They all conspired to take away this privilege of the Garhwal ruler by preventing him, from being the first to bathe, and if need be, by the use of arms. This intention of theirs was conveyed to Medni Shah. He sent them a message saying that it does not behove the "Kshatriya" clan to spill blood unnecessarily at this holy place on the day of the "Kumbh". Therefore, they may have their bath at Har-ki-Paori at the appointed time as he will not be there. The message further stated that if the Ganga considered him (Medni Shah) as one of her true believers she will come to him.

On the morning of the "Kumbh" it was seen that the Ganga had changed its course, leaving Har-ki-Paori dry and flowing along the Garhwal ruler's camp. The Raja, after offering prayers to Mother Ganga, had his bath at the appointed time while those at Har-ki-Paori were unable to do so. They then realised the worth of the Garhwal Raja and went and apologised to him. Since then a current of the river is running along Chandi hill and is known as "Neel Dhara" or the "Blue Rivulet", because of the colour of the water at that place. Probably a flash food at night, which is quite common in the hills after a shower of rain, took place causing the river to change its course.

Another incident regarding the flow of the Ganga waters occurred in the 19th century. The East India Company had sanctioned the construction of the Ganga canal from Haridwar to Kanpur. The work on it had commenced around 1840 when Lord Ellenbrough was the Governor-General. It was Lord Dalhousie who at the urgent request of Thomoson the Lt. Governor of North-West Province and Cautley, the Engineer-in-charge of the project secured the vigorous implementation of the plans. The canal was completed in 1854. When the course of the canal at Haridwar was being dug the local "Pandas" (Priests) objected to the flow of canal waters, at Har-ki-Paori (the main bathing ghat), as they were not free flowing but canalised or controlled or bound by the "Bandh" at the headworks, "Bandh" in Hindi meaning bound). According to them this would result in Har-ki-Paori losing its sanctity. An agitation was launched against the project. Cautley overcame the objection by diverting a distributary from the main stream at a point above the place from where the canal was to take off. Thus a branch of the main river flows past Har-ki-Paori and the cremation ghat, whilst the canal waters flow alongside without touching the main bathing ghat. Thus the Ganga is flowing in three streams at Haridwar.

66

It was in the year 1675, that Guru Ram Rai came and settled in the Doon Valley. He may be considered the man who laid the foundation of the nucleus of the present city of Dehra Dun. The Doon has always been a place, to take shelter in, for ascetics, exiles and refugees. The most important of them all, in modern times is Guru Ram Rai, the impact of whose presence in the Valley has left an everlasting mark. More about him later.

Fateh Shah succeeded Medni Shah. He is credited with fighting a number of actions on the battle field. He led a raid from the Doon Valley into Saharanpur from where he was expelled after great difficulty by the Mughal General Sayed Ali. He is also credited with the extension of his power into Tibet. A head gear, coat, sword and matchlock, said to have belonged to him, were kept in a monastery at Daba in Tibet and worshipped as mementos of a warrior.

He had to fight a number of battles against his traditional enemies, the rulers of Kumaun and Sirmur. In 1686 Fateh Shah occupied the forts of Kalsi and Vairat in Sirmur territory. The Sirmur ruler represented to Emperor Aurangzeb that the Garhwal ruler had seized some of his territory, whereupon the Emperor sent a force to help the Sirmur ruler in recovering his lost areas. As a result, the Garhwal ruler withdrew his troops without any fight. The withdrawal of Garhwali troops without giving a fight encouraged the Sirmur ruler to try and annexe some of the enemy's territory for himself. In this he was unsuccessful and was told by Aurangzeb not to attack the Raja of Garhwal in future.

During the reigns of Fateh Shah and Medni Prakash of Sirmur, the Sikh Guru, Govind Singh, came to Sirmur State from Anandpur because of his rift with Raja Bhim Chand of Bilaspur. The rift between the Guru and Bilaspur Raja occurred over an elephant named Prasadi of the Guru and given to him by Raja Man Singh of Bangala. Bhim Chand, of whose domain Anandpur formed a part, asked the Guru for the elephant which he refused. As a result of the refusal the Guru was banished from Anandpur. The Guru came and camped at Mirpur village near Nahan. Medni Prakash invited the Guru to Nahan where he stayed for some time. From Nahan he moved down to Paonta, on the west bank of the river Yamuna, in Kyarda Dun. Here with the Raja's permission he built a fort, the remains of which are still seen in the locality. The ladies of Govind Singh's family heaved a sigh of relief in getting a suitable place to rest, and thanked the Almighty for having given them a safe site to keep their feet on (Paaon-than). Thus the place got its name Paonta. While the Guru was at Paonta, the marriage of a son of Raja Bhim Chand was settled with the daughter of Raja Fateh Shah of Garhwal, who was also a friend of the Guru.

On this occasion Guru Gobind Singh sent gifts for the bride to her father Fateh

Shah. Raja Bhim Chand learnt about this and wrote to Fateh Shah reminding him about the old estrangement between him (Bhim Chand) and Guru Govind Singh. The Garhwal ruler was threatened that the marriage would not take place if the friendship between him and Guru Govind Singh continued. Consequently Fateh Shah, much against his wishes, had to return the gifts of the Guru. The Guru was cut to the quick by this unprovoked indignity and he threw down the gauntlet when Bhim Chand was returning from Srinagar via the Doon Valley after the wedding of his son. As a result a battle was fought at Bhangani about nine miles north of Paonta. Raja Kirpal Chand of Katoch (Kangra), Kesri Chand of Jasanwala, Sukhdev Chand of Jasrota, Hari Chand of Hindur and others who were in the marriage party took part in this battle as Bhim Chand's allies. The fight lasted three days and ended in favour of Guru Govind Singh. Rajas Hari Chand, Kesri Chand and Sukhdev Chand fell in the field. Although some Sikh chroniclers mention the presence of Fateh Shah at this battle, it seems improbable as he would not have left Srinagar immediately after the wedding.

At Bhangani there are monuments (Chattries) over the spots where the Ranis of the fallen Rajas, probably committed "Sati" or the Rajas were cremated. Guru Govind Singh then made his camp at Bhangani where a Gurudwara still exists. After sometime the friendship between Medni Prakash and the Guru incurred the displeasure of the Emperor Alamgir (Aurangzeb). This resulted in the Guru leaving Sirmur territory and the severance of relations between him and the Sirmur Raja.

During Fateh Shah's reign the Doon Valley had a peaceful time and the people by and large prospered. There were no raids by the marauders from across the Shiwalik and the Yamuna. Fateh Shah was succeeded by his son Dalip in 1717. He reigned for a few months when he was succeeded by his brother Upendra Shah.

Upendra Shah ruled for a period of nine months and was succeeded by his nephew Pradip Shah, son of Dalip Shah. Pradip Shah is supposed to have ruled for over 50 years from 1718 to 1772.

According to Mola Ram, the poet-cum-historian of Garhwal State, Pradip Shah was five years old when he came to the throne. Because of his minority his mother who was a Himachal princess ruled as the Queen Regent. Right from Medni Shah's time there were two factions at court namely the Khasia Rajputs (the original inhabitants of Garhwal) and the other Rajputs who had come and settled there, from other parts of the country, as mercenary soldiers. Amongst the latter category were five Katoch brothers from Kangra. They had worked their way into the Queen Regent's confidence (because of being Himachalies like her), and were appointed to all the important and high offices. Because they were in power they started harrassing the local populace by imposing a number of taxes. Some of the taxes imposed by them were:-

(a) Married women's Tax. This was a tax levied on a family, according to the number of married women in it. The family had to give one measure of grain, per woman, per year, to the royal granary.

(b) Tax on cooking places. This was a tax of one rupee per cooking fire place, per year, in a household.

(c) Income Tax was levied on the family's income as in the present times; and

(d)   Cattle tax on the number of animals owned by a person.

Because of the atrocities committed by them the five brothers were eventually assassinated.

According to tradition, a number of families who could not afford to pay these taxes would make do with one woman being married to all the brothers. Some would cook their meals at one place, and only one milk animal would be kept.

On Pradip Shah's taking direct control of his government matters started improving. During the latter part of his grand-father's reign and the earlier part of his own, the Doon enjoyed a season of exceptional prosperity. Large numbers of Rajput and Gujar settlers reclaimed the waste lands and new villages came up. At one time (in 1729) there were as many as 400 of them in the Doon, and the gross revenue from them amounted to nearly Rs. 95,000/-. In 1747 the Valley was assessed at Rs. 97,465/- of which Rs. 42,845/-was assigned away in revenue free grants to religious establishments and individuals. This prosperity of the Doon attracted the attention of Najib-ud-Daula, better known as Najib Khan, a Rohilla and Nawab of Saharanpur. Roh is a region in Afghanistan famous for its soldiers who were known in India as Rohillas. Because of the Chief and a large number of Rohillas living in the Moradabad, Rampur, Bareilly region it was renamed Rohilkhand, the original name being Katehar. There is still a railway station by this name, and a small Zamindari in Oudh. By the end of 1754 Najib Khan had brought the upper part of Saharanpur district under his control by dislodging the last of the local chiefs, Chait Singh of Bahsuma. In 1757, the Rohilla led an expedition into the Valley and occupied it after meeting a feeble resistance from the Garhwali forces. In 1755 Najib Khan had established his seat at Najibabad, the town named after him. In the vicinity of this town he built a fort called "Pathar Garh" - Fort of stone. It was built mostly from the remains of the large Buddhist stupas, of Moradhawaj, situated between Kotdwar and Najibabad. He was the general who defeated Safdarjang after whom are named the aerodrome, hospital and housing colonies near his tomb in New Delhi, and did not allow the latter to capture Delhi. For this service to the Mughal king Najib Khan was given the Doab area from Meerut to Saharanpur districts between the Yamuna and the Ganga rivers. His occupation of the area east of the Ganga was also recognised by Delhi.

Towards the end of his active career Najib Khan was too busy guarding his borders against the incursions of the Sikhs from across the Yamuna. As a consequence, he could not devote much time to the administration of his outlying district of the Doon. His administration was considered to be benevolent and progressive in character. Although a large number of Muslims were encouraged to settle in the Valley, he favoured no particular community to the prejudice of another. The original sons of the soil in the Valley received protection from him which, they being the conquered people, was necessary for them. Canals and wells were dug, agriculture got a boost and as a result the land revenue increased as also the number of villages. There were as many as 500 estates under horticulture and agriculture.

Trade also increased along with agriculture. There were Hatnalas ("Haat" meaning a shop or market and "Nala" meaning a pass) at Nagal, Rajpur, Bhagwantpur, Thano and Bhogpur towns through which the trade between the plains and the hills passed. The peaceful days for the Valley ended with the death of Najib-ud-Daula in October 1770 A.D. His son Zabitah Khan who succeeded him could not hold his father's legacy. Gujars, Sikhs, Rajputs and Gorkhas, one after the other, started harrassing the people of the Valley till, from a flourishing district, it became a barren waste. To a large extent Pradip Shah, who had retaken the areas lost to Najib Khan, was responsible for this state of affairs. Having become old and feeble he had come under the influence of the Mahant of Guru Ram Rai's gurudwara in the Valley. Under the Mahant's advice, the seat of the district's administration was shifted from Nawada to Dehra Dun town. Nawada declined and is now a small village. Pradip Shah died in 1772 after suffering a paralytic stroke.

Lalat Shah (also known as Lalit Shah) succeeded his father Pradip Shah in 1772. Quite a few details are available about his family from Mola Ram's history of the House of Garhwal.

Lalat Shah had three Ranis. The senior most was the daughter of the house of Keonthal in Himachal. She bore him a son named Jaikirti or Jai Kirat Shah. The father's relations with the son and his mother were not very cordial although he was the eldest son. The second Rani was the daughter of the Raja of Doti (in Nepal). She was his favourite Rani and bore him two sons Pradyuman and Prakram Shah. The third Rani was the daughter of some local Zamindar or one of the ministers of Garhwal. She had a son called Pritam Shah. One of Lalat Shah's daughters was married to a Zamindar of the Doon Valley. He was Gulab Singh Pundir. He probably was also the Raja's local governor in the Doon.

According to a legend, Shankracharya after restoring the temple at Badrinath, had entrusted the performing of the daily puja and temple rituals to his disciple Trotakacharya. He and his disciples carried out these duties till the end of the 15th century. Thereafter, the Sadhu sect known as Dandi-Swamis took over these tasks and performed them till 1776 when the last of them, Swami Ram Krishna (not to be confused with Ram Krishan Paramhansa) suddenly died. The problem of interruption in the daily routine of the temple was feared. Luckily Lalat Shah was in camp, at Badrinath, at the time. He, by the authority vested in him as the temporal head of the temple, ordained that the temple's cook, who was a Namboodri Brahmin (like Shankracharya) conduct the puja and other rituals in the Sanctum Sanctorum of the temple. He was appointed the Rawal and bestowed with a ceremonial Khilat and a gold brocade umbrella. His name was Gopal and on being appointed Rawal he had to give up his wife and children and live a life of celibacy. He petitioned to the Raja that as a result of this new office his children were going to suffer both socially and financially since they would neither be able to work being young, nor would they be able to marry being poor. Thereupon his family was given the grant of Dimer village and were allowed to collect the offerings at the Lakshmi temple inside the compound of the Badri temple. The descendants of Gopal's family are known as Dimris (named after their village of Dimer) and in addition to performing the puja at the Lakshmi temple assist the Rawal in his labours. On the Raja's orders the local Brahmins agreed to inter-marry with these people.

70

Since then, till to-day, the priest or the Rawal at Badrinath is a Brahmin from Kerala, belonging to Namboodri, Choli or Mukani castes. He has to practice vows of celibacy, has to be a Sanskrit scholar and well versed in Vedantic philosophy. At one time he was the uncrowned ruler of Badrinath and its various estates donated by the various Rajas to the temple. Because of degeneration in the lives of some of the Rawals and mismanagement by them their role was reduced to that of a paid priest and the management vested in a committee appointed for that purpose. More about it later.

After the death of his father Najib-ud-Daula, Zabitah Khan was able to keep a hold on only the districts of Meerut and Saharanpur. The rest of the estates were retaken by their former chiefs. In order to extend his fiefdom he attacked the fort at Bhogpur in the Eastern Doon. The attack was repulsed by the Garhwalis. Later on he was driven to penury because of a Mughal action against him, for the recovery of Imperial revenues. After losing the fight he escaped across the Yamuna and became a Sikh convert taking the name of Dharam Singh whilst his family was imprisoned by the Mughal.

Lalat Shah was keen to give a kingdom to each of his favourite Rani's sons. With this aim in mind he started campaigns to annexe the territories of Sirmur and Kumaun. First he attacked the fort of Bairat and set it to the torch. Then the fort at Kalsi was attacked where the Sirmur forces put up a stiff fight and defeated the Garhwalis, who had to withdraw and a treaty was signed between the two rulers. Lalat Shah had to liquidate his personal treasure in order to pay the troops for this action. The next fight was against Kumaun where he was successful because of the help given by the Joshis of Almora. The second son Pradyuman Shah ruled over Kumaun as Pradyuman Chand for a short period before coming back to Garhwal.

Williams, in his Memoir of Dehra Dun has the following to say about this action in Kumaun.

"I confess my utter inability to unravel the politics of this period with any degree of satisfaction to myself. According to one account, Deep Chund, king of Kumaon, Kulyan Chund's successor, was treacherously murdered, (together with his minister, Jey Kishen Joshee) by his spuriously descended cousin, Mohun Singh, who himself ascended the throne of Kumaon. Then Lulat Sah and the Raja of Dotee, leaguing with the family of unfortunate Jey Kishen and other malcontents, expelled the usurper, and placed Pardooman Sah on the throne in his stead. The new king reigned in Kumaon for nine (?) years, one of his principal Minister being Hurruk Deo, Jey Kishen's brother. After that Lulat Sah dies, leaving Garhwal to Jey Kurt Sah. The latter, favouring Mohun Singh's pretentions, desired to depose Purdooman Sah, who, reciprocating the feelings of his brother was anxious to establish Prakarm Sah, his own and full younger brother, at Sreanugur. Jey Kurt Sah dying in the meantime, Purdooman Sah therefore occupied Garhwal, and entrusted Kumaon to Hurruk Deo's care. The Viceroy was soon driven out by Mohun Singh, but regained his footing, and put the usurper to death. Then again, Lall Singh, Mohun Singh's brother, once more drove him out, with the aid of Faiz Ullah Khan's Rohillas from Rampore. He soon, however, regained possession of Almorah with Purdooman Sah's assistance, until Prakarm Sah (!) took Lall Singh's part, when he was compelled to retreat to Sreanugur, where he ended his days in retirement. Hurruk

Deo Joshee must have been a patriot with a very elastic conscience, for he enjoyed a place of trust in the immediate household of Nujeeb-ud-Douluh."

Because of Lalat Shah's neglect or as some say from his oppression of the Muslim peasantry the affairs in the Doon deteriorated. The Doon became the happy hunting ground of Gujar and Sikh marauders. In 1775, the Sikhs swept through the Valley, plundering, murdering and burning as they went. Again in 1783 the Sikh chief Baghel Singh and his raiders after being checked, by the troops of Asaf-u-Daulah, the Nawab Vazir of Oudh, at the Ganga turned towards the Doon. Crossing the Shiwaliks they came into the Valley, and carried out their raid unchecked since the inhabitants fled like sheep. Some of them who had the intelligence consigned their valuables to the sanctuary of Guru Ram Rai's temple. This device proved beneficial, because the Sikhs respecting the temple spared it while ransacking the houses around it. The raiders did not settle in the Valley but went back after burning a few villages.

Various raiders came and went as they pleased from the Valley, although badly impoverished, because it still paid them to raid it. Dehra had become a populous town and the Garhwal Raja even went to the extent of buying peace from some Sikh Sardars, by paying them an annuity of Rs. 4000/- in return for protection. This payment was called "Rakhi" by the Sikh's, or protection money in allusion to the Hindu custom of a sister tying a "Rakhi" on her brother's wrist for protection. The amount of Rakhi for the peasantry was one-fifth of the land produce at each harvest. The Sikh Sardars had divided the countryside amongst themselves and each one collected his share in his area. It was sometimes called "Kambali" (Kambal = a blanket) or the price of a blanket being paid by every farmer for his protection.

Forester, an English traveller, happened to be at Sahaspur, in the Western Doon, when two Sikh tax collectors came to receive the customary levy. By their behaviour and the treatment they got from the locals he was constrained to remark, "From the manner in which these men were treated, or rather treated themselves, I frequently wished for the power of migrating into the body of a Sicque for a few weeks". Even their horses were fed green barley, pulled out of the standing crop. From this action it can be inferred how well they must have fared, prompting the Englishman to write the remark that he did.

The raids of the Rajputs and Gujars from Saharanpur did more mischief than those of the Sikhs. Theirs were no petty enterprises of common gang robberies, but regular invasions, on a small scale, by men of consequence, who were able to lead small armies composed of infantry and cavalry. Those were the days when a Rajput or a Gujar leader could, at a pinch, muster a thousand troops. Against such a force the public of the Doon could hardly offer much of a fight, although it occasionally attempted reprisals. The excursions of the plainsmen in the second half of the 18th century were the acts of wanton aggressors, and the people of the Doon had no more chance against them than they (the Rajputs and Gujars) had against the more powerful Sikh Sardars. The raiders mostly came into the Valley through the Timli and Mohand passes.

The passes of Kansrao and Haridwar were at first less frequented. When the Gujars bacame more powerful than the Pundirs, Raja Ramdayal Singh of Landhaura, near

Roorkee, took control of these two passes. Once he was in possession of them he started his old profession of robbery and dacoity during the intervals when he found time from his chores in the capacity of a Zamindar. The Garhwal Raja was far too weak to attempt resistance and bought peace from the raiders by handing over a few villages, in the Valley, to each of their leaders as "Jagirs", on condition of their guarding each pass against other raiders, belonging to their own or other groups. In this way the Pundir's chief and son-in-law of Lalat Shah, Gulab Singh, got twelve villages and his son Bahadur Singh was given the fiscal management of the Doon in 1787. Raja Ram Dayal got five villages. The Raos of Kheri, Sakhrauda and Raipur (in the Saharanpur district) were also given villages in the Doon. All these "Jagirs" were resumed by the British after their conquest of the Doon.

Raja Ram Dayal originally had seven villages, but the Garhwal Raja resumed two, on account of some misconduct by the former's followers. Ram Dayal's descendant Koushal Singh laid a claim to them which was rejected by the British administrator Mr. Shore in 1823.

Lalat Shah died in 1780 A.D. and was succeeded by his eldest son Jai Kirti Shah.

In 1786 A.D. Ghulam Qadir, the grandson of Najib-u-Doulah, thought of re-annexing the Doon. Accompanied by his adviser Raja Munyar Singh, he entered the Doon from Haridwar in the month of June. His progress through the Valley was marked by fire and bloodshed. He not only looted Dehra but set fire to Guru Ram Rai's Gurudwara. He showed his contempt for the Guru and his followers by slaughtering a cow and splashing its blood in the holy shrine. He went to the extent of breaking the Mahant's "Sitar" and lay with his shoes on the Guru's bed on which he had slept and died. This bed, having silver legs, is preserved and worshipped in the Gurudwara, even now, as a relic of the Guru.

Jai Kirti Shah's reign of five years was one of intrigues, conspiracies, fighting and sorrow for him. Because of his father's ambition to provide independent states for the brothers Pradyuman and Prakarm the Garhwal courtiers including the army commanders and ministers were divided into two camps. One camp sided with Jai Kirti Shah and the other with his two step-brothers. For a brief period Pradyuman had gone as the Raja of Kumaun. His younger brother had accompanied him. They were keen to dispossess Jai Kirti of the Garhwal Raj and instal one of themselves in his stead. Intrigues and conspiracies were being hatched all the time between the two groups and their respective supporters. The Joshis of Almora were also playing their dubious role in these proceedings. At the time the army commander of the Doon was one Ghamand Singh and his brother was his deputy. One group of ministers requested these two brothers to come to Srinagar and take over the administration from Diwan (chief minister) Kripa Ram Dhobal, who had reduced the Raja's power to zero. He had become the de-facto Raja himself.

Ghamand Singh went with his troops and after killing Kripa Ram took his place. He proved a bigger despot than his predecessor. A conspiracy was hatched against him by some of the other army commanders and he had to make his escape in the dead of night. His brother Kedar Singh also disappeared from the Doon as he had no troops to protect him.

Probably it was at this time that the Raja appointed Umed Singh as the military governor of the Doon, although he is supposed to have offered the post to Ajab Ram, the man responsible for Ghamand Singh's ouster.

Ajab Ram turned down the offer and secretly joined hands with Prakarm Shah and Ghamand Singh who was recalled to Srinagar. The Raja was forced into appointing Ajab Ram as Chief of the Army, Ghamand Singh as Chief Minister and his brother Kedar Singh as Governor of the Doon. Whether he took up his post or stayed on in Srinagar is not known. Ajab Ram now promised the Garhwal "gaddi" to Pradyuman who was in Kumaun, on condition that he invade Garhwal and give Ajab Ram the revenues of the Salan area. The two brothers marched against the elder brother. Jai Kirti Shah asked the Sirmur ruler Jagat Prakash for help. Jagat Prakash started with his troops for Srinagar, but before he could reach it the town had been surrounded by the Kumaunese army of the two brothers. A fight between the Sirmur and Kumaun troops took place at Kaproli, a little distance from Srinagar. In this battle the Kumaunese were defeated, the two traitor Garhwali Generals Vijay Ram Negi and Ghamand Singh were killed at the orders of Jagat Prakash. The two brothers Pradyuman and Prakarm fled back to Kumaun. Jagat Prakash suggested to Jai Kirti that they should persue the fleeing brothers and finish this chronic problem, once and for all.

The Garhwali ministers and courtiers, who were in league with Pradyuman and his brother, advised the Raja against such action. The reason given was that, as it was the war had been a strain on the exchequer, another action would result in Jagat Prakash appropriating the entire revenue of the state, for his troops' expenses. The Raja fell in line with this thinking and after thanking Jagat Prakash bade farewell to his saviour. As a thanksgiving gift, apart from other items, Jagat Prakash was given the Doon as "Jagir". The other items were rupees one and a quarter lacs in cash, a jewelled Tiara, robes of honour and the Garhwal Raja's own pearl necklace. Thus the Doon passed from Garhwal to Sirmur rule.

Williams places this episode during the reign of Pradyuman Shah instead of Jai Kirti Shah. The reason for this anomaly is that the history of Garhwal by Mola Ram who lived through this period was not available to Williams or subsequent British historians. According to Williams the Raja of Sirmur proclaimed his government over the Doon three years after the death of Rohilla Ghulam Qadir and during the reign of Raja Pradyuman Shah. Ghulam Qadir, after annexing the Doon in 1786, appointed Umed Singh (the man appointed as governor of the Doon by Jai Kirti Shah) as his deputy in the Valley. Umed Singh served Ghulam Qadir faithfully till his death in 1789. Thereafter Umed Singh courted Pradyuman Shah, to whom the district once again became nominally subject and the former continued to enjoy its fruits. The Sirmur ruler probably reclaimed his Jagir rights after the death of the Rohilla and posted a representative at Prithipur in the Western Doon.

After the return of Jagat Prakash, the Garhwal ministers again wrote to Pradyuman to come and attack at Dewalgarh where Jai Kirti Shah had gone to pray at the temple of the family "Devi". The attack came and the Raja barely escaped with his life. He is supposed to have gone to Devprayag where after praying at the temple he died on the fourth day of his arrival. Some said he was murdered while according to others he died of chagrin and fatigue. This was in 1785.

During his reign an account of a tragedy, in 1784, at Haridwar is given by Eliot based on "Chahar Guljar Shujai" — by Munshi Hari Charan Das. It is as follows:

"Every year in the month of Baisakh (April) the people of India, particularly Hindus, resort to Haridwar, a place of great sanctity, for the purpose of bathing and fair which lasts for several days. It is said that in Jumadad Awwal, 1198 AH (April 1784 AD) in the Hindi month of Baisakh, when the people had collected as usual, such a deadly blast arose that fifteen hundred persons died from it in two hours. In the same month and year thousands of people lost their lives from starvation in Delhi in a space of 5 or 6 days on account of the dearth of corn. The famine raged from Multan down to Bengal and Maksudabad, with such violence that people were reduced to a very deplorable state. They laboured under double difficulties, one the scarcity of grain and the other the want of employment which equally affected both the soldier and the tradesman".

A similar tragedy took place in the 1938 Kumbh Mela at Haridwar when hundreds of pilgrims perished in a fire.

Another incident connected with the Haridwar Kumbh Mela took place in April 1796. Sardar Sahib Singh of Patiala and Sardar Rai Singh of Bhuria with their families came to the mela with about 1400 armed horsemen. Haridwar in those days was under the administration of the Mahrathas. Because of the Kumbh the Gosai Sadhus (a sect of the Hindu ascetics) had temporarily taken over the administration of the town. A verbal exchange took place between the Sikh's Udasi Guru and the Gosais on 19th April, resulting in unpleasantness. The Sikhs, on the last day of the mela, sent their families out of Haridwar and divided themselves into several armed groups. These groups then attacked all and sundry, who came their way as a reprisal on account of the earlier exchange between the Gosais and the Guru. There was general looting and plunder of the pilgrims and over 500 persons were killed. Lots of people escaped across the Ganga. The Sikhs did not cross over because of the presence of Capt. Murray, of the Nawab of Oudh's army, and his native troops who were camping there.

Pradyuman now ruled Garhwal as well as Kumaun, for a whole year, but harassed on the one hand by the pretensions of his brother Prakarm and on the other by attacks of the party favourable to Mohan Singh the Kumaunese. As a result Pradyuman abandoned Kumaun altogether in 1786. Thereafter he took up his residence, permanently, at Srinagar.

The Sirmur State Gazetteer states that Dharam Prakash, brother and successor of Jagat Prakash, proclaimed himself the ruler of the Doon and it was he who posted a representative at Prithipur and Umed Singh started owing allegiance to him. Prakarm Shah, who thought himself to be the ruler of Garhwal and hence of the Doon, on hearing of this action went with his troops into the Valley. They were able to bring Umed to book, threw out the Sirmur troops from Khushalpur fort in the Western Doon and occupied it. On getting these news Dharam Prakash despatched Kunwar (Prince) Ishwari

Singh with an army. He was able to throw out the Garhwalis and recapture the Valley for Sirmur. Prakarm went back to Srinagar and Umed Singh was re-installed in his office.

Pradyuman Shah then entered in an alliance with the Marathas, who glad of an opportunity for plunder agreed to come to his assistance. They merely amused themselves and went back after a few skirmishes with Sirmur troops, without achieving any results. Umed Singh was thus able to maintain the authority of Sirmur over the Doon for another eight or nine years. The Garhwal Raja again lured him over to his side by giving him the hand of his daughter in marriage. The result was that the Valley once again came under the authority of Srinagar at the beginning of the 19th century. Umed Singh was preparing to declare independence when his plans were upset by the Nepalese invasion of the Doon.

The Valley, all this time, belonged to any one bold enough to overcome the little opposition that could be made.

The Sikh, Rajput and Gujar raids continued into the Valley. Whenever delay occurred in payment of "Rakhi" money, 50 to 100 Sikh troops would come and sweep through the Valley collecting the dues. The actions of others were more ambitious. The "Amil" (official revenue collector) and other government officers were their own masters and collected as much booty as they could, in as short a time as possible, not knowing when they might be replaced. Hence every one was busy lining his pocket. Amongst the more notorious of these oppressors were Hari Singh of Guler, a son-in-law of Pradyuman Shah and Ramdayal of Landhaura who between them stripped the people of the Valley bare. The revenue from the district fell to Rs. 8000/- per annum, which was only double the amount paid as "Rakhi" (Protection money).

In 1800 A.D. or thereabouts the Marathas entered the Valley from Saharanpur and looted all that they could before going back. On this occasion they met no resistance at all and they had a free run of the place. There is a folk tale about a Maratha chief named Raghunath Rao. He is supposed to have gifted the Doon Valley to the Badrinath temple. Probably he was the man who led the above mentioned raid and on withdrawing from the Valley gifted it in order to attain salvation. It was the public property of every free-booter who wanted to have it.

Pradyuman Shah sent Rama and Dharni, two Brahmin brothers who were his ministers and were later murdered at Prakarm Shah's orders, to improve the administration in the Valley. They were replaced by the Zamindar of Sahaspur in the Western Doon. He in turn was replaced by Shib Ram Saklani on Prakarm Shah's orders, who was running a parallel administration to that of his brother. One of Shib Ram's ancestors was given the area of Saklana as a revenue free grant in recognition of his services, to the Garhwal Raja in the action against the Rohillas.

Saklana is situated on the border of the present administrative district of Dehra Dun and of the erstwhile Tehri State. The river Song takes its rise in this area. The British had also confirmed the grant to the descendants of Shib Ram Saklani (named after the village). Apparently this family had a lot of influence at the Garhwal Court as well as in the Doon. As an example of the family's importance the following story is told about Sis Ram Saklani (whose grandson Sobha Ram served the British as a subordinate revenue collector) and Mahant Har Sewak of Gurudwara Ram Rai. The latter was accused of having committed a murder and Sis Ram in his capacity as the administrator of the Valley ordered the Mahant's trial by ordeal. The accused's hands were plunged into boiling molasses and on being burnt was declared guilty. As a punishment, apart from the burnt hands, a heavy fine had to be paid by him.

In 1796 Captain Thomas Hardwicke of the East India Company visited Srinagar. Instead of taking the direct route through the Doon, which was more arduous, he went via Kotdwar and Lansdowne (though this town did not exist then). His account of the travels in Garhwal is given below. It gives an objective view of every thing in Garhwal and the Valley.

For the country side he had to say, "Depopulation and misery are the striking features throughout, and a greater share of the country seems in the undisturbed possession of the birds and beasts of the forest than appropriated to the residence of man".

He goes on to say, "the royal family, consisting of the Raja and his two brothers, Prakarm Shah and Pritam Shah, did not stand on ceremony, and visited him in camp, accompanied by a small retinue. The Raja appeared to be about 27 years of age, low in stature, slender in body with regular features, and effeminate air, nervous in speech, and altogether, judging from his exterior, not made of the metal fit for coping with the hardy Gorkhas, who had already made decided advances in this direction. The manners of the brothers denoted great simplicity. Their clothing had none of that ostentatious gaudiness so conspicuous in the dress of the Indian nobility, and the dress of the Raja differed in no respect from that of the other princes". To Hardwicke the Raja seemed to be a man of fair intelligence, possessing some knowledge of contemporary politics, and taking an interest in it. He conversed about British progress in the East, about the Rohilla war, and expressed much admiration of European proficiency in military art. He knew nothing, however, of the tactics of civilised warfare and for the first time saw the movements (drill) of a disciplined soldiery by the party of sepoys guarding Hardwicke's camp.

According to Hardwicke in Srinagar town the houses were built of rough stone masonry, with slated roofs, being generally two stories high. The streets were so narrow that two people walking from opposite directions could hardly pass abreast anywhere, except in the Bazaar. The palace, situated in the centre of the town, was very old and dilapidated. The annual revenue of the whole kingdom comprising of the Doon, Garhwal and Kumaun, including income from all sources namely land revenue, taxes on exports, imports, royalty from mine and gold washing hardly exceeded five lakh rupees. The land revenue of the Doon was only rupees eight thousand. Land revenue was generally paid partly in cash and partly in kind, in the proportion of fifty-fifty of the produce from the land. Very little money reached the royal coffers, after the necessary deductions to meet the local expenditure. Most of the land tax went in the payment of troops' wages. Certain state employees, musicians and dancing girls were paid by Bills of Exchange on the Zamindars. Hardwicke met several such persons travelling upto 30 kos (60 miles) to have the Bills for their arrears of pay, encashed. A further alienation of land revenue arose from constant donations to Brahmins and endowments to temples during successive reigns.

The fiscal management of gold washing was extremely simple. Each gold-washer paid Rs. 100/- a year to the government for the right to prospect, without reference to the quantity of gold found. Apart from the other localities, this precious metal was found in Rishikesh, Lukhurghat and some rivers of the Doon Valley, Rispana being one of them. There were copper mines, north of Srinagar, which were worked eight months in the year, the rest of the time the place being snow bound. The ore was of 50% purity and half of the value of the pure metal went to the ruler and the balance to defray the expenses of obtaining it. There was a lead mine in the State which was worked by the Raja according to the requirements of the metal. The iron mines of the region were left to any one who chose to extract it, for they were not commercially viable.

The principal items of import into Garhwal were rock salt, borax, musk in pods, "chouries" (fly whisks) hawks and slaves from the country north of Niti and Mana passes or the Bara Hati plateau. Wool and woollen products, cotton textiles, and common salt were imported from the plains. The average import and export duties levied on certain items were six percent of the value of the merchandise. The principal source of the ordinary revenue of the Raja was the traditional offerings made to him by the people at the time of various Hindu festivals. On extraordinary occasions like a marriage of a member of the Raja's family a general tax was levied on all the government allotted lands. Yet the Rajas were miserably poor compared to their contemporaries' standards in the rest of the country.

The standing army consisted of not more than 5000 men, a motley force, armed with the weapons commonly used in the area to which each group of soldiers belonged. Thus they had bows and arrows, swords, bucklers while some had matchlocks. One thousand troops were quartered in Srinagar whilst the rest were scattered all over the State to assist the local administration in collecting government revenue. Dress, discipline or rather the lack of it, irregularity in paying the troops were treated with complete disregard by government and it had to pay dearly for it, in the course of time.

For the maintenance and pay of the troops their Group Commanders were assigned some lands, the income from which was meant for this purpose. The jobs of these Group Commanders, apart from military administration in their respective districts were to superintend the collection of revenue, dispense justice in petty civil and criminal disputes while referring the important ones to Srinagar court. Fines and confiscations were the ordinary punishments for almost all crimes. Even murder was seldom punished by death. The convict, if a Rajput, was severely fined, if a Brahmin, banished from the State, but treason, cow killing and violation of caste laws were generally given capital punishment. For example, if a Dom (Harijan) smoked a Rajput's hookah, the Harijan's life was forfeit. The methods of execution, a rare event, and mostly of the Harijans, were either by hanging or beheading. The Gorkhas later added impalement. The punishment of chopping of a hand or nose was occasionally resorted to in cases of theft. Adultery with a woman of the lower classes was a petty misdemeanor punishable by fine, but if the adulteress happened to be a lady of rank, the rule was to cut off her nose and kill her lover. To make the punishment more signal its execution was left to the injured husband.

The government was a simple monarchy yet the Raja's power was not absolute, but controlled by a council of ministers consisting mostly of officials designated as Dewan (Chief Minister), Vazirs (Ministers), Daftaries (Secretaries), Faujdars (Army Commanders) and Negis (A family title from the old days, as these people were from Naga or Scythian stock and predominated in those days. This title was hereditary in some families who were the locals as opposed to the later Caucasian settlers.) The Negis were the local administrators.

In January 1775 A.D. Singh Pratap (or Pratap Singh) came to the Gorkha throne in Nepal. His uncle Daljit Shah and younger brother Bahadur Shah conspired to seize the throne from him. But the plot was foiled and the uncle left the kingdom whilst the brother was imprisoned. After some time he was banished from Nepal and went to live in exile at the border town of Bettiah in the British province of Bihar. The Gorkha troops who had been fighting and conquering the neighbours of Nepal, could not be kept idle for long. Therefore, they were employed in skirmishes along the borders of Nepal including that with China. Singh Pratap died in 1777 and his two and a half year old son, Ran Bahadur was put on the throne under the Regency of his mother Rajendra Lakshmi. On hearing the news of his brother's death Bahadur Shah came back to Nepal and tried to rule in the name of his minor nephew. Again he was imprisoned by his sister-in-law and later released on the intervention of the family Guru (Priest) Gaj Raj Misra. A ding-dong fight continued between the two in-laws for supremacy. The queen-regent ruled till her death in 1786 and during this period added more territory to her country. In achieving these successes she utilised the services of a young 31 years old soldier, Amar Singh Thapa, son of Bhim Sen Thapa who was a troop Commander under her late husband. On her death the brother-in-law Bahadur Shah took over the regency and started ruling the country in the name of his nephew Ran Bahadur as the boy had turned out to be a weakling. Bahadur Shah not only extended the rule of Nepal upto the border of Garhwal but also made the ruler of Garhwal a vassal of Nepal. Amar Singh Thapa who had conquered Kumaun for Nepal was made the military governor of the newly conquered territory.

In 1792 the Chinese attacked Nepal and Amar Singh Thapa and his troops were recalled from the Garhwal region to defend the country. Amar Singh Thapa had besieged the fortress of Langurgarh in the Salan district of Garhwal and for over a year was unsuccessful in capturing it. Amar Singh Thapa and Capt. Kaloo Pandey, who were commanding the Gorkha troops made a diversion and went with a small contingent to Srinagar and were successful in occupying the place. The Garhwal ruler, Pradyuman Shah, had abandoned Srinagar on the approach of the Gorkhas and had gone across the Alaknanda to Ranihat. Here he was joined by one of his commanders Dharni Dhar Khanduri, who was sent to the Nepalese to try and bring about a peace treaty. The Garhwal ruler was in the dark about the orders to the Gorkha Commanders to immediately return to Nepal and they in turn were keen to make an honourable retreat from Garhwal. Thus a treaty was signed under which an annual tribute of Rs. 3000/- was to be paid to the Nepal government. In order to have the treaty ratified Dharni Dhar Khanduri was sent with the Gorkha Commanders to Nepal. The treaty was ratified by the Nepalese ruler and he sent a Khilat and a Saropa for Pradyuman Shah. Orders were also passed to release all Garhwali men and women who had been made prisoners during the year long siege of Langurgarh, in Garhwal. Embassies were exchanged between the two courts. According to the Garhwal archives Ramapati Khanduri, Dharni Dhar's brother, was appointed ambassador to Nepal. A government department to deal with Nepal affairs was opened and placed under the charge of Dharni Dhar. Whilst in Nepal he had married the daughter of the Raj guru (family priest) of the ruler, and because of this alliance Dharni Dhar had gained the confidence of the Nepalese court. Bahadur Shah, who had been incarcerated by his nephew on his assuming full ruling powers, died in 1795. Ran Bahadur who was more interested in wine, women and song abdicated in favour of his one and half year old son. This son was born of a Brahmin widow who belonged to Tirhut in the Terai area. His name was Governyudh Vikram Shah. Ran Bahadur and the child king's mother took 'sanyas' (renounced the world) and went to live in Devpatan. The boy king was under the regency of his step mother. This change took place in March 1799. In spite of having taken 'sanyas' and renouncing the throne Ran Bahadur could not keep himself away from political intrigue and women. He kept interfering in the affairs of his country both overtly and covertly. It resulted in a piquant situation and a kind of anarchy prevailed in the administration of Nepal and its territories.

The Doon, which was a part of Garhwal Raj, must have felt the repercussions of the happenings in the rest of the Kingdom, especially at Srinagar the capital.

As per the peace treaty of 1792 with Nepal the Garhwal Raj had to pay an annual tribute of Rs. 3000/-. On various pretexts the Nepalese increased this sum to Rs. 9000/- and in addition the Garhwal exchequer had to bear the full expenses of all the Gorkha officials who would come to Badri Nath and Kedar Nath on pilgrimage as also the expenditure of the Nepalese ambassador and his embassy in Srinagar. All this amounted to between 25 to 30 thousand rupees annually. This expense was a big drain on the state's treasury especially when in 1795 a famine took place in the state, the like of which had never occurred before.

Capt. Hardwicke, an English traveller who arrived in Srinagar in 1796 describes the conditions prevailing in the land in the following terms:—

"The Raja is surrounded in such a pitiable economic condition that he can not even obtain clothes, for himself, as are usually worn by his contemporary rulers in this country. He has to satisfy himself with clothes like those worn by his subjects. Villages have been abandoned and where there were habitations wild animals are roaming about. The ruler has had to mortgage villages to the Badrinath temple and borrow money from the temple funds. Sometimes he has borrowed even from the traditional money-lenders. There are no signs of any economic improvement in the near future."

On top of all this, to add to Pradyuman Shah's woes his younger brother Prakarm Shah had started a revolt in the state against him. There was a regular civil war going on in Srinagar, the capital, between the followers of the two brothers since the year 1800 onwards. Among the nobility those who were siding with Prakarm Shah mention must be made of the two Saklani brothers, Shish Ram and Shib Ram, who were the jagirdars of Saklana village on the border of the Doon and Garhwal. They played quite a role in the subsequent events in and around the Doon. Skirmishes between the two groups went on for months. Twice Prakarm Shah imprisoned his brother in the fort and fought his nephew Sudarshan Shah, who was able to get the better of his uncle and obtain the father's release. A truce took place between the two sides.

Thereafter Prakarm Shah talked of partitioning the state and even went to the extent of having his coins minted and got the memorandum of partition drawn up. Once again Prakarm Shah arrested the brother through treachery and took him across the river, to Ranihat, and cut off the rope bridge on it thus isolating him from his capital. The Raja was able to send a message across the river to his ministers and supporters that they should somehow cross over and have him released by force. A conference was held amongst the ministers and Sudarshan Shah. Whilst the conference was on, the gate keeper reported that the Nepalese ambassador had arrived. He was called in and was told the whole story. He informed the assembly that the Nepal ruler had sent sealed letters for the two warring brothers and that he (the ambassador) was to ensure that Pradyuman Shah was allowed to rule in peace. The ambassador sent word to Prakarm Shah that he should make arrangements to have him conveyed across the river in order to meet him and receive the embassy. He was taken across and received ceremoniously by Prakarm who was read out the letter addressed to him from the King of Nepal. In the letter he was admonished for having kept his elder brother in confinement and ordered to release him forthwith to rule his land. If these instructions were not carried out at once he (Prakarm) himself would have to leave the country or face imprisonment. Prakarm and Pradyuman once again agreed to bury their differences and a compromise was signed between them. As soon as the ambassador withdrew to Kumaun, Prakarm started collecting his troops and encircling his brother's palace. Thereupon Pradyuman reported to Bom Shah, the Nepalese military governor of Kumaun and requested him to send the ambassador again. Bom Shah called Pradyuman to meet him at Badhangarhi. At this meeting Pradyuman was told in no uncertain terms that since he could not look after his country and because of some misunderstanding over the movement of the Garhwali troops against the Nepalese, the governing of Garhwal would be taken over by Nepal in spite of the treaty of 1792 A.D.

After this meeting Pradyuman Shah was sure that the Nepalese had decided to annexe Garhwal and that his life was in danger. Therefore at night he along with his ministers escaped from the fortress and made their way back to Srinagar. In the morning the Raja's troops, who were mostly Pathan and Rohilla mercenaries, were in a quandry without any one to guide them. Bom Shah told them to go away if they valued their lives. They went towards Langurgarhi where they were met by Prakarm who was on his way to meet Bom Shah. The soldiers were bought over, by Prakarm, to his side.

The Raja not finding Prakarm at Srinagar, sent Rama Khanduri after him to call him back to Srinagar so that the two brothers could plan their strategy vis-a-vis the Nepalese threat. Prakarm without meeting Rama had him murdered when he was spending the night with a courtesan. Prakarm with his troops started back for Srinagar and before reaching there had the other Khanduri brother, Dharni, also murdered. The two brothers had earned his enmity for having sided with the Raja and preventing Prakarm from gaining the throne of Garhwal. On the night of 8th September, 1803 an earthquake of such intensity that its tremors were felt as far as Calcutta, shook the earth all over Garhwal and Kumaun region. The tremors continued at intervals for seven days and nights. The Gurudwara building in the Doon also suffered damage. This event having occurred shortly after the murders of the Khanduri brothers made the people take it as a retribution for the crime of killing innocent Brahmins.

The Doon Valley proper, a province of the Garhwal Raj, was at the time governed by Umed Singh, Pradyuman Shah's son-in-law. The Mahant of Guru Ram Rai's gurudwara was Har Sewak, and the Gujar raja of the neighbouring Zamindari of Landhaura, near Roorkee was Ram Dayal Singh. He was a friend of the Tehri raja, who had given jagirs, in the Doon Valley to Ram Dayal and to the Raos of Kheri, Sakhroda and Raipur. The Zamindars Mian Dulel Singh of Prithipur, Surjan Singh of Dalanwala, and others were his (the Raja's) loyal subjects. The Governor Umed Singh, stayed in the present village of Nawada. At the beginning of the 19th century, according to Capt. J.A. Hodgson, who conducted a survey in the Doon Valley proper, in 1813-1814, there were forty odd inhabited villages scattered from the Ganga to the Yamuna, and the Shiwaliks to the Himalaya.

In view of the Nepalese threat Pradyuman Shah decided to transfer his documents and valuables, including his gold throne, jewellery, the gold and silver utensils and plate of the Badri/Kedar temples, out of Srinagar. He felt that the Gorkha invasion could be stopped in the Doon Valley with his own resources and the help of his friends. Therefore under the charge of his youngest brother Pritam Shah and sons Sudarshan Shah and Devi Singh, he (the Raja) sent all the stuff to Nawada in the Doon Valley. The ladies of the household were also evacuated and only Pradyuman Shah and Prakarm Shah stayed on in Srinagar. The probable route taken by these evacuees was via Teri (Tehri) across the Bhagrithi and from there to Chamuwakhal, Saklana, Nagal and then down to Nalapani (Khalanga or Kalinga fort) from where Nawada and the town of Dehra are quite close.

Three weeks after the September earthquake the Nepalese forces entered Srinagar, the capital of Garhwal Raj. The troops were under the command of Amar Singh Thapa, whose orders were to annexe for Nepal, the entire hilly region upto Kashmir. His Deputy was Hastidal Chauntra who was to be assisted by Randhir Singh Basnait during this campaign. There were three thousand musket bearing regular troops and an equal number of irregulars, in the invading force.

On hearing of the approach of the Gorkha forces the Garhwal ruler and his ministers thought that it was futile to put up a fight. They decided to leave Srinagar and joined their families in the Doon Valley. The Gorkha commander, on learning about the escape of the ruler, sent out troops in search of him. In due course, after meeting sporadic resistance on the way from the locals, the Gorkha troops occupied the Valley from Rishikesh to Dehra Dun town. Pradyuman Shah with his entourage escaped into Saharanpur district via the Mohand Pass. A few weeks earlier Col. Burn had occupied

82

Saharanpur town and brought the district under the rule of the East India Company. Pradyuman Shah went to Kankhal and sought refuge with his family priest at Haridwar. Haridwar in those days was a small township, the main bazar was 1 1/2 furlongs in length and 15 feet wide (this is the lower bazar in Haridwar and is till the same in size). The pilgrims face a lot of difficulty in getting accommodation to stay during the mela season especially at the time of Kumbh Mela. After Haridwar came under the Company's rule, Henry Wellesley had a bathing ghat and an inn built for the benefit of the pilgrims. The boundaries of the English and Garhwal territories probably met at Bhimgoda where there were check posts on both sides. Jawalapur also was no bigger than a large village. Kankhal on the other hand was a flourishing town - the largest in size.

Even today one can see in Kankhal the old "Havelies" with paintings on their walls and massive doors in Mughal style. The family priest or "Panda" of the house of Tehri-Garhwal was Maya Ram, who was also the leader of the other "Pandas" of Haridwar. For giving refuge to his father and to his own family during their adverse times, Sudarshan Shah, on gaining the state of Tehri-Garhwal gave a Jagir to Maya Ram. This consisted of 1500 Bighas of land at Khara and Pradeep Nagar, near Raiwala, part of which is still in the possession of his descendants.

Knowing that Pradyuman Shah would make attempts to regain his state Amar Singh Thapa had the Timli, Mohand and Kansrao Passes strongly secured against any intrusion. In order to keep the goodwill of the local leadership Amar Singh did not disturb the privileges given to the local leaders like the 'Sayanas' and 'Lambardars'. They in return cooperated with the Gorkha administration.

In the meantime Pradyuman Shah left his family in Kankhal and went to Saharanpur. There he mortgaged his throne for a Lac of rupees and the Badrinath temple jewellery and plate for another fifty thousand rupees. With this money and with the aid of the Gujar Raja Ram Dayal he raised a force of twelve hundred Ranghar, Pundir, Gujar and Rajput mercenary soldiers. With this force he came back into the Doon Valley and gained control over a part of it. On hearing of this intrusion Amar Singh Thapa who was in Srinagar came down to the Valley with his troops.

In January 1804 the forces of Amar Singh and Pradyuman Shah met on the plain of village Khurbara in Dehra Dun, (today this is a thickly populated locality between Tilak Road and the Bindal river) and a great battle ensued. According to the Tehri state archives present at this battle were the two brothers of Pradyuman Shah, Prakarm and Pritam Shah, and the two sons Sudarshan Shah and Devi Singh. On the Nepalese side beside Amar Singh himself there were Bhakt Vir Thapa and Prince Ranjit Kanwar. Pradyuman Shah had a copy of the "Gita" tied to his left arm and a small "Shiv Ling" on the right. In the fight his personal Standard Bearer Kishen Singh got such a severe sword cut that his face was nearly severed in two. Pradyuman Shah fell to a bullet from Ranjit Kanwar's fire while in conversation with Mian Dulel Singh of Prithipur. On hearing of his death, the four princes of his family made good their escape. Prakarm went to his in-laws in Hindur (Nalagarh) whilst the other three made their way to Kankhal. There was complete rout of the Garhwali force.

Amar Singh had Pradyuman Shah's body conveyed to Haridwar, with full military honours, for cremation under the charge of the Dalanwala Zamindar Surjan Singh Rawat. Amar Singh Thapa himself covered the Raja's body with a woollen shawl, which in the Hindu tradition is the highest form of honouring and respecting the dead. Only Pritam Shah, the Raja's brother, was at Haridwar and in the absence of the sons he carried out the last rites of the brother. After the funeral Pritam Shah was made prisoner by the Nepalese and sent to Kathmandu. A more probable account is that he never escaped, with his nephews, but was taken prisoner on the battle field and made to go with the body to do the last rites. It seems that no other member of his family was present and none of the Raja's widows, who were in Kankhal committed "Sati", on his pyre, as was the custom those days. The reason for this could be that Kankhal being in English territory the Gorkha troops did not want to enter it and inform the family or else for political expediency kept the cremation a secret.

After this battle there was complete chaos in the Doon accompanied by plunder, arson and rape by the Gorkha soldiers. Mahant Har Sewak of Darbar Guru Ram Rai was confined in the Gurudwara on suspicion of being a collaborator of Pradyuman Shah and all the Gurudwara lands confiscated. For a whole year the land in the Valley lay bare and desolate.

According to tradition the Brahmins of Palia Garh, on the road to Yamnotri (the source of the river Yamuna), are the worshippers of Devi known as the goddess Ketitali. It is believed that at the beginning of each year the Devi predicts the good and bad happenings for the ensuing year through the dreams of a chosen Brahmin. The misfortunes of Pradyuman Shah, the rise of Gorkha power and their defeat at the hands of the British were foretold by these Brahmins at the beginning of 1803.

In April 1804 Amar Singh returned to Srinagar leaving a Gorkha governor to administer the Doon Valley which was now completely under Nepalese control. Amar Singh reorganised the administration of Garhwal. The members of the two famous Garhwali families the Saklanis and the Khanduris became the most obedient and loyal servants of the new rulers and carried out their orders as they had done under their previous masters. Amar Singh was now ordered by the Nepalese Darbar to carry his campaign of acquisition and or annexation, west of the river Yamuna. He was to bring the area right upto the river Satluj, after conquering the fort of Kangra and the intermediate areas, under the Nepalese flag. Once this was achieved he was to make plans to invade and conquer Lahore and Delhi.

Across the Yamuna was the state of Sirmur and at this time its ruler was Karam Prakash. He was an unpopular ruler with his subjects. On getting an opportunity, his courtiers surrounded him in his fortress of Kangor 32 kilometers from Nahan. In the fight that ensued a person named Cholumian, who was Karam Prakash's double, was killed and word spread that the Raja was dead. During the confusion that followed Karam Prakash, with his family, managed to escape to Kalsi. His younger brother Ratan Prakash was placed on the Sirmur throne. Karam Prakash requested the Gorkhas to come to his aid in regaining his state. They took advantage of this situation and invaded Sirmur and instead of giving the territory back to Karam Prakash added it to their conquests. In this fashion the Gorkhas went on conquering territories in the hills right upto the boundary of Kangra. Here they were halted and kept in check by the forces of Sansar Chand of Kangra forcing Amar Singh Thapa to come to terms with him. A treaty was signed whereby the Gorkhas were to remain in Nalagarh (Hindur) on the east bank of the Satluj river which would be the boundary with Kangra. In the meantime a lot of political changes took place in Nepal, after the assasination of Ran Bahadur in April 1805. This slowed down the progress of Amar Singh's campaign in Himachal.

In December 1805 he renewed his campaign against Kangra and crossed the Satluj after all the Hill Princes of Himachal, barring Sansar Chand, had accepted the suzerainty of Nepal. He reached the citadel of Kangra and surrounded it from all sides but could not block the river side entrance to the fort. This siege continued for three years. One version is that this was purposely done because of Amar Singh and Sansar Chand having come to a secret understanding. According to it, the Gorkhas had the run of the country around the fort on the eastern side while Sansar Chand had his door open on the river side. However four attempts were made by Amar Singh to gain the fort which failed, and he had to ask for reinforcements from Nepal. Sansar Chand was besieged from the west by the Sikh ruler Ranjit Singh who was able to gain control over the Kangra fort and thus frustrated the Gorkha ambition of conquering Northern India.

The following story is told of the valour of the widow of Kirti Chand (Singh), the Commander of the Kangra army, at the battle of Tira Sujanpur, and the Nepalese Commander Nain Singh Thapa.

Kirti Chand, a Garhwali, was in the service of the Kangra Raja and was commanding his troops. He (Kirti Chand) was killed in battle. When the victorious Gorkha Commander was entering the town, astride an elephant, a musket shop hit him in the thigh. He fell off the elephant. Another bullet hit his deputy Dalbam Shah in the shoulder. Their escort went in search of the assailant and on coming in sight of the assailant they were fired upon also, killing three of them. The person firing, on being over-powered, was found to be the widow of Kirti Chand. On being questioned by Nain Singh as to the reason for her firing at him, she replied that as he had killed her husband, his (Nain Singh's) life was forefeit to her and that she had every right to kill him. She was sorry that she could not die in battle but would now like to be killed in order to join her husband who was waiting in the next world. Dalbam Shah wanted her to be hanged immediately but Nain Singh was so impressed by her valour and loyalty to her husband that he made her an offer. He wanted her to go to Nepal and he would see that a pension was given to her, for maintenance, but she declined. He then ordered that Kirti Chand's body be found and its proper cremation arranged. She became a Sati. Nain Singh succumbed to his injuries a few days later.

The Doon Valley was being governed by Balbhadar Singh who was Amar Singh's nephew. The civil administration was entrusted to Sis Ram Saklani who had been made an ''Amil'' (collector of revenue) by the Gorkhas. He is reported to have had the hands of Mahant Har Sewak plunged into boiling molasses, when he was suspected of having committed a murder. The proceedings, though summary, were strictly judicial, being in the nature of a trial by ordeal - a remnant of medieval times. The hands were burnt and the Mahant had to pay a heavy fine for his assumed crime and also lost his Zamindari lands.

As a consequence of the Gorkha invasion and the resulting loot and plunder, the people of the Valley had left their homes, some going up in the hills and others to the plains across the Shiwaliks. There was hardly any cultivation carried on and the annual revenue receipts, from the Valley, came down to Rs. 9000/- from Rs. 1 lac the amount collected before the Gorkha occupation. When Hastidal Chauntara became the Nepalese viceroy of Garhwal conditions slowly started improving in the area. The Doon Valley, which had become more or less completely desolate because of the tyrannical behaviour of the Gorkha soldiers and the revenue collectors, once again attracted people back to their lands. Mahant Har Sewak was the only Zamindar of the Valley who still commanded respect among the public. Hastidal gave back the Mahant's lands to him who in turn persuaded his tenants to return and start cultivating the lands. In a couple of years the revenue of the district increased from Rs. 9000/- to Rs. 16000 annually.

During the reigns of Pradyuman Shah and his two predecessors the Doon Valley did not have any administrator worth the name for more than six months at a time. After the death of Najib-ud-Daulah in 1770 A.D., the people of the Valley were subjected to constant raids for the purpose of looting and plundering by the Rajput, Gujar and Sikhs hordes from the surrounding areas. These raids stopped the day the Gorkha governor announced that for every raid into the Valley he would send out his troops to burn one village of the raiders. Once some Sikhs took a chance and came into the Valley, to plunder as before, ransacked a village and carried away many young women and cattle. When the Gorkha commander of the area heard of this incident he sent a couple of hundred of his troops after the raiders. Their village was surrounded and put to the torch. Every escaping human being was killed in cold blood, except young good looking women who were brought as spoils of war. Such methods may have been barbarous but they had a salutary effect on the raiders.

The Gorkha administration was more or less on the same pattern as the Garhwali's. The local Gorkha governors exercised the same powers as their Garhwali predecessors. The Thapas, who were considered low born because they were agriculturists as opposed to the Chauntras who were aristocrats, had gained supremacy over others at the Nepalese court. The Thapas had started replacing their opponents in all important offices. In the Doon, Hasti Dal was replaced by Bhairon Thapa as governor. Capt. Raper, an English traveller and surveyor, met Bhairon Thapa in company with Hasti Dal at Kharkharee, near Bhimgoda in Haridwar on 8th April 1808. Capt. Raper was camping there on his way to find the source of the Ganga along with Lt. Webb and Capt. Hearsey. At some time Hearsey had treated Hasti Dal after he had been mauled by a bear and hence he not only knew him (Hearsey) but was obligated to him. Hastidal told Raper that as he was no more the governor he would not be able to give him much help in his travels in Garhwal. The new governor appeared suspicious and obstructive, pointing out insurmountable difficulties on the way, and tried to dissuade Raper from proceeding further. The party however got as far as Bhatwari and then had to return because the path beyond was inaccessible for their heavy bagagge. Actually the survey work was entrusted to Lt. Webb who was from the East India Company's Survey department. From Bhatwari he sent a local person from his party, who was clever enough to be able to use a compass and to make a rough drawing and measure distances by the number of paces walked, to go upto Gangotri. This man was able to bring back useful information to Webb. Webb and party in the meantime went upto Badrinath, charting the course of the Alaknanda River and on returning to Joshimath they were told by the Gorkha Subedar to get out of the territory without delay and to by-pass Almora. After having a rough time enroute they arrived at their headquarters at Bareilly where Webb fell ill. As a result the tabulations and drawings of his tour's survey data were delayed. The Surveyor General was impatient to get the maps of Gangotri and the other areas, surveyed by Webb, because Hearsey in the meantime had privately sent his own general map of the areas to England, to be passed on to the Directors of the Company, through Rennell another surveyor. Hearsey had asked Rennell to inform the Court of Directors that this tour of the Ganga basin in the mountains had been undertaken by him at his personal expense, hence he should be either suitably rewarded for his labours or else be permitted to privately publish the map.

When the Surveyor General sent Webb's map to England it was discovered that Hearsey had pirated it, at the time Webb was lying ill at Bareilly, calling it his own. Rennell had to apologise to the Directors.

Earlier to this survey a Frenchman, Michel Pierre Gacoin, who was a mercenary and a surveyor had entered the Doon around 1804. He came up the Yamuna Valley travelling along the banks and making a map of the area showing all the towns, forts and villages on the river's banks. He travelled 30 miles up the river up to where it enters the Shiwaliks and stopped as he felt unsafe to proceed further. This map he passed onto the East India Company's Surveyor General Col. Colebrooke as he had given Gacoin a sum of Rs. 1000/- for surveying the Yamuna north of Delhi, since it had not been surveyed before. This map was a great help to the British in planning their war, against the Gorkhas, in the Western Doon.

In spite of the Gorkha occupation of the Doon, surveyors in the Company's pay were able to get into the Valley and do their work. In 1811 Surveyor Blake proceeded beyond the Doon upto the interior Himalaya, surveying all the way. He had accompanied a Dr. Rutherford as his assistant. Rutherford was a merchant trading in timber, hemp and other valuable articles produced in this area, and was also the Civil Surgeon of Moradabad. In February 1814 another Surveyor, Hodgson, came into the Valley through Haridwar.

Here he procured a "hill carriage" (probably a bullock or a horse cart) and went from Rishikesh towards Deoprayag"..... about 20 or 30 kos of mountain road along the course of the Ganges, but I find the snow is middle deep on the hills I must pass." Perforce he had to postpone the trip and instead took a ten day trip in the Shiwaliks through the Kansrao Pass area and went back to Saharanapur. On March 29th, 1814 he again came into the Valley via the Timli pass. The Gorkha Commander at Dehra Dun, Balbhadra Singh Thapa, was insolent and rude to him because he was suspicious of the British and did not approve of their survey work. Hodgson tried to reassure him by saying that he will not be using his Perambulator (surveying instrument) but was only going to shoot tigers. The Commander refused to meet him but agreed to give him guides and protection to any other place except Haridwar. Hodgson in the meantime had got permission to survey from Kazi Ranjor. He, therefore, did not worry too much about the local administrator, and decided to go up the Yamuna Valley to survey Bhadraj mountain, round which the river flows into the Valley. On getting to the top, after a stiff climb, he was disappointed in not being able to see the eternal snows at the back. They were hidden in clouds. However, he got a good view of the neighbourhood and through a telescope the river Tonse appeared to be three times the size of the Yamuna. He and another surveyor Mackenzie camped on Bhadraj and carried out their work. During winter it seldom snows on Bhadraj. However a local belief is that if it has snowed in Mussoorie the weather will not clear till it has snowed on Bhadraj. Nine times out of ten it turns out to be so. Copies of his map of the Doon were in great demand by the army that was to invade the Valley later in the year.

However the first European to reach Gangotri and Yamnotri was James Baillie Fraser who was on a visit to his brother William, an assistant to the British Resident at Delhi. Later William was given political charge of Garhwal.

There were 84 Commandants, each in-charge of a Sub-division in the three provinces of the Nepalese controlled areas of Kumaun, Garhwal and Himachal. Amongst the Governors looking after these provinces Bhairon Singh Thapa was in-charge of Garhwal. Since the war in Kangra was raging with full force the Governors were occupied in its conduct and they left the administration of their territories to their deputies and assistants. Bhairon Singh Thapa also went to the battle front leaving behind his son, Shisht Thapa to manage the affairs during his absence. The Deputies holding assignments in the districts and their sub-divisions exercised their unlimited powers in a summary manner. Intricate law suits were decided by having recourse to ordeals of different kinds, as in the case of the Mahant and sometimes by the "toss of a coin." In order to recover arrears of government revenue the household effects or even the families of the defaulters were sold. The Gorkhas had an inherent contempt for human life and thought less of a human being than of a cow whose slaughter could only be expiated by the offender's death. Being sold into slavery was a common feature and a regular slave market flourished at Haridwar on the boundary with British India. Courts condemned defaulters, who had been sentenced to pay a fine and could not do so along with their families to life long bondage to the state which in turn sold them to the public.

Besides, parents sold their children under pressing circumstances, uncles their nephews or nieces, and anyone over whom the seller had a physical hold. According to J.B. Frazer, something like 2,00,000 Garhwalis were sold by auction into bondage, during the Gorkha rule over Garhwal. This figure may be an exaggeration but it cannot be questioned that a slave market existed. During the annual fairs held at Haridwar usually in the month of April, hundreds of wretches, varying in age from 3 to 30 years, were brought down from the hills and sold. They fetched from Rs. 10/- to Rs. 150/-per head whereas the average price of a camel was Rs. 75/-, a horse fetched from Rs. 250/- to Rs. 300/- and elephant Rs. 200/- to Rs. 300/-. According to Hearsey 30,000 Garhwali men, women and children were sold, by Gorkhas in the slave market, because of their inability to pay either the revenue or the fines imposed on them. According to him 80,000 Garhwalis left their houses and fled to the interior mountains because of the Nepalese oppression.

The Nepalese Governor of the Doon Balbhadra Singh ordered that all old "Jagirs" and land grants sanctioned to some people by the previous government be cancelled and new ones sanctioned after review of each case. The district of the Doon (excluding Jaunsar-Bawar) was divided into five sub-divisions namely Sabalpur, Basantpur, (in

89

the east) Santaur, Kalyanpur and Soiree (in the West) and a revenue settlement was made by the new rulers. The revenue levy in the Doon was less than in the Garhwal region because of the benign outlook of the local Nepalese Governor. The temples mentioned below had been endowed with the revenue from some of the villages in the Valley from the days of Garhwali rulers. These endowments were honoured by the Nepalese. They were:-

Badrinath Temple - Village Dobhalwala

Kedar Nath Temple - Prempur and Jakhan villages,

Bharat Mandir in Rishikesh - Rishikesh and Tapoban,

Gorakh Nath Temple - Jogiwala and Gorakhpur villages.

In those days the limits of village Dobhalwala extended up to Garhi where the present cantonment is situated. A part of this village was taken on lease by the British Government to build the new cantonment and annual rental is paid to the Badrinath temple committee by the Government of India. Recently a couple of lakhs of rupees were paid as arrears of rent.

The Gurudwara of Guru Ram Rai had been endowed with the villages of Khurbara, Rajpur and Chamesari (Chamya) by Raja Fateh Shah and Dhamawala (which is a part of the main bazar of the town of Dehra), Mayanwala (Mehunwala Mafi,) Panditwari and Dhartawala villages by Raja Pradeep Shah. In addition to these there was an endowment of six villages, across the Ganga in Garhwal, the recorded income from which in 1827 A.D. was Rs. 35/-. The Nepalese on taking over the Valley revoked these endowments and started managing the villages and collecting revenue. Balbhadra later on relented and restored the endowments, and issued two copper plate "Sanads" (endowment warrants) in favour of Mahant Har Sewak, in the name and on behalf of Maharajadhiraj Governyudh Vikram Shah Bahadur. The first one was for Dhamawala village. One of the directions in it was that 50 paise worth of "Prasad" Halwa, a sweatmeat made from wheat flour, after being offered to the Guru's memory, was to be distributed amongst the devotees every day. In those days the price of wheat was about one rupee per quintal. Therefore it can be assumed that every day about twenty to thirty kilograms of "Prasad" was made and distributed. The second plate was in respect of the other villages whilst there is no record of the ones across the Ganga. The Mahant was given the management of the villages and by his persuasion a number of villagers, who had fled at the time of the Gorkha invasion, came back and resettled on their lands.

In 1811 another land grant was given by Balbhadra Singh to one Naik Sukhbir Gosain at the time of the establishment of the Kali temple at Asarori, on the Dehra Dun-Saharanpur road, on the Doon Valley side of the tunnel. This temple was established by the Gorkhas for the benefit of the troops who were quartered there to guard the pass. There is a novel feature of this place. The temple is at the highest point of the hill and next to it is a fresh water well, dug by the Gorkha priest at the time of building the temple. It is very seldom that one comes across such a phenomenon, in geography. Wells are usually found at the bases of hills or in valleys and very rarely at the highest point. Sukhbir Gosain was allowed to clear the forest and establish a village in an area

90

of one mile circumference around the temple, for the upkeep and maintenance of it and his family. He was also allowed to name the village Sukhbirpur and it would be his property to be inherited by his descendants. They are still the priests and in possession of the temple and have built another temple across the tunnel. The credit for the second temple goes to Cautley, the Englishman who made the Ganga canal and built the Asarori tunnel.

The Gorkhas, after occupying the Doon, killed hundreds of able bodied youngmen and carried away innumerable women and children mostly girls. The result was that the population, in the Doon went down sharply as a consequence of the exodus, the killings and capture by the invaders. The dread of the Gorkhas taking away their female child, once she grew up, forced parents to strangle them at birth. In 1814 when the British occupied the Valley they found that the number of old widows and bachelors below thirty years were far more than the rest. There were hardly any children to be seen. The Gorkha soldiery would buy a woman for ten to fifteen rupees and use her as a slave. She, and any children born during her slavery, accompanied the solider wherever he went. Any one resisting this kind of action was mercilessly beaten into submission. Women were treated like any other household goods and for sexual satisfaction. The oldest profession on earth flourished. Enterprising locals would run organised brothels in places where there was a good population of soldiers. In Dehra Dun town such an establishment existed till as late as 1947 and was served by Garhwali and Jaunsari women. Here one paid the fee and had his fun. The organisers would even send the women to the customer's place for a slightly extra charge. The going rate, before World War II was 25 paise for an hour and rupees two for the night. Flesh trade in the Valley was quite common. Even today the Jaunsar-Bawar area is notorious for it. Poverty and illiteracy are the main reasons for this state of affairs.

Some times if a culprit was unable to pay the fine imposed for his misdeed by the Gorkha Officer in-charge of the district, he was sold into slavery along with his family. Parents driven to desperation sold their children, and under certain circumstances uncles sold their nephews and nieces and elder brothers their younger brothers and sisters.

Raper, the Englishman who passed through Haridwar in 1808 has written the following in his journal, regarding the conditions prevailing at the time:-

"The Gorkhas ruled Garhwal with a rod of iron and the country fell into a lamentable decay. Its villages became deserted, its agriculture ruined and its population decreased beyond computation. It is said that two lakhs (2,00,000) of people were sold as slaves, while a few families of consequence remained in the country; but, to avoid the severity of the tyranny, they either went into banishment or were cut off or forcibly driven away by their tyrants, yet some of the individual rulers of these conquerors were mild and not disliked. Bam Shah and Hastidal, the governors of Garhwal, were disposed to indulgence; and in some situations the country towards the close of Gorkhali rule was again improving and getting reconciled to its new state. Ranjor Thapa was also a well disposed man and a mild governor, and inclined to justice, but the executive officers were severe. Their manners as conquerors were rough, and they despised the people they had conquered (this attitude amongst the present day Gorkhas is still discernible towards the Garhwalis), so that at some distance from the seat of government exactions went on, insults and scenes of rapine were continually acted, and the hatred of the people to their tyrants was fixed and exasperated; the country was subdued and crushed, not reconciled or accustomed to the yoke; and, though the spirit of liberty was sorely broke, and desire for revenge was checked by the danger of avowing such sentiments, a deliverance from the state of misery groaned under was ardently, though hopelessly wished for.''

The administration of justice was on no regular system. It depended on each of the officers exercising jurisdiction according to his position and the number of men at his disposal to ensure the execution of his orders. All petty civil and criminal cases were disposed off by the Commandant of the troops to whom the particular tract of the district was assigned, while cases of importance were disposed off by the civil governor of the province assisted by the military chiefs who happened to be present at the headquarters. The Commandants who were frequently absent on active duty delegated their powers to their Deputies called ''Becharis''. Garhwal was divided into three provinces or commands, the Doon being one of them. The procedures followed in dispensing with the cases was the same as was followed by the Garhwalis and common to most Hindu states of the time.

A brief oral examination of the parties was conducted in the presence of the court. In case of doubt a volume of the ''Gita'' was placed on the head of the deponent, who was then enjoined to speak the truth. Where the evidence of eye-witnesses was not available or the testimony was conflicting the defendant was asked to undergo a test by ordeal in which if successful his defence was established. Common forms of ordeal in use were (a) the 'Gola dip' in which a bar of red-hot iron was carried by the person in his hands for a certain distance; (b) 'Karahi dip' in which the person's hands were plunged into boiling oil or molasses, and as in the former case the evidence of innocence was that no physical harm resulted to the person; and (c) the 'Tarazuka dip' in which the person undergoing the ordeal was weighed against a number of stones which were carefully sealed and deposited in some secure place and again weighed the next morning. If the person undergoing this test proved heavier than the previous weighing, his innocence was considered established.

Judgement was delivered and recorded on the spot, in the presence of the onlookers and handed over to the successful party, while the loser was fined, more in proportion to his means than the importance of the case.

Cases of disputed inheritance or of commercial dealings were dealt with by 'Panchayats', or a council of arbitrators, who frequently disposed the case by drawing lots. The names of the litigants were written on slips of paper of equal size, shape and material, which were then placed before an idol in a temple; the priest then went in and picked one of the papers, and the person whose name was written on it was declared successful. Many matters were simply decided by the plaintiff proceeding to some well known temple and there swearing by the idol that his statement was the true one.

In the 'Teer ka dip' the person remained with his head submerged in water while another ran the distance and back covered by an arrow shot from the spot where the trial was being held. If the person did not drown in the meanwhile he was declared successful. Poison was in very particular cases resorted to as the criterion of innocence. A given dose of a particular root was fed to the person concerned and if he survived, his innocence was considered proved. Another mode of appeal to the interposition by the Deity was the placing of either a sum of money, or a bit of earth from the land in dispute, in a temple before the idol; and the party volunteering for such test, would then, after heaping curses on himself, took home the article so placed. If death was a curse named and none occurred within six months, in his immediate family, he gained his cause.

The day of reckoning arrived for the oppressors when they (the Gorkhas) were overthrown by the forces of the East India Company. The treatment meted out to the Gorkhas, by the liberated Garhwalis is described by J.B. Frazer, in his book "Himalaya Mountains", in the following words:-

"It was usual during the time the Gorkhalis were in power to station parties in the different districts for the purpose of collecting the revenue, and in progress of time many of them took daughters of the Zamindars in marriage; not always with the good will of the latter, but the connection formed a tie between the conquerors and the conquered which though far weaker, from the savage and treacherous nature of the people, and circumstances of violence under which it was formed, than a similar one in most other countries would have been, was still sufficient, during its existence, to guarantee the life and prevent the murder of the son-in-law. When the power of the Gorkhalis was broken in the remoter districts, who were thus connected, choose to domesticate with their wives and families rather than run the hazard of retreating through a country of hostile savages, ripe for revenge upon tyrannical but now foreign masters. Others too in like manner, although not enjoying the security resulting from any such tie, choose rather to trust to the protection of some Zamindars whom they had known, and had possibly once obliged, and by whom they believed that their lives would not be attacked, than risk their safety in a more dangerous flight, although the loss of property in both cases was nearly certain. Thus individuals of this wretched people were found in the hills in every district, and almost every one was stripped of his property even till they were in want of clothes to cover them from the weather. Many were more deplorably situated. Some wounded and neglected were found languishing unassisted and wanting even necessaries. Others had fled to the jungles to escape the massacre to which their comrades had fallen victims and for a long time subsisted on the roots and fruits found in thick forests. Even the marriage tie did not always ensure good treatment, and not unfrequently when terrors of consequences ceased, the Zamindars reclaimed their daughters and forced them to leave their husbands, although the stipulated prices had been paid for them."

Captain Hearsey described the Gorkha commanders as, "ignorant, subtle, treacherous, faithless and avaricious to an extreme; after conquest and victory, blood-thirsty and relentless; after defeat, mean and abject. Their soldiers are badly armed and can bear no comparison to the Maratha troops.'' This assessment of Hearsey's was proved wrong at the battles of Kalanga, Jaithak and Almora. On the other hand Fraser describes the Nepalese as men and soldiers in these terms.

"The regular army of Nepal has been for so long a time accustomed to active service, to a series of constant warfare and victory, that the men have become really veteran soldiers, under the advantages of necessary control and a certain degree of discipline; and from their continual success they have attained a sense of their own value - a fearlessness of danger and a contempt of any foe opposed to them. They are cheerful, patient of fatigue, industrious at any labour to which they are put, very tractable and quiet, and from what has fallen under my own observation and knowledge, not, I think, wanton or cruel. This, however, is a dubious part of their character: in various situations they have behaved in different ways, and have given reason to presume that their natural description, whatever it may be, is swayed by situations and circumstances; even as a nation their character seems various and unsettled. The individuals must exhibit a greater variety still. At the same time the many acts of cruelty committed by them and their tyrannical treatment of the Garhwalis should not be forgotten.''

Reverting back to the ruling family of Garhwal it is noticed that from 1804 onwards, Raja Sudarshan Shah, and his family with their entourage, were living in the house of their family priest at Kankhal (Haridwar) in British territory. Pradyuman Shah had liquidated all his valuables to raise money for his last campaign against the Gorkhas, hence his son Sudarshan was not well off financially. It was around 1810 that Sudarshan Shah came in contact with Major (then Captain) Hyder Young Hearsey. He was the man who had gone with Captain Raper and Webb to survey the upper reaches of the Ganga and had pirated Webb's map of the Gangotri area, when he was lying ill at Bareilly.

Hearsey or to give him his full name Hyder Jung (later anglicised to Young), was born in India in 1782 of an English father, probably Lt. Col. Andrew Hearsey, and an Indian mother. After being educated at Woolwich, England, he was taken in service by the Nawab Wazir of Oudh, at the young age of sixteen, through the influence of Col. Andrew Hearsey who had been appointed Commandant of the Company's garrison at Allahabad. In 1799 Hyder entered the Maratha service under the French General Perron who made the lad his aide-de-camp. By his capability Hyder at the age of seventeen was appointed Deputy Commandant of the Fort of Agra after its occupation by Perron. When Perron started showing partiality to his fellow countrymen, in the matter of appointments, a number of Anglo-Indian and English officers left his service. Hyder was one of them. He now joined George Thomas, another freebooter, who like Perron was carving out a kingdom for himself from the ruins of the Mughal empire. Since their aims were similar and the territories to be won being limited to the area around Delhi a confrontation between the two took place at Thomas' citadel at Hansi in Haryana. In this fight Thomas was defeated at the hands of Perron's officers amongst whom was another soldier of fortune James Skinner (founder of the Skinner's Horse, the 1st Cavalry Regiment of the Indian Army to-day) and his brother Robert. Later on Hansi was to become the fief of the Skinners. Now Hyder decided to become a freebooter himself and raised a force of 5000 men, which he held ready to use in favour of the first power which might make a satisfactory bid for his help. Lord Wellesley, the Governor General, ordered General Lake to (a) liquidate Perron's fief (b) take Emperor Shah Alam under British "protection" and reduce Perron's army. In other words Perron had to go. Hyder joined the Company's service at the age of twenty-one and was given a salary of eight hundred rupees a month. He disbanded his 5000 men with the exception of one regiment of Cavalry (800 men) which he was permitted to bring to Lake's army.

In 1805 Hyder was ordered to go and subdue a revolt by some Zamindars of Bareilly. He fought a decisive action against the rebels in the neighbourhood of Kareli, an estate which subsequently became his and his descendants' Zamindari. He married a daughter of one of the deposed Nawabs of Cambay. She, being an adopted daughter of the Mughal Emperor Akbar II, brought a lot of property in her dowry. Her elder sister married another English soldier of fortune Col. William Linnaeus Gardner (founder of Gardner's Horse, 2nd Lancers, another cavalry regiment of the present Indian Army). Gardner was sensitive to any comment on his marriage to a native and on one occasion published the following statement in an Indian newspaper:-

"A Moslem lady's marriage with a Christian by a Kazi is as legal in this country as if the ceremony had been performed by the Bishop of Calcutta, a point lately settled by my son's marriage with the niece of the Emperor. The respectability of the females of my family amongst the natives of Hindustan has been settled by the Emperor many years ago, he having adopted my wife as his daughter; a ceremony satisfactorily repeated by the Queen on a visit to my own house at Delhi."

From the above statement it will be seen that in pre 1857 days there were quite a lot of intermarriages, in India, between the natives of Hindustan and Europe.

Hearsey met Sudarshan Shah at Anjani Ghat, in Kankhal (Haridwar). He (Hearsey) was shown the "Firmans" granted by Aurangzeb to the Raja of Garhwal, in respect of the Doon and Chandi Pargana across the Ganga. At the time the Doon was under the Gorkhas, and the possibility of the Gorkhas leaving the area, and Sudarshan Shah re-gaining the territory, were remote. However Hearsey concluded a bargain with the Raja and purchased the Doon and Chandi, along with the 'firmans' in respect of them, for a paltry sum of Rs. 3005/- as per the Deed of sale dated 22.6.1811, a translation of which is reproduced below:-

" I, Raja Soodersun Sah, son of Raja Hardut Sah, grandson of Raja Aleep Sah, great grandson of Raja Hardut Sah, do hereby solemnly declare that whereas Pergunnas Doon and Chandee were settled on my ancestors (without there being any co-parcenery rights with any other person) by the Firmans of His Majesty Emperor Aurungzeb (may God shed heavenly lustre on his grave), at this present time being in a sound and healthy state of mind, and not being swayed by the false persuasions of others, but of my own free-will and accord, do hereby sell the above Pergunnas, with all the rights accruing therefrom, such as revenue, Sayer, Firewood, and all other Zamindari rights, together with the Imperial Firmans, to Captain Hearsey in consideration of rupees 3005/- (three thousand and five), the half of which will amount to one thousand five hundred and two eight annas only (1502-8).

I hereby acknowledge to have received the whole of the aforesaid sum in full from Captain Hearsey; the whole sum has been paid by him, and I have received and made use of it. I also acknowledge to have put Captain Hearsey in possession of the above Pergunnas, together with the Imperial Firmans relating to them. Nothing is due to me from him (not a dam, not even a diram). If I or any of my successors or heirs should set up a claim for any balance of the above mentioned sum, it should be rejected as false; and no cognisance whatsoever should be taken of it; I myself alone am responsible for this act.

With this view I have executed this deed in order that it may serve both as deed of sale and a receipt for the above mentioned sum of money; also that it may be made use of as documentary evidence in case of any litigation.

Written this day, the 22nd June, 1811, corresponding to 30th Jaumadul sanl 1226 A.H. and 17th Asadha Fusli and Bikramajeet Sumwut 1818.

(Signed and sealed)   Raja Soodersun Sah.

Witnessed by
(Signed)
Chunee Lall, Moonshee, son of Diara Sahaie.
Thakoor Dass, in charge of Office Records.

On 28th October, 1815 by a Deed of sale, Hearsey sold the area of Chandi to the East India Company. The translation of the Deed is as under:-

''I, Hyder Young Hearsey, Major, a resident of the town of Bareilly, do hereby solemnly declare that whereas all the villages detailed below belonging to Pergunna Chandee, Zillah Moradabad, province Shahjahanabad, which under the Imperial Firmans of their most magnificent Majesties, Mohomed Shah, Aurungzeb, and Alumgeer Shah (may God illuminate their graves) were settled on and held for generations by the ancestors of Soodersun Sah, and which have been sold to me by the aforesaid Raja, I now at this present time being in a sound and healthy state of mind, and not being swayed by persuasion or force, but of my own free will and accord do agree to sell all the villages detailed below to the Right Honourable the East India Company (may their glory rise) in consideration of the annual sum of rupees 1200 (one thousand two hundred), half of which equal to 600 rupees current coin. This sum to be made payable to me and my heirs and successors from generation to generation in perpetuity commencing from the first day of January 1812 A.D., corresponding with the 3rd Margh, 1219 Fusl, and 15th Ziulhujj 1226 Hejera. And from that date all the rights and interests thereof, Dhakillee as well as Khariji, small as well as great, all the produce of fruit-bearing and other trees, also Julkur and Bunjer lands Jheels and Jhaburs, all revenue accruing from grazing contracts, bamboos, timber, Kutha, lime, wax, honey, lac Kundas and bunslochun and all other rights, with the exception of mosques, graves, public roads, bye-paths, and all such like public properties.

The Honourable East India Company have purchased the villages mentioned in this deed in a fair and honourable manner, and they have been made over to them and are now in their possession.

After the execution of this deed nothing is owing to me from the said East India Company. I have made over to the Government officials the Imperial Firmans together with the deed of sale executed in my favour by Raja Soodursun Sah. Although the Imperial Firmans are for both the Pergunnas Dhoon and Chandee, yet I have only sold the Zamindarrie and the rights and interests accruing thereon of the Pergunna of Chandee. But I here promise that when the Pergunna Dhoon shall come within the possession of the Honourable East India Company I will sell the villages belonging to it to the aforesaid Company.

With this view I have written this deed to serve as documentary evidence in times of need.

Below is a detail of villages of Pergunna Chandee and their boundaries.

(Signed) Major Hyder Young Hearsey

Witnessed by:

(Signed) Major Rogers, Adjt. 42nd N.I.

Capt. Bullock

Capt. Boder

Goolam Ali, Moonshee

Lt. Hamilton

Chunie Lal

The above mentioned deed was executed on the 28th day of October, A.D. 1815, corresponding with 1223 Fuslee in the month Kartik equivalent to 1233 Hazeria on a Saturday.''

(True copy of translation)

A.W. Hearsey, Captain Retd. List.

After the Gorkha war of 1814 the English government reinstated Sudarshan Shah on the throne of a truncated part of Garhwal. He was given the rule of the lands west of the Alaknanda river and upto the river Yamuna in the west. The Company retained the Doon Valley, lands east of the Alaknanda and or the Ganga (including the Pargana of Chandi). Hyder Hearsey now asked the Company to purchase the Doon according to the condition mentioned in the sale deed of Chandi. But the Company's government and its successors repeatedly turned down Hearsey's and his family's claim over the Doon. The Hearsey, till as late as 1939, kept on representing to the government of India and the Secretary of State for India, in London, regarding their ownership rights of the Doon on the basis of the Firmans purchased by Hyder from Sudarshan Shah, without either of them, at the time, being in actual possession of the property. The Hearseys contended that by buying Chandi from Hyder, whose title to it was the same as that to the ownership of the Doon, the Company had recognised the validity of his ownership to both the areas.

Najib-ud-Daula had annexed the Pargana of Chandi to his dominions. It continued in his territories till it was annexed by the Nawab of Oudh, and from whom the East

India Company took it. The Company gave physical possession of it as a "Jagir" to Hearsey before he bought the "Firmans" from Sudarshan Shah as is evident from the following extract of a letter written by the former to Ross the British Resident on 28.4.1820. This letter was obviously written by Hyder after his selling the rights in Chandi to the Company and putting in his claim for the sale of the Doon which had been rejected by the Company.

"It was merely for the sake of the proprietary rights of the Jagir that had been granted to me by the government (the Company), I was induced to purchase these Firmans, which were of no use to the Rajah at that period, 9 years ago, when he was in a state of starvation and all his family naked, and it was at the request of Harak Dev Joshi, who introduced the young Rajah to me at Unjanee Ghat, I assisted him with money, food and clothes."

The Hearseys further contended that the Company did not retain the Doon by right of conquest from the Gorkhas, but in virtue of Hyder Hearsey's purchase from the Garhwal Raja. In support of this it was asserted that, in the Treaty of Segowli of 2nd December, 1815, all the actual conquests made by the Company in the fight with the Gorkhas, and retained by them at the close of that war, are distinctly mentioned and that the Doon is not amongst them. The Hearseys therefore maintained that the Indian government did not own the Doon by conquest, but by the agreement which it had entered into with Hyder Hearsey as per the sale deed dated 28th October, 1815 for the Pargana of Chandi. The words of the Deed on which this contention is based are, "But I here promise that when the Pergunna Dhoon shall come within the possession of the Honourable East India Company I will sell the villages belonging to it to the aforesaid Company". The whole thing hinged on the interpretation of the words 'shall come within the possession of....'" The question was how? Was Hearsey to first take possession from the Gorkhas and then give to the Company or was the Company to get it on its own from them, and then buy the Valley off him (Hearsey). The Company's and therefore the Government of India's interpretation was the former as is evident from the following entry in the official "Gazetteer of Himalayan Districts of the North Western Provinces" issued in 1880 after the eclipse of the East India Company.

"In the year 1811, Sudarshan Shah had promised Major Hearsey to grant to him the Dehra Dun and taluka Chandi, should he procure the restoration of the country then occupied by the Gorkhalis. Major Hearsey now brought forward this claim, but it was rightly held by both the Raja and government that, as the conditions precedent to the grant had not been fulfilled, Major Hearsey had no claim, legal or moral. Moreover the Raja on receiving back a portion of his ancient possessions from the British expressly relinquished his sovereign and proprietary rights in those tracts to the British Government. At the termination of the war Mr. W. Fraser in 1815, was authorised to hand over to Raja Sudarshan Shah those portions of Garhwal which were situated to the west of the Alaknanda river with the express reservation of the Doon and the Pargana of Rawain lying between the Alaknanda and the Bhagirthi rivers. Mr. Fraser was directed to consult with Mr. Gardner as to the actual boundary which should be fixed with a view to control the route to Tibet by the passes available for commercial intercourse". The division of Garhwal took place accordingly and both the Mana and Niti passes came under British territory along with the holy shrines of Badrinath and Kedarnath.

Hyder Hearsey was responsible for getting a regular bathing ghat made at Haridwar. In April 1820 he witnessed a dreadful accident on the Ganga during the annual fair. He describes the occurrence in the following words:-

"The stone steps leading down to the bathing place being very precipitous, broad at top and narrow below, the multitude, striving who should get first to bathe at the propitious moment made a sudden rush and swept down the Gorkha guard; and above 370 men and women, beside the guard were jammed together, quite entangled in a most extraordinary manner, and died a most horrible lingering death. Being dark, the multitude still went over the heads and bodies of those who had first fallen, impelled by the crowds following them. At break of day I was present, and beheld a shocking sight. I strove to drag out many that were alive and below, and their bodies nearly immersed in water; but it was impossible, and that the dead bodies had first to be dragged away from the top. By 9 or 10 A.M. the fermentation from the heat and moisture was so very great that those few who were extracted alive were covered with blisters, and but a few of them lived. The greatest number who perished were Bairagis and Gossains, who wearing long hair, were seized by others below them, and this extraordinary entanglement took place. There were also a few very fair Sikh women amongst the killed."

Such accidents are still repeated at practically every "Kumbh Mela". In 1986 "Kumbh Mela" over 50 odd persons died in a similar stampede. Hearsey represented the cause of the accident to the Governor-General Lord Hastings who at once ordered a broad and safe bathing place to be made.

In the Anglo-Gorkha war Hyder Hearsey was fighting the Gorkhas in the Pilibhit-Kali-Kumaun Sector of one of the three battle fronts opened by the British. Some of his descendants still reside in Mussoorie.

Another character connected with the Doon and contemporary of Hearsey's was Lt. Col. James Skinner, C.B. (1778-1841). At the battle of Kalanga, which gave the British the Doon there was one "Rissalah of Skinner's Horse" fighting for them. Later his descendants settled in the Doon and own properties in Dehra and Mussoorie. James and his brother Robert were born of a Scots father and a Hindu Rajput mother who had been rescued by the father under romantic circumstances. She committed suicide when James was twelve. He was apprenticed to a printer, of Calcutta, but ran away after a few weeks. His sole ambition was to become an officer in the Company's army. The British army would not have him because, by a decree of 1792, a half breed was debarred from holding a King's Commission in the army, even though his father was an officer in the Bengal British army. Like Hearsey he also joined the Maratha Standards, under General Benoit de Boigne. Following General Perron's defeat Skinner too, like Hearsey, came under General Lake's wings. In spite of having crossed over to the British side James refused to take up arms against his former employer the Scindia.

After the battle of Delhi and their defeat the Maratha troops, leaderless and demoralised, crossed over to the British side and a thousand of them stood before Lake wanting to see Sikandar Sahib. (Skinner, because of his victories in the past had earned the nickname "Sikandar" after Alexander of Macedonia who is called Sikandar in India.) They said that they would only serve under him and none else. Thus at the age of twenty-five James Skinner was given the command of a cavalry regiment under the Union Jack. In 1814 the regiment was expanded and Robert Skinner also got an independent regiment of his own called the 3rd Bengal Cavalry (Skinner's Horse) the former being 1st Duke of York's own Regiment of Bengal Lancers. In 1921 the two were amalgamated and are now known as the "Skinner's Horse" and forms an integral part of the Indian army.

Robert, committed suicide in 1821, after killing his wife for infidelity and beheading her paramour.

To-day Lt. Col. Michael Alexander Robert Skinner, descendant of James' 4th son, lives in Mussoorie, in one of the Skinner houses. The Dehra Dun property was sold fifty years ago and is now part of the Doon School campus. "Mike", as he is known amongst the family and friends is the last of the clan to have commanded Skinner's Horse in 1960.

Sudarshan Shah, while in exile had married the daughter of Raja Karam Prakash of Sirmur. He had also lost his kingdom of Sirmur to the Gorkhas and was living in the British territory at Bhuria, in to-day's Haryana. In adversity the traditional enemies had become friends.

In 1803 some of the courtiers of Karam Prakash, led by the sons of Mian Kushal Singh, had conspired to dethrone Karam Prakash. On learning of this he and his family left Nahan and went to live in a fort in his territory of Kyarda Dun. In the absence of the ruler from the capital the disloyal courtiers started plundering the people in the state. The Raja's two brothers Ratan Singh and Kishen Singh led two groups of courtiers and influential people. The former wanted to usurp the throne and the latter plunder the state. There was maladministration all around and even the army was aroused against the Raja. To arrest or assassinate him they besieged the fort where he was living. An entry was forced into the fort. The Raja and a few faithful followers offered resistance. In the fight, one of the Raja's servants who closely resembled his master was killed and a rumour was spread that the Raja had been slain. Taking advantage of this confusion the Raja and Rani Guleri escaped to Kalsi.

In Nahan, Ratan Singh was put on the throne by his supporters whilst Kishen Singh continued his activities of looting and plundering. Karam Prakash went to Dehra Dun and met the Gorkha governor Amar Singh Thapa and told him his tale of woe and the turmoil created by the state officials. Raja Karam Prakash also complained that according to the treaty between Nepal and Sirmur the Ganga was the boundary between the territories of the two countries and that Amar Singh Thapa had encroached upon Sirmur's area of Dehra Dun in defiance of the treaty. Nevertheless, if aid to suppress the rebels and to restore order in the state was given, mutual good relations would continue. Gorkhas in their expansion programme were looking for such opportunities. They promptly agreed to help, and invaded Sirmur, expelled Ratan Prakash, established their own government leaving Karam Prakash in no better position than before. Amar Singh then annexed the state of Handur (Nalagarh). Although Ratan Prakash had been ousted from Nahan yet the rebellion and confusion prevailed, and peace could not be restored in full measure.

Amar Singh Thapa, instead of restoring Karam Prakash to the Sirmur throne, appointed his own son Ranjor Singh as the administrator and sent him to Nahan. Ranjor Singh sacked the capital, demolished a number of buildings and got a fort constructed on the hill at Jaitak where he established his seat. Karam Prakash then went to Subathu in Ramgarh district of Sirmur state. This place had been granted as a "Jagir" to one Kushal Singh for his faithful services to the Sirmur Darbar. By the terms of the grant the grantees were to come to the aid, with men and material, of the ruler in time of need. But the sons of Kushal Singh renounced their allegiance and told Karam Prakash to leave Subathu. The Raja complained about this attitude of Kushal Singh's sons to the Patiala chief, and requested him for help but to no avail. The Raja then appealed by a ''Mazharnama'' or protocol dated 1st May, 1812, to the neighbouring rulers, but nothing came of it. The Raja with his family and entourage was compelled to seek asylum at Bhuria, a town and a small Sikh principality in the British district of Ambala. The state of Sirmur broke up and some of the local administrators of some areas became the lords thereof. Nahan and its adjoining area became a part of the Gorkha empire.

While Karam Prakash was at Bhuria, his wife called the Guleri Rani, a wise and courageous woman, took upon herself the administration of the Raja's affairs. She appealed to Col. Ochterlony, the British Political Agent at Ludhiana, for help. This appeal by her coincided with the British declaration of war against the Gorkhas. After the Anglo-Gorkha war in 1815 the native chiefs and Rajas whose territories had been usurped by the Gorkhas, were re-installed on their thrones by the British, but not Karam Prakash. He was excluded because of his notorious profligacy and imbecility. Instead his six years old eldest son, Fateh Prakash, was placed on his father's throne under the Regency of his mother Rani Guleri. Karam Prakash continued to reside at Bhuria till his death in 1826.

Once it became known that the Company had decided to remove Gorkha rule upto the Kali river, the two Saklani brothers, Jawala Ram and Kashi Ram, descendants of the earlier traitors Sheesh Ram and Shib Ram who had let down Pradyuman Shah by siding with Prakarm Shah, went to Delhi seeking an interview with the Assistant Resident Mr. Fraser. The Saklanis at the time of the Gorkha invasion of Garhwal had turned traitors and had joined hands with the invaders and gained favours from them. Now their descendants' game was to convince the English that they and they alone were the rightful and legal claimants to the Garhwal throne. This information was conveyed to Sudarshan Shah by one of his well wishers. Sudarshan went to consult his friend and benefactor the Nawab of Rampur. He advised him to go to Delhi and place the correct facts before the Resident. For this purpose the Nawab outfitted him in robes as became his position, gave an elephant and horses and a letter addressed to Fraser. Sudarshan Shah pleaded his case before Fraser. Kashi Ram Saklani also happened to be there at that time realised that their game was up. When Sudarshan Shah was leaving Fraser, Kashi Ram fell at the Raja's feet and asked for forgiveness, and was pardoned. Although Fraser had accepted Sudarshan Shah's claim to the Garhwal throne he was advised to go to Farrukhabad and meet the Governor General's Agent, Sir Edward Colebrooke, who told him to accompany the Company's army which was to invade the Doon and create insurgency, in the Valley, against the Gorkhas.

After it was decided by the British to go to war with the Gorkhas Lt. Col. Gardner (Hyder Hearsey's brother-in-law) at the beginning of 1814 entered Dehra Dun not as a soldier but as a shikari and an angler. He was to be accompanied by his cousin Hon. Edward Gardner (one of the Asstt. Residents at Delhi) who could not come. While in the Valley he got into trouble with Balbhadra Thapa who was suspicious of his intrusion into the Valley. He was suspected of spying which suspicion was confirmed by the British invasion a few months later. For some time Gardner was in danger of losing his life. The Mahant of Ram Rai's gurudwara—"The Bishop", as Gardner called him and who was friendly towards him, intervened, and because of his influence Gardner was deported instead of being shot as a spy.

According to contemporary accounts by British writers, of the period, the main cause for the East India Company attacking the Gorkhas was aggression by them on its territories along the Himalaya foothills in Bihar, Uttar Pradesh and Himachal Pradesh. Most of the aggressions were entirely without excuses, and as they produced no worse results than occasional feeble remonstrances on the part of the British, the Gorkhas persevered in systematic encroachment on British territory at every favourable opportunity.

The immediate cause, vide the Proclamation of the British Government dated Lucknow 1st November, 1814 of the Anglo-Gorkha war, was a wanton attack on the main Police Station in the disputed frontier territory of Butwal in Gorakhpur district of Uttar Pradesh. This attack took place on 29th May, 1814 in which eighteen of the Company's policemen were killed and six wounded. Munraj the Gorkha leader, of the attack, personally supervised the murder of the Police Inspector-in-charge, although he had surrendered himself as a prisoner. He was tied to a tree and pierced with arrows like a pin-cushion till he died.

The capture of another police station with more loss of life followed. Because of the rainy season the Governor General only lodged his protest by writing a letter to the Raja of Nepal, instead of launching the attack for which preparations were already afoot. The Raja treated the letter with disdain and sent an aggravating reply.

Another reason for war mentioned in the November Proclamation was that between May and November 1814, "The Nepalese with a baseness and barbarity peculiar to themselves endeavoured to destroy the troops and the subjects of the Company on the borders of Saran (in Bihar) by poisoning the waters of wells and tanks in a tract of considerable extent. The fortunate discovery of this attempt baffled the infamous design and placed incontrovertible proof of it in the hands of the British Government".

The Gorkha charge was that as the Company was wanting direct access to Tibet, in order to increase its trade, it was looking for an excuse to over-run Nepalese territory hence these border skirmishes. Judging by the subsequent securing of Mana and Niti passes, in Garhwal, by the British, the Gorkhas may have had a point.

The Company having decided on war resolved that the Nepalese should be attacked simultaneously from several points. In Bihar a force of about 8000 men was placed under the command of Major General Marley, who was to march on to Kathmandu the Nepalese capital. In Gorakhpur Maj. Gen. J.S. Wood was to attack with a force of 4000 men while Major General Gillespie, with a force of 3500 men was to capture the Doon. In Haryana and Himachal Major General Ochterlony, with 6000 troops, was to attack the enemy's positions between the Satluj and Yamuna rivers. Lord Moira (Hastings) the Governor General, who before taking over the Government of India had insisted on combining the offices of Governor General and Commander-in-Chief, was to direct the entire operations from Lucknow.

Mr. Prinsep describes the commencement of Marley's and Wood's campaigns on the eastern end as "nothing short of disgraceful, betraying a carelessness, timidity and want of scientific knowledge which happily seldom occurs in the annals of the British army. The latter (General Wood), though his force was beyond doubt greatly superior in number to that of the enemy opposed to him, attempted little beyond defensive measures, and in what little he did attempt of a more active nature he failed. General Marley's division had now been raised to 13000 men, a force more than adequate to encounter the whole Gorkhali army, (which at this time was no more than 4 to 5 thousand) even if its numbers had approximated to the exaggerated estimates to which that had been raised by vague reports and loose computation. After two serious disasters and the loss of two guns and a thousand men his campaign ended, on 10th February. He fled the field by abandoning his army without even making any arrangements for the command of the troops on his departure. It was fortunate for the honour of the British arms that Generals Gillespie and Ochterlony were men of a different stamp, though even in their case the latter alone showed that he possessed the true qualities of a great Commander".

Major General Sir Hugh Robert Rollo Gillespie K.C.B. (postuhmous), to give him his full title, took over the command of East India Company's army at Meerut in October 1813. He had been a regular soldier of the British army having seen action in both West and East Indies - from Jamaica to Java.

In 1794 a British force was sent for the capture and occupation of the French island of Haiti in the West Indies. Since the British were in a winning position it was decided to demand the surrender of Port-au-Prince from the French Commissioner Monsieur Santhonax. Gillespie was a member of the party sent ashore for this purpose. Immediately on landing at the port they were made prisoners and produced before Santhonax who charged them with espionage, and ordered that they be shot. The chance discovery of a Masonic emblem dangling from the Frenchman's paunch, by Gillespie, saved the British from mutilation and death. Gillespie, at once, made himself known as a fellow Freemason by signs. Immediately the attitude of Santhonax changed. Gillespie and his companions, instead of going to the gallows were lavishly treated with French hospitality. Since betrayal by poisoning seemed a suspicion likely to be harboured in the mind of his guests, Santhonax pointedly tasted the dishes, at dinner, before offering them to his visitors. Masonic protection included the safe return of the British emissaries to their ship, but not, to the credit of the Frenchman, the surrender of the town. Such is the bond of brotherhood amongst Freemasons who practice the tenets of Freemasonary.

In the Anglo-Gorkha war Gillespie was to take part in a campaign in a country on which adequate information was lacking. It was moreover a country of mountains, forests, and restricted valleys defended by a people of proved fighing value and who were now to be attacked by troops lacking all knowledge of mountain warfare. From the onset he was not very optimistic of success, and was doubtful of the adequacy of his force. "I am inclined to think" he wrote before moving upto his concentration point, "that Lord Moira will find the present undertaking more arduous and difficult than he imagines as the country itself is so difficult of access; every yard is a post and the Gorkhalis are a very active, warlike people. I shall have to move in several columns, and my force is so small that I feel disaster".

Gillespie's original force consisted of:-

Artillery - 2 Twelve pounders, 8 six pounders, 4 Howitzers and 247 men,

Infantry - H.M's 53rd Regiment - 785 men, 1/6th, 1/7th and 1/17th Battalions of Native Infantry 2348 men, 1 Platoon (100 men) of 8th Royal Irish Dragoons (Gillespie's old regiment) and Pioneers 133 men.

This force had to be afterwards re-inforced and the final figures of combatants and non-combatants were:-

Ist Battalion of H.M's 53rd or Shropshire Regiment	785 men
1 Platoon of 8th Royal Irish Dragoons (Gillespie's old Regiment)	100 men
Native Infantry approx.	3,000 men
Pioneers	200 men
Detachments of Horse and Foot Artillery, 7th Native Cavalry and 1 Rissalah of Skinner's Horse	4,400 men
Non-Combatants	10,000 men
Camp followers and Officers' Personal Servants	5,000 men

(John Ludlow's personal effects in this campaign required 6 camels, and even then his stock of liquor had to be left behind.)

In those days the British army in India did not have branches like the Army Service, the General Service and Ordnance Corps. It depended for all the necessities of life upon a vast army of camp followers, a system inherited from the Mughal regime. According to his rank, every officer was allowed from ten to twenty-five personal servants to look after his clothes, his equipment and his laundry, to pitch his tent, cook and serve his food and his drinks as well as an overseer over those who performed these tasks. If he kept a palanquin - and senior officers often reclined in them rather than ride all day in the hot sun he needed six bearers. For every horse he was allowed two servants, a groom and a grass cutter; and for every elephant another two. For each three camels he hired to carry his personal baggage he had one servant—camels and elephants were marks of status, and senior officers would have forty or fifty of them.

Every regiment was accompanied by non-combatant stretcher bearers, veterinary surgeons, water carriers, saddlers, blacksmiths, cobblers, tailors, milk-girls, and often, for entertaining the sepoys, dancing girls and their fiddlers. This personnel would sometimes be as many as six hundred people. A Commissariat officer of that period described the camp-follower system thus:-

"First comes a bevy of elephants.... laden with tents of European soldiers; then follow long strings of camels, carrying the spare ammunition... and the tents of the native troops. Then again, more camels, carrying hospital stores, wines, medicines, beddings, beds, pots and pans.... Imagine a county infirmary, its contents to be removed daily some ten or fifteen miles on the backs of camels, and you have some faint idea of this very small portion of our luggage.

Then come doolies, or litters... Another long string of camels carrying the day's supply of grain for the cavalry and artillery horses comes next, as well as what are called troop stores—horse clothing, head and heel ropes, pickets, nose-bags, spare shoes, etc. The supply of grain for the day for two hundred horses would need two hundred camels, and for the troops stores as many again. And now comes the private baggage and the tents of the sybarite officers. Finally, the varied groups of women, children, ponies, mules, asses, bullocks and carts laden with all sorts of things.''

How lavish was the life style of these British officers can be judged from the following incidents:-

Once an English journalist, travelling with an army of invasion, offered a few boxes of cigars as a present to the Officers' Mess which had entertained him. Politely, he was advised that they would be scarcely appreciated since the mess had a stock of two camel-loads of the best Manilas.

At times even wives of senior English Officers accompanied their husbands into battle. On 26th December, 1843 the British Commander-in-Chief General Sir Hugh Gough attacked the Gwalior State forces. The senior officers' ladies were mounted on elephants to witness the battle, but the gun fire and the explosion of an ammunition dump nearby stampeded the beasts across the country. They were found in the afternoon and none the worse the ladies were taken, for tea, to a tent pitched on the ground held earlier by the Marathas. Suddenly a squad of British troops rushed into the tent and carried the occupants out. They were hardly clear when an enemy mine exploded and the tent was blown to pieces. After the campaign ended the Governor General Lord Ellenborough celebrated the escape by presenting each of the ladies with a commemorative war medal like the one given to the Company's troops.

Metcalfe, the British Resident at Delhi, had received instructions from the Government of India to institute enquiries, of a political nature, about Sudarshan Shah the claimant to the Garhwal throne. Metcalfe deputed his assistant Fraser to do this job. who went to Haridwar where Sudarshan Shah was living in exile. Metcalfe also wanted Sudarshan Shah to accompany the English force and create insurgency, against the Gorkhas, in the Doon. When Fraser was at Haridwar his life was saved by Sudarshan Shah at a tiger hunt in the Chandi Forests.

Fraser who was riding an elephant fired at a tiger as the animal came out in the beat, and wounded it. The tiger attacked Fraser's elephant which panicked. Sudarshan Shah, also on an elephant, and at some distance on seeing this rushed to their aid and shot the tiger.

By 18th October, 1814 Gillespie's force was concentrated at Saharanpur. On the 19th Lt. Col. Carpenter of the 17th Native Infantry marched with a small column, including two companies of the 53rd HM's regiment under Lieut. Young, towards the Timli Pass and entered it the next day. Lt. Col. Mawby, following with another column came up the Mohand Pass. The Kheri Zamindars and Rana Jeewan Singh, also accompanied the troops with their followers in the hope of recovering their Jagirs in the Doon. Both columns entered the Valley and met in the town of Dehra on the 24th, without having had to fire a shot.

The Gorkha troops, numbering a mere 300-400 regular Nepalese troops were under the command of Captain Balbhadra Singh Thapa. Balbhadra was a nephew of Amar Singh Thapa, while according to another historian he was Amar Singh's daughter's son. He had withdrawn his troops to the fortress of Kalanga on the Nalapani hill. It was a crude structure hastily constructed on the highest point of the spur south-east of Rajpur, and ten kilometers north-east from Dehra, on the Sahastradhara road. It was built of boulders and reinforced with stockades. Its building was started probably after the Gorkhas received intelligence of the Company's intentions to attack the Nepalese forces along their borders, as it was still being completed at the time of the British attack. It was surrounded by a tableland some half a mile in extent. The approaches were difficult—its front being covered by a stream running through a deep ravine and its flanks and rear protected by hills and thick forests.

Col. Mawby sent a messenger, on the night of 24th, to Balbhadra, demanding the surrender of the fort. He, at mid-night when the messenger arrived, was woken from a well earned sleep. The Gorkha commander read the letter and tore it up. "It is not my custom or habit to carry on a correspondence at so late an hour," said the Commander to the English messenger. Those familiar with the Gorkha character can imagine easily enough the squat, mongoloid features of the small hillman, suffused with the perverse humour of his tribe as he added, "I send my salaams (Greetings) to the English Sardar and assure you that I shall be paying you a visit, soon, in your camp." This act of defiance created much astonishment in the British camp, for so little had any one reckoned upon encountering serious opposition in Dehra Dun, that General Gillespie had evidently considered his presence there quite unnecessary.

On the 25th Col. Mawby thought to punish the insolence of the Gorkha, and mounting a couple of 6 pounders and two howitzers on elephants proceeded to take the fort by assault. A few rounds were fired when the task was given up as impracticable and the British force returned to Dehra with less contempt for the enemy and a more positive appreciation of the work before them. General Gillespie joined the force on the 26th and took command. His Junior's failure against a position believed to have been of minor strength completely changed Gillespie's plan.

"Me Voici", he wrote on the 28th October from the position before Kalanga," in the far famed Dhoon - the temple of Asia; and a most beautiful valley it is, the climate exceeding every thing I have hitherto experienced in India. It was not my intention to have advanced so far into the valley had not Col. Mawby, whom I sent forward with a force I thought sufficient to completely take possession of the whole by a *coup-de - main*, failed. I was on the banks of the Yamuna, and within the valley, with the intention of reconnoitring and examining this line when I received Mawby's report that he had failed from want of correct information and that it was impracticable to take the place. At this moment the greatest part of the troops, excepting 1300 infantry, 5 guns, and 300 cavalry in advance with Mawby, were at Saharanpur, and below the

ghauts, ready to pass the Jamuna into the Sikh country for the purpose of moving westward to support Ochterlony's movements.

You may imagine this check completely changed by plans: and here I am, with as stiff and strong a position as ever I saw, garrisoned by men who are fighting *pro aris et foicis* in my front, and who have decidedly formed the resolution to dispute the fort as long as a man is alive.

The fort stands on the summit of an almost inaccessible mountain; and covered with an impenetrable jungle; the only approaches commanded and stockaded. It will be a tough job to take it; but by the first proximo I think I shall have it, *sub auspice deo* (Sic).''

Apart from the question of the fort Gillespie was confronted with a problem of a peculiar difficulty. He was pledged to co-operate with Ochterlony westwards on 1st November, but obviously could not do so till a key position on his flank, which as soon as he advanced westwards would become a threat to his rear, had been taken or 'masked'. His force was insufficient to detach troops to contain it and still co-operate with Ochterlony. He must, therefore, take the fort. There remained the question of method or methods to be employed. To reduce the fort by bombardment would require a battering train, the arrival of which from Delhi would take four to five weeks. Gillespie had but four days before he was due to go to the aid of Ochterlony. The utmost importance of his attack on Nahan to coincide with Ochterlony's advance had been emphasised by Marquis of Hastings (Lord Moira) the Commander-in-Chief, when he wrote ''... No measure appears of more immediate importance towards the general success of the operations.'' This kind of admonition from his chief, could not be easily ignored by any subordinate. The matter was too urgent if the whole plan of campaign was not to be jeopardised, to allow of any reference back to the Commander-in-Chief who was in Lucknow. Gillespie decided to storm the fort.

On the 29th detailed and through orders were issued, by him, for attack. There was to be controlled musketry, a determined use of the bayonet, avoidance of straggling in column, a short rest to regain men's breath before the assault, strict silence and the passing of orders in whispers from front to rear, a warning against the dexterity of the Gorkhas with the ''Khukri'' and the advice to keep them at bayonet's length, the importance of synchronising the various attacks, and a host of pertinent wisdom was given in what turned out to be Gillespie's last orders.

''In all attacks (generally speaking)'', he added, ''against entrenched or stockaded posts firing and halting to reload often cause severe loss—this may be avoided by an undaunted and spirited storm. In ambuscade—coolness. Let emulation actuate all, but corrected by steadiness and coolness—no breaking of ranks or running for who is to be foremost. Each column must be a mutual support and every soldier actuated by principle of cool and deliberate valour which will always have the advantage over wild and precipitate courage.''

Mr. James Baillie Fraser, the first European to reach Gangotri and the brother of William Fraser, the political assistant of Metcalfe, accompanying Gillespie's expedition, in his ''Journal of a tour through part of the snowy range of the Himalaya mountains

108

and to the source of the rivers Jamuna and Ganga'', London 1823 states that, ''a more careful reconnaissance was made and orders at once followed for an assault, the preparations for which show a remarkable contrast to those made by Lt. Col. Mawby''. Fascines (long bundles of sticks bound together, used in building earthworks and batteries) and gabions (a cylinder of wicker work filled with earth, used as a military defence) were prepared beforehand. All the howitzers and 12-pounders and half the 6 pounders were sent on elephants to the table-land, across the Rispana river, and occupied it without opposition. Batteries were at once prepared for the guns and four separate storming parties and a reserve were formed under (a) Col. Carpenter with 611 men; (b) Captain Fast with 363 men; (c) Major Kelly with 541 men; (d) Captain Campbell with 283 men and the reserve of 939 men under Maj. Ludlow. These were all to ascend, on a gun being fired, from four different points and so distract the attention of the enemy. The attack was fixed for the morning of 31st October, although war was formally declared by the Governor General on 1st November, 1814.

The Gorkha Commander had done everything possible with the scarce men and material at his disposal. The wall, of the fort, although not yet complete, was raised sufficiently to render its scaling or mounting without ladders practically impossible. Gaps were filled up with stones, stockades were erected along the lines of approach, and at a wicket open, but cross-barred, a gun was placed, which covered the main side of attack.

At 2 A.M. on 31st October Major Kelly's column moved out of its detour round the village of Karsali while that of Captain Fast moved on Danda Lakhaund and Capt. Campbell moved on Astul. At seven o'clock the gun signal, warning all troops that two hours later the general assault was to be made, was fired.

Just before nine, the hour for the assault, a Gorkha detachment, which during the night had occupied a hill outside the fort on the right of the batteries, made a threat against Gillespie's flank. They were driven back with the bayonet. This success uniting with the eagerness of a sanguine temper and a close pursuit of the retreating Gorkhas induced Gillespie to give the signal for assault, sooner than it was intended, to the main attacking column and the reserve to storm the fort forthwith. The consequence was that three out of four columns took no part in the attack, and the column under Col. Carpenter with the reserve under Col. Ludlow had to bear the whole brunt of the fighting.

The troops advanced steadily to the foot of the fort wall, the dismounted Royal Irish Dragoons doing valiant work by driving the enemy right through the stockaded village into the fort itself. Here came a serious check. The gun at the gateway swept away the pioneers before the ladders for escalade could be placed in position. The leading files of the assaulting troops, too, melted away under the fire from this gun. An attempt was made to force the out-work and the gateway itself, but was foiled by the well-directed fire of grape, musketry and arrows by the defenders. Even women were to be seen hurling stones to repel the assailants. The British troops were forced to fall back to the shelter of the huts within the stockade. Lt. Ellis of the Pioneers was shot dead, while in the act of putting the first ladder against the wall, and the rest of the ladders were burned in the village where the Pioneers and the whole of the storming party had retreated.

109

Two Companies of the 53rd Regiment were present on this occasion. They did, indeed, show a disposition to retire from the stockade itself, but express orders from Gillespie categorically bade them hold on.

By now the time fixed for the general assault was past. Yet there were no signs of the converging columns. Gillespie, harrassed by the possibility that they had not heard the signal again and again sent duplicate messages by different routes to each of the three columns to assault immediately. Not one of these messages ever reached its destination. Nor, evidently, had any of the columns heard the gun signal.

At 10.30 A.M. the troops in the stockade were reinforced with two guns, three companies of British Infantry, and the remainder of the Royal Irish Dragoons. Gillespie himself, at the head of his staff, entered the advanced position. The guns, served with the greatest gallantry by the Horse Artillery, were pushed upto within 25 yards of the fort walls, and under their supporting fire a further attack to storm the fort was launched. The attack failed. The men of the 53rd British Infantry on getting to within 30 yards of the wicket sulked and refused to stir a step further. They were not afraid, but, it is said, hated their Commanding Officer from some grievance, real or imagined, over excessive parade exercise and fatigue duties. According to Ludlow, who was commanding the reserves, only four men of this regiment would go forward in the final attack.

Gillespie, all his life, had acted on the principle that to attack, attack and again attack was the one sure method to victory. A retreat was unthinkable, the thought probably never entered his head. So far he had been successful in every action that he had led. According to him a personal example was what was needed.

Placing himself at the head of the attacking column, he once more ordered an attack. The British troops, of the 53rd again hung back, only the Irish Dragoons and the native sepoys followed. Vainly Gillespie, far in advance of the line waving his hat in one hand, and the sword presented to him by his old regiment the 8th Royal Irish Dragoons in the other, yelled to them, cajoled them to come on. There he went, a shortish, stocky figure, his sword occasionally reflecting the sunlight, accompanied by his aide-de-camp Lt. O'Hara, and followed only by the Dragoons. He could be seen to gain the very entrance to the wicket gate of the fort.

Suddenly the sword no longer glinted aloft. Gillespie fell, shot through the heart, on the threshold of the fort he had sworn either to take or die for. Young O'Hara, died by his General's side. Colonel Carpenter, who succeeded to the command on the death of Gillespie, deemed it prudent to retreat. By this time Campbell and his troops had reached the fort and covered the retreat which enabled the British to bring back the dead and the wounded as well. The gun at the gate did much damage to the attacking party, and when the reserve advanced and got within the line it defended, the first discharge brought down the whole front line, killing seven and wounding eleven. Several persons penetrated to this very wicket, but unsupported, could produce no effect. A very heavy fire was kept up from the walls by the garrison within and showers of arrows and stones were discharged at the assailants, and many severe wounds were received from stones which they threw very dextrously. Women were seen throwing them regardless of the danger of exposure to the enemy's fire. Five officers, including Gillespie,

110

were killed and fifteen were wounded, of whom several died subsequently of the injuries then received; 27 non-commissioned officers and men were killed and 213 were wounded. Out of the detachment of the 8th Irish Light Dragoons (the General's old regiment) four men were killed and fifty wounded. It was the Dragoons and Charles Kennedy, a horse gunner and a fellow Ulsterman of the General, who under heavy fire, bore his body away in the retreat. Presumably this is a list of British casualties only as no mention is made, in the various accounts of the casualties of the native Infantry Battalions taking part. Their casualties have been ignored by all the contemporary historians, of that period, who were British. At that juncture to play up casualties of native sepoys may not have been politically expedient.

This inglorious repulse must be mainly attributed to Gillespie's impatience. Success would not have added much to his reputation, as he was already acclaimed the hero of Vellore (in South India), Cornellis, Palimbang (in West Indies) and Djoejocarta (in Indonesia), and his death only prevented such a failure from being disgraceful. Overlooking the strength of the enemy's position, he apparently expected a repetition of his brilliant Coup-de-main at Vellore. One moment's reflection would have made him change his plan, for with the resources at his command, he might have easily blockaded the fortress, as was done subsequently, and starved out the garrison in a few days. All these conclusions are from hindsight. The defeat had psychological effects of great magnitude. A handful of Gorkhas had withstood the power of British arms and had routed them. They too had, killed a General of great reputation for winning wars. The British had lost prestige in every native eye; they had moreover, lost something even more important. They had lost confidence in themselves.

But these, as the Marquis of Hastings said in his personal diary, were "...light disadvantages in comparison to the loss of Maj-Gen Gillespie. His zeal, his energy, and his resources rendered him infinitely material for the conduct of operations in a country the features of which are so novel to officers unaccustomed to the plains of Hindustan. Genius like his would have soon fashioned others to a just conception of the system to be persued in mountain warfare; and, deprived of him, I fear they will have to poke out their way amid many errors and oversights before they attain such experience as may give them due confidence in themselves." So great was the general sense of loss that on receipt, at Calcutta, of the news of Gillespie's death, the garrison flag was flown at half-mast from sun rise to sun set and forty-five guns were fired at noon, corresponding to his age, in his memory.

Gillespie's remains lie buried at Meerut, where they were conveyed in a barrel full of rum to prevent putrefaction. His monument is the most conspicuous in the cemetry, consisting of a high pillar, about 30 feet high surmounting a pedestal, in the western side of which is a bas-relief plaque and a skull and cross-bones surmounting an urn. The inscription on the plaque reads:-

VELLORE CORNELLIS PALIMBANG.
SIR R.R. GILLESPIE,
DJOEJOCARTA,

On the east face is another plaque on which is inscribed: "Repaired in 1862 by his old Corps, the 8th King's Royal Irish Hussars".

Col. Mawby, being the senior-most officer on the spot, succeeded to the command of the British forces. His caution was as excessive as his predecessor's rashness. He withdrew the force to Dehra with the intention of awaiting the arrival of a battering train and other reinforcements from Delhi. It was nearly a month, before the train arrived, during which time the Gorkhas got an opportunity to procure supplies, and repair the fort, whilst the British passed the time in purposeless inactivity.

It was not until the 24th November that the arrival of a siege battery from Delhi enabled the British to resume the attack on the fort. On the following day active operations recommenced and batteries were erected with 18 pounders within 300 yards of the wall of the fort. By the 27th, a practicable breach was effected almost without any loss of the British, though the Gorkhas kept up a regular well-directed fire. The British fire power was very effective and an attack by the Gorkhas was repulsed with losses to them. Everything promised well for the assault launched by the British. The storming party was led by Major Ingleby of the 53rd Regiment and consisted of two companies of his regiment and all the Grenadiers of the Native Corps. They advanced to the breach. Being wounded Ingleby had to retire to the rear and Capt. Coultman took his place. He never got beyond the breach which Lt. Harington alone ascended, at the expense of his life. Some of the men followed his example but although the remaining Companies of the regiment were brought to support the attack, no advantage was gained. The breach was not sufficiently large and the Gorkhas standing in it defended it with every thing that came to hand from fire balls and arrows to stones. The British refusing to make a dash, were compelled to retreat.

The troops of the 53rd showed the same sullenness as before whereas their opponents fought like demons. According to the regimental history, "Sullenness, not cowardice held them back; for no one turned to fly; but none went onwards; they stood to be slaughtered." The officers on the other hand showed devoted gallantry. Harrington died at the breach while Lt. Luxford, of the Horse Artillery, was shot near him as he was in the act of attempting to clear the way with a gun. Two other officers who lost their lives were Capt. Campbell of the 6th and Lt. Cunningham of the 13th Native Infantry. Seven officers were wounded, of whom six were from the 53rd. Against this number 33 men were killed, and 636 including 12 sergeants, 3 drummers and 184 privates of the 53rd, were either wounded or missing. Again there is no mention of casualties amongst the natives both combatants and non-combatants.

Thus the disastrous results of the first attack were repeated. It was only now discovered that there was no water supply within the fort, and that the inhabitants were obliged to get it from a spring (the Nalapani Spring) which was some distance from the fort. The British made arrangements to cut off the water supply route. The batteries resumed firing the next day doing great damage to the besieged garrison and its shattered defences.

On the night of 30th November at around 3 A.M. three days after blocking of the water supply route, Balbhadra Thapa with 70 men, all that remained of his garrison, evacuated Kalanga fort. Tradition has it that on abandoning his stronghold the Gorkha Captain triumphantly exclaimed, from the rampart in a loud voice; "to capture the fort was a thing forbidden, but now I leave it of my own accord." Thirst and not the might of arms forced him to withdraw and leave his bastion. The Gorkhalis cut their way through the chain of posts placed to intercept them and escaped to a neighbouring hill.

Fraser gives the following description after British took over the fort's possession.

"At three o'clock that morning, Major Kelly entered and took possession of the fort; and there indeed the desperate courage and bloody resistance they had opposed to means so overwhelming were mournfully and horribly apparent. The whole area of the fort was a slaughter-house, strewn with bodies of the dead and wounded and the severed limbs of those who had been torn to pieces by the bursting of the shells; those who yet lived piteously calling out for water, of which they had not tasted for days. The stench from the place was dreadful. Many of the bodies of those that had been early killed had been insufficiently interred; and our officers found in the ruins the remains and the clothes of several thus incompletely covered staring into view. One chief was thus found out, who had fallen in the first attempt, and had received this wretched semi sepulchre. The bodies of several women, killed by shot or shells, were discovered; and even children mangled yet alive, by the same ruthless engines.

One woman, who had lost her leg, was found and sent to the hospital, where she recovered. A young child was picked up, who had been shot by a musket ball through both his thighs, and who also perfectly recovered. There was also a fine boy of only three or four years old, whose father, a Subedar had been killed, and who was left in the fort when it was evacuated; he was unhurt and was taken care of. Upwards of 90 dead bodies were burnt by our native troops; and about an equal of wounded were sent to the hospital and carefully treated; several prisoners were also taken.

The determined resolution of the small party which held this small post for more than a month, against so comparatively a large a force, must surely wring admiration from every voice, especially when the horrors of the latter portion of this time are considered; the dismal spectacle of their slaughtered comrades, the sufferings of their women and children thus immured with themselves, and the hopelessness of relief, which destroyed any other motive for the obstinate defence they made, than that resulting from a high sense of duty, supported by unsubdued courage. This and a generous spirit of courtesy towards their enemy, certainly marked the character of the garrison of Kalanga, during the period of its siege.

Whatever the nature of the Gorkhalis may have been found in other quarters, there was here no cruelty to wounded or prisoners; no poisoned arrows were used, no wells or waters were poisoned; no rancorous spirit of revenge seemed to animate them: they fought us in fair conflict like men, and, in the intervals of actual combat, showed us a liberal courtesy worthy of a more enlightened people. So far from insulting the bodies

113

of the dead and wounded, they permitted them to lie untouched till carried away; and none were stripped, as is too universally the case.

The confidence they exhibited in the British officers was certainly flattering. They solicited and obtained surgical aid, and on one occasion this gave rise to a singular and interesting scene. While the guns were firing a man was seen on the breach, advancing and waving his hand. The guns ceased firing for a while, and the man came into the batteries. He was a Gorkha whose lower jaw had been shattered by a cannon shot, and who came thus frankly to solicit assistance from his enemy. It is unnecessary to add that it was instantly afforded; and when discharged from the hospital, signified his desire to return to his corps to combat us again: exhibiting thus, through the whole, a strong sense of the value of generosity and courtesy in warfare, and also of his duty to his country, separating completely in his own mind private and national feelings from each other, and his frank confidence in the individuals of our nation, from the duty he owed his own, to fight against us collectively".

Balbhadra and his followers on leaving the fort made their way to "Nalapani" (water course), the stream after which the hill derives its popular name, to quench their thirst and for a brief well earned rest and some refreshment. Spies carried word of their presence to the British camp, and Balbhadra, being surprised in an ambush was compelled to flee. He was joined by some more Gorkhas, about 300, who had been seen hovering about in the neighbourhood endeavouring to find a way into the fort. Major Ludlow was sent after them with some 400 troops. He attacked their camp at night and succeeded in dispersing them with the loss of over 50 killed. In the action two of the British officers and 15 men were wounded. This was on the night of 1st/2nd December. Now Balbhadra escaped into Sirmur and went to the fort at Jauntgarh which he successfully defended against a British force sent under Major Baldock. Subsequently he joined the Gorkhali forces at Jaithak. This was around the middle of February, 1815.

On 4th December, 1814 Capt. Fast attacked and occupied the fortress of Bairat in Jaunsar. It was situated at a height of 7000 feet above sea level and was impregnable in comparison to Kalanga. Yet it was abandoned without a casualty amongst the attackers. The Jaunsaries were fed up under the Gorkha rule and siding with the British starved the enemy out by intercepting and looting their supplies. With the evacuation of Bairat and the occupation of Kalsi by Col. Carpenter, the conquest of the Doon and Jaunsar was complete.

On 5th December Col. Mawby after having Kalanga fort razed to the ground, as per his orders, left Dehra Dun and going via Saharanpur reached Major General Martindale's camp near Nahan and handed over his command to him. Martindale's forces occupied Nahan town on 24th December after Amar Singh Thapa's son Ranjor Singh left it and moved to Jaithak. Jaithak fort perched at a height of 5000 feet above sea level defied all attacks by the British.

According to Fraser the people of Garhwal, including the Doon, and Sirmur were quite indifferent to the outcome of the fight between the two forces although their fate depended on it. After the second repulse of Kalanga, in a letter to Tula Ram, an employee of Fraser's, Prithi Singh of Koolee expressed the general feeling on the apathy of the people when he said, "You ask us to come to the Valley and fight the Gorkhas and that we will find the conditions in the place as they existed before the Gorkha occupation. How can this be possible when a few hundred Gorkhas could not be dislodged from Nalapani. Our economic condition to-day may be worse than our servants', in 1803, yet in the last ten years we have reconciled ourselves to our fate." The people, badly off may have been, feared something worse if they aroused the suspicions of the Gorkhas, who the people felt would make a come-back. This line of thinking was quite logical judging from the way the British had been taking a beating at the hands of the Gorkhas. A letter dated 2nd March, 1815 allegedly from Amar Singh Thapa to his king was intercepted by the British at Almora. From this letter, reproduced below, it will be seen that the Gorkha General, in spite of the loss of the Doon and his Sovereign's instructions, was cherishing hopes of defeating Ochterlony and the English. In case he was able to do so Maharaja Ranjit Singh would surely join hands with him. Then a joint Gorkha-Sikh army would cross the Yamuna and make a two pronged attack. One attack would be directly on the plains and with the other, after recovering the Doon join up with the Nawab of Oudh, who would be happy to cooperate. The reason for this was that he had been made to part with 25,000,000 rupees by Lord Hastings ostensibly as a loan, which was never meant to be repaid. Furthermore the British Resident Major Baillie had made the Nawab's life miserable by placing various restrictions on him. When the Company decided to go to war with the Gorkhas its financial condition was in a deplorable state. The credit of the government bonds, for monies borrowed was, so low that twelve percent discount was the regular calculable rate in the market. Therefore the money received from the Nawab came in handy in prosecuting the Nepalese war.

TRANSLATION OF LETTERS INTERCEPTED DURING THE NEPAL WAR

From Amar Singh and his sons, Ramdas and Arjan Thapa, to the Raja of Nepal, dated Rajgarh, 2nd March, 1815.

A copy of your letter of the 23rd December addressed to Ranjor Singh under the red seal was sent by the latter to me, who have received it with every token of respect. It was for the following purport:—

"The capture of Nalapani by the enemy had been communicated to me from Garhwal and Kumaun as also the intelligence of his having marched to Nahan; having assembled his force he now occupied the whole country from Baraparsa to Sabotari Mahotari. My army is also secretly posted in various places in the jungles of the mountains. An army under a general has arrived in Gorakhpur from Palpa and another detachment has reached the borders of Bijipur. I have further heard that a general officer has set out from Calcutta to create more disturbance. For the sake of a few trifling objects some intermediate agents have destroyed the mutual harmony, and war is waging far and wide. All this you know. You ought to send an embassy to conciliate the English, otherwise the cause is lost. The enemy making immense preparations have begun the war, and, unless great concessions are made, they will not listen to terms. To restore the relations of amity by concessions is good and proper: for this purpose it is fit, in the first place, to cede to the enemy the districts of Butwal, Palpai and Sinraj and the disputed tracts, already settled by the Commissioners towards Bareh. If this be insufficient to re-establish harmony, we ought to abandon the whole of the Tarai, the Dun and the lowlands, and, if the English are still dissatisfied on account of not obtaining possession of a portion of the mountains, you are herewith authorised to give up with the Dun, the country as far as the Satlaj. Do whatever may be practicable to restore the relations of peace and amity, and be assured of my approbation and assent. If these means be unsuccessful, it will be very difficult to preserve the integrity of my dominions from Kanka Tista to Satlaj. If the enemy once obtain a footing in the centre of our territory both extremities will be thrown into disorder. If you can retire with your army and military stores, to pursue any other plan of operations that may afterwards appear eligible, it will be advisable. On this account, you ought immediately to effect a junction with all the other officers on the Western service and return to any part of our territory which, as far as Nepal, you may think yourself capable of retaining. These are your orders.''

In the first place, after the immense preparations of the enemy he will not be satisfied with these concessions, or, if he should accept of our terms, he would serve us as he did Tippoo, from whom he first accepted of an indemnification of six crores of rupees in money and territory, and afterwards wrested from him his whole country. If we were to cede to him so much country, he would excite another disturbance at a future opportunity and seek to wrest from us other provinces. Having lost so much territory we should be unable to maintain our army on its present footing, and our military fame being once reduced, what means should we have left to defend our eastern possessions? While we retain Basahr, Garhwal is secure; if the former be abandoned, the Bhotiyas of Rawain will certainly betray us. The English having thus acquired the Dun and Rawain, it will be impossible for us to maintain Garhwal, and being deprived of the latter, Kumaun and Doti will be also lost to us: after the seizure of these provinces, Acham, Jumla and Dulu Dwalekh will be wrested from us in succession. You say that a proclamation has been issued to the inhabitants of the Eastern Kurats; if they have joined the enemy, the other Kurats will do so likewise, and then the country from the Dudh Kosi on the east to the Beri on the west cannot be long retained. Having lost your dominions, what is to become of your great military establishment? When our power is once reduced, we shall have another Major Knox's mission under pretence of concluding a treaty of alliance and friendship and founding commercial establishments. If we decline receiving their mission they will insist; and, if we are unable to oppose force and desire them to come unaccompanied with troops, they will not comply and they will begin by introducing a company, a battalion will soon after follow, and at length an army will be assembled for the subjection of Nepal. Thus you think that if, for the present, the lowlands, the Dun and the country to the Satlaj were ceded to them, they would cease to entertain designs upon the other provinces of Nepal. Do not trust them. They who counselled you to receive the mission of Knox and permit the establishment of a commercial factory will usurp the government of Nepal. With regard to the concessions now proposed, if you had in the first instance decided upon a pacific line of conduct and agreed to restore the departments of Betwal and Shiuraj as adjusted by the Commissioner, the present contest might have been avoided; but you could not suppress your desire to retain these places, and having murdered three revenue officers, a commotion arose and war was waged for trifles.

At Jaithak we have gained a victory over the enemy. If I succeed against Ochterlony and Ranjor Singh with Jaspao Thapa and his officers prevail at Jaithak, Ranjit Singh will rise against the enemy. In conjunction with the Sikhs my army will make a descent into the plains, and our forces crossing the Jamuna from two different quarters will recover possession of the Dun. When we reach Hardwar, the Nawab of Lucknow may be expected to take a part in the cause and on his accession to the general coalition we may consider ourselves secure as far as Kanka. Relying on your fortune, I trust that Balbhadar Kunwar and Rewant Kaji will soon reinforce the garrison of Jaithak, and I hope ere long to send Panth Kaji with eight companies when the force there will be very strong. The troops sent by you are arriving every day, and when they all come up, I hope we shall succeed both here and at Jaithak.

Formerly, when the English endeavoured to penetrate to Sandauli, they continued for two years in possession of Baraparsa and Mahotari; but when you conquered Nepal they were either destroyed by your force or fell victims to the climate with the exception of a few only who abandoned the place. Orders should now be given to all your officers to defend Chaudandi and Chaudena and the two Kurats and the ridge of Mahabharat; suffer the enemy to retain the lowlands for a couple of years: measures can afterwards be taken to expel them. Lands transferred under a written agreement cannot again be resumed; but, if they have been taken by force, then force may be employed to recover them. Fear nothing, even though the Sikhs should not join us.

Should you succeed in bringing our differences to an amicable termination by the cession of territory, the enemy in the course of a few years would be in possession of Nepal, as he took possession of the country of Tippoo. The present therefore is not the time for treaty and conciliation; these expedients should have been tried before the murder of the revenue officers, or must be postponed till victory shall crown our efforts. If they will then accede to the terms which I shall propose, it is well; if not, with the favour of God and your fortune and that of our country, it will be my business to preserve the integrity of my country from Kanka to the Satlaj. Let me entreat you, therefore, never to make peace. Formerly, when some individuals urged the adoption of a treaty of peace and commerce, I refused my assent to that measure, and I will not now suffer the honour of my Prince to be sullied by concessions and submission. If you are determined on this step, bestow the humiliating office on him who first advised it, but for me call me once more to your presence. I am old, and only desire once more to kiss your feet. I can recollect the time when the Gorkhali army did not exceed 12,000 men! through the favour of heaven and the renown of your fore-fathers your territory was extended to the confines of Kanka on the east. Under the auspices of your father we subjugated Kumaun, and through fortune we have pushed our conquests to the Satlaj. Four generations have been employed in the acquisition of all this dignity and dominion.

117

At Nalapani Balbhadar Singh cut up 3 or 4,000 of the enemy; at Jaithak, Ranjor Singh, with his officers overthrew two battalions. In this place I am surrounded and daily fighting with the enemy and look forward with confidence to victory. All the inhabitants and chiefs of the country have joined the enemy. I must gain two or three victories before I can accomplish the object I have in view of attaching Ranjit Singh to our cause; on his accession and after the advance of the Sikhs and Gorkhalis towards the Dakhan, the Chiefs of the Dakhan may be expected to join the coalition, as also the Nawab of Lucknow and the Saligrami Sadh. Then will be the time for us to drive out the enemy and recover possession of the low countries of Palpai as far as Bijipur. If we succeed in regaining these, we can attempt further conquest in the plains.

There has been no fighting in your quarter yet. The Chaudandi and Chaudena of Bijipur, as far as the ridge of Mahabharat and Kiliana, should be well defended. Countries acquired in four generations, under the administration of the Thapas, should not be abandoned for the purpose of bringing matters to an amicable adjustment without deep and serious reflection. If we are victorious in the war, we can easily adjust our differences; and if we are defeated, death is preferable to a reconciliation on humiliating terms. When the Chinese army invaded Nepal we implored the mercy of heaven by offerings to the Brahmans and the performance of religious ceremonies, and through the favour of one and the intercession of the other we succeeded in repelling the enemy. Ever since you confiscated the jagirs of the Brahamans, thousands have been in distress and poverty. Promises were given that they should be restored at the capture of Kangra, and orders to this effect under the red seal were addressed to me and Nain Singh Thapa. We failed, however, in that object, and now there is an universal commotion; you ought, therefore to assemble all the Brahmans and promise to restore to them their lands and property, in the event of you conquering and expelling the English. By these means many thousands of respectable Brahamans will put up their prayers for your protection and the enemy will be driven forth. By the practice of charity the territory acquired in four generations may be preserved and, through the favour of God, our power and dominion may be still further extended. By the extension of territory our military establishment may be maintained on its present footing and even increased. The numerous countries which you propose to cede to the enemy yielded a revenue equal to the maintenance of an army of 4,000 men, and Kangra might have been captured. By the cession of these provinces the fear of your name and splendour of your court will no longer remain; by the capture of Kangra your name would have been rendered formidable, and though that has not happened, a powerful impression has nevertheless been made on the people of the plains by the extension of your conquest to the Satlaj.

To effect a reconciliation by the cession of the country to the west of the Jamuna would give rise to the idea that the Gorkhalis were unable to oppose the English, would lower the dignity of your name in the plains, and cause a reduction of your army to the extent of 4,000 men. The enemy will therefore require the possession of Basahr, and after that the conquest of Garhwal will be easy, nor will it be possible in that case for us to retain Kumaun, and with it we must lose Doti, Acham and Jumla. He may be expected to penetrate even to Beri. If the English once establish themselves firmly in possession of a part of the hills, we shall be unable to drive them out. The countries towards the Satlaj should be obstinately defended. The abandonment of the disputed tracts in the plains is a lesser evil. The possession of the former preserves to us the road to further conquests; you ought therefore to direct Guru Rangnath Pandit and Dalbhajan Pande to give up the disputed lands of Butwal and Shiuraj and the twenty-two villages in the vicinity of Bareh, and, if possible bring our differences to a termination. To this step I have no objection and shall feel no animosity to those who may perform this service. I must however declare a decided enmity to such as in bringing about a reconciliation with the English consult only their own interest and forget their duty to you. If they will not accept these terms, what have we to fear? The English attempted to take Bhartpur by storm, but the Raja Ranjit Singh destroyed a European regiment and a battalion of sepoys, so that to the present day they have not ventured to meddle with Bhartpur and one fort has sufficed to check their progress. In the low country of Darma (perhaps Burma) they establish their authority, but the Raja overthrew their army and captured all their artillery and stores, and now lives and continues in quiet possession of his dominions. Our proffers of peace and reconciliation will be interpreted as the result of fear, and it would be absurd to except that the enemy will respect a treaty concluded under such circumstances; therefore let us confide our fortunes to our swords, and by boldly opposing the enemy compel him to remain within his own territory, or if he should continue to advance, stung with shame at the idea of retreating after his immense preparations, we can then give up the lands in dispute and adjust our differences. Such, however, is the fame and terror of our swords that Balbhadar with a nominal force of 600 men destroyed an army of 3 or 4,000 English. His force consisted of the old Gorkha Kurakh companies, which were only partly composed of the inhabitants of our ancient kingdom and of the people of the countries from Beri to Garhwal, and with these he destroyed one battalion and crippled and repulsed another. My army is similarly composed, nevertheless, all descriptions are eager to meet the enemy. In your quarter you are surrounded with the veterans of our army, and therefore cannot apprehend desertion from them. You have also an immense militia, and many jagirdars who will fight for their own honour and interests. Assembling the militia of the lowlands and fighting in the plains is impolitic; call them into the hills and cut them up by detail (a passage here the sense of which cannot be discovered).

The enemy is proud and flushed with success and has reduced under his subjection all the western Zamindars. The Rajas and Ranas of Karnal and the Thakurain will keep peace with no one. However, my advice is nothing. I will direct Ramdas to propose to General Ochterlony the abandonment on our part of the disputed lands, and will forward to you the answer which he may receive. All the Ranas, Rajas and Thakurain have joined the enemy and I am surrounded; nevertheless we shall fight and conquer, and all my officers have taken the same resolution. The Pandits have pronounced the month of Baisakh as particularly auspicious for the Gorkhalis, and by selecting a fortunate day we shall surely conquer. I am desirous of engaging the army slowly and with caution, but cannot manage it, the English being always in a desperate hurry to fight. I hope however to be able to delay the battle till Baisakh, when I will choose a favourable opportunity to fight them when we shall have driven the enemy from hence, either Ranjor Singh or myself, according to your wishes, will repair to your presence. In the present crisis, it is very advisable to write to the Emperor of China and to the Lama of Lahsa and to other Lamas, and for this purpose I beg leave to submit the enclosed draft of a letter to their address. Any errors in it, I trust, will be forgiven by you, and I earnestly recommend that you lose no time in sending a petition to the Emperor of China and letter to the Lamas.

ENCLOSURE

Translation of draft of petition to be addressed to the Emperor of China by the Raja of Nepal.

"I yield obedience to the Emperor of China, and no one dare invade my dominions; or if any force has ventured to encroach on my territory, through your favour and protection I have been able to discomfit and expel them. Now, however a powerful and inveterate enemy has attacked me and, as I am under allegiance to you, I rely on obtaining your assistance and support. From Kanka to the Satlaj, for a thousand kos war is waging between us. Harbouring designs upon Bhot, the enemy endeavours to get possession of Nepal, and for these objects he had fomented a quarrel and declared war; five or six great actions have already been fought, but through the fortune and glory of your Imperial Majesty I have succeeded in destroying about 20,000 of the enemy. But his wealth and military resources are great, and he sustains the loss without receding a step; on the contrary numerous reinforcements continue to arrive, and my country is invaded at all points. Though I might obtain a hundred thousand soldiers from the hills and plains, yet without pay they cannot be maintained, and, though I have every desire to pay them, I have not the means: without soldiers I cannot repel the enemy. Consider the Gorkhalis as your tributaries; reflect that the English come to conquer Nepal and Bhot; and for these reasons be graciously pleased to assist us with a sum of money that we may levy an army and drive forth the invaders or if you are unwilling to assist us with subsidies and prefer sending an army to our aid, 'tis well. The climate of Darma is temperate; and you may easily send an army of 2 or 300,000 men by the route of Darma into Bengal, spreading alarm and consternation among the Europeans as far as Calcutta. The enemy has subjugated all the Rajas of the plains and usurped the throne of the King of Delhi, and therefore it is to be expected that these would all unite in expelling the Europeans from Hindustan. By such an event your name will be renowned through Jambu-dwipa; and whenever you may command, the whole of its inhabitants will be forward in your service. Should you think that the conquest of Nepal and the forcible separation of the Gorkhalis from their dependence on the Emperor of China cannot materially affect your Majesty's interests, I beseech you to reflect that without your aid I cannot repel the English; that these are the people who have already subdued all India and usurped the throne of Delhi; with my army and resources, I am quite unable to make head against them, and that the world will henceforth say that the Emperor of China abandoned to their fate his tributaries and dependants. I acknowledge the supremacy of the Emperor of China above all other potentates on earth. The English, after obtaining the possession of Nepal, will advance, by the route of Badrinath and Manasarovar and also by that of Digarcha, for the purpose of conquering Lahsa. I beg therefore that you will write an order to the English, directing them to withdraw their forces from the territory of the Gorkhali state, which is tributary to and dependent upon you: otherwise you will send an army to our aid. I beseech you, however, to loose no time in sending assistance, whether in men or money, that I may drive forth the enemy and maintain possession of the mountains; otherwise in a few years he will be master of Lahsa.''

Subsequent events however turned out to be very different. Balbhadra, the hero of the Doon, after the surrender of Jaithak fort, where he was one of the defenders, escaped to Nepal. Balbhadra, while in Nepal, formed an illicit connection with the wife of another which relationship became publicly known. Under the Nepalese law for his crime of committing adultery Balbhadra's life became forfeit to the aggrieved husband. Balbhadra expatriated himself from Nepal, took employment in Ranjit Singh's army at Lahore, and died fighting for him at the battle of Naushahar near Peshawar in the war with the Afghans.

The fort of Kalanga was razed to the ground by the British troops, before leaving the place, as it had become a symbol of their shameful action in the Doon. To-day the spot where it stood cannot be distinguished even by its debris. However at the southern end of the spur on the Sahastradhara road, two small monuments in the shape of twin obelisks were erected by the conquerors. One is to the memory of General Gillespie, his officers and men who died there and the other to Balbhadra and his Gorkhas. The inscriptions on them are as under:-

Obelisk (1) (WEST SIDE)

To the Memory of
MAJOR GENERAL SIR ROBERT ROLLO
GILLESPIE, K.C.B.,
LIEUT. O'HARA, 6th N.I.,
LIEUT. GOSLING, LIGHT BATTALION.,
ENSIGN FOTHERGILL, 17th N.I.,
ENSIGN ELLIS, PIONEERS,
KILLED ON THE 31st OCTOBER 1814.
CAPT. CAMPBELL, 6th N.I.,
LIEUT. LUXFORD, HORSE ARTILLERY,
LIEUT. HARRINGTON, H.M. 53RD
REGT.,
LIEUT. CUNNINGHAM, 13th N.I.
KILLED ON THE 27th NOVEMBER
AND OF THE NON COMMISSIONED
OFFICERS AND MEN WHO FELL
AT THE ASSAULT.
(EAST SIDE)
Troops engaged

DETACHMENTS HORSE AND FOOT
ARTILLERY.
100 MEN OF THE 8th ROYAL IRISH
LIGHT DRAGOONS, WHO WERE DIS-
MOUNTED, AND LED TO THE ASSAULT,
BY SIR R.R. GILLESPIE.
H.M. 53RD REGT.
5 LIGHT COMPANIES FROM CORPS IN
MEERUT.
1st BATTALION 6th N.I.
Do. 7th Do.
Do. 13th Do.
Do. 17th Do.
7TH NATIVE CAVALRY.
1 RISSALAH OF SKINNER's HORSE.

Obelisk (2) (WEST SIDE)
ON THE HIGHEST POINT
OF THE HILL, ABOVE THIS TOMB,
STOOD THE FORT KALUNGA.
AFTER TWO ASSAULTS,
ON THE 31ST OCTOBER AND 27TH
NOVEMBER,
IT WAS CAPTURED BY THE BRITISH
TROOPS,
ON THE 30TH OF NOVEMBER 1814,
AND COMPLETELY RAZED TO THE
GROUND.
(EAST SIDE)
THIS IS INSCRIBED
AS A TRIBUTE OF RESPECT,
FOR OUR GALLANT ADVERSARY,
BULBUDDER,
COMMANDER OF THE FORT,
AND HIS BRAVE GOORKHAS,
WHO WERE AFTERWARDS,
WHILE IN THE SERVICE
OF RUNJEET SINGH,
SHOT DOWN IN THEIR RANKS,
TO THE LAST MAN
BY AFGHAN ARTILLERY.

Today out of the four plaques the one on the east side of the obelisk towards the north is missing. There is a blank in the side of the structure. The missing plaque contained the list of "British and Indian" troops engaged in the action. Since this inscription is given in William's "Memoir of Dehra Dun" published in 1874, it means it got destroyed or removed after that. Probably it may have been removed, during Mahatma Gandhi's 1921 agitation against British Imperialism, by the Congress agitators, before the monument was declared "Protected" under law. Since then it is under the charge of the Archaeological Department of the

Government of India. Unfortunately the powers that be, today, have completely neglected this and the other "Protected" monuments, in the district, like the rock edict of Emperor Ashok at Kalsi.

Thus after the occupation of Kalanga fortress on the night of 30th November, 1814 the Union Jack started flying over the Doon and it flew uninterrupted till the night of 14th August, 1947.

The Gorkha had a lot to teach to the British in the art of warfare. It was only when the English learnt the Gorkha methods of warfare that the latter found themselves outmatched not so much by military tactics of their opponents as by their fraud and long purse. Prinsep writes:-

"It must be allowed to the Gorkhas that they were an experienced as well as a brave enemy: they had been continually waging war in the mountains for more than fifty years, and knew well how to turn every thing to the best advantage. Caution and judgement were, therefore, more required against them, than boldness of action or of decision;.....

It will be perceived that little advance was made in the campaign until we had learnt to turn the same advantages to account against the enemy, by the help of which he foiled us so often at the commencement; for with all the Indian warfare, combined with the professional science of Europe, our officers found yet something to learn from these Gorkhas. We adopted from them the plan of stockading posts, which the nature of the campaign frequently rendered it necessary to place beyond the limit of prompt support.

The strength of the stockades was originally greatly miscalculated: made up of rough hewn wood and stones, heaped together between an inner and outer palisade, they were in appearance so contemptible as to invite assault without even seeming to require breaking....... The lighter artillary made little or no impression, and the difficulty of bringing up heavy guns, rendered them in truth, most formidable defences. (Does this not remind one of the Indian army taking tanks up the Zojila Pass in the 1947 war with Pakistan?). The wood and materials for raising them were everywhere at hand, and the celerity with which they could be prepared in any position formed a main source of the strength of the country. But this was a resource equally available to an invader, and one which placed the issue in the power of continuance, that is, in the length of the purse."

Ochterlony was the first English General to adopt these tactics in battle.

It does not require much intelligence to understand the causes which principally contributed to the success of the British over the Gorkhas. The latter could not boast of such a long purse as their enemy and, moreover, they were numerically inferior to him. Add to these, the wonderful capacity which the English possessed for intrigues and conspiracies and for raising traitors by holding out temptation and specious promises in the camp of their opponents and no wonder need be expressed at their final triumph over the Gorkhas.

A Calcutta newspaper report, dated 17th November, 1814, on the failure of Gillespie blamed "the very defective topography of that district contained in our maps". Defending the English Surveyors of that time another English Surveyor, a hundred odd years later, remarks, "even if a copy of Hodgson's survey had reached Gillespie, it will surely not have affected the issue". In other words the course of the battle would have been the same.

In 1903 and 1912 two British army officers Col. W.G. Hamilton, D.S.O. and Col. L.M. Shakespeare respectively writing in the United Service Journal made the following comments on the Gorkha war.

Col. Hamilton attributes the success in the war to Ochterlony, whose fame rests mainly on his outstanding qualities as commander and leader of men and to Dr. Rutherford. The latter was the trade agent for the Company and Civil Surgeon at Moradabad. He had free access into the Doon and Kumaun during the course of his trading activities with the locals. He provided the best and most accurate information regarding the Gorkha army, its leaders, its organisation and fighting value and the topography of Kumaun and Garhwal. He employed Pandits, Gorkhali soldiers and others as paid spies. His services in the Kumaun campaign were invaluable, yet his sound advice and opinions expressed before the war do not appear to have carried the conviction, they deserved, with the authorities.

Col. Shakespeare was at one time Commanding Officer of the 2nd Gorkha Rifles or the Sirmoor Battalion formed, after the Gorkha defeat, in Dehra Dun. He lived in the house, next to the Circuit House (Dun Court), known as No. 10 Cantonments till his death. To-day this house is the property of 5 and 8 Gorkha Rifle Regiments. The 2nd Gorkha Rifle Regiment went into British service in 1947 after severing its link with the Indian Army. He writes:—

"Unlike other Asiatic enemies the Nepalese showed a remarkable spirit of courtesy towards us, worthy of a more enlightened people. The cases of poisoned wells or arrows, or cruelty to wounded, is only recorded in one or two cases, no rancorous spirit of revenge appeared to animate them, they fought in fair conflict like men, and abstained from insulting the bodies of dead or wounded. In no case was there any interference with the dismal duty of collecting the casualties at the close of an action."

The Company's officers and men did not receive any medals for taking part in the war with Nepal. Col. Shakespeare further writes:—

"It is curious to note that this war, which lasted in its first phase from October 1814 to May 1815, and in its second phase from January 1816 to May that year, was full of hard fighting, losses and hard work, produced no medals, nor is it inscribed on the war honours of the numbers of regiments, English and Native, who took part in it. How different to the lavish distribution of such (Honours) in our day."

Regarding the wisdom of Amar Singh Thapa Shakespeare writes:—

"It is also worthy of note that Amar Singh's policy of keeping out the English at all costs from Nepal, so gravely impressed by him on Durbar (the Nepalese ruler) then is still kept up; and who shall say that he was not wise."

Col. Shakespeare could not have been very popular, for his last remarks, with his fellow country men like the ones who years later "refused to preside over the liquidation of the British Empire."

The testimonials given, by the British, to Balbhadra and his men for their gentlemanly behaviour towards the enemy's dead, wounded and prisoners are in sharp contrast to the behaviour in their fight and rule over the Gorkhalis as recorded by the contemporary English chroniclers.

After the fall of the fortresses of Malaun and Jaithak, in Himachal, a convention for peace was signed, on 15th May, 1815, between Ochterlony and Amar Singh Thapa. Under this convention the Gorkha Commanders and their troops along with their camp followers were allowed to withdraw to Nepal. For his safety Amar Singh was provided an escort of Company's troops under Lieutenant Murray. This was necessary as the victims of Nepalese oppression, were now all out to wreck their vengeance on their former oppressors. Thus the Gorkha withdrew from Himachal, Garhwal and the Doon going back to Nepal via Kurukshetra, Haridwar and Pilibhit.

Back in Nepal Amar Singh Thapa, the valiant and loyal soldier was so badly humiliated, at court, that some say he committed suicide, by swallowing a diamond. According to another story he retired to Neelkanth (Gosain kund) and died on 29th July, 1816 of a broken heart. Of his two wives one committed Sati on his pyre while the other who was at Rasputnath immolated herself in the quadrangle of a temple there.

Balbhadra had gone to Lahore and died fighting for Maharaja Ranjit Singh. Thus ended the Nepalese saga of the Doon.

William Fraser of the Delhi Residency had accompanied the British forces into the Doon for the purpose of setting up a civil administration, collecting revenue and policing the area. Initially he was unable to find people who were willing to be enrolled in the Company's service to do these jobs. The reason for this was the uncertainty created in the minds of the people, about the outcome of the war, because of the defeats suffered by the British in the first two attacks on Kalanga fort. However after a couple of months he was successful in recruiting men who had left Gorkha services or who under Sudarshan Shah's instructions had acted as guides to the English. One such person was Shib Ram Saklani, who was appointed as Sudarshan Shah's representative in the Doon with Fraser's approval. Fraser, while giving his approval, wrote to Shib Ram on 16th April, 1815 that, "as the Raja's representative you are to spare no efforts in bringing peace and confidence amongst the people of the Valley". He was entrusted with the job of bringing people back to their abandoned villages, see that the local leadership was weaned away from Nepalese influence and cooperated with the new rulers. He was further told that when he successfully completes the tasks assigned to him, his old jagir would be restored to him. Shib Ram worked so diligently that Fraser was pleased.

Fraser restored the Jagir (grant) of Saklana to Shib Ram Saklani and also gave him, for his lifetime, the village of Bajawala in the Doon Valley as a revenue free grant. Saklana is an area situated in Tehri Garhwal on the north-east boundary of Dehra Dun district bounded on the north-west by the Bandal river and on the south by the Song. Shib Ram, through his influence with Major Baldock and Fraser, was able to get jobs for his relations with the British. Two of his nephews Nand Ram and his elder brother

125

Kashi Ram who were sons of Shib Ram's brother Sheesh Ram were employed in the Company's service. Nand Ram became the Tehsildar of Dehra Dun while Kashi Ram, who was Shib Ram's cow herd, was appointed a peon. Shib Ram died in 1818 and the Tehri ruler wanted to resume the Jagir but it was restored to Shib Ram's minor son Hari Ram and his cousin and guardian Kashi Ram. Kashi Ram died in 1829 without an issue and a dispute about succession again arose. Devi Dutt, son of Nand Ram, claimed that as Kashi Ram was his foster father he (Devi Dutt) had succeeded to his estate. His claim was violently contested, and the subsequent disagreements became such as to warrant the attachment of the property by Young, who was also the Political Agent for Tehri State, till a decision was made by a higher authority. Unluckily the attachment was carried out through Nand Ram the Tehsildar of Dehra Dun and Devi Dutt's father. Therefore Nand Ram also had an interest in encouraging the feud. Finally an order dated 3rd August, 1830, of the Delhi Resident, put Hari Ram and Devi Dutt, the two cousins in joint possession of the Mafi (grant) as vassals of the Tehri Raja. Nand Ram's descendants through his son Narain Dutt settled down permanently in Dehra and came to be known as "Mafidar Saklanis." Two of them, Hirday Narain and Maharaj Narain, were considered as some of the loyal subjects of the British crown in the Doon. The former was bestowed with the title of Rai Bahadur. Their progeny are still flourishing in the Doon.

Because of a number of complaints of corruption amongst Young's staff, particularly against Munshi Bakar Ali and Subedar Jawan Singh who had Young's ear, the Garhwal political agency was reverted back to the Commissioner Kumaun Division in 1842. An Assistant Political Agent was posted at Dehra Dun for the convenience of the Garhwalis.

In the first week of June 1815 a British contingent under Major Baldock, accompanied by Sudarshan Shah and his retinue had marched towards Srinagar via Tehri. Fraser, on reaching Ranihat, after a few skirmishes enroute with Gorkha commanders who had not heard of the Malaun convention, sent for Bhakhtawar Singh Basnait, the Nepalese governor of Srinagar. He was made aware of the convention and offered safe passage to Nepal like his other compatriots. Bhakhtawar Singh went back home via Kumaun and the British forces occupied Srinagar. On 14th July, 1815 Fraser and Sudarshan Shah (who had been camping at Ranihat) entered Srinagar. The next day Fraser announced that people living upto Rudraprayag on the east of Alaknanda and Mandakini rivers should henceforth consider themselves as the Company's subjects. This area was to be a Sub-division of Kumaun under its Commissioner Edward Gardner. The remaining part of Garhwal barring the Parganas of Chandi, Doon and Rawain, was given as "Garhwal Jagir" to Sudarshan Shah, his descendants and successors in perpetuity. Thus Sudarshan Shah became the ruler of a truncated Garhwal of his forefathers, later known as the native state of Tehri Garhwal—so named because Sudarshan Shah established his seat at Tehri. The pargana of Rawain was given back to him in 1824.

The holy shrines of Badrinath and Kedarnath came under the British part of Garhwal. The head priests of these temples thought that they had become independent Rajas, and started acting as such. The result was that mismanagement of finances, debauchery of the Rawal (Head Priest) and corruption became so rampant that the general administration

126

of the temples was again entrusted by the British to the Tehri Raja. This arrangement did not prove very successful because all temple disputes and employees were subject to British law and jurisdiction thus making the Raja only an administrative figure head. Ultimately by public demand, the Uttar Pradesh government of the time passed the Badrinath Temple Management Act, 1939. Under this Act, a Management Committee was appointed and the Rawal's position became that of a paid employee of the Committee. The first meeting of this Committee was held at Kirtinagar, in Tehri State on 5th March, 1941 under the chairmanship of the Honourable Dr. Sir Sita Ram, the then President of the United Provinces Legislative Council. Since then these shrines are being managed by this Committee.

Similar was the fate of the Himachal states. Sirmur lost Jaunsar-Bawar, Keonthal Sabathu Fort and Pargana, and Bushair had to part with Raien and Sindhuk Parganas. Jauunsar-Bawar was merged with Dehra Dun district while the other Himachal areas were merged with their adjoining British territory.

By a resolution, of the Company's government, dated 17th November, 1815, the Doon was formally annexed to the British district of Saharanpur. Till then Dehra Dun was being administered on an ad-hoc basis by Fraser of the Delhi Residency while Jaunsar-Bawar was placed under the charge of Captain Birch who reported directly to the Resident at Delhi.

By an order dated 20th January, 1816 Mr. Grindall, District Magistrate of Saharanpur was asked to take over charge of the district from Fraser and make arrangements for the organisation of the police force. The Assistant Collector Mr. Chamberlain was made responsible for collecting the district's revenue. These jobs were later entrusted to Mr. Calvert, Assistant Collector of North Saharanpur vide order dated 15th March, 1816.

On 28th February, 1817 the Governor General-in-Council passed the regulations for the governance of, "the tract of country called Dehra Doon, formerly composing a part of the territories of the Raja of Nepal".

At this time the total population of the Valley was 17,000. For the establishment of a Police force in the Valley a budget of Rs. 229/- per month, towards salary, of the personnel was sanctioned. The total number of men employed were 49. Against these the figures in 1863 had gone up to 224 men at Rs. 1786/- a month.

On the signing of the Malaun convention the British started recruiting Gorkha troops from the disbanded Nepalese army. The Sirmoor Battalion, later known as the 2nd Gorkha Rifles was raised in 1815 by Capt. Young, of the 68 Native Infantry, as an Irregular Native Infantry Regiment. He was its first Commandant.

During the Anglo-Gorkha war Young (then a Lieutenant) had been captured by a small band of Gorkhas after his troops had run away. The Gorkhas, admired his courage at not trying to escape with his men, treated him well, made friends with him and finally released him. In turn, full of admiration for their manly qualities he asked for permission to raise a battalion from the Gorkha prisoners held at Dehra Doon. At first the battalion so raised was stationed at Nahan, the chief town of Sirmur, hence the name Sirmoor Battalion. It was directed to join the force assembled at Sitapur in Oudh and destined to invade Nepal, but had only reached Moradabad when the order was countermanded, and it returned to Dehra, which had been selected as its future cantonment. When first formed the Battalion had ten companies of one Subedar, four Jamadars, eight Havildars, two Buglers, and 120 Sepoys each. This was reduced in 1818 to eight companies of 80 men each. It was again on duty at Sitapur and in October 1817, served under General (later Sir) David Ochterlony in the Maratha campaign.

After Mr. Calvert's deputation to make the revenue settlement, the Doon was left completely to itself with occasional visits by the Saharanpur Magistrate (North) who was authorised to deal with all matters of police and criminal jurisdiction. The Diwani

Adawlut (Civil Court) of Meerut, was to deal with civil litigation. This was changed, in 1818, to the Diwani Adawlut of North Saharanpur. A hasty land settlement had been carried out in the Saharanpur District and which was imperfectly revised. This and repeated droughts had reduced the peasantry of the district to a wretched condition financially. The result was that the people were discontented. The village leaders rallied under the guidance of Rani Dhun Kaur. She was the widow of Raja Ram Dayal of Landhaura, a woman of great cunning, some ability and considerable hereditary influence in the district. These leaders did their best to foster discontent and a desire for a change of government became very general. It should not be forgotten that the Mughals were still occupying the Red Fort at Delhi, hence British rule was still looked upon as temporary and subject to change. With their minds thus unsettled the Rajputs and Gujars of the area, many of whom had seen better days, neglected agriculture and went back to their old profession of dacoity and thugee. They were expecting the British Raj to last for a short period and were sure that lawlessness as of yore would prevail. Incidents of dacoity, in the beginning, were few and far between, and in a short time their incursions into the Doon increased to alarming proportions. It was at this point of time that the Company appointed the Hon'ble Mr. F.J. Shore as Joint Magistrate and Revenue Superintendent of the Doon under Mr. Grindall, the Commissioner. Mr. Shore's tenure lasted nearly six years from 1823 to 1829, and his headquarters were at Dehra. Mr. Shore was eccentric in his habits and ideas. For instance, his affectation of dressing himself in native style, like his contemporary Metcalfe at Delhi, drew forth a general order from their Government addressed to officers in the Western Provinces, prohibiting such practices. At the same time he (Shore) possessed a vigorous well trained intellect, and his physical energy far surpassed his mental powers. An indication to assert his own individuality made him somewhat impatient of control, but his appointment at Dehra gave him a rare opportunity of carrying out his own views without prejudice to himself and with benefit to others. He was the second son of Sir J. Shore, (later Baron Teignmouth) of the Company's Civil Service, who became the Governor General of India in 1793 at the age of 43 years.

The following description of Dehra and Mr. Shore by Captain Mundy, Aide-de-Camp to Lord Combermere, who came from Meerut into the Doon via Haridwar through the Kansrao Pass, is worth recording:—

"On the 12th of April 1828, Colonel Dawkins and I left Haridwar, and commenced our march through the valley of Deyra Doon. Our route was most beautiful, and reminded me much of some of the milder and least wild regions of the Alps. The road, which is made with great art, winds through a woody declivity, sometimes closely hemmed in by abrupt rocky banks, and at others traversing a luxuriantly wooded plain. We found our tents pitched in a thick forest near the small chokee Karsrah (Kansrao).

On the summit of the hill above our encampment is a small bungalow, built for the accommodation of persons travelling without tents; and similar buildings are established at nearly every stage through the Doon. From this point we enjoyed a magnificent prospect. Below us lay the beautiful valley of Deyra, luxuriant with many-tinted forest, and refreshed by the rippling little rivers which run in a meandering course through the whole length of the vale, from the Ganges to the Jumna. The view is bounded on all sides by mountains. In the north and west, those of Garhwal and Sirmoor rise, series after series, till they are terminated by the snow-capped peaks of the Himalayas. In the south the prospect is abruptly closed by the range of woody hills which form the boundary of Deyra Doon, and cut it off from the plains of Hindustan. During breakfast a hurkarah (messenger) arrived with a note from a gentleman who passed by this same route yesterday, informing us that, as he was fishing in a mountain-stream near at hand, a tiger came to drink at it within pistol-shot of him, and retired without seeing him. We determined to look for him in the evening, though our chance of success is small in a country so full of ravines, by which the tigers can sneak away to the woods when they hear the crashing approach of the elephants.

April 14th - Marched eleven miles to the town of Deyra, whence the name of the Valley. The first half of the day's journey led through a thick forest of very lofty trees, many of them strangers to the plains of India. The underwood was formed of richly flowering plants, among which the corinda sent forth its well-nigh sickening fragrance; and parasites of the most gigantic proportions twined round the trunks and branches of the larger trees, resembling in their grotesque writhings, the folds of huge boa-constrictors. In the immediate neighbourhood of the town of Deyra the jungle has been cleared away, and the wheat crops are remarkably fine.

On arriving at our tents we received a polite invitation from Mr. Shore, the political agent for this province, to pass the day in his house. He is a remarkably tall and handsome man, has adopted the Mussalman costume and wears a long beard. He is also distinguished as the scourge of all the brigands and wild beasts that infest his province. In bringing the former to justice he seldom trusts to inferior agents, but, taking one or two determined assistants, mounts his camel or his horse, slings his rifle on his shoulder, and with no better food then rice, and no more efficient nightshelter than a blanket, makes two or three forced marches to the lurking-place of the robbers. His most remarkable exploit was the following:—

A numerous and determined banditti, being persued by the battalion of Gourkahs cantoned at Deyra, took refuge in a small fortress. Mr. Shore, with Major Young, the Commandant of the corps above-mentioned, arrived before the walls, but having no guns capable of effecting a breach, Mr..S. proposed that they should cut down a tree, and, forming a battering-ram force the gates in this primeval method. The machine was prepared and carried upto the gate in spite of the fire of the garrison. The instrument did its work-down went the gates, and in rushed my hero and Major Y. at the head of their men.

The verandah and rooms of this active persecutor of the wild animals of the forest are adorned with the grim skulls and stuffed skins of tigers, bears, boars, monkeys, and other characteristic drawing-room furniture; and while we were at breakfast two black bears, with silver collars round their necks, strolled quietly into the room and took possession of the posts of honour on the right and left of our host."

Mundy further describes his journey to Landhaur and Mussoorie:—

"The distance from the base of the hill to Landour, the most elevated of the two stations (Mussoorie being the other station in those days), is eight miles, and the road, which, for the sake of necks and nerves I rejoice to say is in progress of improvement, sometimes winds round the edge of the rocks, sometimes zigzags up the face of the hill, plunges into the depths of a ravine, or creeps over the giddy summit of a naked crag. It is, in its present unfinished state, in most parts not more than three feet wide, not unfrequently diminishing to one foot, and even six inches". (The original road went through the grounds of what is now the Oak Grove Railway School. Higher up, it passed to the east of Bala Hissar, not the west as it does now, and rejoined the line of the present road further up. From here it went on to Landhaur. The road past the Himalaya Club and Municipal office was made later; the Masonic Lodge road later still.) "We were an hour and a half reaching a little half-way hamlet, situated, or rather perched, in a small nook of cultivation. On a narrow but elevated platform of earth on the right hand of the road, we passed the new made grave of Sir Charles Farrington of the 31st regiment, who died of consumption on his way to Landour, whither he was repairing as a last hope, about a fortnight ago. In this romantic spot, surrounded with trees, and overhung with black rocks, a monument is to be erected to his memory. We reached the little half built colony (Landour) without accident, and breakfasted with Major Brutton of the 11th Dragoons who commands the Depot of European invalids. During the building of the bungalows the hospitals, the Major and the rest of the officers, and the invalid men amounting to eighty, are living in tents, and many of the sick are already, from the effects of the delightful climate, recovering. The establishment of this station, so convenient for the invalids of Meerut, and the great northern cantonments, will be a great saving to Government, who were obliged, before its creation, to send their sick servants to the Cape of Good Hope or at least to sea.......The oak and the rhododendron are the largest timber trees; and of the latter, which in Europe and America is a mere shrub, the beams of the Landour houses are formed."

Talking of bears the following story was doing the rounds a hundred years ago, as recorded in a Mussoorie publication of that time:—

"It would appear that Master Bruin (Bear) was enamoured of a certain young woman in a village, and he had been known to make frequent visits to her cottage, but without success. Bruin however came down the hill one evening earlier than usual, and finding the young damsel by herself in a field, made a bold dash and, amid shouts of the villagers, carried her off in triumph to his craggy home. Now is this elopement, kidnapping or abduction? If it were only cognizable, the police and the legal profession might have made a harvest out of it. As the cave was inaccessible the men were helpless; they despaired of the life of the young woman but cherished ideas of bitter revenge. Deep plans were laid to this end. It was not long before Bruin fell into the trap, and when he came down for his afternoon feed of cucumbers, Indian corn and Mandua, of which he is said to be fond, his retreat was cut off. He made a good fight for liberty but was overpowered and fell at the hands of his enemies. The next thing was to ascertain the fate of the unfortunate woman, and this the villagers did by climbing a cliff overhanging the cave in which the bear was known to have lived. One of the men, bolder than the rest, descended by means of a long rope secured to a rock, and when he arrived opposite the cave to his great surprise he found the woman alive. The difficulty that now presented itself was to get the woman away from the cave. It was impossible for her to climb up the way the man had descended, so more help and more rope had to be procured and sent down to the cave. The woman was finally let down by means of a basket, and all returned to their homes amidst great rejoicings.''

If Guru Ram Rai can be called the founder of the old town of Dehra, Mr. F.J. Shore may be called the architect of the present towns of Dehra and Mussoorie, the foundations of which were laid during his tenure.

Long before Mr. Shore's arrival in the Doon mismanagement of revenue along with repeated seasons of poor crops had a disastrous impact on the people of Saharanpur district. Because of poor economic conditions people had taken to dacoity. A gujar named Kallua or Kulloo became the leader of a large gang of disciplined and armed robbers. This gang was active on both sides of the Ganga and lived by pillage. No one seemed to know his background and some of those who had seen him did not admit it for fear of reprisals at his hands. Initially his name rather than his actions created more fear amongst the peasantry. This rendered his reputation incomprehensible and Shore was inclined to regard him as the creation of a fertile imagination.

The gang, however, continued to terrorize the district and first Mr. Glyn, the magistrate, and then Mr. Shore himself were obliged to ask the aid of the Commandant of the Sirmur Battalion. The jungles of the Shiwaliks were fruitlessly ransacked for the free booters. In May 1824 a gang entered the Dun by the Kaluwala Pass, plundered the village of Nawada and retreated hurriedly the same night without securing the whole of their booty. The men of the Sirmur Battalion were mobilised with utmost rapidity and, lightly equipped, followed the track of the dacoits into the Saharanpur district without once catching sight of them. The pursuers returned to Dehra much disheartened, and Mr. Shore, in consequence of this fruitless expedition, officially announced his utter disbelief in the existence of the great brigand chief. The Gurkhas, he argued, had scoured the jungles in every direction for months, and had never come upon any large band of robbers, nor could a numerous body of professional thieves possibly subsist upon the proceeds of such robbery as had occurred. Again, the victims were always either inhabitants of the Dun or banias or travellers whence he inferred that the real culprits were the people at the south base of the Shiwaliks: their fathers had held jagirs in lieu of blackmail, theft was their heirloom and Kallua he concluded was a mere bugbear invented by them to throw the police on the wrong scent. Mr. Shore was correct as to the actual culprits though wrong in treating Kallua as a myth. The motive of the dacoits was perhaps not so much mere plunder as the desire of a return to the old lawless way of living unencumbered by the regulations of superior authority. In short, the presence of the armed bands implied rebellion rather than mere law-breaking. The leaders of the movement had ample resources, and whenever these happened to fail the reign of terror which they had established rendered requisitions easy, and prevented sufferers from volunteering information against their oppressors. The police on the other hand were few in number and poorly armed, so much so that after the sack of Nawada Mr. Shore felt himself compelled to ask Mr. Ewer, a Pluralist, who combined the offices of Surperintendent of Police and third member of the Board—to arm his police with carbines. On the 30th May, 1824 the band again invaded his district and this time converging upon Raipur, a large village near Dehra. About sunset Gujar after Gujar came dropping into the village until a goodly company was assembled. A few questions judiciously put to the strangers proved their inability to give any satisfactory account of themselves, and all were captured before they had time get their arms, which they had concealed in the neighbouring jungle. This misadventure does not seem to have discouraged Kallua for by the autumn of the same year he had, assisted by his lieutenants, Kuar and Bhura, also Saharanpur Gujars, assembled a very respectable force, recruited from among his own clansmen and the more turbulent Ranghars. They were armed with swords, spears and matchlocks, and affected a sort of military discipline. Their headquarters were at the fort of Kunja (Bahadurpur), a village a few miles west of Rurki belonging to Bije Singh, a connection of the Landhaura family and Taluqdar of forty four villages. He was in league with other powerful landholders and had confederates in Meerut and Moradabad, if not in more remote districts. Their first act of defiance to the Government was an attack on the police outpost at Katarpur, which they attacked and plundered: their next was the sack of Bhagwanpur, a town situated immediately to the north of Kunja, five days later. In the latter enterprise 80 or 90 dacoits were engaged. Mr. Grindall, the Magistrate of Saharanpur, failed to appreciate the grave import of this attack. He directed the police to investigate the case in the usual manner. The course of their enquiries led them to Bije Singh's fort of Kunja, from the walls of which they were saluted with a volley of bullets. They prudently retired and sent in a report to the Magistrate, who contended himself with issuing a summons to the refractory taluqdar. Bije Singh naturally paid no attention to the process and Kallua was encouraged to fresh exploits. On the 1st October a police guard of 200 men bringing in a large sum of money from Jawalapur Tehsil to Saharanpur met an overwhelming force of the insurgents at Kalalhati, east of Bhagwanpur; they were speedily routed and forced to leave their treasure in the hands of the enemy. Kallua now assumed the style of Raja Kalyan Singh and began in royal fashion to despatch messengers in various directions to exact tribute from the villages within his kingdom. His band exceeded one thousand, and he announced his intention of throwing off the foreign yoke and releasing the prisoners in the jail. His proceedings caused considerable alarm, and an attack upon the city of Saharanpur was in the popular estimation no remote contingency. The affair of Kalalhati was speedily reported to Mr. Grindall. He sent an express to Captain Young for reinforcements. His messenger arrived just as Mr. Shore heard that Amritgir, Zamindar of Raiwala on the Ganga, had received a requisition for the payment of Rs. 400/- from the self styled Raja. On hearing the grave news Mr. Shore abandoned his plans for the interception of the messenger and determined to accompany the Commandant of the Gorkhas. They left with 200 rank and file early the next morning and joined Grindall at Sikandarpur, five miles north of Kunja, on the 3rd October. The rebels with incredible presumption determined to await the attack outside the fort, but the death of Kallua killed at the first discharge disheartened them and they retreated into the fort. One sally was made, which the Gorkhas vigorously repulsed. Success

133

encouraged the bseiegers to attempt a coup de main. The walls were too high to escalade without ladders and the force had no guns. The Gorkhas cut down a tree with their khukris and roughly trimmed the branches, leaving enough to afford a good hand-hold. This they used as a battering ram and quickly broke in the door. Much hand-to-hand fighting ensued in which Mr. Shore, armed with sword and buckler, greatly distinguished himself, receiving a severe wound. After resistance in the fort had ceased many of the rebels found an escape by the postern and hid in a sugarcane field. Thence they were driven out and suffered severe slaughter. In all 152 were killed and 41 taken prisoners. Amongst the Gorkhas 16 men were killed and 29 wounded.

The rising so promptly suppressed was popularly called the "Kalwagirdi." The remainder of the band however rallied round the two lieutenants, Bhura and Kuar, who had escaped from the fort. They continued to give trouble. Early in January 1825 they ventured to show themselves again and made a swoop at the small but rich village of Rishikesh. Another hard season in Saharanpur had given them an accession of new recruits, and on the night of the 12th a dismayed chaukidar reported the investment of Thano by 200 men. Gorkhas were sent out to watch the roads to the plains, but, contrary to their instructions, they attempted to surprise the outlaws. They were only partially successful and the gang scattered through the jungle and escaped into the Saharanpur district through the Kansrao Pass. The band was next heard of in the Moradabad district, but it dispersed before the arrival of the soldiers.

On the 9th April a band of about 300 pilgrims travelling northwards from Haridwar was attacked and plundered, and a few killed and wounded. Mr. Shore's attempts to intercept the dacoits failed: and he proposed to establish a permanent line of Gorkha outposts between Lachhiwala and the Motichur hill near Haridwar. At the same time, writing to Mr. Ewer at Kalsi, he complained of the advantage the dacoits derived from having their haunts in the debatable ground near Jawalapur (south of Haridwar), where the four districts of Kumaun, Saharanpur, Moradabad and the Dun meet. This circumstance rendered escape easy, while the police gladly availed themselves of the plea of want of jurisdiction to conceal their own cowardice or incompetence; and he suggested the establishment of a Joint Magistrate in Jawalapur with concurrent jurisdiction in the four districts. The expedient was not proved necessary by the result for the band energetically hunted by the authorities of both districts began to decline in prestige. Mr. Shore's activity in this respect drew a remonstrance from the Judges, who requested him to observe moderation in sending them dacoits' heads. Bhura's arm had been broken by a musket ball at Kunja and, the wound mortifying, he died. Kuar's last expolit was the sack of Sokalpur near Roorkee on 11th May, 1825. His band ceased to trouble the district after receiving somewhat severe treatment at the hands of Zamindars of Hansuwala and Doiwala. Kuar himself was ultimately captured in 1818 and hanged. Gang robberies continued on a small scale. Early in 1827 a line of chaukis (guard posts) along the road between Dehra and Haridwar was established. Ten havildars, two jamadars and seventy men of the Sirmur Battalion were appointed to hold them. In spite of these precautions three villages of the Dun were plundered in June that year. Meanwhile Mr. Shore had been active in developing the resources of his district.

In 1825 the Governor General passed a Regulation for "annexing to the jurisdiction of the Commissioner of Kumaun the tract of the country called the Dehra Doon, and also the pargana of Chandee, which were heretofore forming part of the districts of Saharanpur and Moradabad. According to a communication dated 8th December, 1825 to Mr. Shore "....the Governor General in council has this day been pleased to remove you from the office of Register of Saharanpur and Joint Magistrate stationed in the Dehra Doon and to appoint you to be Assistant to the Commissioner of Kumaun, with a salary of Rs. 1500/- per mensem". Thus the Doon and Mr. Shore came under the administration of Mr. Traill instead of Mr. Grindall. This tenure of Shore as Magistrate and Collector of the Doon was marked by a decided improvement in the condition of the district and the inhabitants themselves.

The points he himself most frequently insisted upon in proof of the general progress were the fact that on his arrival in the District, the whole of the agricultural community could not muster among them much more than half-a-dozen carts, whereas, when he gave over charge to Captain Young on the 10th December, 1828, they possessed upwards of one hundred; again, in 1822 the Doon was absolutely without roads, but before his departure, thirty-nine miles of roads (valued at Rs. 300/- a mile) had been made by convict labour with little or no assistance from the Government, while the Government itself had, at his instance, expended from Rs. 50,000/- to 60,000/- in such improvements as opening up the Haridwar and Kheree passes, and other works of utility; finally, the people had, under his influence, shaken off some of their characteristic apathy. They, too, had actually made roads (in all some ten miles long) at their own expense; Dehra, through which one used, during the rains, to wade along in gutters knee-deep with mud, could now be traversed with perfect comfort; the waste land was gradually brought under cultivation; and labourers, whom nothing could have once induced to work more than six hours in the twenty-four and who often declined to work at all on a cloudy day, were willing to toil from sunrise to sunset.

Mr. Shore belonged to a class of officers destined, some feared to become extinct under a less sympathetic Government. His abilities have been often excelled, but his official morality commanded unqualified admiration. Eminently possessing what he himself defines as the essential qualification for a good district officer, "not so much great talent as a determination to submit to perpetual annoyance in various petty ways," he was full of physical energy, and unceasingly devoted the whole of that energy to the performance of his duty and the benefit of those around him. Frequently, his loyalty to his employees went beyond the strict performance of duty. For instance, he advanced the money to build the Dehra jail out of his own pocket, and after the settlement of the European residents at Mussoorie and the establishment of the convalescent depot at Landhaur in December 1827, had increased the influx of visitors from the plains, his generosity extended to such minute details as having banias' shops set up along the high roads for the convenience of travellers, by means of advances (hardly ever repaid) out of his own private purse, and paying a Chowdhri (headman) whose duty it was to supply labour, for which the demand had suddenly risen to a degree probably unprecedented in these provinces. Yet many misunderstood him, and some even accused him of vexatious interference.

Although a repetition of the disturbances of 1824 seemed no longer possible, gang robberies were still not unknown, and in June 1827, five villages were plundered in Saharanpur and three in the Doon. The employment of the Gorkhas as a constabulary (under orders of Government, dated 21st July, 1825) appears to have been again necessary, but the banditti soon withdrew to the Sikh territory, whence they had made an irruption into this and the adjoining district.

The Doon started growing by leaps and bounds attracting people, both British and native plainsmen, who came and settled in the Valley. The natives came as farmers, businessmen, artisans and government employees. They came mostly from the neighbouring areas of Saharanpur, Muzzafarnagar, Meerut and Ambala districts. The English who came to live in the Doon were largely covenanted civilians, military officers of the Company and also some inevitable 'Box-wallahs' or the merchants. The population of the district, comprising of Dehra Dun, Mussoorie and Jaunsar-Bawar had grown from 17000 in 1815 to 1,02,830 in 1865, a period of fifty years. The people, except for the European and well to do Indians, lived in thatched mud huts or made of grass screens. In 1829 when Shore left the district there were only nine masonary houses, three at Dehra, one at Rajpur and four at Rishikesh belonging to Indians. Shore was so satisfied with the progress of his charge that he remarked, "Had not private considerations rendered my departure to England necessary, I would have consented to remain permanently in the Doon, without hope of preferment to a higher appointment, the increase in my salary being dependent on the increase of the revenue, such is my confidence in the potential of the District."

Capt. (now Major) Young, who was the Commandant of the Sirmur Battalion as well as Superintendent of Jaunsar-Bawar area, had been made Assistant to Shore in early 1827. Young now succeeded Shore, becoming Assistant to the Commissioner of Kumaun and Superintendent of the Doon including the Sub-division of Jaunsar - Bawar. Part of Government Order dated 12th May, 1829 to Mr. Ewer, Commissioner of Revenue, Meerut, appointing Young reads as under:—

"Mr. Shore having embarked for England, I am directed to acquaint you that the Governor General-in-Council had been pleased to appoint Major F. Young, of the 68th Native Infantry, Commanding the Sirmur Battalion, to be Superintendent for the affairs of Dehra Doon and its dependencies, with a consolidated salary of Rs. 500/- Sonat per month including the allowance now drawn by him in the Political Department as Superintendent of Jaunsar and Bawar." He was also the Agent for Political Affairs of Garhwal Raj.

The word "Sonat" is actually the Persian word "Sanwat" meaning the coin minted during the current year. The value of currency those days was determined by the year when it was minted. The older coins were less valuable than the newer ones. The older ones through usage, got worn out and lost a percentage of the metal and hence were reduced in value. Therefore payment to Young was to be made in rupees, minted in the year of payment to him, so that he did not lose money on the depreciation of the coins. All government revenue and dues were also paid in "Sanwat" coins. For this purpose Gold and Silversmiths kept sealed bags, full of such coins, of varying amounts. These were exchanged for the old coins after discounting them for their depreciated value. Even at weddings and other celebrations new coins were used. Since Young's time the District Magistrate and Collector of Revenue of District Dehra Dun was designated as Superintendent of the Doon. He was so designated, till 1947, because he was responsible for police duties, also, in Jaunsar-Bawar.

In the beginning so little was known about Jaunsar-Bawar that once a Superintendent of the Doon was called to account for being absent from his district without leave, when his duties rendered his presence at a distant corner of Jaunsar-Bawar necessary. This tract of the district is better known for its peculiar social and religious customs which have earned its people the distinction of being a Scheduled Tribe like the Nagas of North East India.

Young was appointed on a salary of Rs. 500/- Sonat per month. Against this Shore, who was only Assistant Magistrate and Collector of Dehra Doon, was paid Rs. 1500/- per month. Young was incharge of the District from 15th August, 1826 till 30th December, 1841, perhaps the longest period that any officer had held this appointment. The disparity in the pay of the two smacks of nepotism because Shore's father was a former Governor General and hence had influence with the Directors of the Company.

Under Young's appointment order the Doon was once again placed under the jurisdiction of the Commissioner Meerut Division who was to hold sessions for jail sentence, at least once a year, in Dehra Dun for the trial of prisoners committed by the Superintendent of the Doon. The Commissioner was to refer cases for final sentence either to the Resident at Delhi or to the Judges of the Circuit Court.

The people of Jaunsar-Bawar are a polyandrous society and the majority of them worship Mahasu and Parshu Ram the sixth incarnation of Vishnu, unlike the Vaishnavaits and the Shivaits.

The principal features of Polyandry are that the husbands must all be sons of the same mother or by the same set of husbands. The advantages of the system are locally said to lie in the fact that land does not become subdivided and quarrels are prevented. When the eldest brother is at home he shares the bed with the wife, and in his absence the next eldest brother takes his place, and so on. The other brothers have to take their opportunity of approaching the wife in the day time in the fields. A brother may take a separate wife and in such a case, may continue to enjoy the common wife as well, if the other brothers do not object. Or, he may separate, and obtain his share of the family property, but if children have been born his share is reduced. It sometimes happens that a household has several wives in common. One case was reported in which the family consisted of eight brothers, six being sons of one mother, and two of another. The family first married three wives who were possessed in common, but subsequently one of them took another wife. Later the six real brothers appropriated the first three wives and the other two sons the new wife. There is no prohibition on the marriage at the same time of two sisters, though this is rare, and a specific reason was given in one case, viz., that the first wife bore only daughters. Polyandry is usually said to be the effect of an excess of males over females, and it is certain that there is such an excess in Jaunsar-Bawar where there were in 1901 only 814 females to 1,000 males, and the excess was still more marked in the birth-rate which gave during three years ending 1908 only 762 females per 1,000 males. It has been said that polyandry generally results from female infanticide, but there is no trace of this ever having existed in Jaunsar-Bawar. A considerable number of females were married to persons in Tehri State and in Garhwal, and there did not appear to be any excess of unmarried women. From this brief account it will appear that the polyandry of Jaunsar resembles the patriarchal system of Tibet, and not the matriarchal system of the Nairs of Southern India. This appears more clearly from the customs of inheritance. If a man dies his brother or brothers succeed. If there are no brothers surviving the son takes all. Failing a son, the widow takes, but only for her life time, and she forfeits this right if she marries again in a village other than the one her deceased husbands belonged to. If there is no brother or son, and the widow is disinherited, first cousins on the father's side if there be any, may succeed.

Mahasu is the collective name of four deities, namely Basak, Pibasak, Buthiya or Baitha and Chalta. The first three abide in temples dedicated to them at Hanol in Khat Bawar, at Tahnu in Khat Panjgaon and at Anwar. The fourth or Chalta Mahasu took up his residence at Bairat in Khat Kuru and moves from Khat to Khat as occasion arises. These deities according to a local legend came from Kashmir some time in the hoary past in this way:—

Una Bhat lived in village Maindrath and had a large family of relatives and dependents. At this time, a demon named Kirbir Danav made his appearance at the confluence of the Tonse and Yumuna near Kalsi and day by day ate Una's people until only Una, his three sons and one daughter remained. Una fled to the forests of the Yumuna and wandered about from place to place seeking means to destroy the demon and revenge the death of his relatives. One night the Deota Mahasu appeared to him in a dream and said:— "Be of good cheer, O Una, proceed to Kashmir where the four Mahasus dwell and invoke their aid; they will destroy the demon, for no one else can." Una set out for Kashmir the next day and arrived at the place where the watchman of Mahasu lay fast asleep with two great iron clubs some hundred maunds in weight beside him. No one could approach Mahasu without the watchman's permission, so Una took up one of the clubs and placed it at the foot of the sleeping watchman, who soon awoke and demanded the name of the intruder and his business. Una at once answered:— Mamu (Uncle) I am thy nephew." The watchman replied:! "Bhai, you are not my nephew, but as you have chosen to address me what has brought you here?". Una told his story and the watchman dissuaded him from attempting the perilous journey, but finding Una resolved to proceed, gave him some rice and lentils and told him that he should first reach the forest of Ghagti and if troubled by storms a handful of the rice and lentils sprinkled in the air would cause the storm to abate. He would next reach Kanani Tal, the lake of Kanana, into which he was to spit and throw some of his hair. If his saliva turned into cowries and his hair into snakes, he would know that he was in the miracle-working land of Kashmir. There were but two dwellings in the great plain, one of the Mahasus' and the other of Kelu Bir, an attendant and athlete. On Saturday he was to hide himself in Kelu Bir's house and about ten at night the four Mahasus might be seen arriving in palanquins and retiring to their house to rest. Early in the morning the Mahasus went out to the sound of drums: first Basak to hold his court, then Pibasak, then Baitha and then Chalta. When the last came out, Una should go to him and lay his case before him and be guided by his advice. Una followed the instructions of the watchman and his petition was favourably received by the Mahasus, who eventually told him to return to his own country and they would destroy Kirbir. Chalta gave Una a handful of rice, an earthen vessel and his own staff, and told him when hungry he need only strike the staff on the earth and water would come forth with which the rice might be prepared for food. This, too, would prove that Mahasu was with him, and if in addition when he arrived at Maindrath he threw some of the rice into the Tonse Kirbir could do him no harm. On the first Sunday after his arrival he should yoke an unbroken heifer to a plough and have it driven by an unmarried boy who had never before driven a plough, and he would find that the plough would turn to gold and the share to silver. He should then plough five furrows, in each of which a stone image would be found representing the four Mahasus and their mother Deolari. Una on his return did as directed and the images appeared in the furrows. Basak appeared first with his thigh transfixed by the ploughshare, then came Pibasak with a wound in his ear and then Baitha with his eye injured. They are so represented in the temples of Jaunsar-Bawar. Chalta alone appeared sound and free, and hence the first three remain in the temples dedicated to them whilst Chalta is able to move about. Deolari, the mother, appeared in the fifth furrow and a temple to her name was erected in the field. Una worshipped the Mahasus and ordered his youngest son to serve them. He obeyed and became a Deopujari or priest. The second son was directed to strike a gong and became a musician or Bajgi. Then the Mahasus formed a garden and filled it with narcissus plants from Kashmir to serve as offerings to them on festivals. Una then built houses for Kelu Bir, Kadasiri Bir, Sakrar Bir, and sixty-four other Birs, who attended the Mahasus. The Mahasus then sought for Kirbir, but as he did not appear Sakrar was sent to seize him, and was promised a loaf and sweetmeat on every ''Sankrant'' should he be successful. Kirbir still remained at large and Kelu Bir was then sent with a promise of four times the amount of offerings and that goats sacrificed to the Mahasu would be killed at the door of his house. Kelu killed Kirbir and hung up his head in Mahasu's temple. Basak and Pibasak took Garhwal as their share and have temples in Bijoli and Rawain parganas of Garhwal. Jaunsar-Bawar fell to Baitha and Chalta. The temples to Mahasus in Jaunsar were built by the Zamindars long after Una's time. There are temples to Sangry at Mandhan in Khat Koru and Udpalta, where he is carried about Khats Semalta, Udpalta, Koru and Seli. The temples of the Mahasus are now served by Sarswat Brahmans and the offerings consist of male kids (young goats), coins, rice, water and narcissus flowers.

The origin of the Mahasu as given by Hamilton and reproduced by Williams is rather different. Hamilton supposes him to be of Scythian descent and relates that according to Brahmanical tradition, at a remote era of time, a man ploughing in the pargana of Bucan saw a snake which erecting itself before him said: ''I am sent by the divinity: raise near this place an image to be worshipped, call it the Mahasu Deota and it will reveal to you laws that are to be obeyed.'' On learning of this vision of the cultivator some Brahmans made an image and placed it in the field where the snake had appeared, and after some time had elapsed, it was inspired to give them the following instructions, the observance of which secures the devout from the evils of the present world and insures their happiness in the next, viz.:— First never to sleep in a bed with four legs; second, never to drink pure milk. Butter milk is permitted, but it is meritorious to abstain from eating the butter, it being more praiseworthy to burn it at the places appointed for the worship of the Mahasu Deota or demi-god: third, always to sacrifice the finest goats at the demi-god's shrine and if similar sacrifices elsewhere be abstained from, so much the better. The abstinence from milk enjoined by the Mahasu connects the Jaunsaris, according to Mr. Atkinson, with the people in Indus Valley to the present day and with the old Kators of Chitral; the latter of whom the same authority on somewhat slender evidence identifies with the Katyuris of the Almora District. Of the original four Mahasus introduced from Kashmir two Basak and Pibasak, are said to have migrated to Tehri as mentioned earlier. The remaining two Chalta and Baitha still exercise a most important influence over the daily life of the Jaunsari. According to Major Young the headquarters of the gods were situated at Hanol, ten miles north of Bawar in the erstwhile

Tehri-Garhwal state. The temple contains two idols, one of which was stationary while the other was the travelling or Chalta Mahasu. The god, when on circuit, observed both state and etiquette. His palanquin was invariably accompanied by a train of 60 or 70 men and dancing girls; but he never visited a village unless he received an invitation through his Wazir, at that time the head man of Bawar. The terror inspired by the god, however, always procured him the necessary invitation. If a village had suffered a misfortune the god was requested to pay a visit. He attended seated in a palanquin surrounded by silver vessels followed by his own retinue to which all chance idlers invariably attached themselves. The throng was fed for one day by the inviting village and kept for six months by collections levied on the Khats (sub-divisions) in the division, who were also obliged to furnish their quota of ghee and goats. The god used to divide his favours between Jaunsar-Bawar and the neighbouring state of Jubal, residing in each for twelve years alternately. His exactions ruined the superstitious inhabitants; so much so that Young reported that they were unable to pay the revenue. He therefore interdicted the levy of contributions within the British territory and ordered the Wazir to accept no more invitations from any village in the Pargana.

The power of the god was not, however, broken by these summary proceedings. Both Mr. Cornwall and Mr. H.G. Ross one time Superintendents of the Doon, describe his malign influence over the whole Pargana of Jaunsar-Bawar. According to them, "Cases are commonly decided by compurgation in his temple, to which the parties proceed and swear to the righteousness of their cause. Any misfortune which may afterwards occur is attributed to the wrath of the god against the perjurer, with the result that the land which was the subject of the dispute is given up and lies permanently waste as under a curse. If a villager has a grudge against an enemy he takes a clod out of his field and lays it on Mahasu's altar with prayers and offerings; and if the owner of the field afterwards falls into any trouble he imagines it to be due to the displeasure of the god and abandons the field. Persons between whom oaths have been passed and their descendants are permanently out of caste; they can have no dealings of any sort, though personally they may be on excellent terms; and as the people are naturally prone to litigation such excommunication is common, and proceeds to such a degree that the children of such enemies may not even attend the same school." The hillmen of Jaunsar share a characteristic with all dwellers in countries where the forces of nature are obtrusive: they are extremely superstitious. All misfortunes are believed to be due to the machinations of one or other of their devil gods; and in Mr. Ross's time around the year 1869-70 the people of Chijal, being afflicted with small-pox, burned down four hundred deodar trees as a sacrifice.

The ages of the Sirmur Battalion and the present town of Dehra Dun were about the same. The troops' barracks were around the area now occupied by the Forest Rangers College and the two open spaces in the centre of the town were the "Parade grounds" of the troops. The present clock tower and thereabouts the locality was called Lashkar (in Persian meaning cantonment) and of course the name Paltan Bazar is self-explanatory, Paltan = Regiment + Bazar = Market, (Regimental Bazar). Young lived in the oldest building of the present day St. Joseph's Academy's campus, and had a country house at Nala Pani. The water for the construction of the Dehra house was transported by mules from the Rajpur canal three miles away. The City Board office locality was called "Faltu Lines" as here were situated the lines for the camp followers and troops' families.

In 1874 the Dehra Cantonment was shifted to its present site. The old cantonment lands were taken over by the Municipality as per the Boards's Resolution dated 11th August, 1874 which reads as, "With reference to No. 179 dated 3.7.73 from Government of India the Military Deptt. to Secretary to Government N.W.P. (North West Province as Uttar Pradesh was then known) No. 450 dated 4.8.74 from Officer Commanding II Gorkhas to the Superintendent of Dehra Dun. Resolved that the Committee is ready to take over the old Dehra Cantonment on Monday 17.8.1874. Further resolved that Secretary write to Commanding Officer and request him to kindly make over all Books, Registers, Agreements etc. connected with the old Cantonment". The town of Dehra Dun was made a Municipality in 1867 whilst Mussoorie had already become one in 1842.

A new road was made to connect the Cantonments with Rajpur road called the Hathibarkhala Road (now New Cantonment Road). The name Hathibarkhala has its origin in a tradition to the effect that there was here a large Pipal or Banyan or Bar *(Ficus indica)* tree, which had an opening between its trunks through which an elephant tried to pass, and in doing so rent the tree asunder, whence the name of the village, khala being the ravine crossing the road.

The British, on taking control of the Doon, directed their energies towards its development. Apart from carrying out periodic land settlements efforts were made to introduce irrigation and new crops, apart from the traditional ones grown by the local population. As the Valley's geology rendered the profitable construction of wells impossible the very existence of villages, except those near perennial streams, depended upon the canals which intersect the Valley. Mr. Shore had a well constructed in the Kutchery compound at a cost of Rs. 11,000/- which is 228 feet deep. Because of its depth it had to be abandoned. Yet all along the base of the Shiwaliks, in Clement Town, Bharuwala and Mohobewala areas there are artesian wells in peoples' compounds. The average depth of wells in the Valley is around 100 feet. Therefore, the Administrators having found the ancient Rajpur canal (believed to have been built by Rani Karnavati) in existence soon turned their attention to the possibility of constructing canals in other parts of the Doon. The value of canals in the Doon is not restricted only to irrigation. To many villages they carry water for drinking purposes, though not for irrigation; and so people are able to live on and cultivate land which would otherwise, for lack of drinking water, be unpopulated and barren.

In 1823 Lieutenant de Bude was deputed to make a canal survey with a view to the construction of new canals and the repair of those that had fallen into a state of decay. Because of neglect a number of villages which depended on them for their water supply, had been deserted by the inhabitants. In 1826, a water tax was imposed on the gardens of Dehra, the money so collected being applied to the repair of the Rajpur Canal. Later under Young's administration, Capt. Cautley (the builder of the Roorkee or the Ganga Canal) and Capt. Kirke (also Adjutant of the Sirmur Battalion) were placed in charge of the canals. Improvements and extensions took place, more and more villages came to be settled. In the year 1900 there were approximately 83 miles of canals in the Doon.

Tradition credits the construction of the Rajpur canal and the locality of Karanpur to Rani Karnavati and her consort Kunwar Ajab Singh alias Ajbu Kunwar (after whom village Ajabpur is named), who administered the Doon district on behalf of the Rajas of Garhwal. He had his headquarter at the village of Nawada. Later, the work of maintaining and repairing this canal was entrusted to the Mahants of Guru Ram Rai's Gurdwara. In 1817, Mahant Har Sewak claimed full proprietary rights over the canal. This claim was rejected by the Company's Government on the ground that it was built by the Rani long before the arrival of Guru Ram Rai into the Doon. Later again, the Sirmur Battalion undertook its repairs. This water course was originally designed to convey drinking water to the people of Dehra. Later its waters were used less for drinking purposes than for irrigation of flower gardens and lawns in the town. The canal consists of two branches, the Dehra branch flowing past the Head Post Office and the Dharampur or the East Canal branch.

When the East Canal branch was being made the English engineer in charge decided to take French leave and go up to Mussoorie. The view from there of his project was so clear that he started supervising the construction by means of messengers and a pair of field glasses. While still at Mussoorie an unexpected visit by his boss at the work site, exposed his game, resulting in an immediate transfer to some god forsaken place. During the rains the view from Mussoorie is at its best. In the old days, when regular horse racing was in vogue in Dehra, people with good binoculars could follow the racing horses. The lights of Haridwar, Roorkee, Saharanpur and at times Ambala are visible at night with the naked eye. Once again the Rajpur canal waters are being used purely for drinking purposes as they have been merged with the town's main water supply from Bandal river.

Capt. Cautley, apart from being a geologist, can be compared to Ferdinand de Lesseps, the Frenchman, who built the Suez canal, as Cautley built the Ganga and other canals in North West Province. In 1840-41 Cautley designed the Katapathar canal which gets its supply of water from the Yamuna and irrigates a large area in the Western Doon.

The Bijapur canal was designed by him in 1837 to irrigate the triangular tract between the Tons, the Asan and the Bindal rivers. Its waters flow past and through the Forest Research Institute and the Indian Military Academy. In addition to the canals already mentioned, including his main one the Ganga canal, he also made the Eastern and Western Yamuna canals in the Saharanpur and Ambala Districts. As mentioned earlier he was also a geologist of international repute.

In 1859-60 the Kalanga canal was constructed while in 1863-64 the Jakhan canal was completed.

Before the opening up of the Valley by the British to colonists, it was mostly covered by primeval forests and the climate by consequence excessively unhealthy and the locals were indolent due to continuous bouts of Malaria. According to Williams, ''such was the laziness of the cultivators that they were in a most wretched condition, living from hand to mouth and completely at the mercy of petty money-lenders. Nothing else could be expected of men who thought it a torture to work on a cloudy day, remained idle altogether on a rainy one, and never went through more than six or seven hours honest toil out of twenty-four. The great demand for agricultural labour, due to the large proportion of waste lands encouraged their indifference.''

Mr. Shore when making his land revenue settlement was careful to acquaint himself with the condition of the people and their land. No village was assessed which he had not first carefully inspected, and he explained that his undoubtedly low assessments were based on a consideration of the poverty and indolence of the people and their proneness to desert. In short his object was to keep the tenantry on their newly broken lands. At that date the number of villages in the Doon was 156. The highest rate of revenue was Rupee one per acre and in most villages it did not exceed 10 annas 6 pies per acre and in some the rates were nominal.

The European settlers who came forward were given thousands of acres of land on very favourable terms. The land was to be held rent free for three years, and was not to reach the maximum of Rupee one per acre till after 20 years, and then this rate was only to be charged on three-fourth of the whole culturable area, one - fourth being left unassessed. These rates were later revised. The first set of Grants issued in 1838 were nine and the Grantees eleven. The Grantees were to clear the whole of their grants within twenty years with the exception of the irremediably barren land. The Grants were Attics or Attic Farm 6072 acres, Arcadia 5499 acres, Markham 5861 acres, Innisfail 7462 acres, Endeavour 977 acres, Hopetown (consisting of East, Central and West Hopetowns) 18,813 acres and Kargi, Bughant Bharuwala Nagleh 1589 acres. The total area of the Grants amounted to approximately 72 square miles which is about one-sixth of the Valley, exclusive of the strips of highland that go towards making up the total area of the district. All of these, except the Markham, Endeavour and the last, were in the Western Doon. Markham was partly to the East of Nagsidh Forest, on the tongue of land between the Suswa and the Song rivers near Doiwala Railway station and partly south of the Suswa along the base of the Shiwaliks. The Endeavour Farm was started by a Mr. Vaughan who selected as the scene of his enterprise the edge of the Ganga

Khadar along the right bank between Raiwala and Rishikesh. He perished with all his family of malaria in a few years.

In March 1838 Lord Auckland, the Governor-General accompanied by his sisters Lady Emily Eden and Lady Fanny Eden visited the Doon. He was the first Governor-General to do so after the annexation of the Valley by the British. Being a bachelor, his sisters had come out to India with him as his First Ladies and spent six years travelling with him throughout. During her stay in India Emily had kept a regular diary, "written solely for the amusement of my own family".

Reproduced below are the pages pertaining to the Governor-General and his party's visit to the Doon on its way from Saharanpur to Nahan in Sirmur:-

Saharanpore, Sunday, March 11, 1838.

This is a small station, only two ladies, one of whom is Miss T.: she came out last year to join a brother here, who is quite delighted to have her, and she seems very contented with her quiet life; but every body is contented with their stations at the foot of the hills. They stay the cold season here, and go in twelve hours up to Mussoorie, where most of them have their regular established homes, so they escape all hot weather. Miss T and her brother and the other Saharanpore gentlemen came out to meet us, and G. and I stopped at Captain C.'s to see an immense collection of fossils, all proving that our elephants of the present day were 'Little Chances' of the olden time. G had a durbar, and in the afternoon we went to the Botanical Gardens, which are very shady and nice; and we sent the band there as the Saharunporites do not often hear music. It is a pretty little station.

Kerhi, March 15.

G. has been out tiger hunting from the two last stations. They never had a glimpse of a tiger, though here and there they saw the footprints of one. One of the days the thermometer was at 90°F in our tents, but G. stayed out the whole day, and said he did not feel the heat.

Mussoorie, Sunday, March 18.

On Thursday evening we went on to Deyrah, too late to see anything, but Friday morning the beauty of the Himalayas burst upon us. We were encamped just under the mountains—too much under them to see the snowy range, but still nothing could be more beautiful than the first view of the range, and no wonder one hates plains. Colonel Y. had us out early in the morning to see his little Ghoorkha regiment manoeuvre. Most of the men are about five feet six, with little hands and feet in proportion. All the mountaineers are very small creatures, but they make excellent little soldiers; and the Goorkhas beat our troops at this spot twenty five years ago and killed almost all the officers sent against them. Now they are our subjects they fight equally well for us, and were heard to say at Bhurtpore that they really thought some of our soldiers were nearly equal to themselves. They look like little black dolls. They are quite unlike natives. There is a regular fool attached to the regiment, who had stuck a quantity of wild flowers in his helmet, and came up and saluted G.with a large drawn sword in most ridiculous manner. After that we went to see a Sikh temple, where there was a great festival, and about a hundred fakeers, the most horrid-looking monsters it is possible to see. They never wear any clothes, but powder themselves all over with white or yellow powder, and put red streaks over their faces. They look like the raw material of so many Grimaldis. At eleven, the two ladies and five gentlemen of the station came to visit us; and at four G. and I set off under Colonel Y's auspices, to see a cavern that has just been discovered about four miles from this, and which was found out in a very odd way. One of the soldiers had murdered his havildar out of jealousy, and escaped, and was taken, after a fortnights search, in this cave, nearly starved to death. It is just the place where Balfour of Burley would have hid himself. I have not enjoyed a drive so much for ages, and it was through such a beautiful country—such hills and valleys. I wish we might settle at Deyrah for the rest of the term of our transportation. One of the worst parts of this journey is that we never can go even two yards from the camp without an officer with G. on account of the petitioners. When we got near the cave we found Colonel Y., Dr. G., and Captain M. at the entrance of a dark grotto, through which a stream was running. 'Nothing to walk through', Colonel Y. said, 'not more than two feet deep, or two feet and a half at most', and so in they all went; but my bearers luckily declared they could carry the tonjaun through, and they contrived it, though sometimes one tumbled down, and then another, and I had once to sit at the bottom of it to prevent my head being knocked off by the rocks. It was a beautiful cavern about 500 yards long, and at the other end there was a tent, where G. and Colonel Y. had wisely established dry clothes, but the others who had not taken this precaution were glad to gallop home as fast as they could.

Yesterday we started at half past five in the carriage, came five miles to the foot of the hills; then the gentlemen got on the ponies, and F. and I into our jonpauns, which might just as well be called tonjauns - they are the same sort of conveyances, only they swing about more, and look like coffins. The mountaineers run up the hills with them in a wonderful manner. We were two hours going up precipices which, as Vivian Grey says, were completely perpendicular, but with perhaps a slight incline inwards at the bottom, and then we reached Colonel G.'s bungalow at Mussoorie. Such a view on all sides of it: Nothing could be grander - good fires burning - and a nice sharp wind blowing. Pleasant!

We found our Bengalee servants, who had come on the day before, very miserable. They had slept in the open air and were starved with the cold, and were so afraid of the precipices that they could not even go to the bazaar to buy food. I dare say to people who have never even seen the smallest rise in the ground, not even a molehill, these mountains must be very terrific.

While she was dressing me, Rosina was mimicking F.'s jemadar who is in a particular state of fear. 'There was poor Ariff, he buy great stick, and he put stick out so, and then he put his foot by it, and then he say, "Oh! what me do next, me tumble if we move me stick or me foot." 'I thought we should have been alarmed by what Miss T. said of her fears, but we went out on our ponies in the evening and cantered along the paths quite easily, though it is ugly looking down. One stumble, and horse and all must roll down out of sight. But, to be sure, how beautiful the hills are! I am certain

I shall grow strong again in a week at Simla, and as for ever being well in the plains, that is an evident impossibility, so far as I am concerned.

Mussoorie, Monday, March 19.

We went to the little Mussoorie church yesterday morning. The bearers are steady men, I have no doubt, but still I wish they would not race with each other; for at the sharp corners where they try to pass, the outer jonpaun hangs over the edge, and I don't altogether like it. In the afternoon we took a beautiful ride upto Landour, but the paths are much narrower on that side, and our courage somehow oozed out; and first we came to a place where they said, 'This was where poor Major Blundell and his pony fell over, and they were both dashed to atoms,' - and then there was a board stuck in a tree, 'from this spot a private in the Cameronians fell and was killed.' Just as if there were any use in adding that he was killed, if he fell any body might have guessed that. Then ...., who lived up here for three years, said he would take us home by a better path, and unluckily it was a worse one, and we had to get off our ponies and lead them, and altogether I felt giddy and thought much of poor Major Blundell! But it is impossible to imagine more beautiful scenery. This morning we went to breakfast with Colonel M. and saw the whole extent of the snowy range, and very fine it is. It is a clever old range to have kept itself so clean and white for 5,000 years. As we came back we met Mars, who is quite happy here, with Ariff after him. I asked him what he was doing. 'Jo veux absolument faire monter ce pauvre Ariff la haut.' - 'Do you like going, Ariff? I said,-'No ladyship' - ''Don't you think the hills are beautiful?'' - ''No, ladyship, very shocking;'' and he made a face of such utter nausea it was impossible to help laughing. Mars said afterwards that Ariff flung himself on the ground and declared nothing should induce him to take another step. My jemadar in consequence was particularly puffed up about it, though I believe he disliked his walk quite as much. 'I been to the Hospital, been to Macdonald Sahib, been everywhere where ladyship has been. Poor Ariff, he fear much!' and he walked out with a smile of self-complacency at his superior courage.

Rajpore, Wednesday, March 21.

We came down from Mussoorie Monday afternoon with great success, but the change in an hour from cold to heat made us all deaf to begin with, and half the servants were sick, and in the middle of the night I took one of my attacks of spasms. I always think Dr. D. in his heart must wish that they would begin twelve hours sooner. He always had to get up at one in the morning, and the spasms lasted till past three - such an inconvenient time when we have to march at half-past five. I really thought this time I should not have been able to go on, but somehow it always can be done when it cannot be helped; and as all the tents were ready at the next station, I went for the first time in a palanquin - it saves the trouble of dressing, and I just moved from the bed into it. G. went out shooting again this morning on positive information of a tigress and three cubs, but as usual they could not be found. However, they have had some very good shooting.

Thursday, March 22.

We had a great deal of rain last night; and so when we came to cross the Jamuna this morning it was not fordable, and there never was such a mess - only three boats for all our camp. Two poor men drowned in the night trying to swim over, and one or two camels were carried away, but found again. Then the road was so bad the carriage was not available, and I came part of the way on the elephant, which as I was not strong, shook me to atoms. We crossed at last, and then it appeared that everything had been drenched in the night, and there was not a bed nor a sofa to lie down on. Luckily, Rosine lent me her charpoy, a sort of native couch, and Dr. D. got a medicine chest, and gave me some laudanum and now I am better again; but of all the troubles in life for 'an ailing body,' I think a march the most complete. It is a pouring day, but luckily very cool. Chance has been very ill for the last week, and I have made him over to-day to the surgeon of the body-guard, who has bled him, and says he can cure him.

Friday, March 23.

We must luckily halt here three days, for half the people and things are still on the other bank. I am better to-day, and Chance in a more hopeful state. As you will hear from us several times by the overland packet before this comes to hand, I may as well send this off without coming to the interesting crisis of Chance's fate; but as the inflammation in his dear little chest is supposed to be subdued, you may feel tolerably easy, I, as usual, wind up with the observation that your last letter was dated August 5—seven months and three weeks old.

Camp, Nahun, March 26, 1838.

I sent off my last journal from Rajghaut, March 23. We got all our goods over the river on Friday evening, and marched Saturday, 24th. The regiment and the cavalry went the straight road, and we made an awfully long march of seventeen miles towards the hills. It was the last day of the dear open carriage, which has been the only comfort of my life in this march. Nothing is so tiresome as all the miserable substitutes for it—three miles of elephant and four of tonjaun, and then a pony. Both men and cattle get so tired in a long march, or when they are employed every day. The road is very pretty all through the Dhoon, and much cooler than the plains. Chance is better, thank you. I knew you would feel anxious about him. His constitution is dreadfully Indianised; but perhaps the hills, and a judicious change of diet, may be of use. However, he is done for as an English dog; he is just the sort of dog you see at Cheltenham.

We came up to Nahun yesterday morning by means of elephants and jonpauns. The road was very steep, but nothing like that to Mussoorie. The Rajah of Nahun met us at the last stage, and came up the hill with us to-day. He has his palace at the top, a sort of hill fort, and about 100 soliders—imitations of our soldiers and a band of mountaineers, who played 'God save the Queen' with great success. He is one of the best looking people I have seen, and is a Rajpoot chief and rides, and hunts, and shoots, and is active. Nothing can be prettier than the scenery, and altogether Nahun is the nicest residence I have seen in India; and if the Rajah fancied an English ranee, I know somebody who would be very happy to listen to his proposals. At the same time, they do say that the hot winds sometimes blow here, and that his mountains are not quite high enough; and those points must be considered before I settle here.

This morning we have been to see the palace, which is an odd collection of small rooms, painted and gilded in curious patterns - of course no tables and chairs; and indeed the only piece of furniture in the house was an English barrel-organ, and in one of the rooms downstairs there was a full grown tiger, tolerably tame, and a large iron pot full of milk for his dinner.''

Some of the characters in the narrative are identified as under:—

Miss T is Miss Bacon, G is George Eden Lord Auckland - the Governor General, Capt. C is Cautley, the builder of Canals, Colonel Y is Colonel Young of Dehra Dun while Dr. G is Dr. Grey, Young's Assistant Surgeon in the Doon. Captain M is Macgregor from the Governor General's staff while F is Lady Fanny Eden, his sister. The cavern referred to, which the party went to see, is the canyon of the Tons river now known as "Robbers Cave" and a favourite picnic spot in Dehra Dun Cantonment. Kaluwa, the dacoit and his comrades are also supposed to have used this place for hiding - hence the name. The Sikh temple referred to is Ram Rai's gurudwara and the occasion probably the Jhanda fair. Col. G and Col. M are Colonel Young, again, whose house was "Mullingar" where the Edens stayed.

The following pages are reproduced from the book "Wanderings of a Pilgrim" by Fanny Parks. She was a contemporary of the Edens and followed the Governor-General's party into the Doon on 16th March, 1838. Fanny Parks travelled in India during 1822 and 1845 making Allahabad her headquarters. She was a cousin of Captain (later Major) Edmund Swetenham who married a Garhwali belle of Mussoorie and settled at Cloud End, after commanding the Invalids Establishment at Landhour. Compared to the brief account of Mussoorie by Emily Eden, Fanny Parks gives a vivid picture having spent two and a half months in the station:—

1838, March 16th — We drove out twenty miles, to the place where the palanquins awaited us, travelled dak (mail-cart) all night, found a buggy ready for us at the last stage, and reached our friend's house at Saharanpur the next morning by 8 A.M. On the road, about five o'clock in the morning, I was much delighted with the first view of the snowy ranges; I never anticipated seeing mountains covered with snow again, and, as I lay in my palanquin, watching the scene for miles, breathing the cool air from the hills, and viewing the mountains beyond them, I felt quite a different being, charmed and delighted. Mr. and Miss B (Mr. and Miss Bacon) received us very kindly; and I had the pleasure of meeting an old friend, Captain Sturt, of the Engineers; the man whose noble conduct distinguished him so highly, and who was shot during the fatal retreat of the army in Afghanistan. In the evening we visited the Botanical Garden; it is an excellent one, and in high order; some tigers were there, fiercely growling over their food, several bears, and a porcupine. The garden is well watered by the canal, which passes through it. The Governor-General broke up his camp at Saharanpur, and quitted, with a small retinue, for Mussoorie, the day before we arrived.

14th— We took leave of our friends, and resumed our dak journey at 4 P.M.; during the night we passed Lord Auckland's camp, which was pitched in a very picturesque spot at Mohun-chauki: the tents, the elephants, and the camels formed beautiful groups among the trees, and I stopped the palanquin a short time to admire them. We passed through a forest, or Sal Jangal, as they call it, - in which wild elephants are sometimes found, and met with a little adventure: a tiger was lying by the road-side; the bearers put down the palanquin, waved their torches, and howled and screamed with all their might: the light and noise scared the animal, - he moved off. I got out of the palanquin to look at a tiger 'au naturel', saw some creature moving away, but could not distinguish what animal it was; the bearers were not six feet from him when they first saw him; it was a fine, clear moonlight night. The jangal looked well, and its interest was heightened by the idea that you might now and then see a wild beast. A number of fires were burning on the sides of the hills, and running up in different directions, these fires, they tell me, are lighted by the Zamindars, to burn up the old dry grass; when that is done, the new grass springs up, and there is plenty of food for the cattle; the fires were remarkable in the darkness of the night. For some miles up the pass of Keeree, our way was over the dry bed of a river; on both sides rose high cliffs, covered with trees; the moonlight was strong, and the pass one of great interest; here and there you heard the noise of water, the pleasing sound of mountain stream turning small mills for grinding corn, called "Panchakki". In the morning we arrived at the Company's bungalow at Rajpur.

Rajpur is situated at the foot of the hills: I was delighted with the place; the view from the bungalow put me in mind of Switzerland. We went to Mrs. Theodore's hotel, to see her collection of stuffed birds and beasts; a complete set costs 1600 rupees (Pounds Sterling 160). At the bottom of the valley between the Hills I heard the most delightful sound of rushing waters: taking a servant with me, I went down the steep footpath, irresistibly attracted by the sound, and found the mountain rill collected into a mill-dam, from which, rushing down, it turned several mills; and one of the streams was turned off into the valley, forming the little cascade, the sound of which had attracted me. How bright, clear, cold and delicious was the water! Being too unwell to bear the fatigue of climbing the hills, I sent for a hill pony, called a 'gunth'; he was brought down; the little fellow never had a woman on his back before, but he carried me bravely up the sheep-path, for road there was none. Moti, the name of the handsome gunth, is an iron-grey hill-pony,—more like a dwarf-horse than a pony; he has an exceedingly thick, shaggy mane, and a very thick, long tail;—the most sure footed sagacious animal; he never gets tired, and will go all day up and down hill; seldom fights, and is never alarmed when passing the most dangerous places. Give your gunth his head, and he will carry you safely. Horses are dangerous,—even the most quiet become alarmed in the hills. Captain S—bought this gunth at the Hurdwar fair; he came from Almora, cost 160 rupees (Pounds Sterling 16); and 300 rupees have been refused for him.

The following history was related to me concerning the gunth: — Colonel P—, to whom the animal was lent, took him to the snowy ranges; "In some pass, by some accident, the gunth fell down a precipice, and was caught upon an oak tree. There he swung; one struggle would have sent him to the bottom, and to certain death; he never moved. Colonel P—, who was walking at the time, got some people, who descended to the place where the gunth hung, dug out a standing-place in the side of the hill, just big enough to hold the pony, and contrived to get him off his tree into the spot: the gunth was so much alarmed, that they left him to recover from his fright on this spot the whole night; and the next morning got him up the precipice in safety to the road."

Any horse would have struggled and have been killed; these gunths appear to understand that they must be quiet, and their masters will help them. He is a queer-tempered little fellow; he kicked my 'sa'is'over one day, and always kicks at me if I attempt to pat him; but he carries me capitally: nevertheless, he is "vicious as he is little".

The whole day I roamed about Rajpur; the 'Paharis' (the Hill-men), who had come down to bring up our luggage, were animals to stare at: like the pictures I have seen of Tartars, little fellows, with such flat ugly faces, dressed in black woollen coarse trousers, a blanket of the same over their shoulders; a black, greasy, round leather cap on their heads, sometimes decorated all round their faces with bunches of Hill-flowers, freshly gathered; a rope round their waists. Their limbs are stout, and the sinews in the legs strongly developed, from constantly climbing the hills. They are very honest and very idle; moreover, most exceedingly dirty. Such were the little Hill fellows we met at Rajpur.

16th— This morning the gunth came to the door for my companion to ride up the Hills: I was to be carried up in a jampan. A jampan is an arm-chair, with a top to it, to shelter you from the sun or rain; four long poles are affixed to it. Eight of those funny little black Hill fellows were harnessed between the poles, after their fashion, and they carried me up the hill. My two women went up in dolis, a sort of tray for women, in which one person can sit native fashion; these trays are hung upon long poles, and carried by Hill-men. The ascent from Rajpur is seven miles, climbing almost every yard of the way. The different views delighted me: on the side of the Hills facing Rajpur the trees were stunted, and there was but little vegetation; on the other side, the northern, we came upon fine oak and rhododendron trees—such beautiful rhododendrons: they are forest trees, not shrubs, as you have them in England. The people gathered the wild flowers, and filled my lap with them. The jangal pear, in full blossom, the raspberry bushes, and the nettles delighted me; I could not help sending a man from the plains, who had never seen a nettle, to gather one; he took hold of it, and, relinquishing his hold instantly in excessive surprise, exclaimed,— "It has stung me; it is a scorpion plant." Violets were under every rock; and the wild, pleasing notes of the Hill birds were to be heard in every direction. The delicious air, so pure, so bracing, so unlike any air I had breathed for fifteen years, —with what delight I inhaled it! It seemed to promise health and strength and spirits: I fancied the lurking fever crept out of my body as I breathed the mountain air; I was so happy, so glad I was alive; I felt a buoyancy of spirit, like that enjoyed by a child.

The only bungalow we could procure was one on the top of the hill of Landowr; it was an uncomfortable one, but a roof was not to be despised in such cold weather: we had a fire lighted instantly, and kept it burning all day. Where now was the vile fever that had bowed me down in the plains? It has vanished with the change of climate, as if my magic. The Hill air made me feel so well and strong, we set off on our ponies in the evening to visit Mr. E—'s house; it is beautiful built with great taste, and highly finished; its situation is fine, on a hill, at the further end of Landowr. Thence we went to Colonel P—'s bungalow, a good house, well situated, but very far from supplies; he offered it to me for the season for 1200 rupees—i.e. 120 Pounds Sterling for seven months. From the barracks, at the top of Landowr, the view of the snowy ranges is magnificent. In any other country these hills would be called mountains; but, being near the foot of the Himalaya, that in the distance tower above them, they have obtained the title of "The Hills." Landowr, Bhadraj, Ben Oge, are covered with oak and rhododendron trees; the valleys between them, by the Hill people called 'Khuds', are extremely deep: at the bottom of these khuds water is found in little rills, but it is very scarce. About two thousand feet below Landowr water is abundant, and there are some waterfalls. The Hills are very grand, but have not the picturesque beauty of the valley of Chamouni:—and yet it is unfair to make the comparison at Landowr; Chamouni is at the foot of Mont Blanc: to compare the two, one ought to proceed to the foot of the snowy Ranges, where their solitary grandeur would overpower the remembrance of Mont Blanc. I long to go there: the difficulties and privations would be great; I could not go alone, and the fatigue would be excessive; nevertheless, I long to make a pilgrimage to Gangotri, the source of the Ganges.

17th—Started on our ponies at 7 A.M. to ride to Mussoorie, which is only a short distance from Landowr. The scenery at that place is of a tamer cast; the southern side of the hill, on which most of the houses are situated, puts me in mind of the back of Isle of Wight, but on a larger scale; the projecting rocks and trees, with gentlemen's houses in every nook, all built on the side of the hill, give the resemblance. The northern side is called the Camel's Back, from a fancied resemblance of the hill to the shape of that animal; there the scenery differs entirely. The southern side, on which Mussoori is situated, has few trees, and looks down on the valley of the Dhoon; the northern side is covered with fine trees the hills abrupt; a wildness and grandeur, unknown on the southern side, is all around you; the valleys fearfully deep, the pathway narrow, and in some parts so bad, only one foot in breadth is left for a pony. At first I felt a cold shudder pass over me, as I rode by such places; in the course of a week I was perfectly accustomed to the sort of thing, and quite fearless. A pathway three feet in width at its utmost breadth, is a handsome road in the Hills; a perpendicular rock on one side, and a precipice, perhaps three or four hundred feet deep, may be on the other. It is all very well when the road is pretty open; but when you have to turn the sharp corner of a rock, if looking over a precipice makes you giddy, shut your eyes, and give your gunth the rein, and you will be sure to find yourself safe on the other side. The little rascals never become giddy; and after a short time you will turn such corners at a canter, as a thing of course. I was delighted with the wildness of the scenery,—it equalled my expectations. In front of Mussoori you are in high public, the road called the Mall is from eight to ten feet wide, covered with children, nurses, dogs and sickly ladies and gentlemen, walking about gaily dressed. I always avoid the Mall; I go out for enjoyment and health, and do not want to talk to people. The children: it is charming to see their rosy faces; they look as well and as strong as any children in England; the climate of the Hills is certainly far superior to that of England. Not liking my bungalow, I changed it for another half way up the hill of Landowr.

17th—Lord Auckland and the Misses Eden arrived to-day, and took up their residence at Colonel Young's, a little below, on the hill of Landowr.

From my bungalow the view is beautiful, and we have as much air as man can desire. The first thing was to get 'Purdas', stuffed with cotton, for very window and door; the next, to hire a set of Hill-men, to cut and bring wood from the khuds, and water and grass for the ponies. A long ride round Waverly was the evening's amusement; then came a dinner of excellent Hill-mutton, by the side of a blazing fire of the beautiful rhododendron wood. The well closed doors kept out the cold, and my kind relative congratulated me on having lost my fever, and being so comfortable in the Hills.

Visited Mr. Webb's hotel for families; it is an excellent one, and very commodious. There is a ballroom, and five billiard tables with slate beds; these slate beds have only just arrived in India, and have very lately been introduced in England.

19th—During the time I was waiting for my relative, who had accompanied Lord Auckland, to show him the hospital and the different buildings at Landowr, which were under his charge, my attention was arrested by a great number of Hill-men, carrying large bundles of moss down to the plains; they grind up the moss with barley-meal, and use it as soap; it is in great repute at weddings.

Rode my little black horse, but found him not so pleasant in the Hills as a gunth, and more fatiguing. At the foot of Landowr there is an excellent bazar: every thing is to be had there,—Patee foie gras, becasses, truffles, sola hats covered with the skin of the pelican, champagne, Bareilly couches, shoes, Chinese books, pickles, long poles for climbing the mountains and various incongruous articles. Many years ago, a curious little rosary had been brought me from the 'santa casa' of our Lady of Loretto; a facsimile of the little curiosity was lying for sale in the Landowr bazar, amongst a lot of Hindustani shoes!

The Governor-General and his party quitted Landowr, and returned to Rajpur, on their march to Simla, up the valley of the Deyra Doon.

In the evening I rode out to see Ben Oge and Bhadraj; at the foot of Ben Oge is a boy's school; a number of little fellows were out at play. There is also a girl's school at Mussoori. Here English children can receive some education in a fine climate.

20th—Rainy; thermometer in the varandah at noon, 56°F; at 3 o'clock p.m. 54°F.

21st—The Hills covered and hidden by deep clouds; thunder and lightning, with some rain. Thermometer, 8 a.m. 46° evening fine, heavy rain at night.

23rd—Captain E S....has an estate in the Hills, called Cloud End, - a beautiful mountain, of about 60 acres, covered with oak trees: on this spot he had long wished to build a house, and had prepared the plan, but his duties as an engineer prevented his being long enough at a time in the Hills to accomplish the object. I offered to superintend the work during his absence, if he would mark out the foundation: a morning's ride brought us to his estate, situated between a hill, called "the Park" and Ben Oge, with Bhadraj to the west; the situation is beautiful, - the hills magnificent and well-wooded. Having fixed on the spot for the house,—the drawing room windows to face a noble view of the Snowy Ranges,—the next thing was to mark a pathway to be cut into the Khud, a descent of two miles, for the mules to bring up water.

The plan of the house was then marked out, and a site was selected for my hill-tent, commanding a view of the Himalaya: this little tent was made to order at Fathegarh,

—it is twelve feet square, the walls four feet high, and has two doors. A stone wall is to be built around it, a chimney at one end, and a glass door at the other; a thatch will be placed over it, and this will be my habitation when I go to Cloud End, or when I make excursions into the Hills; my kitchen will be an old oak tree. The Hills are so steep, a single pole tent of the usual size can be pitched in very few places. Under an old oak, on a rock covered with wild flowers, I sat and enjoyed the scene: the valley of the Doon lay stretched before me, and the Hills around me. There is a rhododendron tree on this estate that bears white flowers,—it is a great rarity, and highly prized; all the flowers of the other rhododendron trees are of a magnificent crimson. The Hill-men are fond of sucking the juice from the petals, which, it is said, possesses an intoxicating quality.

Stormy looking clouds were rolling up from the valley towards the Hills: returning home, we were caught in as fine a storm as I almost ever beheld; it was a glorious sight,—the forked lightning was superb, the thunder resounded from hill to hill, the hail and rain fell heavily: for about two hours the storm raged. We took shelter in a Europe shop; towards night it decreased; wrapped in black blankets, which we procured from the bazar, we got home in safety; the rain could not penetrate the black blankets, the wool of which is so oily. The storm raged with violence during the night, but I heard it not: in the morning the Hill-tops were covered with snow: at 7 a.m. the thermometer 38°F in the verandah; in the room at noon with a fire it stood at 57°F.

25th—My relative left me, taking back all useless servants, and the camels from Rajpur.

Visited the hospital, of which Mr. Morrow is the steward, to see his collection of birds. The specimens are very well preserved with arsenical soap, and they sell well on that account: he had two pair of the Moonal pheasants alive, their plumage bright and beautiful. The collection was large; I selected only a few specimens, as follows:—

The Golden Eagle of the Himalaya: a bird I have often seen flying around Landowr; and a remarkably fine one. Also the Black Eagle of these mountains.

The Loonjee, or Red Pheasant, from the deep forests of the Himalaya: a bird rare and valuable; the skin on the neck is peculiar; in confinement they are timid and quiet, but the light annoys them, from being accustomed to the shade of the forests.

The Moonal, Duffeah, or Blue Pheasant of the Himalaya: these birds are brought from the interior, they are seldom found so far down as Landowr; nevertheless, one was shot at Cloud End, Bhadraj; they are timid at first in confinement,—after a few days, they will eat wheat in your presence, and show no signs of alarm. The eggs they lay when in cages might be brought to England; why should they not thrive in our climate, since they are inhabitants of a cold region? The hen-bird, although less splendid in plumage than the cock, is very game.

The Koklas Pheasant, common in the Hills, is also a very game-looking bird.

The Callige Pheasant, with its peculiar top-knot, is, as well as those before mentioned, excellent food. Other Pheasants are found in the Himalaya, of which I was unable to procure specimens.

Black Partridges: The most beautiful in the world are found in most parts of India, they are a great delicacy.

The Chakor, or Red-legged Partridge: very similar to the French Partridge; excellent food: they may be rendered so tame, they will run about the house and garden. Chakor, the Bartavelli, or Greek Partridge (Perdix chukar, Gould. Perdix rufa, Lath): said to be enamoured of the moon, and to eat fire at the full of the moon. This bird is also called "ātash-khwār" (fire eater), a variety of *Tetrao fufus,* Lin.; called, in Hindi, Chakor. It is also denominated "Moon Bird," and "Minion of the Moon". The common grey partridge is coarse and inferior.

Bush Quail and Rock Quail: beautiful and delicious. When buying a number of quail, which are caught in nets, you will rarely find a cock bird, if caught near Lucnow, or any native court; they are taken out, and sold as fighting birds. Quail are numerous all over India, and generally sold twenty-five per rupee.

A Jangal Cock and Hen: the wild cock and hen of the woods, common over all India; the stock to which all common fowls owe their origin. There are various kinds of fowls in India; the ghagas are large, fine, and very long legged, like game birds; the chatgaiyan are fine also; the karaknath are considered very delicate by the natives, but the purple colour of their bones has a disagreeable appearance.

Green Pigeons: beautiful birds. Blue Pigeons: which inhabit the wells; it is said the fare of an aide-de-camp is "hard work and blue pigeons!"

The Barbet, the Blackbird, the blue-winged Jay, the Long-tailed Blue Jay, the Woodpecker, Humming Birds, the Shah Humming Bird, the Mocking Bird, and the Cuckoo, whose note is delightful in the Hills, recalling thoughts of early youth and home.

The Chand Chuck, the King Crow: a most courageous little fellow, fights and bullies all the crows in admirable style: hence his name, King Crow.

Flycatchers, Dhobi Birds, Magpies, and the Rana Chiriya: the colour of the cock is a brilliant scarlet; that of the ranee, the hen-bird, is a bright yellow. They appear during the hot winds.

The Mango Bird: so called as they are seen during the mango season.

The Rocket Bird: with the most elegant long white feathers in its tail.

The birds brought from the interior by the Paharis must have the moss taken out with which they are stuffed, and be prepared with arsenical soap; otherwise, the feathers will fall off.

28th—Some Hillmen brought me two pair of the Moonal pheasants alive; I bought them. They eat wheat, and live very quietly in their cages.

31st—Spent the day at Cloud End, overlooking the workmen. The mountain on which they are building the house will supply almost all the materials: the stones, which are cut out of it for the walls of the house, are at first so soft, they appear to be rotten; but exposure to the air will harden them in a fortnight. The beams are from the old oak trees; the lime is burned from the stones; but the slates are to be brought from a neighbouring mountain; and the frames for the doors and windows will be procured, ready made, from Rajpur.

The day was very hot, but the breeze delightful: returning home, I was seized with illness, and my pulse being one hundred and twenty, called in medical aid. It is not agreeable to be suffering from illness, on the top of a mountain, far away from all one's friends,—depressed, and out of spirits, with nothing to amuse one but the leeches, hanging, like love-locks, from one's temples.

A recovery from illness is a pleasant state, where you have around you beautiful scenery and pure air. The Hills have all that secret treasury of spots, so secluded, that you seem to be their first discoverer; lonely glens and waterfalls, on which the sun's rays scarcely rest one hour in the twenty four; cold hidden basins of living water; and all so shut out from intrusion of the human race, that, in spirit, you become blended with the scene.

April 16th—Spent the day at Mr. E—'s: in the evening, as we were going down the hill, which is exceedingly steep, I was so nervous, from recent fever, that I could not ride down the descent; therefore the gunth was led, and I walked. The pathway, or rather steep track, not one foot in breadth, is covered with loose stones, and on the edge of a precipice. Miss B—rode down perfectly unconcerned. From the bottom of the Khud I rode up the next hill, to see a house, called Newlands; which has been struck and burned three times by lightning. The hill is said to contain a quantity of iron, which attracts the electric fluid. A lady and her ayha were killed there by lightning. On my return I rode up the hill I had not had the courage to ride down; even that was enough to make me nervous, after having suffered from recent fever so many days. A short time ago, as Major Blundell was going to that very house, Newlands, by some accident, his gunth fell over the precipice, and they were both dashed to pieces. At one place I dismounted and climbed the side of the bank, whilst the servants held the gunths during the time three mules had to pass them. The passing was effected with great difficulty, and one of the mules was nearly over the precipice, so narrow was the pathway.

1838, April 17th—Started on my gunth, the day being cloudy and cold, to make a call some miles off down the hill, at Jerripani. The elevation of Jerripani is much less than that of Landowr, and the difference in the vegetation remarkable: here, the young leaves of the oaks are just budding,—there, they are in full leaf; here, the raspberry is in flower,—there, in fruit.

> "The Clematis, the favoured flower,
> That boasts the name of Virgin's Bower,"

was at Jerripani in beautiful profusion, sometimes hanging its white clusters over the yellow flowers of the barbery. The woodbine delighted me with its fragrance, and the remembrance of days of old; and the rhododendron trees were in full grandeur. Near one clump of old oaks, covered with moss and ivy, I stopped to listen to the shrill cries of the cicala, a sort of transparently-winged beetle: the sounds are like what we might fancy the notes would be of birds gone crazy.

> "The shrill cicalas, people of the pine,—
> Making their summer lives one ceaseless song,
> Were the sole echoes, save my steed's and mine."

156

The road was remarkably picturesque, the wind high and cold—a delightful breeze, the sky cloudy, and the scenery beautiful: I enjoyed a charming ride, returned home laden with wild flowers, and found amusement for some hours, comparing them with Loudon's Encyclopedia. A pony, that was grazing on the side of Landowr close to my house, fell down the precipice, and was instantly killed: my ayha came to tell me that the privates of the 16th Lancers and of the Buffs ate horseflesh, for she had seen one of them bring up a quantity of the pony's flesh in a towel;— I ventured to observe, the man might have dogs to feed.

VIEW FROM THE PILGRIM'S BANGLA

19th—The view from the verandah of my bangla or house is very beautiful: directly beneath it is a precipice; opposite is that part of the hill of Landowr on which stands the sanatorium for the military, at present occupied by the invalids of the 16th Lancers and of the Buffs. The hill is covered with grass, and the wild potato grows there in profusion; beyond is a high steep rock, which can only be ascended by a very precipitous path on one side of it; it is crowned by a house called Lall Tiba, and is covered with oak and rhododendron trees. Below, surrounded with trees, stands the house of Mr. Connolly; and beyond that, in the distance, are the snow covered mountains of the lower range of Himalaya. The road—if the narrow pathway, three feet in breadth, may deserve so dignified an appellation - is to the right, on the edge of a precipice, and on the other side is the perpendicular rock out of which it has been cut. This morning I heard an outcry, and ran to see what had happened; just below, and directly in front of my house, an accident had occurred: an officer of the Buffs had sent a valuable horse down the hill, in charge of his groom; they met some mules laden with water-bags, where the path was narrow, the bank perpendicular on the one side, and the precipice on the other; the groom led the horse on the side of the precipice, he kicked at the mules, his feet descended over the edge of the road, and down he went—a dreadful fall, a horrible crash; the animal was dead ere he reached a spot where a tree stopped his further descent: the precipice is almost perpendicular.

22nd—Found a glow-worm of immense size on the side of the hill: a winged glow-worm flew in, and alighted on the table; it is small, not a quarter the size of the other.

23rd—During the night, some animal came into the verandah, killed one of the Moonal hen pheasants, and wounded the cock bird so severely that he will die. There is a wild beast track on the side of the hill opposite my house, along which I have several times seen some animal skulking in the dusk of the evening.

25th—Accompanied some friends to breakfast in my cottage-tent at Cloud End. We laid out a garden, and sowed flower seeds around the spot where my little tent is pitched, beneath the trees; while thus employed, I found a scorpion among the moss and leaves where I was sitting, which induced me to repeat those lines of Byron:—

"That mind that broods o'er guilty woes
Is like the scorpion girt by fire,—
In circle narrowing as it glows,

The flames around their captive close,
Till, inly search'd by thousand throes,
And maddening in her ire,
One sad and sole relief she knows,
The sting she nourish'd for her foes,
Whose venom never yet was vain,
Gives but one pang, and cures all pain,
And darts into her desperate brain.''

My memory was a source of woe to the scorpion at Bhadraj; they surrounded him with a circle of fire; as the heat annoyed him he strove to get over the circle, but the burning charcoal drove him back; at last, mad with pain, he drove his sting into his own back; a drop of milk-white fluid was on the sting, and was left on the spot which he struck; immediately afterwards the scropion died: Mr. R—saw him strike the sting into his own back. When it was over we felt a little ashamed of our scientific cruelty, and buried the scorpion with all due honour below the ashes that had consumed him: a burnt sacrifice to science. In a note in "the Giaour," the idea is mentioned as an error, of the scorpion's committing suicide, but I was one of the witnesses to the fact.

29th—Saw a fine mule for sale for £ 10, and bought him immediately for my own riding; mules are generally very safe on these dangerous roads. Also purchased two smaller ones for the estate for £ 9, water-bags and all. A man brought a number of fine fat Karral sheep, fit for table, from the interior, where they are fattened on acorns; I purchased four of them for twenty four rupees eight annas; the mutton is delicious; they have short tails and large horns, are very strong, and their fleeces, long and warm, are suited to their own hill climate.

30th—The weather constantly fine, cool and pleasant; we have a little fire lighted merely in the morning and evening. Purchased Sancho, a handsome retriever, from a private in the Lancers.

May 1st—My friend Mrs. B—and her four children have arrived; I invited them to come and stay with me; the children are most interesting,—nevertheless, their noise drives me half crazy; my life has been so perfectly quiet and solitary of late, the change makes my head ache.

Sunday, 6th—Unable to go to church at Mussoori; constant rain, very cold and chilly; the clouds are hanging over the mountains in white heavy masses, or drifting on this powerful wind up the valleys, or rather between the ridges of the Hills. I went into the verandah, to see if the Italian greyhounds were warmly housed, and could not help exclaiming, "How delicious is this coldness in the Hills!—it is just as wet, windy and wretched as in England:" thus mingling the recollected misery of a wet, raw day in England, and the delight of a cold day in India. The boys are calling me to have a game of marbles with little apples,—the small sweet apples we get from Meerut.

My mule, who has been christened Don Pedro, carries me beautifully; we canter and trot up and down hill at an excellent pace; he has but one fault,—a dangerous one in the Hills,—that of shying; he would be worth two hundred rupees if he were not timid.

The conical form of the Hills is their great peculiarity; in order to gain sufficient level ground, on which to build the house at Bhadraj, it was necessary to cut off the top of the hill, - a work of labour and expense. A khud is a valley between two hills, which is generally very narrow, so much so that a horse might leap across the bottom of several of the khuds I have seen near Landowr. The building of the house at Cloud End has proceeded at a great rate; five hundred Hill-coolies are constantly employed under the eye of an European, to keep them at their work. The house has been roofed in and my relative has come up from Meerut, to have the slates put on after some peculiar "hikmat" (fashion) of his own.

7th—The storm of yesterday rendered the air so pure and clear, it was most refreshing; I mounted my mule, and went to spend the day at Bhadraj. The Snowy ranges were distinct and beautiful, the wild flowers lovely on every rock; the ride was one of great enjoyment. The wild notes of the Hill-birds were heard in every direction, and the cuckoo was sending forth its old familiar note. On my arrival I found one of the ponies at the estate had been killed by a fall over the precipice when bringing up water from the khud.

14th—Capt. S—says, a very severe earthquake was felt at his estate during the storm the other night: he was asleep in the outer building, and was awakened by the shock, which threw down the gable end of it; fortunately, the large stones fell outwards, or he would have been killed on his bed; he ran out, and took refuge in the little tent. The shock also split open the stone wall of the mule shed. Although his estate is only six miles off, we did not feel the earthquake at Landowr.

18th.—My fair friend and myself having been invited to a picnic at a waterfall, about two thousand feet below Landowr, we started on our gunths at 5 a.m.; none of us knew the way, but we proceeded, after quitting the road, by a footpath that led up and down the steepest hills: it was scarcely possible for the gunths to go over it. At 8 a.m. we arrived, completely tired, and found an excellent breakfast ready. The waterfall roared in the Khud below and amidst the trees we caught glimpses of the mountain torrent chafing and rushing along. After breakfast the gentlemen went out to explore the path to the waterfall; we soon grew too impatient to await their return and followed them.

We descended into the khud, and I was amusing myself jumping from rock to rock, and thus passing up the centre of the brawling mountain stream, aided by my long "pahari" pole of "rous" wood, and looking for the picturesque, when my fair friend, attempting to follow me, fell from the rocks into the water,—and very picturesque and very Undine-like she looked in the stream! We returned to the tents to have her garments dried in the sun, and while the poor little lady was doing penance, I wandered down the stream, of which the various water-falls are beautiful; and, although there was a burning sun on the top of the Hills, down below, by the water, it was luxuriously cool. The path I took was straight down the torrent; I wandered alone for three hours; refreshing myself with wild strawberries, barberries, raspberries, and various other Hill fruits that hung around the stream on every side. The flowers were beautiful, the wild ferns luxuriant, the noise of the torrent most agreeable, - in fact, all was charming. On my return, I found the party at the foot of a beautiful waterfall, eighty feet in height; the spot was lovely, it was overhung with trees, from the topmost boughs of which gigantic climbers were pendant. How gaily did we partake of excellent wine and good fare on that delicious spot! It was nearly sunset ere we mounted our gunths, and took the path through the village of Buttah.

This village is inhabited by Hill people; I saw a very good-looking woman at a cottage door, in a very picturesque dress, and wished to go and speak to her, but was deterred from so doing, as the Hill-men appeared to dislike the gentlemen passing near the village: I must go alone some day, and see her again. By mistake we lost the path, and got into paddy fields, where we were obliged to dismount, and take the ponies down the most dangerous places. My fair companion was on a mare from the plains; we were obliged to tie a rope to the animal, and leap her down those places over which the ponies scrambled; we went down the dry bed of a torrent for some distance, and it was most curious to see how the gunths got over and down the rocks. Walking fatigued me to excess; I mounted my gunth, and rode up some frightful places, up the bed of a small torrent, where there was no path; the gunth clambered up the rocks in excellent style. Presently Mrs. B—thought she would do the same; she had not been on the mare ten minutes when I heard a cry, "The mem sahiba has fallen into the khud!" Her horse had refused to clamber up a rocky ascent, I suppose she checked him, he swerved round, and fell down the khud; fortunately he fell on his right side, therefore her limbs were above him, and they slipped down together, the horse lying on his side, until, by the happiest chance, his downward course was stopped by a tree. The saises ran down pulled her off, and brought her up the Hill; afterwards they got the horse up again in safety. But for the tree, the lady and her steed would have been dashed to pieces; she was bruised, but not much hurt. Her scream alarmed me,—I thought it was all over. We returned completely tired, but the day had been one of great delight, the scenery lovely, and the air delicious.

From Landowr, looking towards Hurdwar, the isolated Hill of Kalunga or Nalapani, with its table-land and fortress on the highest extremity, is visible. When the steady coolness and bravery of the Ghoorkhas, united with insurmountable obstacles, compelled our troops to fall back, General Gillespie determined to carry the place; and, at the head of three companies of the 53rd Regiment, reached a spot within thirty yards of a wicket defended by a gun; there, as he was cheering the men,—waving his hat in one hand. and his sword in the other, he was shot through the heart, and fell dead on the spot. Thus died as brave and reckless a cavalier as ever put spur on heel; his sword is one of the interesting relics of my museum. I never meet a hardy, active little Ghoorka, with a countenance like a Tartar, and his kookree at his side, but I feel respect for him, remembering the defence of Kalunga. The women showed as much bravery as the men; showers of arrows and stones were discharged at the enemy: the women threw the stones dexterously,—severe wounds were inflicted by them; and they undauntedly exposed themselves to the fire of the enemy; they acted with the natural courage inherent in us all, never having been taught that it was pretty and interesting to be sweet, timid creatures! Perhaps, after all, the noble conduct of these Ghoorka women may be traced

160

to a reason given by a modern European author, who covertly asserts, that women, not having souls as men have, are guided in all their actions by instinct: The Hindus are equally complimentary, and assert,— "A woman cannot be kept in due subjection, either by gifts, or kindness, or correct conduct, or the greatest services, or the laws of morality, or by the terror of punishment,—for she cannot discriminate between good and evil"!

The "kookree" is a semicircular, long, heavy knife, always carried by the Ghoorkas; sometimes the sheath is curiously embroidered with strips from the quill of the peacock's feather: two small crooked knives are generally in the same sheath. The kookree is used for war as well as for all domestic purposes.

The sword used by the Ghoorka officers called a "korah" or a "bughalee", is also used by the executioners in China for decapitation, with a backhanded drawing cut.

The sling used by Hill-men is made of a thick long cord of worsted, having a little breadth in the centre, in which, having placed the stone, they whisk the sling round, and launch it. Specimens of all these weapons I brought from the Hills. The sling above described was doubtless used by the Ghoorka women at Kalunga.

22nd—We mounted our gunths so early we were at Cloud End by 7 A.M. to breakfast. Ben Oge, the hill adjoining, is the highest point at Mussoori. The day was bright and clear. Captain S—asked us to ride to the summit; he accompanied us on foot. The view from the top of Ben Oge was beautiful: the Snowy Ranges were so clear and distinct, you could see every peak. I thought of Captain Skinner's journal as I looked at the peaks of Jumnotri, the source of the Jumna, and traced the river as it wound below through the khuds at the foot of the mountains, its course doubling like a hare. Beyond was the peak of Gangotri, from which the Ganges rises. I longed to march into the interior, to behold the grandeur of the scenery of the Himalaya. Ben Oge is quite tree-less at the summit, but the ground was covered with wild lavender, thyme, and various mountain flowers of great beauty, while numberless butterflies flitted over them. My relative found the breeze very chilly, but the sun was so hot it made my head spin; we returned to his house: he was seized with cholera, from the heat of his body being suddenly checked by the cold air, and the sun pouring on his head; he was very ill, and in great pain for two hours. We returned home, determined not to ascend another hill during the heat of the day.

26th—My little widow and I were out riding at seven in the morning; on our return we were surprised to find a very severe earthquake had been experienced at Landowr and Mussoori, which had frightened all the people; there were three distinct shocks. We on our gunths did not feel the shocks; there are but few hours in the day in which an earthquake could catch us off our ponies.

I have never put on a bonnet since I came to the Hills; like the steeds in the "Lay of the Last Minstrel," which "stood saddled in the stable day and night, "so am I saddled in my hat and riding-habit, always on my pony; my visits are made on horse back. I have a jampan, (a sort of chair, with poles, carried by Hill-man) but this is a disagreeable kind of conveyance; and I like the independence of my pony much better. The earthquake was charming; we seem to have all the eccentricities of nature around us. A Landowr

Etna or Vesuvius would figure well in my journal, could we be lucky enough to discover a burning mountain in these Snowy Regions.

28th—I gave a picnic party by the side of a mountain stream, in a deep khud at Jerripani: the barberries were quite ripe, in shape much thicker than the English, in colour black, very good in taste. The wild dog-rose hung its clusters of white flowers from almost every tree in the richest profusion;—it is a beautiful climber.

June 1st.—The weather is hot during the middle of the day, the thermometer 70°F; one cannot go out with comfort, unless the day be cloudy or stormy; it is very hot for the hills.

5th—A very hot day;—the Hills covered with a foglike smoke, occasioned by the burning of the jangal in the valley below; hot and smoky air comes up in volumes. Mrs. M—was riding this evening, when a leopard seized her spaniel, which was not many yards in front of her pony; the shouts of the party alarmed the animal, and he let the dog drop; however, the poor spaniel died of his wounds. Some officers laid wait for the leopard, and shot it; I saw it, coming up the hill, fastened on a bamboo, to be stuffed and prepared with arsenical soap.

7th—Mr. D—invited us to a picnic at Bhadraj; we selected a spot under a fine oak tree on the estate at Cloud End; numberless amusements were provided for us; a champagne tiffin was pleasant under the old oak tree; and a dinner, rich and rare, finished the amusements of the day. When the moon arose we mounted our gunths; and, as the road lay through the dark shade of trees, and on the edge of precipices, we determined to be careful, and agreed to muster three times on our journey of six miles, to see that none of the party had fallen into the khud. Away we cantered through the beautiful moon-light, almost racing our ponies. At the last muster, Mr. H—was thrown by his mule; but as he was scarcely hurt, it was only a laughing matter. We reached home at half past eleven, after a beautiful ride and a pleasant day.

10th—One of the officers of the Buffs met a bear the other day, and was glad to get off unhugged; bears as well as leopards abound in the Hills. I must not take my pet dog out riding with me; at this time of the year wild beasts are numerous, and render it dangerous.

We have a great number of visitors every day in the Hills; people have nothing to do but to run about calling and amusing themselves. A third earthquake has taken place; but as ususal, I on my gunth was unconscious of the quaking of the earth. A storm of thunder, lightning, and hail has cooled the air, and it is very pleasant weather. The Hills look so beautiful at night, when they are on fire; the fire never spreads, but runs upto the top of the Hill; they fire them below in several places at once, to burn the old long grass, and make way for the new to sprout up.

11th—A letter from Allahabad tells me, — a more severe storm took place there on the third of this month—more severe than the one in which the Seagull was wrecked; it only lasted an hour. It blew down one of the verandahs of our house, unroofed the cow house, the meat-house, the wild-duck-house, the sheep-house, etc. the repairs will not cost us less than seven hundred rupees (Pounds Sterling 70).

162

13th—Accompanied Mr. R—to see the Botanical Garden, which is small, but interesting: I ate cherries from Cashmere, saw a very fine Hill lily from the interior, and gathered many beautiful flowers. Some peaches, from the Dhoon valley, very large and fine, like English peaches, were sent me to-day.

18th—Our party being engaged to dine at Cloud End to-day, under the old oak tree, we got up at 6 A.M., when we found the Hills covered with thick white clouds from the bottom of the khuds to their summits; the clouds were so thick, and we were so completely in the midst of them, you could not see beyond the verandah; the thunder rolled and the sheeted lightning flashed. After a while the wind blew off the clouds, and the Hills re-appeared, but only for a few moments, when fresh clouds rolled up from the valley and every thing was again hidden in the white foggy cloud. The rain fell heavily, straight down from the heavens: I trust the rains have set in this day; without them the famine, and the sickness which is raging in the plains below, will continue.

This specimen of what the rains will prove has quite horrified my fair friend, and she is wishing herself back again at Meerut. I—who am fond of storm and tempest—have enjoyed the day; I like these hurly-burly scenes; too frequent repetition might perhaps render them annoying, and the dampness might be productive of rheumatism. Thermometer 1 p.m. 69°F.

19th—At half past 7 a.m. our party were at Cloud End, seated on the rocks under the old oak, enjoying breakfast after the ride. The delicious mountain air made me feel so well, I proposed to Captain A—to visit the summit of Bhadraj, seven miles off. The rest of the party thought the exertion too great, and would not join us. On-quitting the made road we entered a track on the side of the mountain, overhanging a deep precipice. We lost our way, and found we could neither turn our mules round, nor proceed any further. We dismounted; Captain A—with some difficulty, turned my mule; he then attempted to do the same to his own,—the animal became skittish, and, slipping from his hand, went down the side of the hill; how he kept his feet was wonderful. The mule looked quietly up at us from below; to have attempted to catch him would have sent him down the rock to certain death, we therefore walked off, leaving this most beautiful mule, for which £ 20 had just been paid, to his fate. As we expected, when he found the other mule had gone off, he ascended the rock with the utmost caution, and rejoined his companion; I was glad to see his bridle in his master's hand again.

After much toil we arrived at flag-staff on the top of the hill; thence the view was such as is seldom seen in such perfection, even in these mountains: —looking down towards the plain of the Deyra Dhoon, instead of the beautiful valley in all its emerald green, interesected by rivers pouring down from the Hills,—instead of this, white clouds entirely filled the plain, giving it the appearance of being filled with hills covered with snow; beyond were the dark hills of the lower Range; the next minute the clouds changed their appearance, and rushed up the Hills on a strong wind, covering several mountains at a time in a most extraordinary manner with volumes of white clouds; then, driving on, left them bright in the sunshine. The river Jumna, in the khud or valley, at times visible, at times concealed by clouds, wound its tortuous course below. I have seen the Hills under almost all forms, but the grandeur of the view on this stormy day exceeded any thing I had before beheld, and well repaid the fatigue. At times it rained a little, at times there was a scorching sunshine, then came gusts of wind and clouds, wrapping every object around us in dense white vapour. A little further on we found a Hindu idol, rudely cut in stone; this idol is now neglected, but was formerly much worshipped. Near it is a large stone, on which is chiselled, "Lady Hood, 1814:" on speaking of this to the political agent, he laughed and said, you were more enterprising than Lady Hood; you visited the spot,—she only sent a man to chisel out her name, and that of Colonel B—on the top of Bhadraj; she never visited the place in person." We returned to dinner at Cloud End: how glad we were of a glass of champagne after our fatigues! and how glad we were we had brought the beautiful mule back in safety! After tea, remounting our steeds, we returned to Landowr: I rode in the course of that day twenty six miles, up and down hill,—a pretty good distance for a lady; — but who can feel fatigue in the bracing, most enjoyable air of these delightful mountains ?

21st—At twenty-two minutes after 4 P.M., an earthquake shook the ground and the house; I was sitting at table and felt the shocks, which were very powerful. Rain, rain storms, storms, thunder and lightning daily: truly, saith the proverb, "There are storms in high places".

24th—A delightful day! How fine, how beautiful are the snowy ranges! In consequence of the heavy rain the roads have become very rotten and dangerous; in many parts, half the road has fallen into the khud; and where the path is often not three feet in width, it leaves but a small space for a man on his gunth. Mr. T—, of the artillery, met with a serious accident this morning; the road was much broken, and as he attempted to ride over it, it gave way; he and his pony went down the precipice. Mr. T—was stopped in his descent, after he had gone one hundred feet, by a tree, was brought up, and carried to a surgeon. He was much hurt in the head, but is expected to recover in two or three weeks; no bones were broken; the pony went down two hundred and fifty feet, and was found alive.

One of my men was brought in for medical aid, he had been employed in charge of a gang of Hill-men, cutting slates for the roof of the new house, in a deep khud, and had caught a fever. The slates found in the Hills are very good, but more brittle than those of Europe. The houses formerly were all thatched at Landowr; a thatched roof is dangerous on account of the lightning which so often strikes and sets fire to it. Captain S—introduced slated roofs, and several people have followed the good example he has set them".

164

According to a minute dated 23rd March, 1838 Lord Auckland found that the Grants given in the Doon were doing well. On one Grant 600 acres had already come under the plough and in a few months it was expected that 2000-3000 acres would be cultivated, where a year ago was only forest. The Grantees were going in for Mauritius sugar cane, cotton and indigo. They were also contemplating producing wool from Bhutan sheep. Auckland objected to the distance from a market (as is the situation even to-day), and the answer was, "we shall build boats from the timbers of the Hills and the sale of boats will fully pay the carriage". His admiration for the energy of the colonists was tempered by the discovery that the best sites had been appropriated by the officers of the district or persons connected with them. Col. Young, the Superintendent of the Doon and Commandant of the Sirmur Battalion held 10 or 15 thousand acres in the name of one Mr. MacGregor, a west Indian of excellent character and much experience. Similarly his (Young's) Joint Magistrate Captain Fisher, his Adjutant Lieutenent Kirke and his Assistant-Surgeon Dr. Gray held about as much and more in partnership with others.

Besides these there were allotments and applications for allotments, to the extent of 70-80 thousand acres, and amongst them one from an engineer, of two years standing in the army posted at Mussoorie, for 4000 acres. This Auckland very rightly held to be wrong, but, on the other hand these transactions had been carried on with the knowledge, if not express sanction, of Sir Charles Metcalfe (who himself had commandeered a large chunk of land in Delhi) and the Board of Revenue. Auckland therefore contended himself with calling for an exhaustive report of the Grants, and the matter was dropped for the time being. The present government servants can quote this precedent and tell their detractors in similar situations that they are only following one of the age old traditions of their service.

Shortly after obtaining the grants the grantees of Arcadia, Hopetown, the Attic Farm and Markham united their interests in a joint stock agricultural company (called Maxwell, MacGregor & Co.) consisting of 40 shares with a paid up capital of £ 20,000, subsequently raised to £ 50,000 when they added Innisfail and a vast grant in the Saharanpur district to their acquisitions, which thus covered an area of over 100 square miles. In 1842 troubles began. The home government in a despatch censured firstly upon the special irregularity of allowing civilians to hold grants within their own jurisdictions and secondly upon certain general irregularities such as the grant of lands to non-residents and non-cultivating Europeans in contravention of the instructions conveyed in a previous despatch of May 1838. The Court concluded "by desiring that all grants, which had been in that or in any other respect irregularly made, should, as far as practicable, be cancelled". The Government of India appears to have neglected or overlooked the conditional nature of the order, and the result was that all covenanted officers were required to relinquish their interests in the grants by 1st January, 1845 or to resign the service. This order is open to criticism on more grounds than one. The general prohibition against holding land within their jurisdictions was directed only against officers in civil employ, whereas many of the grantees were officers of the army; and in view of the peculiar circumstances of the Dun the desire of a former government had been to attract capital at any cost, and it had deliberately ignored the breach of the rules.

This decree was fatal to the company. The shares were all thrown simultaneously on a most contracted market: Arcadia and East Hopetown were sold for Rs. 20,500, Central and west Hopetown for Rs. 5,000, Attica for Rs. 1,000. Such was the end of a speculation which had involved an expenditure of more than Rupees four lakhs. The Government of India and the Court of Directors in 1850 admitted the arbitrary and unjust nature of their orders, and granted compensation to the extent of over a lakh and a half rupees.

The grantees were probably on the whole lucky in that their venture was suppressed before it had absorbed more capital. Writing in January 1844 the Lieutenant-Governor remarks: "Hopetown, Arcadia and the Attic Farm are well known to all who have visited the Dun as interesting and apparently thriving establishment." But he adds: "as a speculation the attempt has failed, disease has carried off their labourers, murrain has destroyed their cattle; unthrifty and careless management by agents has disappointed their hopes. The persons who first engaged in the undertaking are now on the point of withdrawing from it, owing to the disappointment of their expectations of profit." Mr.G.H. Smith, a shareholder in the company, admitted in October 1843 that upto date the undertaking, far from giving any return, had yearly swallowed up much more than it had yielded. Up to August 1843 more than rupees four lakhs had been spent on it. Indeed the speculators seem to have rather freely indulged in what the Board of Revenue styled with a happy facility of expression "an anticipative incubation of profits." The factors against the success of the undertaking were the want of an indigenous or naturalized population, the extraordinary insalubrity of the climate, the lack of irrigational facilities, and lastly the size of the grants, which rendered inevitable their supervision by hirelings with no stake in their success. Other large grants of later date failed from exactly similar causes; while Mr. Powell's Bharuwala grant, also assigned in 1838, was not too large for his own supervision and with careful and economic management, it prospered.

In spite of this early fiasco speculators, both European and Indian, came forward to take waste land grants on substantially the same conditions as those which governed the 1838-1840 grants. These are from the circumstances of their progressive revenue technically known as "rasadi" grants. The main point in which they differ from the earlier grants is their comparative smallness. The largest were the Markham Grant resumed and re-assigned, the Jolly Grant, and Lister's Majri Grant, and none of them proved a successful venture: a circumstance which points the argument of those who attribute the failure of the 1838 grants to their unwieldiness.

Twelve estates with an area of over 20,000 acres, including the lands of the two Tea Companies, were held in fee simple under Lord Canning's rule of 1861, which provided for the purchase of the fee simple of unassessed lands at rates not exceeding two rupees and eight annas per acre for uncleared land or Rs. 5/- per acre for land unencumbered with jungle, subject to a deduction for swamps or unculturable land, and also for the redemption of land revenue already assessed. Lord Canning proposed to limit the permission of redemption to such a number of estates as would in their aggregate not exceed ten percent of the total revenue in the district, and the price of the redemption was fixed at 20 years' purchase of the existing assessment.

In addition to these there were three estates whose land revenue had been redeemed, and three good service grants, Raynorpur given to the widow of Captain Raynor, killed in the defence of Delhi, for his good and gallant services during the Mutiny of 1857, which earned him the Victoria Cross posthumously; Balawala granted to Captain Forest's children and Barasi granted to Subedar Singbir Thapa of the 2nd Gorkha Rifles. A small tract of land near Phanduwala in Eastern Dun, was given out as a good service grant to Subedar Major Judhbir Singh in 1902-1903, and is now known as Semalas.

The Mahant of the temple of Guru Ram Rai in Dehra held free of revenue Dehra Khas, Dhartawala, Mihunwala, Panditwari, Rajpur and Chamansari. Dubhalwala was dedicated to the temple of Badrinath, Prempur and Jakhan to Kedarnath, Rishikesh and Tapoban to Bharatji, Gorakhpur and Jogiwala to Gorakhnath temples respectively.

Amongst these Grantees was also Mr. Samuel Cunliffe Lister (created Baron in 1891 and took the name Lord Masham). His "Lister Grant" of 970 acres was in the Lachiwala area and he was the first person in the Doon to experiment with Sericulture. He was a patentee of numerous inventions, which included the compressed-air brake for railways, and a wool combing machine. There is a village called Listerpur in the Eastern Dun.

The descendants of the Raynors are still living in Dehra Dun and a village named Raynorpur still exists. Another person General Sir Robert Dick took the Dalanwala estate of 492 acres. Genl. Dick was killed in the war against the Sikhs in 1846, at the battle of Sobraon. This estate was later sold by his widow to a group of Indian businessmen who converted the area, including the portion growing tea, into the now well known Dalanwala locality of the town of Dehra. Dick House is till there and is the nucleus of the campus of Col. Brown's School which was started in 1926 by Col. Brown, a retired British army officer.

An interesting story about Col. Brown is that he in partnership with a Dr. Balbir Singh had started the Cambridge Preparatory School in 1921. This institution was being run in the campus known as White House, which is next door to Dick House, and is to-day housing the Welham Boy's School. In 1926 the two partners fell out and Col. Brown started a new school taking with him some boys, from the former school, who formed the core of the new one. It is said that one night he led the Senior boys to White House and got them to steal desks and chairs to furnish his classrooms. It resulted in a long drawn out court case between the former partners. Unfortunately this practice seems to have become a tradition, over the years, amongst the partners owning Col.

Brown's, whoever they may be at any point of time—robbing Peter to pay Paul! Vishwanath Pratap Singh, one of the country's Prime Ministers and owner of Manda House on Rajpur Road, studied in this school for five years.

While on the subject of land grants mention should be made of the Tea Industry in the Doon. Hardly a handful of people know that the first tea garden in India was laid out in the Doon, in the Public Sector, by the East India Company. The origin and the progress of the industry in the district was due to the efforts of Dr. Royle, Superintendent of the Company's Botanical Garden at Saharanpur. In 1827 he first recommended to the Indian Government to experiment with tea cultivation in the Himalaya foot hills. Again in 1831, he expressed his views in a report to the Governor-General Lord William Bentinck during the latters visit to Saharanpur. At about the same time Dr. Wallich presented a paper to the Committee of the House of Commons on the affairs of India, urging the cultivation of tea in the districts of Kumaun, Garhwal and Sirmur. Royle felt that Jharipani, halfway between Rajpur and Mussoorie would be one of the most favourable places for conducting an experiment of this kind.

Meanwhile Bentinck, having decided to give tea cultivation a fair trial, appointed a committee to go into the mechanics of carrying out the project. The Committee came to the conclusion that, "the proposed experiment might be made, with great probability of success, in the lower hills and the valleys of the Himalayan range,—since in the mountainous tracts of northern and eastern frontier, several species of plants are found indigenous, which are also natives of China, and are not met within other parts of the World." In 1835 tea plants reared from seeds brought from China were distributed to the most promising districts. Dr. Falconer, Dr. Royle's successor chose Garhwal for his first experiments. In 1838 he reported that some plants which were the produce of seeds from the Koth nursery, in Garhwal, were actually growing at Saharanpur itself, and that tea would flourish in the Doon seemed certain.

Eventually a government plantation was started in 1844 on a 400 acre plot of land at Kaulagarh village near Dehra, under the charge of the Superintendent of the Saharanpur garden, Dr. Jameson. For laying out this and other experimental tea plantations Chinese labour and supervisors were also imported. In 1846 the London brokers reported in flattering terms on a sample of Kaulagarh tea sent to them. The tea was found to be as well made and declared to be as good as Chinese tea in aroma, smell, colour of infusion and taste. It was carried on with fluctuating success for the first 23 years. In his report of 1850 Mr. Fortune, who had been to China and was deputed by the government to visit the various plantations, commented on Kaulagarh that "the plants, generally, did not appear to him to be in that fresh and vigorous condition which he had been accustomed to see in good Chinese plantations". However, his report of 1856 was much more favourable, and he attributed the improvement in the condition of the plantation to his own suggestions. This brought a strong rejoinder from Dr. Jameson who pointed out that, whereas Mr. Forturne now admitted the plants to be equal to any in China, he had previously condemned the Doon as unfit for tea cultivation on insufficient data. With regard to his suggestions, the improvement could hardly be attributed to them, because far from being new they were all contained in some notes prepared by Jameson himself, some years before, for the information and guidance of tea planters. It was due to Jameson's efforts that tea at one point of time had become the principal commodity of the district.

Once the East India Company started winding up its affairs in India the Kaulagarh tea estate was purchased by His Highness Sirmur from the Government, in 1867, for a sum of 20,000/- Sterling. It continued to be the personal property of the Sirmur Ruler even after 1947 and to-day the area is a housing colony known as Rajinder Nagar, named after the last ruler. In 1857 His Highness Sirmur purchased the Annfield Grant (692 acres), including the villages of Baitwala and Gangbhewa for a sum of Rs. 1,40,000/- from the Annfield Tea Company owned by Genl. R. Macpherson. He, H.H. Sirmur, established a market for the locality's trade at Choharpur (now known as Vikas Nagar). The estate had 400 acres of land under tea. To-day there is not a single tea bush surviving.

The British Government endeavoured to encourage private enterprise in this direction. It offered land to planters on exceedingly favourable terms from the beginning. The Kaulagarh tea estate was established with the same object. It was not sold till tea culture had taken a firm root in the district. Under Lord Canning's Rules of 1861 Dehra Dun Tea Co. Ltd. (incorporated in 1863) alone had a Fee Simple Grant of 9002 acres. For this land the price to be paid was Rs. 38,015/-. Similarly a number of individuals who had taken grants of land went in for tea cultivation.

In 1847 there were only eight acres under Tea but in 1853-54 a number of Indians and Europeans began planting large areas under Tea when experiments should have been carried out on a smaller scale. The result was disastrous for all failed. The causes of failure were various. The planters were quite ignorant of the nature of the tea plant and the treatment it required, and how the green leaf is to be manufactured. All imagined that they had merely to sow the seed and reap a golden harvest. Few possessed any reserve capital sufficient to carry them over the years of initial experiment and loss. They could not subsist without an immediate return of their capital which was, in the nature of things, impossible. In 1857 Dr. Jameson calculated that in the Doon there were 1,00,000 acres land capable of bearing tea. However in 1947 there were 22 tea estates covering an area of about 5,500 acres producing nearly 9,00,000 kilograms of tea. Unfortunately, because of urbanisation pressure on land and government apathy tea in the valley is on its way out, unless a miracle happens and the tea industry is revived.

Rhea cultivation was also attempted in the Doiwala region. It is a plant which is a native of China and Japan and was probably brought into the Doon along with tea. It is known as China Grass, Ramie or Rhea grass in English, Kankura in Hindi and Rhea in Assamese. It is a low hairy shrub and grows in warm temperate regions of lower Himalaya of Assam. The plant is known for its fibre which is 3 to 16 inches long, beautiful, lustrous and stronger than cotton fibre. The fibre is hardly affected by climatic conditions, chemicals or sea-water, is neither elastic nor flexible and does not stretch or shrink when washed. The thread made out of the fibre can be used in the manufacture of non-creasable and rot proof textile fabrics, carpets, plush, gas mantles etc. and as a substitute for cotton wool and flax. In Japan it was a favourite fibre for making fishing nets and paper pulp for Bank note paper. The plant's Botanical name is *Boehmeria nivea* of the Family-Urticaceae. The experiment failed and its cultivation in the Doon was abandoned.

By the beginning of the current century the Doon had become famous for its five Cs—Chobe (timber), Chuna (lime-stone), Chawal (Basmati rice), Chai (tea) and Chestnuts.

In 1823 Shore and his military counterpart, Capt. Young, erected a shooting box on Camel's Back hill, the first house in Mussoorie. Another small house was built shortly afterwards somewhere on the Kulri hill. The splendid climate and the good sport obtainable gradually attracted other Europeans, as the Doon became better known. In 1827 the Company's Government established a convalescent depot for British soldiers at Landhaur. On the establishment of the Depot Capt. Young, as Commandant of Landhaur Cantonment, built Mullingar as his residence. This building is still recognisable and inhabited. Below it another house came up as a chummery and was called White-Park-Forest named after the three men who chummed up (shared) in this house.

By 1829 there were a number of houses in Mussoorie. The park was built by Col. Whish in 1827. About this time Capt. Kirke, and one or two others whose names are amongst the first in the old Municipal "householders' register", had commenced building. It is recorded that a merchant named Lawrence came up in 1828 with a stock of miscellaneous goods for sale and built a hut for himself and his goods on the Camel's Back. From this it is evident that there must have been something of a European population by that time to purchase from him. The two, Landhaur and Mussoorie, were, at first entirely separate. The convalescent depot was on top of the Landhaur hill; Mussoorie showed a tendency to keep well to the west in the direction of Hatipaon and Cloud End. The station is supposed to have been named after the Mansur or Mansuri (*Coriaria nepalensis*) shrub which grew in abundance on these hills. Probably the story is the same as the naming of Calcutta where an Englishman pointing towards a freshly cut tree, asked a native the name of the place. The native thinking that the Sahib wanted to know as to when the tree had been cut answered "Kaalcata" (Kaal = Yesterday + Cata = Cut). Similarly it seems that when the name of the locality was asked for from the native, he thinking it was the name of the plant being asked for, answered "Mansuri". The government officials eventually dropped the 'n' calling the place Masuri or Mussoorie. To-day the Landhaur section is also known as Mussoorie except that the military part of it has a separate civic Cantonment Board. The Mussoorie Municipal Board was established in 1842 having its office in the Kutchery compound.

Early in May 1833 Col. Sir George Everest, F.R.S., C.B., Kt., established his office in Mussoorie, on being appointed as the Surveyor-General and Superintendent Great Trigonometrical Survey. He was to spend the next ten years of his life in India, with Mussoorie as his summer headquarters, and moving to Dehra for the winter. In December 1832 he had bought the estate called the Park, near Hatipaon (elephant's foot) in Mussoorie from Col. Whish who had built a house there in 1827. Working from here he brought the Great Arc, in the next eight years, 500 miles north from Central India to the Himalaya. Everest was one of those officers who at work spared neither himself nor anyone else. He was also the first departmental head who had direct access to the Company's government at Calcutta and reported only to the Adjutant-General of the Bengal army. Everest had purchased the Park as his personal property for residence. Mr. Morrison, Everest's Office Registrar was accommodated in the old brewery of Henry Bohle north-east of the Park which had been taken on rent. The brewery situated in the Mackinon Park area, had been started by Bohle, who had come up from Meerut, in 1830, but had to be closed in 1832 when the estate was purchased by a Mr. Parsons who sold it in 1835 to John Mackinon, Bohle's son-in-law. John Mackinon was a retired army school master from Elgin in Scotland. After buying the property he opened the first school in Mussoorie calling it the Mussoorie Seminary. Everest offered to use his influence with the Superintendent of the Doon, Col. Young, to obtain ground for building on the range west of the Park and adjoining it, for any of his subordinates who would apply to him. In the interim Everest was willing to allow such persons as desired it, and could not otherwise accommodate themselves, to erect temporary structures on suitable spots on his estate on the express understanding that the ground would be vacated at two month's notice and the building removed. His office was established at the Park with accommodation for the staff. Water was a problem, as it still is, and he had to engage eight mules for transporting it every day. He wanted to build an observatory and a workshop at the Park, but the government turned down his request as it was not intended to have his office permanently at Mussoorie. Everest again wrote giving various reasons and hoping the government may relent, but on 1st February, 1834 a firm order was issued forbidding all civil and military departments to have their offices permanently in the hills. Perforce he had to move his staff down to Dehra where they were accommodated in tents and the office of the Surveyor-General was established on a ground near the Rispana river, where the Old Survey Road now runs. The site was acquired from a Zamindar of Karanpur. The office of the Great Trigonometrical Survey remained at Hatipaon where Everest would retire during the monsoons along with his field staff and do his calculations. From time to time he erected various buildings of a temporary nature at the Park.

For this purpose, in his usual peremptory way Everest ordered the Kotwal (Police Chief) of Saharanpur to immediately send four wood sawyers to Mussoorie as they were required there for "Public Service". The Kotwal placed the order before his District Magistrate. The Magistrate wrote to Everest pointing out that though it was the duty of the civil authorities to aid the Survey department in every legal way yet it is doubtful if the Surveyor-General has the authority to issue such orders without routing them through the proper channel. At another time Everest was addressed as "Kumpass Wala Sahib" (Officer-in-charge of the Compass) in an application for pension from one of his native employees. The application had been sent through Young, the District Magistrate of the Doon, who forwarded it in original. Everest took offence at being addressed as such and wrote back to Young that the correct designation is Surveyor-General and Superintendent of the Great Trigonometrical Survey of India, and that no correspondence should be sent wherein the low, familiar appellative "Compasswala", which may be in common use in the bazar language, is used. The vernacular title is "Surveyor General Kishewar Hind".

Everest's Dehra office, under the Registrar Mr. Morrison was situated alongside the office-cum-residence of Lieutenant Henry Kirke, who was Young's Station Staff Officer and Adjutant of the Sirmur Battalion. Incidentally Kirke was one of the first lot of officers who had been given a grant in the Doon. The Survey Field Party's camp followers were also living, in grass huts, in their office compound along with the Department's transport animals. This started a battle royal between Morrison and Kirke over some cattle and mules straying into Kirke's adjoining compound and vice versa.

One Sunday morning one of Morrison's mules strayed into Kirke's compound and was tied up by the latter's staff. On learning of it Morrison wrote a polite note asking for the return of the mule and offering to pay for any damage that it might have done. Kirke demanded two annas (2 annas = 12 paise today) as fine which was paid, and the mule was released. A few days later a herd of cattle, belonging to Kirke, strayed into the Survey compound and destroyed some of the huts of the staff living there. The cattle had been coming almost daily to feed on the grass of the huts.

Morrison had four of the cattle tied up under the charge of the Gorkha sentry on duty in the Survey compound and waited for the owner to come and have them released. Kirke instead of following his own example, of paying a fine, ordered one of his havildars (Sergeants) and four men with fixed bayonets to enter the Survey compound, forcibly release the cattle in defiance of the sentry under whose charge they were placed. This was accordingly done and Kirke in a note to Morrison commanded him to send the cattle to the Station pound, which was situated in the former's compound. Because the Gorkha guard hesitated in handing over the cattle to Kirke's men, and because the guards at the Survey office were from the Sirmur battalion, Kirke ordered extra drill to their havildar-in-charge because the sentry had taken orders from Morrison, who was a civilian. After this incident Kirke removed the old guard detachment from the Survey compound and posted a new one. Explicit instructions were given to the Guard Commander that they were to guard only the government treasure chest kept in the office. The guard was not to accompany the Survey party bringing money from the Treasury or guard the money going from the office to the Surveyor-General's camp. The guard commander was further directed to report to Kirke and take orders only from him.

When all this was reported to Everest in writing he lost no time in drafting a report to the Commander-in-Chief. Before sending it on, a copy of it was sent to Young for information. Young immediately reacted and put his adjutant in his place, who apologised profusely to Everest. The guard would in future be directly under Major Everest's command. Young, however, did not close the affair till he had explained to Everest his subordinate's side of the whole affair and put the blame on Morrison. In spite of this unpleasant episode Kirke named his grant of land "Arcadia" in honour of the Great Arc of Triangulation for measuring the size of the earth. This land is four miles west of Dehra and two miles north of the east end of Everest's base line. It is now known as Arcadia Tea Estate, and forms a part of the land belonging to the Dehra Dun Tea Co., Ltd., some area of which has been acquired by the Indian Military Academy. This was a typical case of the supercilious attitude of army-men towards their civilian counterparts.

Everest had another tiff with Young, this time in the latter's civil capacity as Collector of Excise. The Survey "Khalassies" or "Lascars", as the native Class IV employees were called, were supposed to be distilling their own country liquor for their personal consumption, thereby depriving the government of excise revenue. Young informed Everest that except under the authority of a license from government, it was unlawful for anyone to manufacture any excisable product, and for this purpose government had issued licenses to two local Indians to distil liquor for sale. Young also suggested that in order to check illicit manufacture, a regular liquor shop may be permitted to be opened in the Survey Estate, as the local brew was as necessary to many natives as a dram of Rum to the European soldier. In case the shop was not allowed to be established Young would have to report to the Commissioner the loss that government would incur by way of excise revenue. To this Everest replied that in his own Regiment, which was Bengal Artillery, European troops were debarred access to shops where alcoholic liquor or intoxicating drugs were sold and this prohibition was general in the army. The consumption of such articles was considered detrimental to discipline and health. As for the opening of a shop and the loss of government revenue, in the absence of it, he asked Young to quote the Rule by which it was incumbent on a government department to open such a shop. He further assured that as soon as the Rule was quoted it would be complied with. No shop was opened.

In February 1835 and then again later in the year Everest became seriously ill and was confined to bed, totally deprived of the use of his left leg from the hip downwards. During his second illness he was once bled to the verge of fainting, had more than 1000 leeches attached to the hip, over 30 cupping glasses, 3 blisters and medicines. Fortunately with this treatment he was able to recover the use of his limb and to carry on his work of triangulation. While in the field, Everest once spent fifteen days on the Gwalior-Dholpur frontier because the former ruler, in spite of prior information, had not sent a suitable escort to receive him with ceremony and accompany him into the State territory. He crossed over only when he was ceremonially escorted across. Because of his illness Everest requested the Governor-General, Lord Auckland, whom he met at Saharanpur on 11th March, 1838, to give an Assistant who would help with the heavy office work. Auckland asked for a medical opinion on Everest's health and on the basis of this a Deputy Surveyor-General was appointed at Calcutta and an Assistant Surveyor-General was posted to Dehra Dun. Everest was promoted Lieutenant Colonel in March, 1838 and he wrote a memorial, to the Court of Directors pressing to be made a Companion of the Bath. In it he mentioned the names of 22 brother officers of the Company's service who had been so honoured whilst he had been deprived of it. He had to wait 20 years before he got the honour. In 1839 he put up a temporary observatory and workshop at Hathipaon for training his assistants in astronomical observations. In 1837 the Directors had provisionally approved of Major Thomas Jervis to succeed Everest in case his health failed and he had to quit. Jervis in his impatience had a pamphlet, containing some papers and addresses praising his own work as Surveyor and that of Everest's as a thing of the past and including an address of the Duke of Sussex, President Royal Society, printed and circulated amongst scientists connected with survey work. A copy of it was sent to Everest also. On reading the publication he was cut to the quick. Since he and the Duke were Freemasons, Everest wrote a series of letters to him remonstrating against the conduct of the Royal Society in praising Jervis. On realising that Everest was not going to quit in a hurry Jervis left India in 1841. The same year Everest completed his field work on the Great Arc. A pressman of that time writes about it, ''Measuring an arc of the meridian-----In this stupendous work the Surveyor-General has surpassed the European astronomers----but unless the arc is used as the backbone of a web of triangles to be thrown across the continent of India it is of little practical value.---- He (Everest) might have combined----the Revenue and trigonometrical operations, and furnished a map of India as correct as there is of any part of the world. ---- Completed one of the most stupendous works in the whole history of science. No scientific man ever had a grander monument to his memory than the Great Meridional Arc of India.----The whole conception of the Survey as it now exists was the creation of his brain''.

In September, 1843 Everest left the Doon which had been his headquarters for ten continuous years and sailed for home from Calcutta on 16th December, 1843. Before leaving Mussoorie he appointed Capt. Murray, one of his neighbours, as his attorney to sell his house in Dehra and ''The Park'' in Mussoorie.

Col. Robert Thatcher of Bengal Infantry bought ''The Park'' in 1861. He also bought the adjoining estate of Dobri with its luxuriant Sal forest. In 1863 ''The Park'' was purchased by Col. James Skinner, who re-sold it almost at once as his family found it too remote. It was bought by John Mackinnon who left it to his sons the brewers. Their descendants sold it to an Indian a Dehra family—the Shahs. It has now been acquired by the State Government for setting up a tourist complex. A grandson and a grand daughter of Thatcher were living in Mussoorie till thirty years ago. Everest's Dehra house, 9 Old Survey Road, was bought by Murray himself and was sold after his daughter's death in the 1950's. Amongst Everest's neighbours at the time were William Fraser, the Resident at Delhi, owning Leopard Lodge and Major Swetenham who owned Cloud End estate, west of the Park.

At the suggestion of his successor Andrew Waugh Everest's name was given to the world's highest mountain. This naming has been a matter of controversy as it was alleged in some quarters that Everest named it after himself and, Waugh had nothing to do with it. It was further alleged that it was Radhanath Sikdar, one of Everest's computers, who had determined the height and position of the mountain. The best comment came in a letter to the Editor of ''Standard'' in 1905 which concluded: ''It was not Everest but his officers who placed his name just a little nearer the stars than that of any other lover of the eternal glory of the mountains. There let it stay, in witness to the faithful work, not of one man but of scores of men''.

Like so many other Englishmen who made the Doon their temporary home, during their stay in India, Everest was one of them save that he won international fame, more because of the mountain.

The owner of Cloud End was Major Swetenham. How he came in possession of the property is like the fairy-tale of the Sleeping Beauty and the Prince. Major Swetenham who was the Commandant of the Invalids establishment at Landhaur, and some friends were out on "Shikar" (hunting) near the village in the vicinity of Cloud End. Whilst the party was taking a break from the exertions of shikar a feminine voice burst forth into song startling them. The language was Garhwali but the dulcet timbre of the voice compelled Swetenham to investigate. At the sight of the stranger the singer naturally stopped singing and ran away from the scene. On being followed she turned out to be the only child of the local Garhwali Zamindar. Swetenham was so smitten by her that he persuaded her father to allow them to marry. Thus the local village belle became Mrs. Swetenham. The couple settled on her father's estate and built a house which was called Cloud End. Their Zamindari extended right down to the foot of the Bhadraj hill which was also a part of it. All the six sons that she bore became Colonels in the British Indian army. One of them, Col. R.A. Swetenham, was a signatory to the Charter of the Dehra Dun Club when it became a Limited (By Guarantee) Company in 1901. One of the grand daughters Louise Swetenham apparently inherited the old lady's voice and became one of Mussoorie's most popular 'Nightingales'. Another grand daughter married a nephew of the Victoria Cross holder Raynor, a man called H.G. Raynor, whose descendants are still living in Dehra. He and his wife were the joint owners of Udyabagh Tea Estate. The land came in her dowry as her Zamindari, while he cultivated it as a tenant by planting tea bushes on it. They had two children a son and a daughter. Raynor got annoyed with his children and disinherited them and willed his property to his son's children as the daughter was childless. The wife on the other hand willed her property in equal shares to the son and daughter. The son in his turn disinherited his sons and left every thing to his daughters. Darbar Guru Ram Rai is now the owner of the above mentioned tea estate along with the neighbouring one called Goodrich. In the course of time Cloud End estate, in its present size, came to the share of two of the grand daughters of the original Swetenham's. In 1965 Col. E.W. Bell husband of one of them sold the estate before leaving for England to Mr. Durga Ram Agarwal for a sum of Rs. 37,000/-. Mr. Agarwal was the last Manager of Kaulagarh Tea Estate, before it became a housing colony.

The site where the "Mussoorie Library" building is situated once belonged to Mr. Scott and Mr. Pitt who sold it to Major Swetenham. In 1843 a Mussoorie Library Committee was formed with Mr. Vansittart, the then Superintendent of the Doon, as its President. The funds for the project were collected by subscription and a sum of Rs. 2,500/- was collected in the first year. Major Swetenham sold the land for a sum of Rs. 300/- and it was transferred in the name of Mr. Vansittart, "to be held for ever in trust for, and on behalf of the Mussoorie Library Committee". The Library stands on the flat below Savoy Hotel and next to it is the Band Stand. On the ground floor are shops which are a source of income to it while the Library proper is on the first floor. In the days of yore a band, belonging to one of the British regiments, posted either in Mussoorie or in Dehra used to play for an hour every Wednesday and Saturday evenings. On these evenings the upper verandah of the Library was hired to the Savoy

Hotel for use as a Restaurant. Since the Library was the White Man's preserve the Sahib and his Memsahib would partake of cucumber sandwiches and tea while listening to music. A notice at the Library entrance read "Dogs and Indians not allowed" till the end of World War I. A High Court Judge an Indian, who had come from Madras, threatened to take the Committee to court unless the word "Indian" was removed. After a lot of correspondence the words were substituted by the words "Rights of admission reserved"

The Band-Stand bears the following inscription:-

Erected 1915

This Bandstand was presented

To

The Mussoorie Municipality

by

H.H. Jagatjit Singh Bahadur, G.C.S.I.

Maharaja of Kapurthala

"The Chateau" is the Kapurthala palace in Mussoorie, just above the Savoy Hotel. It is one of the most picturesque buildings of the station built in French style, by Jagatjit Singh who was one of the earliest Indian rulers to patronise the hill station, till his death. No other Indian Prince has left behind such a landmark.

When in 1826 the British were unable to enter the fort of Bharatpur, Lord Combermere asked for Gorkha soldiers to lead the assault on the place. The Sirmur Gorkhas having seen action under the British at Sitapur and under Ochterlony in the Maratha campaign, were told to send two Companies to Bharatpur. They led the assault on the fort which was perched on top of a hill, and were the first to enter and capture it. This was their first battle honour. During the battle Capt. Mundy who was present noticed an action of a Gorkha Sergeant which he has recorded. It reads as under:-

"During the siege of Bhurtpore, and after our parallels had been pushed to within 300 yards of the counterscarp, a white horse was observed to be picketed close under an outwork of the fort, and in a situation so exposed to the fire of both besiegers and besieged, that no one on either side seemed willing to run the risk incident upon an attempt to appropriate him. The neutral nag was therefore in a fair way of being shot or starved to death. Our hero—the Gorkha Sergeant doubtless too poor to be well mounted—cast the eye of covetousness upon the snowy charger; and one morning, determined to, 'do or die', jumped over the gabions, and, running across the glacia, reached the horse, cut him adrift, and, under a heavy fire of musketry from the walls, trotted him in triumph into the trenches, himself unscathed, and his prize receiving only one bullet through the nose, which scarcely blemished him. The right of conquest is so well established in British India, that there is no fear of the gallant Sergeant being disturbed in his acquisition."

In 1846 the "Sirmoor Gorkhas" were engaged in the first Anglo-Sikh war and were in time to save Ludhiana from being plundered by the Sikhs, whom they fought at Aliwal on the road from Ludhiana to Ferozepur. The battle took place on 16th January, 1846 at the spot now commemorated by an obelisk inscribed in English, Persian and Gurmukhi, the language of the Sikhs. They fought them again at Sobraon in the same region. In 1848, the Regiment was again on service at Ludhiana, and remained there until the end of the second Anglo-Sikh war.

The town of Dehra started growing along the sides of Saharanpur and Rajpur Roads, from the iron bridge on the Bindal in the south to the Bodyguard lines in the north. The best houses were built in the northern part of the town by people, mostly English, who were intending to establish permanent homes in India. These houses were surrounded by acres of land, often bordered by hedges of wild roses, which would be a sight to behold, when in full bloom in April-May. An example of such a property was the estate called Nashville. The road by that name is still there. Before this estate was broken up it consisted of a solitary house standing in a compound of 16 acres. Its history is interesting as it shows the rapid development of Dehra. The property was sold at the beginning of the present century for Rs. 20,000/- and was divided into building plots. The original boundaries of the estate were Nashville road in the north, the ravine in the west, Rajpur road in the east and the road between Manda House and New Empire Cinema in the south. The purchaser then sold the original building and the central portion of the compound to Fitch & Co. Ltd., a department store. In 1910 there were seven bungalows apart from Fitch's where the Kwality Motel is to-day. The Raja of Manda, the father of Raja Vishwanath Pratap Singh one of the controversials of Indian politics, had bought his property for Rs. 20,000/- with a house built of sun-baked bricks. To-day the original compound is a sprawling residential cum business cum shopping complex. Establishments like Kwality restaurant, Congress Bhawan, the Odeon Cinema Complex, Bombay, Punjab and Lahore Jewellers, Perfection House, Bindrabuns etc., which are well known names in this part of U.P. are all housed in Nashville estate. Similar was the case with the estate, bounded on all four sides by roads, called Astley Hall, which was at one time the property of "Pahari or Raja or Shikari" Wilson, an Englishman who came to Garhwal in the 1840s without any antecedents. Nobody seems to know his full name except the initial F. which appears on his coins. He is known as Pahari (hill-man) because he lived most of his life in the Himalaya mountains, having made his home at Harsil, Raja because he became so rich and powerful in that region that he minted his own currency for his use in his business, and Shikari because he started his career by making a living by hunting and selling wild animals and birds. No body knows exactly where he came from. According to a local legend he either killed a fellow soldier in a quarrel and escaped from being prosecuted under law or else he deserted from the army during the disastrous Afghan War of 1841. Wilson himself seems to have told people that he was a native of Wakefield, in Yorkshire, whose destiny had led him to India and because of poor health had come to Landhaur from where he decided to move into the inner hills. Either way he seems to have deserted his former associations and settled in Tehri State around 1840s. In the beginning his skill as a hunter enabled him to make a living by shooting, preserving and sending to Calcutta for sale skins and stuffed specimens of the exotic birds and animals of the Himalaya including the Musk pod. Within ten years he had established himself as a leading businessman of Garhwal and became the first forest contractor in the area. He made Harsil, a seven day march from Mussoorie, his summer headquarters where he built a huge house which is to-day the Forest Department's rest-house. In this house he had established his harem and the story goes that each of the rooms which opened on to a central court-yard was allotted to a Pahari belle, each one prettier than the other. His favourite, however, was Gulabi who is supposed to have been legally married to him. She bore him a son and a daughter, named Charles and Irene respectively. In the chronicles of Mussoorie one reads about Charles who is referred to as Mr. C. Wilson. He was living at Astley Hall along with his sister and was known to the Gazders, an old Parsi business family settled in the Doon. One of the Gazder daughters Tamy married Noshir Kapadia, the Dental Surgeon, and are now living in a part of Astley Hall. She remembers Charlie Wilson as one of those immaculately dressed individuals, complete with spats, silver mounted cane and a top hat. Gulabi Wilson would be seen, dressed in fashionable hats and gowns brought out from England, driving around Dehra in her carriage and pair. Raja Wilson's fortune, in 1875, was estimated at over £ 1,50,000/-.

It seems that the Wilsons not only owned Astley Hall but other houses also in Dehra and Mussoorie. According to Lady Dufferin, the then Viceroy's wife, who with her family spent a holiday in Dehra had rented "a bungalow here from a native lady who married a white man and who is now enjoying his fortune as a widow." This was in the year 1887. There is a misconception in the minds of some of Wilson's biographers about his owning the "Charleville Hotel" (now Lal Bahadur Shastri Academy) in Mussoorie and have woven quite a story about how it acquired the name. The Wilsons never owned or rented this property or ran a hotel in it. The main building of the hotel was built by General Wilkinson in 1854 on the Chajauli estate. In 1861 the property was purchased by Mr. Hobson a retired Manager of Mussoorie Bank, who started the hotel.

Perhaps in the rest of the world the "Charleville" hotels, restaurants and what not would be correctly called "Sharly-Ville" but in the case of Mussoorie it is not so. The literal pronunciation should be "Charlie-Willy" for it was the combination of the names of the two sons of Mr. Hobson, Charlie and Willy, that gave the hotel its name. In March 1905, the Princess of Wales (later Queen Mary) visited the Doon. In Mussoorie she stayed at the Charleville Hotel-the only hotel in India to be so honoured. Amongst the souvenirs she took home with her were some of Landhaur bazar's walking sticks for her father-in-law, King Edward VII, as he was a collector of them. She also planted a tree, on the morning of March 4th, in the compound of Christ Church which is still standing, with a plaque giving its legend.

It may be mentioned here that around 1870s there was a tea estate called "Charleville" in the Doon Valley. It was owned by the widow of General Dick and formed a part of the Dalanwala grant.

Amongst some of the properties owned by the Wilsons, at some point of time or the other, are "Castle Hill" estate and the skating "Rink" in Mussoorie.

Castle Hill Estate in Landhaur comprises of two properties namely Woodcroft and Green-mount which belonged to Mr. Bleden Taylor. This estate was bought by the East India Company's government in 1853 as a residence for Maharaja Dalip Singh, son of Maharaja Ranjit Singh the 'Lion of the Punjab'. After the annexation of the Punjab by Dalhousie, Dalip Singh was sent to Mussoorie, to reside there whilst his mother escaped to Nepal. The same year he became a convert Christian and a year later he and his cousin Prince Shiv Deo Singh were sent to England. Rani Jindan, Dalip's mother, also joined him there whilst her Chief Minister and paramour, Raja Lal Singh, came and settled in the Doon. On her death Dalip Singh brought her ashes to India for immersion in the Ganga at Haridwar.

After Dalip Singh's departure the government sold the property to Mr. F. Wilson from whom it passed into the hands of Mr. Vansittart, a former Superintendent of the Doon, for a song. On this estate is a tunnel which is not natural but was bored by the Pioneer detachment to carry water from "Khattapani" to Kulri hill for supplying it to Mussoorie residents. In 1908 the government repurchased the Estate for Rs. 3,00,000/- for accommodating some of the Survey of India offices.

The "Rink" was built in 1890 for a Dental Surgeon named Miller. The land for this building was given to the Dentist by one of his patients who could not pay in cash for services rendered, probably a set of artificial dentures. It was run by a person who had started the first Rink in India at Calcutta. It did well at first and a Company called the Mussoorie Skating Rink and Amusement Club Ltd., was formed. A couple of years later the Company failed and the property was purchased by Mr. Charles Wilson in 1894 and the skating Rink, the largest in size in north India, is still a place of amusement for the people. When built, the entire premises were the first ones in town to be lighted by Acetelyne gas.

So much for the Wilsons.

With the advent of the British Raj in the Doon Bell, Book and Candle (the Christian Missionaries) were bound to follow. One such Reverend who has earned a place in the Doon's annals was Mr. J.S. Woodside. He arrived in the Valley in 1853 from the Ludhiana Mission and commenced his holy work by establishing a branch of that mission. In this he was aided by the sole native Christian, then residing in the Doon called Gilbert MacMaster. He was an orphan who had been baptised and educated at the Saharanpur Christian Orphanage. Starting as a scripture reader MacMaster had risen to be the pastor of the Church for the Natives since they were not allowed to the white man's Hall of Prayer. At first Mr. Woodside and his mission met with some opposition. The Missionaries were accused of resorting to illegitimate means of gaining converts, among others, of kidnapping children. They were supposed to be sent to the Mission at Saharanpur, carefully nailed down in boxes for conversion. Woodside also faced difficulty in obtaining land to start a school since the Mahant, who owned most of the land in the native quarters of the town did not want to encourage interlopers by giving them land. To Woodside's good fortune the Lieutenant-Governor of the North-West Province, Mr. Colvin, happened to visit the Doon in early 1854. Woodside presented his problems before him. Colvin ordered that a part of the present Tehsil's compound be placed at Woodside's disposal. Before these orders could be implemented a new Superintendent Mr. Dunlop, took charge of the Doon. He objected to interference with the Tehsil's compound and instead bought a piece of land from his own pocket and gifted it to the Mission. To-day on this land stands the American Presbyterian Mission Boys' High School in the middle of Paltan Bazar and is over 125 years old. Revd. J.S. Woodside was its first Headmaster. In 1859 the Dehra Christian Girls' Boarding School was started under the supervision of Rev. Herron. This is situated off Rajpur Road adjoining the District Magistrate's residence. Woodside's thrust towards conversion was through the medium of education. In 1857 a native Christian colony was established at Annfield in the Western Doon by the Meerut Christian Mission. There the agriculturist converts were established and given land to cultivate. There is quite a sizeable native Christian population in the area and some foreign missionaries are still carrying on their good work of spreading the gospel amongst the heathen. Some of the missionaries at times stray from the path and indulge in playing politics. Government then has to take the unpleasant action of asking them to leave the country.

Woodside thought of expanding the missionary activities on a grand scale. He drew up a plan for colonising, with native Christians, nearly 8,000 acres of land in the Western Doon. Every new convert family was to be given five acres of land in the colony, to build a house and cultivate it, absolutely free of cost. For this purpose he issued a prospectus in the United States and England in February 1873. The synopsis of the scheme as given in 1874, by Williams in his Memoir of the Doon is:-

182

"I may conclude this Appendix by mentioning an enterprise which deserves to be signalised on account of its daring, if for no other reason; the purchase of nearly 8,000 acres of land, forming a part of the Old Hope Town grant at an upset price of Rs. 2,00,000 by the Rev. Mr. Woodside, from the Dehra Doon Tea Company, for the purpose of founding a Native Christian Colony. His plan was to divide the whole into 1,600 shares of 5 acres each. The value of one acre being a fraction under Rs. 24, a five acre share would therefore be Rs. 120/-, and 'parties contributing one share would secure the support of a family'. The word share, however, is calculated to mislead, because, the project not being a commercial, but a charitable, one, each shareholder merely has the right to nominate a Christian family to reside in the Colony, so that the money invested is properly speaking, a donation held in trust by the American Mission. The contributions had reached Rs. 15,595/- on the 1st March, 1873, but Mr. Woodside took leave to England not long after, and it is to be feared, not much has been done since in the way of collecting subscriptions nor do Christian colonists seem over-anxious to occupy the land. In February 1873, three families were located there, and subsequently some others 'calling themselves Christians', strangers to the Doon, accepted employment. Unfortunately, most of these turned out to be really vagrants, and took the first opportunity of absconding. One of the most earnest advocates of the scheme is Mr. Login, C.E., F.R.S.E., who has written a very enthusiatic letter on the subject. The marked succees of his own experiment in cotton farming renders him sanguine about the future of the Colony, to the practical working of which he generously offers the aid of his own experience. I myself, on the other hand, am of opinion that Mr. Login's engineering and agricultural skill, even when backed up by Mr. Woodside's indomitable energy can never make such a project succeed, and I should not be surprised to see the land again in the market before long."

As forecast by Williams, the project failed and the lands purchased from the Dehra Dun Tea Co., Ltd., were sold in 1881 to the East Hope Town Estate Co., Ltd., of which Revd. Woodside was one of the promoters and original shareholders. This Company owns East Hope Town Tea Estate adjoining Arcadia Tea Estate. The area purchased was not 8000 acres but approximately 3500 acres. At one time not long ago the yield and profits of this tea estate were the highest in North India. Thus Woodside ultimately went the way of all flesh by becoming an entrepreneur from a missonary. He and his zealous missionaries were, probably, indirectly responsible for the establishment of Arya Samaj in Dehra Dun in 1879.

Two Hindu boys Baldev Singh and Mohar Singh were students in the Mission School in Dehra. They belonged to the family of Lala Nand Lal, Pratap Singh, Mana Ram and Tulsi Ram, one of the richest Hindu landlords of the town and whose descendants are still living in the Doon. In their school the boys were taught the teachings of Christ to the exclusion of all other faiths. There developed a conflict, within their minds, with regard to their own religious beliefs which could not be resolved by the local Hindu pundits. The boys gave an ultimatum that unless their doubts regarding Hinduism were resolved within six months they would become Christians. The parents were naturally upset and worried. A Brahmin clerk working in the Forest Department wrote to Swami

Dayanand Saraswati, the Reformist and Founder of the Arya Samaj movement, explaining the situation and inviting him to come to Dehra and help the people in solving the problem of conversion of the boys. This was in February 1879. The Swamiji arrived in Dehra on 14th April from Haridwar where he had been attending the Kumbh Mela. He was put up at the bungalow of Miss Dick, on Rajpur Road, which had been hired for his stay. She was the daughter of General Dick of Dalanwala. Dayanand sent for the two boys and had a debate with them and in a short time he was able to satisfy them resulting in their giving up all thoughts of conversion. The missionaries then threatened the boys that the District Magistrate would be offended with them and their family, if they did not convert to Christianity. But the boys and their family did not care about the threats. To show his gratitude to Swamiji their father offered a substantial sum of money to him which he declined, and advised the father to open a Sanskrit language school with it. This wish of Swamiji's was later carried out by Baldav Singh when he gifted a property towards the project.

Swami Dayanand stayed in Dehra till 30th April, 1879. During his stay he delivered nine discourses on various aspects of different religions. In one of these which was on the "Existence of God" he freely commented on the Biblical concept of the Deity. Amongst the audience of about 500 people there were five Europeans present namely, Reverend Morrison, Col. Bright and Messrs Palmer, Guertlain and Crown who owned a chemist shop in town. The missionary was deeply offended at Swamiji's comments, and on the termination of his speech got up and in an angry tone said, "The pundit sahib has done nothing but kick up dust, and hiding his Vedic faith in that dust". After saying these words Morrison started to dispose of the objections which Swami Dayanand had, both directly and indirectly, brought against the Christian concept of God. Dayanand patiently listened to Morrison and after he had finished speaking got up to reply. This was not liked by the irate missionary and in his rage and frustration he started interrupting the speaker. The other Europeans at last could not help remonstrating with the Padree on his strange conduct observing that the Swami was proving his contention in temperate language and in a perfectly rational manner, and that the Doctor should extend the same courtesy to him as he himself had received when speaking. This infuriated the Padree even more and in angry tones he answered: "I am replying to the man in a proper way. If you think my answer is not proper, you had better go and join him". Having said this he went away from the meeting.

After he had gone Palmer and Guertlain approached Dayanand and asked him to give them some time to talk with him in private, to which he agreed. As the meeting started in the verandah of the bungalow Mr. Bipin Bose, a native Christian and Headmaster of the Mission School for boys, in town, came edging in and interrupted the meeting by speaking in favour of the Bible. A dialogue ensued between him and Swami Dayanand. The interruption was not liked by Palmer and Guertlain and a discussion took place between him and Bose, which lasted till midnight.

It was not only the Christians who were upset at Dayanand's lectures, the Muhammadans and Brahmo Smajists also were in a state of agitation. The Mussalmans were more desperate than the others and at one time an irate mob of them marched upto the bungalow, which was made of thatch, and it was feared that they might set fire to it. Better counsel must have prevailed as the crowd peacefully withdrew.

An educated Muslim contractor from Saharanpur was regular in attending Dayanand's public discourses. He was so convinced by Vedic thought that he decided to give up Islam and convert to Hinduism as preached by Dayanand. A request was made to Dayanand who did the first conversion to his faith, at Dehra, by baptising Mohammad Umar son of Khwaja Hussain, as a Hindu and renaming him as Alakhdhari. He became one of the supporting pillars of the local Arya Samaj, which was founded on 29th June, 1879, and continued to be so till his death in 1917. Swami Dayanand paid another visit to Dehra in October 1880. This time there was a public debate between him and Padree Gilbert MacMaster, Woodside's native assistant. Once again the Padree lost his temper and left the meeting in a huff, without concluding the debate. Swami Dayanand even had a discussion with Mr. Hennessy, an Englishman, from the Survey of India on the scientific treatises in the Veds particularly on the construction and use of the telescope and miscroscope.

By 1835 the European population of Mussoorie was large enough to warrant the building of a church. A meeting of the local Christians was held and a site on Kulri hill was proposed for erecting it. This proposal was objected to by Mackinon on account of the distance from his school, and proposed that the church should be erected out to the west of the station. A compromise was effected and the site selected was where Christ Church (near the Library) now stands. Its tower and nave were built in 1836 by Capt. Rennie Tailyour, of Bengal Engineers, Roorkee. The chancel and trancepts were added in 1853 when Mr. L.D. Hearsey, son of Hyder, presented the bell. Fortunately no problem regarding conversion ever arose in Mussoorie.

For years formal education in Dehra Doon was restricted to the two Mission Schools, till a Government School was started in the compound where the city Kotwali now stands. This was only upto the Primary classes. At the beginning of the 20th Century a local lawyer Mr. Jyoti Swarup, took a keen interest in the field of education. Through his efforts a Dayanand Anglo Vedic School (D.A.V. for short) which was started in Meerut was shifted to Dehra in July 1904. It was established on the land, in village Mansinghwala, donated by one of the local Zamindars Mr. Puran Singh Negi. In the course of time this school became a degree college, and to-day the D.A.V. group of institutions are the largest in the district. They are unfortunately administered from Kanpur because of the apathy of the local people. Mr. Jyoti Swarup's wife Mrs. Mahadevi was keen on women's education and at her behest he started the Mahadevi Kanya Pathshala in 1902. Now it is a premier Post Graduate institution for girls in the District.

The Convent Boarding and Day School, now only a Day School, used to be the only European institution in Dehra for primary education where the medium of teaching was in English. It was established in 1901 and is attached to the Dehra branch of St. Joseph's Convent, which has been here since 1863.

Mussoorie can boast of the first formal European school to be opened in the Doon by Mr. Mackinon (referred to earlier), who started his school, The Mussoorie Seminary, in 1832.

At the time of establishing the Landhaur Convalescent Depot in 1827 a dispute had arisen regarding the boundary line between Pargana Jaunpur of Tehri State and the Doon in connection with some encroachments. Some European settlers had encroached on lands of Kyarkuli villagers and others in Tehri State. The boundary between the two areas was fixed along the crest dividing the South-Western from the North-Eastern watershed of the lower Himalaya range. Thus compensation was accordingly fixed for the land appropriated on the northern slope of the hills, and the British government (later the Mussoorie Municipality) paid rent to Tehri State for its lands under individuals' and government occupation. Therefore the British in a part of Mussoorie were mere tenants of Tehri State with rights of occupancy. This fact was first pointed out by Mr.

Bohle, a merchant from Meerut, to Col. Young. Bohle had set up the first brewery at "Frost Valley", besides a distillery, in 1830 and commenced selling whisky without an excise licence. When questioned on this illegal action he defended it on the ground that his establishment was within the jurisdiction of Tehri State and hence outside the purview of British laws. He eventually accepted the British rule of law. He again got into trouble with Young in 1832. The difficulty seems to have been about supplying beer and whisky to British soldiers who came from Landhaur to the brewery with forged passes. Whether on account of trouble with the authorities, or because he did not find the brewery a paying concern in those days he closed it in 1832 and sold the property to Parsons who in turn sold it to Mackinon, Bohle's son-in-law, in 1835. Bohle came back and reopened the old brewery. He continued working there till 1838 when he built a new one on a spur to the north of the old one and transferred his business to the new premises. According to an account Mackinon, invested a lot of money in the new brewery and Mackinon's beer was extremely popular with the British troops. And then as the story goes, an agent of one of the British competitors, put a dead fly in a mug of Mackinon's beer. This mug of tainted beer with the fly was served to Lord Kitchner, the then Commander-in-Chief in India. Kitchner ordered that Mackinon's beer was not to be served to the troops any more. The year was 1901. Thereafter the brewery venture collapsed and Mackinon lost his fortune.

With the reopening of the "Old Brewery" Mackinon closed his Seminary. The Chaplain of Mussoorie at that time was Revd. Maddock, and he, concluding there was a good opening for a school in the station, got his brother out from England, who started a school on the hill above the Library, known at first as Maddock's—and later on as Stokes'. Mr. Maddock had to struggle at first, but eventually established a first class school. On his retirement in 1865, it was purchased by the Diocesan Board of Education, in pursuance of Bishop Cotton's scheme for the establishment of schools in the hills for boys. Hardy was the first Principal. He was succeeded by Rev. Mr. Stokes and it came to be known as "Stokes' Boys School". At the turn of the century the school seemed to be on the wane and the Diocesan Board decided to close it. The estate was purchased by Barrister Lincoln of Lucknow, who also owned the Carlton Hotel there. He dismantled the school and the Chapel buildings and Savoy Hotel was built on the site. It was opened to the public in 1902.

During World War II there was always a big crowd of British, Indian and American military officers, on leave, in Mussoorie. Amongst the places of amusement was the Savoy which had a ballroom and a billiard room. In those days the only Indian whisky produced was Solan No. 1 which was not popular even with the natives leave alone Europeans. Only Scotch whisky was drunk. The cost of an ordinary brand of Scotch was Rs. 150/- for a bottle. Every morning Lincoln would have all the empty Whisky bottles from the previous day's sale, collected and brought down to the cellar. Here he would squeeze out the last drops of the liquor from each bottle and thus collect one to two bottles of whisky every morning, making two to three hundred rupees as pin money. In 1947 this hotel was purchased from Lincoln's sons by Capt. Kirpa Ram whilst the Carlton Hotel was bought by Mr. Ranjit Singh of Lucknow.

In 1845 the Waverly Convent was started. It comprised of two schools Waverly and Belmont. The former took pupils for full fees and the latter at lower rates, children of Christian indigent parents.

St. George's College was started in 1853 through the efforts of Reverend Mc Tye. It was opened in a cottage known as Manor House, — the name by which the Campus is still known. It was founded by the Archbishop of Patna with the object of educating Roman Catholic children. Later it was taken over by the Capuchin Fathers who handed it over to the Patrician Brothers of Ireland in March 1894 who are still running it.

The next school to make its appearance on the scene was "Woodstock". In 1854 the London Society for Promotion of Female Education in the East sent out a teaching staff to open a school at Mussoorie called the Protestant Girls' School. The Woodstock estate was purchased in 1856 and once the school moved there it came to be known as Woodstock School. In 1873, through the efforts of the good old Revd. Woodside, the property passed into the hands of the Board of Foreign Missions of the American Presbyterian Church and has been under their management ever since.

Another school that appeared and, in time, disappeared was Cainville House School. Its place has been taken by the V Centenary Guru Nanak School. St. Fidelis's School and Military Orphanage was transferred from Shimla to Mussoorie in 1866 and it was run as a second school to St. George's till it was closed in 1940. It was purely a Roman Catholic School for children of the local Christians, and army orphans being subsidised by it. Another one was General Biddulph's Summer Home for soldiers' children started in 1870 and closed in 1947. Another such institution was the "Dumbarnie Orphanage" started in 1896 and closed in 1946. In 1888 Garlah's School was started and Mr. Garlah's progeny was living in Mussoorie till the death of Miss Garlah ten years ago. Philander Smith School moved to Nainital where it functioned till 1947 and is now known as Birla Vidyapeeth. Others were Junior Mussoorie School of Bassett Hall, Mr. Moore's Landhaur Boarding and Day School of Sunny Bank and later Mullingar and Mr. Sheehan's Academy where the Civil Hospital now is.

Hampton Court School was started as a strictly undenominational institution in 1876 by Revd. Henry Sells. In 1895 it was purchased by Miss Holland and named Miss Holland's School. She was the first person to do her M.A. in Latin from the Calcutta University, and won the Roychand Premchand Fellowship. Hampton Court Estate was once the Calcutta Hotel and the locals used to call it "Calcuttiya School". In 1922 it was taken over by the Catholic nuns who are still running it. In 1886 "The Wynberg Homes" including "Bala Hissar" were first started by Mrs. Barton West with two pupils, Peter and Mary Cables. Under the school building was a kiln for making charcoal. One day it burst setting the school building afire. Fortunately no one was hurt. The school was then moved to the Castle Hills estate and then finally to its present site in 1894. It is run as a philanthropic undertaking of a Trust set up by an English industrial house of Kanpur namely the Cooper-Allens, and is now known as Allen Memorial Wynberg Homes.

In 1887 an off-shoot of the Lahore Railway School was started at "Fairlawn" in Jharipani and was known as the Sind-Punjab Railway School, having been started by the Railway Company of that name. In 1888 the East Indian Railway Company associated itself with it and the "Oak Grove" estate was bought. The first building on the new campus was designed by and built under the supervision of Mr. Roskell Bayne the Chief Architect of East Indian Railway Company. The girls section was opened in 1897. Today it partly fulfils the needs of the children of Indian Railway's employees, and has an estate of nearly 250 acres.

All these schools catered to the European, Eurasian and natives' children, mostly Christians, whose parents could not afford to send them to England.

The first vernacular medium school was the Islamia school started by Maulvi Mohammed Sayid in a room in Landhaur Bazar in the year 1906. It was followed by the Arya Kanya Pathshala for girls in 1917. In 1927 the Ghananand High School was started by Radha Balabh Khanduri in memory of his elder brother. Ghananand was the successor to Wilson in working the coniferous forests of Tehri State. In 1928 the Sanatan Dharam Kanya Pathshala, another girls school, was established. The schools sustain the economy of Mussoorie to a great extent as the tourist season is now restricted to three months in the year as against eight months before.

In 1854 Lord Dalhousie appointed a Superintendent to look after the forests in the Doon and Rohilkhand and by 1864 a regular Forest Department was established. In 1877 the Inspector-General of Forests, Dr. Brandis suggested the formation of a Cadre of Forest Rangers. In order to impart a systematic technical training to this class of officials, a Forest School—the first Forest School in the British Empire was founded in 1878. It was called "Central Forest School" and was housed in an impressive building and campus along the southern boundary of the Parade Ground in the heart of the city of Dehra Doon. The Forests of the Doon and Chakrata were set aside as "School Training Forests" and formed into a separate circle under the control of the head of the school who was designated as Director. Captain Bailey (later Colonel) of the Army Engineers, and the inventor of the famous Bailey Bridge which is still in use in war and peace, was appointed the first Director. In 1884, the Government of India took over the management of the School from the Government of North-West Province (now Uttar Pradesh) and put it under the supervision of the Inspector-General of Forests and renamed it as the Imperial Forest School. The same year the Government of India sanctioned the establishment, as an experimental measure, of a class in which the entire course of instruction was given in Hindi and which was to last one year only, and at the end of which qualified students were awarded the Forester's certificate. The experiment proved so successful that the course was conducted regularly till it was abolished in 1907.

In 1889 a higher course for Sub-Assistant Conservators' certificate was added. In 1906 with the inauguration of the Forest Research Institute and Colleges, the status of the school was raised to that of Forest College and named the Imperial Forest College. Rangers were being trained till 1933 when the College had to be closed temporarily on account of the cessation of recruitment resulting from the general economic depression. It was reopened in 1935 and since then has been running regular courses. In 1912 the Government of Madras (now Tamil Nadu) started a Forest College of its own at

Coimbatore. It is now called the Southern Forest Rangers College while the one at Dehra is called the Northern.

Freemasonary came to the Doon in 1854 when "Lodge Dalhousie of Mussoorie and Deyrah" was established. It was named in honour of the then Governor-General Lord Dalhousie, and it met in Mussoorie in summer and in Dehra in winter months hence the two names in its emblem. The first Worshipful Master was A.S. Waugh who had succeeded Everest as the Surveyor-General. The first meeting was held at Mussoorie on 13th June, 1854 and at Dehra Dun on 12th December, 1854. The first Indians to be admitted in it were Messrs Randhir Singh and Bikram Singh in the year 1861, and Maharaja Mipendra Narain Bhup of Cooch Behar was the first Indian to be initiated in 1881. Maharaja Jagatjit Singh of Kapurthala joined in 1894 and became the first Indian Master in 1899. He was a member for 55 years till his death in 1949.

In 1903 Lodge Siwalik was founded at Dehra Dun, and it is now known as Lodge Siwalik Dr. Durga Prashad in honour of one of its illustrious members and a prominent citizen and medical practitioner of Dehra Dun. The two Lodges meet in their respective towns independently of each other.

The year 1857 was a momentous one in the country's history when the first national uprising took place against foreign rule. The Doon, however, remained peaceful throughout except for a small incursion by 600 revolutionaries from Jallandhar. They crossed the Yamuna at Rajghat on 16th June and traversed the Valley. In order to stop them a detachment of the Sirmur Gorkha Rifles was sent under Lieutenants Boyce and Edward. Because of lack of support from the local populace the revolutionaries went back without coming into conflict with the troops. On the other hand several pupils and nuns from various convents in the plains were sent to the Waverly Convent in Mussoorie.

When the news of the uprising reached Mussoorie all the European women collected in the Himalaya Club House for security reasons. The next day the panic subsided. It was no longer safe for Indians to move about after dark, near the military establishment, as armed British soldiers patrolled the area. If any one was found in the area without a satisfactory explanation he was liable to be shot. A person on horse-back was shot dead for not answering fast enough to the challenge of the guards. At the other end of the town boys from Maddock's school were armed and made to patrol the area. Precautions were taken to meet any uprising among the people in the bazaars of Landhaur and Library. The British troops at the Landhaur Convalescent Depot were armed and posted in the bazaars and other parts of the station. European civilian volunteers also patrolled the roads in large numbers every night. With the exception of an alarm on the occasions of Id and Bakr-id, when crackers were let off, nothing occurred to disturb the quiet of the place. It should not be overlooked that it was the height of summer and the European population of Mussoorie was at its maximum. At this time Raja Sudarshan Shah helped the British with men and money. He even posted 200 of his troops along the road from Rajpur to guard Mussoorie against intruders. It is said that the Nawab of Najibabad tried to persuade Sudarshan Shah to join hands against the British which he flatly refused and remained loyal to them throughout. In consideration of his loyalty and services the British are supposed to have thought of giving him the Bijnor region including Najibabad but he wanted the Doon Valley and British Garhwal instead, which had formerly formed parts of his ancestors' kingdom. Negotiations in this regard were progressing when Sudarshan Shah died in June 1859 and the file was closed forever.

Apparently, after this event, in 1865 a cannon was placed, atop the Camel's Back hill also popularly known as Gun Hill, where the main reservoir of Mussoorie's water supply is situated. It was supplied by the Cossipore Ordnance Factory and had been cast by H.H. Maxwell in 1865 according to the inscription on its barrel. It was fired daily at noon ostensibly to tell the public the time, but in all probability to remind the people of the might of the English. The man who fired it was paid six pence a day extra by the army, and an equivalent amount by the local Municipal Board which also met the other incidental expenses. The boom was produced by charging the barrel with moist grass, cotton waste and gun powder. The barrel faced the Doon Valley and the Mall road. One day the powder was probably overcharged and a lady departing for Rajpur by dandy, received the unique farewell of the ball of grass being deposited straight into her lap! The jolt the dandy bearers gave her was even more unnerving than the bouquet of grass. The firing of it was discontinued in 1919 as a measure of economy and in 1940, during World War II, the barrel was sent back to the melting pot, the gun carriage wheels stood forlornly on the hill, for years, as a mute reminder of the past glory of the gun.

The Sirmur Gorkha Battalion played a significant part in quelling the 1857 uprising in Delhi. A camel-rider brought the order for them to leave for the plains and within four hours they were on the move. They took two elephants to transport the reserve ammunition while carrying their personal belongings, arms and ammunition on their backs. On arriving at Roorkee they embarked in fifty boats on the Ganga canal which had been completed three years before. Going down this over 300 miles long artificial water-way they reached Nanoo, a point nearest to Meerut. Here they were ordered to carry on downstream to Bulandhshahr, where the uprising was to erupt any minute. They found Bulandshahr destroyed and the treasury sacked. From here they marched across the country reaching Alipur north of Delhi, where they were the only non-European troops in the British force. They were placed alongside the British Artillery, who had orders to turn their guns on them at the slightest sign of mutiny. The Gorkhas fought their way on to the Ridge and held the house of Hindu Rao. During the two weeks of almost daily fighting they lost 103 killed and wounded out of 490 men.

By the middle of July half the Battalion had gone. Their forward outpost was now in a temple courtyard only half a kilometre from the city walls. By the end of August Nicholson's force had arrived and breaches were made in the wall at two places. The Sirmur Battalion, now joined by the Kumaun Battalion (the 3rd Gorkha Rifles) formed part of the force that captured Kishanganj outside the city. Their losses were heavy. Eight out of nine British Officers and 327 men out of 490 were casualties. Lt. Lockart was recommended by the Commanding Officer for the Victoria Cross, but as the recommendation and citation had been sent in pencil instead of ink they were not considered official. The Sirmur Battalion had been at its post unrelieved for over three months under constant fire. The fortunes of war gave them the chance to win undying fame. They were awarded the "Queen's Truncheon" in recognition of their service at the siege of Delhi.

The head of the truncheon had the figures of three Gorkha soldiers standing on top of Delhi Gate of the Red Fort, supporting the Queen's crown. Inside the tower of the gate were two crossed "Khukris"—the Gorkha's native weapon. On rings of silver above and below the gate the words "Main Picquet, Hindu Rao's House, Delhi, 1857" were inscribed in English and Devanagri script. It was presented by the Commander-in-Chief in India at a parade of ten thousand troops in Lahore five years after the events to which it related, and it took the place of a regimental flag. All new recruits would thereafter swear on it their allegiance to the regiment. The Sirmur Gorkhas thereafter saw action in the Momand war in 1864, in the Hazara expedition in 1868, in the Lushai expedition in 1870, in the Malta and Cyprus expedition in 1878, in the battle of Kandhar in September 1880.

In 1876 at the Delhi Darbar, held by the Prince of Wales (later King Edward VII) the Regiment, which was present, was complimented by the Prince. He became its Honorary Colonel and it was thereafter known as "Prince of Wales' Own", which later became 2nd King Edward's Own Gorkha Rifles. As a matter of fact, initially, it should have been named the "Doon Rifles" instead of Sirmur Rifles.

During the second half of the last century Survey of India offices in Dehra Dun grew to considerable proportions. In addition to the original Topographical, Revenue and Trigonometrical Branch, there were the computing section, the photo-zinco, the drawing and printing sections, as well as the photo-helio section in charge of a solar photographer, the Astronomical group, the Tidal and Levelling groups, the pendulum and the Magnetic groups. At the beginning of the present century there were only three observatories in the British Empire at which photographs of the sun were taken. They were at Greenwich, Mauritius and Dehra Dun. There were two observatories in the Survey compound furnished with two different types of telescopes one giving a photograph 8 inches in diameter and the other 12 inches. In Mussoorie many a Survey Officer, who subsequently distinguished himself in geodetic work, made his first acquaintance with a big 36 inch theodolite in the little observatory on top of Camel's Back. This does not exist any more. In 1877 or thereabouts the clock tower on the main building of the Geodetic branch was erected in memory of Major Base, Royal Engineers, who died on duty, while employed in the higher Himalaya. The map publications Division was shifted from Calcutta to Dehra during World War II after the Japanese had bombed that city a couple of times.

Emperor Ashoka's Rock Edict at Kalsi circa 250 BC

The mausoleum of Guru Ram Rai circa 1700 AD

The Persian inscription on the South gate of Guru Ram Rai's mausoleum circa 1700 AD

The Har-Ki-Paori Haridwar circa 1820 AD

Gillespie monument at Kalunga circa 1850 AD

Dehra Dun railway station, with Mussoorie and Gun hill in the background circa 1900 AD

The Journey up to Mussoorie, Rajpur in the distance circa 1900 AD

Half-way house on the road to Mussoorie circa 1900 AD

Centenary Memorial of 2nd Gurkha Rifles Regiment circa 1926 AD

World War I Memorial circa 1920 AD

The Forest Research Institute building with Bhadraj in the background

Supper Scene at a Fancy Dress Dance at the Savoy Hotel circa 1912 AD

According to a folk tale, once upon a time the present polo ground in Chakrata Cantonment, in Jaunsar-Bawar, was a lake. A covey of Chakors (partridges) used to come to quench their thirst at its waters, hence the locals called the place "Chakor That"-a place of Chakors. In course of time it came to be called Chakrata or Chakrauta.

The foundation of Chakrata cantonment dates back to 1866, but no troops arrived there till April 1869. The first ones to arrive were H.M.'s 55th Regiment under the command of Col. (later Lt. Gen. Sir) Robert Hume C.B. in the month of May 1869. The regiment arrived after a 30 days forced march from Ambala where it had been camping to take part in the Viceroy's (Lord Mayo) Darbar in honour of Sher Ali, Amir of Kabul. It came cross country via the Timli pass. They had a difficult task before them as they had to form and build a new station amidst the mountains. The site selected was on a narrow ridge which stretched for twenty five miles below Deoban at an average altitude of 7000 feet above sea level. Only one or two huts were built, except for a small barrack at Kailana where a Sappers detachment was stationed. Consequently the regiment remained in tents for months until gradually, huts arose all around, and roads were made. The huts or barracks were built of stone, slate and wood. The roofs were made of iron sheets or thatch or other grass. Half-way between Chakrata and Kailana a native bazar sprang up with its population of plainsmen.

The work had progressed so well that in February, 1871, Col. Hume and the Regiment received official thanks from the Government of India for their great and successful exertions. In the following May the Viceroy Lord Mayo paid a visit to Chakrata, and personally congratulated and thanked the 55th for the excellent work it had done.

Col. Hume, on retirement from the army (as Lt. Gen. Sir Robert Hume, G.C.B.) settled in Dehra and planted out the Mohkampur tea estate (now Indian Institute of Petroleum on the Haridwar road). He had married the widow of Surgeon-Major Harris, who had been killed in the 1857 uprising at Kanpur. He took a keen interest in the local activities. After some years the tea estate was sold to Sheikh Inamullah who was one of the old land holders owning the building, named after him, on Gandhi Road in Dehra. Hume's step son Harris, was manager of Hurbanswala Tea Estate. It was here that they played host at 'Tea' to the Princess of Wales (later Queen Mary) in 1905. General Hume at that time was the Chairman of the Dehra Doon Tea Co. Ltd. and East Hopetown Estate Co. Ltd. He and his family, the last member dying in 1961, are all buried in the Dehra Dun cemetry.

After the 55th Regiment left Chakrata the Royal Welsh Fusiliers were stationed there, succeeded by the Northumberland Fusiliers who were followed by a number of British regiments, including the famous Black Watch Regiment.

In October 1873, Field Marshal Lord Roberts, V.C., K.P., G.C.B., G.C.S.I., one time Commander-in-Chief in India and hero of Kandhar, then a Lt. Colonel, visited the Gillespie monument in Dehra as his father was present at the battle of Kalanga. Hume relieved Roberts at Kandhar after the last action of the Second Afghan War in 1880.

The regiment posted at Chakrata would come down to Dehra in the winters and was accommodated in tents in the locality known as Ghanghorah.

The last one to occupy the place was the Bedfordshire and Hertfordshire Regiment (called Beds and He(a)rts for short). It left the Cantonment in 1939 at the outbreak of World War II. During the two World Wars the accommodation was used as a Convalescent Depot for the wounded.

A brewery was opened by M/s Dyer Meakins (now Mohan Meakins) for making beer to meet the needs of the troops. It closed down in the 1930s.

Freemasonary came to Chakrata when a Lodge was consecrated and worked by the officers posted there. The Lodge functioned till 1947 when it closed down on the cantonment being abandoned. It was only after the arrival of the Dalai Lama in India, and the Chinese attack in 1962, that the place was reoccupied by the army for starting an establishment for training in espionage. The original buildings and the cart road 77 miles long, connecting the place to Saharanpur, had cost the government Rs. 54 lakhs in those days. Till the arrival of the motor car the Mail tonga, with horses changed every five miles, took a day from Dehra to Chakrata.

A famine, which was no more than a scarcity, affected the Doon in 1861, and this was made a good excuse for famine relief work which was put into effect by the broadening of the road and building the tunnel of the Mohand pass. Before the completion of the tunnel, which was under the charge of Capt. Cautley, travellers had to scramble over the crest of the hill. In 1877, the driest year known in a 100 years, the Doon had another period of famine and a Relief Camp was set up at Lakhibagh where some 250 persons were on "Charitable relief" and about 900 employed on "relief work". But this was chiefly due to an influx of destitute wanderers from beyond the Shiwaliks; and the exercise of a little toughness at the passes to repel the tide of mendicant immigration, kept the number down to an average of 1200. By March 1877 the relief camp was nearly empty; most of the inmates had wandered away, and the bulk of the remainder were drafted off to Bhaniawala near Kansrao to work in real earnest at road making under the District Public Works Department instead of playing at digging holes and filling them up again as they had done in the ravine near Lakhibagh.

Till the road through the Mohand Pass was made fit for vehicular traffic, by building the tunnel at Asarori, all heavy traffic came to the valley through the Timli Pass. With the coming of the railway to Dehra and Rishikesh the traffic on the Timli road became negligible.

In 1873 an English traveller, Andrew Wilson, came to the Doon. The Lieutenant Governor of Uttar Pradesh (then known as North-West Province) Sir William Muir had given him letters of introduction to the Principal of the Thomason Engineering College at Roorkee and to Dr. Jamieson of the Botanical Garden at Saharanpur. After visiting these two persons Wilson went on to Haridwar to see the "Kumbh Mela". From Haridwar he came to Dehra via the Kansrao Pass. On the way he came across the Shikar camp of his namesake "Pahari" Wilson, or as Andrew calls him - "Ranger of the Himalaya", whom he later met at Mussoorie. Andrew Wilson describes his excursion into the Doon and thence to Shimla thus:—

"As the greatest religious fair of the Hindus was being held at this time at Hardwar (Hurdwar), where the Ganges is supposed to issue from the Himalaya, I went over there to see that extraordinary scene, and was fortunate enough to hit upon the auspicious day for bathing.

Hardwar, or, more correctly Haridwar, means the Gate of Hari or Vishnu, and it is also called the source of the sacred Ganges, and is at least the point where that sacred river issues from the mountains upon the plains. With that inconsequence which characterises later Hinduism or Brahmanism, Siva is the proper deity of the Ganges, because he is the Lord of the Himalaya; and when Ganga was unable to pour her flood over India, she obtained the consent of Siva to pour herself over his head, which she did in such an impetuous manner, that "the God grew angry, and locked up her struggling floods amid his labyrinthine hair." In this legend we may see the immense value which was necessarily attached to the fertilising power of the Ganges by the people of India, and the use to which that was turned when Hinduism became a priestly system. The commencement of the yearly melting of the snow on the Himalaya was probably the reason why this particular season was chosen for the yearly pilgrimage to Hardwar, when the sun is in Pisces and enters Aries; but I know not why a particular value should be attached to the pilgrimage every twelfth year, when Jupiter is in Aquarius at the time of the Sun entering Aries. These are the periods specially chosen for the pilgrimage, and high religious merit is ascribed to it, as also, more particularly to bathing in the water at the "auspicious moment," which is calculated by the astrologers and Brahmins, when the Sun enters Aries.

It is a mistake to suppose that Hinduism is not believed in by the people of India, however little relationship it may now have to true religion. On this occasion there were about 1,00,000 people collected at Hardwar, of all ages, and in every stage of physical strength. The bathing was not confined to the auspicious moment. The water, as also the morning wind, was very cold; and delicate young women, children, and old shrivelled grand dames shivered in the stream, but really looked as they were fulfilling a sacred duty, and enjoying an inestimable privilege. Of indecency at the bathing there was not a trace, though, likely enough, in the vast crowd of people camped in the neighbourhood, curious things went on, as they would in any similar crowd in any country; and in no other country that I know of, would a crowd of the same magnitude have presented so much outward propriety of behaviour, whether at the bathing place or in their encampments. The puerility of the whole affair was more striking than any other feature of it. There is scarcely now the enthusiasm which this pilgrimage used to call forth, and British regulations have interfered to prevent the occurrences which redeemed it from common place, and must have made the pilgrims feel that they were accomplishing something wonderful. The Gosains and Bairagis—rival sects of Hindu devotees—are not allowed now to fight as they used to do, and as in 1760, when 18,000 of the latter are said to have been killed at this Hardwar Mela. The steps leading down to the river are crowded enough; but care is taken to prevent such scenes as occurred in 1819, when, at the auspicious hour for bathing, 430 persons were crushed to death, including some of the British sepoys who were placed to preserve order. So careful even are the sanitary arrangements, that there is little chance of cholera breaking out in the camp and spreading its poison all over India as it did on one occasion ten years ago. The doctors at Hardwar, when I was there, were very careful. A youthful pilgrim died, as it turned out, of chest disease, and his relatives, anxious to avoid a medical examination, concealed the death, and had the body carried off secretly; but the medical authorities got wind of the occurrence, and hunted down the corpse ten miles off.

Business is combined with religion at this great gathering. Fruits come from Kabul, Kandahar, Kashmir; turbans, ivory, and metal ornaments are displayed, as also sarsenets, arms of various kinds, and European goods. There are also large numbers of camels, mules, and horses for sale. A number of officers of Punjabi regiments had come to Hardwar in order to purchase horses; and, in the evening, we all assembled for dinner at the bungalow of Mr. Jenkinson, the energetic collector of the district, whose hands were pretty full with all he had to look after. I was indebted to him for the use of an elephant which took me through the fair and all about the place; and the way in which that elephant went up and down steps and over walls which seemed almost impossible for so unwieldy - looking an animal, left a very distinct and lively impression on my mind as to the utter hopelessness of my ever attempting to escape from a wild one. Many and interesting were the stories which the Punjabi officers had to tell of past times; and if the pious Hindus enjoyed themselves—as they appeared to do, whether in the water or out of it - not less did the company of unpolytheistic Englishmen. The spectacle of the bathing was curious, but not very interesting or exciting; and I do not wonder that the Brahmins have announced, by way of getting up a new sensation, that the auspicious properties are about to be transferred from the Ganges to the Jamuna. At night the scene was rendered striking by most magnificent fires in the jungle of the surrounding hills. Some of these blazed in circles, some in long lines, and conveyed the idea of enormous fiery dragons moving on the hillsides; but even these fires did not scare the abundant tigers from the neighbourhood. Round the bungalow and tents of the bronzed English officers were picketed elephants, horses, and camels; beyond that a low, many-voiced murmur rose from the encampment of the vast multitude of

Indians; above and around that, the serpent-like forest-fires gleamed brightly; while, in the thick coverts beyond, there were great powerful forms of beauty and terror, with their cruel hungry eyes "Burning bright, In the Jungles of the night".

From Hardwar I proceeded in a "Duli" along a jungle-path through the Terai to the Dehra Doon and Masuri. This was my first experience of the Himalaya. In vain had I strained my eyes to catch a glimpse of their snowy summits through the golden haze which filled the hot air. Though visible from Rurki and many other places in the plains at certain seasons, they are not so in April; but here, at least, was the outermost circle of them—the Terai, or literally, the "Wet land," the "belt of death," the thick jungle swarming with wild beasts, which runs along their southern base. It is not so thick or so deadly here between the Ganges and the Jamuna, as it is farther to the east, on the other side of the former river, and all the way from the Ganges to the Brahmaputra, constituting, I suppose the longest as well as the deadliest strip of jungle-forest in the world. The greater cold in winter in this north-west portion, and its greater distance from the main range, prevent its trees attaining quite such proportions as they do further east; but still it has sufficient heat and moisture, and sufficiently little circulation of air, to make it even here a suffocating hothouse, into which the wind does not penetrate to dissipate the moisture transpired by the vegetation; and where, besides the most gigantic Indian trees and plants—as the sissu, the seul tree, with its shining leaves and thick clusters of flowers, and the most extraordinary interlacing of enormous creepers - we have, strange to say, a number of trees and other plants properly belonging to far-distant and intensely tropical parts of the earth, such as the *Cassia alata* of Burmah, the *Marlea begoniaefolia* of Java, the *Deeringia celooioides* of Papua, and the *Narium odorum* of Africa. This natural conservatory is a special haunt for wild animals, and for enormous snakes such as the python. The rhinoceros exists in the Terai, though not beyond the Ganges; but in the part we now are—that between the Ganges and the Jamuna—there are wild elephants, and abundance of tiger, leopard, panther, bear, antelope, and deer of various kinds.

My Bombay servant had heard so many stories at Hardwar about the inhabitants of this jungle, that he entered into it with fear and trembling. If the word "Hatti" (elephant) was uttered once by our coolies, it was uttered a hundred times in the course of the morning. Before we had gone very far, my Duli was suddenly placed on the ground, and my servant informed me that there were some wild elephants close by. Now, the idea of being in a canvas palanquin when an elephant comes up to trample on it is by no means a pleasant one; so I gathered myself out slowly and deliberately, but with an alacrity which I could hardly have believed possible. Surely enough the heads and backs of a couple of large elephants were visible in the bush; and as they had no howdahs or cloths upon them, the inference was fair that they were wild animals. But a little observation served to show that there were men beside them. They turned out to be tame elephants belonging to a well known Himalayan character, who was hunting in the Terai, and who seems to have been met by every traveller to Masuri for the last twenty years. I did not see him at this time, but afterwards made his passing acquaintance in the hotel at Masuri, and again in Bombay. It will give some idea of the abundance of game in this part of the Terai to mention, that on this shooting excursion, which lasted only for a very few days, he bagged two tigers, besides wounding another which was lost in the jungle, three panthers, and about thirty deers. He has been called the "Ranger of the Himalaya," and his history is a curious one. About thirty years ago he wandered up to these mountains on foot from Calcutta with his gun, being a sort of superior "European Loafer." There his skill as a hunter enabled him to earn more than a livelihood, by preserving and sending to Calcutta the skins of the golden pheasant and other valuable birds. This traffic soon developed to such proportions that he employed many "Paharris" to procure for him the skins of birds and animals, so that his returns were not solely dependent on the skill of his own hand. He married a native mountain lady, who possessed some land, a few days' marches from Masuri; and finally, by a fortunate contract for supplying Indian railways with sleepers from the woods of the Himalaya, he had made so much money that it was currently believed at Masuri when I was there that he was worth more than £ 1,50,000/-. I was interested in his account of the passes leading towards Yarkand and Kashmir, with some of which he had made personal acquaintance. I may mention, also, that he spoke in very high terms of the capacities, as an explorer, of the late Mr. Hayward, the agent of the Geographical Society of London, who was cruelly murdered on the border of Yassin, on his way to the Pamir Steppe, the famous "Roof of the World". It has been rumoured that Mr. Hayward was in the habit of ill-treating the people of the countries through which he passed; but the Ranger, who travelled with him for some time, and is himself a great favourite with the mountaineers, repelled this supposition, and said he had met with no one so well fitted as this unfortunate agent of the Geographical Society for making his way in difficult countries. I do not think that the least importance should be attached to accusations of the kind which have been brought against Mr. Hayward, or rather against his memory. The truth is, it is so absolutely necessary at times in High Asia to carry matters with a high hand—so necessary for the preservation, not only of the traveller's own life, but also of the lives of his attendants—that there is hardly a European traveller in that region against whom, if his mouth were only closed with the dust of the grave, and there was any reason for getting up a case against him, it could not be proved, in a sort of way, that it was his ill-treatment of the natives which had led to his being murdered. I am sure such a case could have been made out against myself on more than one occasion; and an officer of the staff of the Commander-in-Chief in India told me that the people of Spiti had complained to him that a Sahib, who knew neither Hindustani nor English, much less their own Tibetan dialect, had been beating them because they could not understand him. This was Dr. Stoliczka, a mild, gentlemanly member of the late Yarkand Mission; and the cause of his energy in Spiti was that shortly before, in Lahaul, several of his coolies had perished from cold, owing to disobedience of his orders, and, being a humane man, he was anxious to guard against the recurrence of such an event. But when treating of Kashmir I shall speak more openly about the story of Hayward's death, and only wish to note here the testimony in his favour which was borne by the experienced "Ranger of the Himalaya," who has become almost one in feeling with the people among whom he dwells.

In the centre of this Terai, there is an expensively built police "Chowki", in which I took refuge from the extreme heat of the day; but what police have to do there, unless to apprehend tigers, does not appear at first sight. It is quite conceivable, however that the conservatory might become a convenient place of refuge for wild and lawless men, as well as for wild plants and wild beasts. Hence the presence in its midst of these representatives of law and order, who hailed the visit of a Sahib with genuine delight. The delay here prevented me reaching the cultivated valley of the Dehra Doon till midnight, so torches were lit long before we left the thicker part of the Terai; their red light made the wild jungle look wilder than ever, and it was with a feeling of relief that we came upon the first gardens and tea-plantations. There is no place in India, unless perhaps the plateaus of the Blue Mountains, which reminds one so much of England as the little valley of the Dehra Doon; and Sir George Campbell has well observed that no district has been so happily designed by nature for the capital of an Anglo-Indian Empire. It lies between the Sewalik or sub-Himalayan range and the Himalaya itself. This former low line of hills, which is composed from the debris of the greater range, has its strata dipping towards the latter in a north-easterly direction, and consists of a few parallel ridges which are high towards the plains, but sloping in the direction of the Himalaya where there is any interval between. It contains an immense collection of the fossil bones of the horse, bear, camel, hyena, ape, rhinoceros, elephant, crocodile, hippopotamus, and also of the sivatherium, the megatherium, and other enormous animals not now found alive. At some places it rests upon the Himalaya, and at others is separated from them by raised valleys. The Dehra Doon is one of those elevated valleys, with the Upper Ganges and Jumuna flowing through it on opposite sides, and is about seventy miles in length, and nearly twenty in breadth. It is sometimes spoken of, by enthusiasts for colonisation in India, as if the whole Anglo-Saxon race might find room to establish themselves there; but it is really a very small district, with most of the available land cultivated; and from Masuri we see the whole of it lying at our feet and bounded by the two shining rivers. It is a very pleasant place, however. Being so far north, just about 30° of latitude, and at an elevation of a little over 2000 feet, it enjoys a beautiful climate. Even in the hot season the nights and mornings are quite cool, which is the great thing in a hot country; the fall of rain is not so great as in the plains below or in the hills immediately above; and in the cold season the temperature is delightful, and at times bracing. I saw roses in the Dehra Doon growing under bamboos and mango-trees, and beds of fine European vegetables side by side with fields of the tea-shrub.

In one plantation which I examined particularly, the whole process of preparing the tea was shown to me. It was under the superintendence of a Celestial, and the process did not differ much from that followed in China, but the plants were smaller than those usually seen in the Flowery Land. After having been for long a rather unprofitable speculation the cultivation of tea on the slopes of Himalaya is now a decided monetary success; and the only difficulty is to meet the demand for Indian tea which exists not only in India and Europe, but also in Central Asia. Dr. Jameison of Saharanpur, who has interested himself much in the growth of tea in India, and pressed it on when almost everybody despaired of its ever coming to anything, was kind enough to give me a map showing the tea districts of the Western Himalaya; and I see from it that they begin close to the Nepalese frontier at Pethoragurh in Kumaon. A number of them are to be found from a little below Naini Tal northwards up to Almora and Ranikhet. Besides those in the Dehra Doon, there are some in its neighbourhood immediately below Masuri, and to the east of that hill-station. Next we have those at Kalka on way to Simla from Ambala (Umballa), at or rather just below Simla itself, at Kotgarh in the Valley of the Sutlej, and in the Kulu Valley, so famed for the beauty and immorality of its women. And lastly, there is a group at Dharamsala, and in the Kangra valley and its neighbourhood. The cultivation of tea does not seem to get on in the Himalaya above the height of 6000 feet, and it flourished from that height down to about 2000 feet, or perhaps lower. Some people are very fond of Indian tea, and declare it to be equal, if not superior, to that of the Middle Kingdom; but I do not agree with them at all. When my supplies ran out in High Asia, tea was for some time my only artificial beverage, though that, too, failed me at last, and I was obliged to have recourse to roasted barley, from which really very fair coffee can be made, and coffee quite as good as the liquid to be had under that name in half the cafes of Europe. It is in such circumstances that one can really test tea, when we are so dependent on it for its refreshing and invigorating effects; and I found that none of the Indian tea which I had with me - not even that of Kangra which is the best of all - was to be compared for a moment, either in its effects or in the pleasantness of its taste, with the tea of two small packages from Canton, which were given me by a friend just as I was starting from Simla. The latter, as compared with the Himalayan tea, was as sparkling hock to home-brewed ale, and yet it was only a fair specimen of the ordinary better-class teas of the Pearl river.

Looking from Rajpur at the foot of the hills up to Masuri, that settlement has a very curious appearance. Many of its houses are distinctly visible along the ridges; but they are so very high up, and so immediately above one, as to suggest that we are in for something like the labours and the experience of Jack on the bean-stalk. In the bazaar at Rajpur, I was reminded of the Alps by noticing several cases of goitre; and I afterwards saw instances of this disease at Masuri; at Kalka, at the foot of the Simla hills; at Simla; at Lippe, a cool place, above 9000 feet high, in Upper Kanawar, with abundance of good water; at Kaelang in Lahaul, a similar place, but still higher; at the Ringdom Monastery in Zanskar, about 12,000 feet high; in the great open valley of Kashmir; and at Peshawar in the low-lying trans-Indus plain. These cases do not all fit in any particular theory which has been advanced regarding the cause of this hideous disease; and Dr. Bremley has mentioned in the transactions of the Medical Society of Calcutta, that in Nepal he found goitre was more prevalent on the crests of high mountains than the valleys. The steep ride to Masuri up the vast masses of mountain, which formed only the first and comparatively insignificant spurs of the Himalaya, gave a slight foretaste of what is to be experienced among their giant central ranges.

Masuri, though striking enough, is by no means a picturesque place. It wants the magnificent deodar and other trees of the Simla ridge, and, except from the extreme end of the settlement, it has no view of the Snowy Mountains, though it affords a splendid outlook over the Dehra Doon, the Sewaliks, and the Indian plains beyond. The

"Himalayan Hotel" there is the best hotel I have met with in India; and there are also a club-house and a good subscription reading room and library. Not a few of its English inhabitants live there all the year round, in houses many of which are placed in little shelves scooped out of the precipitous sides of the mountain. The ridges on which it rests afford only about five miles of riding paths in all, and no table land. Its height is about 7000 feet—almost all the houses being between 6400 and 7200 feet above the level of the sea. But this insures a European climate; for on the southern face of the Himalaya the average yearly temperature of London is found at a height of about 8000 feet. The chief recommendation of Masuri is its equality of temperature, both from summer to winter and from day to night; and in most other respects its disadvantages are rather glaring. In April I found the thermometer in a shaded place in the open air ranged from 60° Fahr. at day break, to 71° between two and three o'clock in the afternoon; and the rise and fall of the mercury were very gradual and regular indeed, though there was a good deal of rain. The coldest month is January, which has a mean temperature of about 42°; and the hottest is July, which has 67°F. The transition to the rainy season appears to make very little difference; but while the months of October and November are delightful, with a clear and serene sky, and an average temperature of 54°, the rainy season must be horrible, exposed as Masuri is, without an intervening rock or tree, to the full force of the Indian south-west monsoon. The Baron Carl Hugel mentions that when he was there in 1835, the rain lasted for eighty-five days, with an intermission of only a few hours. It cannot always be so bad as that at Masuri in summer, but still the place must be exceedingly wet, cold and disagreeable during the period of the monsoon, and it is no wonder that at such a season, the residents of the Dehra Doon much prefer their warmer and more protected little valley below.

Notwithstanding the attractions of the "Himalayan Hotel," I would recommend the visitors to Masuri to get out of it as soon as possible, and to follow the example of the American who said to me after forty-eight hours he could stand it no longer, and that he wanted "to hear them Panthers growling about my tent." The two great excursions from this place are to the Jamnotri and the Gangotri peaks, where the sacred rivers, Jumna and Ganges, may be said to take their rise respectively. These journeys involve tent-life, and the usual concomitants of Himalayan travel, but they are well worth making; for the southern side of the sunny Himalaya in this neighbourhood is grand indeed. It is only fifteen marches from Masuri to the glacier from which the Ganges is said to issue, though, in reality, a branch of it descends from much further up among the mountains; and these marches are quite easy except for nine miles near to the glacier, where there is "a very bad road over ladders, scaffolds," It is of importance to the tourist to bear in mind that, in order to pursue his pleasure in the Himalaya, it is not necessary for him to descend from Masuri to the burning plains. The hill-road to Simla I have already spoken of. There is also a direct route from Masuri to Wangtu Bridge, in the Sutlej Valley, over the Burand Pass, which is 15,180 feet high, and involving only two marches on which there are no villages to afford supplies. This route to Wangtu Bridge is only fourteen marches, and that place is so near to Chini and the Indian Kailas that the tourist might visit these latter in a few days from it, thus seeing some of the finest scenery in the snowy Himalaya; and he could afterwards proceed to Simla from Wangtu in eleven marches along the cut portion of the Hindustan and Tibet road. There is another and still more interesting route from Masuri to the valley of the Sutlej over the Nila or Nilang Pass, and then down the wild Buspa valley; but that pass is an exceedingly difficult one, and is somewhere about 18,000 feet high, so no one should attempt it without some previous experience of the high Himalaya; and it is quite impassable when the monsoon is raging, as indeed the Burand Pass may be said to be also. The neophyte may also do well to remember that tigers go up to the snow on the south side of the Himalaya; and that, at the foot of Jumnotri and Gangotri peaks, besides "them panthers," and a tiger or two, he is likely enough to have snow bears growling about his tent at night.

I had been unfortunate in not having obtained even a single glimpse of the snowy Himalaya from the plains, or from any point of my journey to Masuri, and I learned there that they were only visible in the early morning at that season. Accordingly I ascended one morning at daybreak to the neighbouring military station at Landaur, and there saw these giant mountains for the first time. Sir Alexander Burnes wrote in his 'Travels into Bokhara,' & C.-"I felt a nervous sensation of joy as I first gazed on the Himalaya." When Bishop Herber saw them he "felt intense delight and awe in looking on them." Even in these antienthusiastic times I fancy most people experience some emotion on first beholding those lofty pinnacles of unstained snow, among which the gods of Hindusthan are believed to dwell. From Landaur a sea of mist stretched from my feet, veiling, but not altogether concealing, ridge upon ridge of dark mountains, and even covering the lower portions of the distant great wall of snow. No sunlight as yet fell upon this dark yet transparent mist, in which the mountainous surface of the earth, with its black abysses, seemed sunk as in a gloomy ocean, bounded by a huge coral-reef. But above this, dazzling and glorious in the sunlight, high up in the deep blue heavens, there rose a white shining line of gigantic "icy summits reared in air." Nothing could have been more peculiar and striking than the contrast between the wild mountainous country below - visible, but darkened as in an eclipse - and these lofty domes and pinnacles of eternal ice and "neve". No cloud or fleck of mist marred their surpassing radiance. Every glacier, snow-wall, icy "aiguille" and smooth-rounded snowfield, gleamed with marvellous distinctness in the morning light, though here and there the sunbeams drew out a more overpowering brightness. These were the Jumnotri and Gangotri peaks, the peaks of Badrinath and of the Hindu Kailas; the source of the mighty sacred rivers; the very centre of the Himalaya; the Himmel, or heaven, of the Teuton Aryans as well as of Hindu mythology. Mount Meru itself may be regarded as raising there its golden front against the sapphire sky; the Kailas, or "Seat of Happiness," is the coelus of the Latins; and there is the fitting, unapproachable abode of Brahma and of his attendant gods, Gandharvas and Rishis.

But I now felt determined to make a closer acquaintance with these wondrous peaks - to move among them, upon them, and behind them - so I hurried from Masuri to Simla by the shortest route, that of the carriage road from the foot of the hills through the

Sewaliks to Saharanpur, by rail from thence to Ambala, by carriage to Kalka, and from Kalka to Simla in a ''jhanpan'' by the old road, which, however, is not the shortest way for the fast section, because a mail-cart now runs along the new road. Ambala, and the roads from thence to Simla, present a very lively scene in April, when the Governor-General, the Commander-in-Chief, the heads of the Supreme Government, their baggage and attendants, and the clerks of the different departments, are on their way up to the summer retreat of the Government of India. It is highly expedient for the traveller to avoid the days of the great rush, when it is impossible for him to find conveyance of any kind at any price - and I did so; but even coming in among the ragtag and bobtail,—if Deputy Commissioners and Colonels commanding regiments - men so tremendous in their own spheres—may be thus profanely spoken of—there was some difficulty in procuring carriage and bungalow accommodation; and there was plenty of amusing company,—from the ton-weight of the post office official, who required twenty groaning coolies to carry him, to the dapper little Lieutenant or Assistant Deputy Commissioner who cantered lightly along parapetless roads skirting precipices; and from the heavy-browed sultana of some Gangetic station, whose stern look palpably interrogates the amount of your monthly ''paggar'' to the more lilylike young Anglo-Indian dame or damsel, who darts at you a Parthian yet gentle glance, though shown ''more in the eyelids than the eyes,'' as she trips from her ''Jhanpan'' or Bareilly ''dandi'' into the travellers' bunglow''.

Till Government purchased the "Doon Court" (Circuit House), in 1901, situated in the Cantonments, Viceroys and Governors visiting the Doon had to depend on the hospitality of private house-holders. If the stay was for a long period they (the visitors) even hired houses for their stay. The following pages from the journal kept by Lady Dufferin, whose husband was the Viceroy and Governor-General from 1884-88, describe their visits to the Doon in 1885 and 1887 the last being a month's private holiday in the Doon.

On 27th October, 1885 the Viceroy and his party entered the Doon Valley on leaving Nahan. This is what Lady Dufferin writes:-

"It really is much nicer to look up at moderate hills, and to move about on a level world, than to be perched on a high peak and to look down upon range after range of gigantic mountains (obviously a view from Government House, Simla). A river too is a refreshing sight, and the Jamuna is a very rapid one. We crossed it on a pontoon bridge, which had been built expressly for the Viceroy. We lunched half-way, and then drove onto Dehra Doon, the country getting prettier at every step. It is a sort of table-land between the two last ranges of the Himalayas, and its climate is quite pleasant to live in all the year round. In sight of it is Mussoorie, another hill station, which appears to be at a much more reasonable distance from the world in general than Simla is.

Our horses and the Body-Guard spend the summer at Dehra Doon, so, in spite of the long drive we had just had, we started off directly to see the stables and the barracks. We are staying in the very pretty bungalow of the Officer-in-charge of the Body-Guard, Captain Onslow. (This bungalow is now called the "Rashtrapati Ashiana" so named by the late President Fakhruddin Ali Ahmad, the President of India, who once spent ten days in it. Part of the estate now houses the National Institute for the Visually Handicapped and the rest is occupied by the President's Body-Guard. The Governor-General's Body-Guard estate was built in 1831 and the horses arrived the following summer.)

Wednesday, 28th October, 1885:-

We left Dehra at nine in the morning, having a drive of forty-five miles before us. A little way from the village (obviously Dehra was not big enough to be called a town leave alone a city, which it now is) we stopped to see a tea-garden. It belongs to Sir H. Macpherson and is on a small scale, the making (of tea) all done by hand, and not by machinery as it is in large establishments. First we saw the crop growing-low, thick, compact, glossy-leaved bushes; then we saw the young shoots which had been picked, dried in the sun, and rubbed and heated, and made up in their damp state into dirty looking balls which are allowed to ferment, and then more drying and sifting is gone through, and the tea is ready for use. Green tea is not fermented at all, which is the only difference between it and black. The most delicate tea is made from the

204

budding leaf, the second best from the leaf just unfolded, and so on till it is too coarse to be used.

We got through our long drive very well, and reached Sahranpore soon after tea.''

The tea garden referred to is the erstwhile Niranjanpur Tea Estate on the Saharanpur road, just across the Bindal river. It is now completely urbanised thanks to the Uttar Pradesh Government.

The Dufferins came back to the Doon in March 1887 and spent some weeks relaxing from their official chores. She describes the visit as follows:-

''1887, March - Tuesday, 29th - We left the house at 5.30 yesterday morning, and the Maharajah drove me to the station. Blanche and Fred were with me till the middle of the day, when they went off to Delhi, and Mr. Lawrence Gordon and I pursued our way to Dehra, where the children are staying and where we are to spend a quiet month.

Mrs. Charles Gordon met me at Saharanpur and gave me dinner and saw me off in my ''dak gharry'' (mail cart). Oh! what a night I had of it. The gharry itself resembles a hearse more than any other carriage, but instead of being painted a glossy black it is a shabby brown. When you are about to spend the night in it, you put in your pillows and your blankets, and as there are no seats you make yourself as comfortable as you can in a recumbent position upon the floor. There are sliding doors at either side, and these generally slide open when you want them to be shut, and shut when you wish them to be open. In this box you are rattled along and jolted from side to side, changing horses every five or six miles. I came to the conclusion that the journey was not one for a nervous person to make. It was pitch dark, and I had no sooner accustomed to one team of dreadful animals than I had to go through the agony of trying another. When I got well off each time I was happy, but the moment we stopped to change my mind was full of anxiety. There was one particularly bad hour, which is rather amusing to me now to look back on. The new team neighed wildly and made unmistakable signs of wishing to fight; they turned round and presented sometimes their heads and sometimes their tails to my open door. I immediately declared I could not, and would not, go on with them, but no intelligible answer was made me, and all the numerous white figures which were bustling about in the gloom seemed indifferent to my fears. I at last succeeded in waking my servant, who was sound asleep on the roof, and I routed Mr. Lawrence Gordon out of the carriage in which he was following me. He appeared in a miserable suit of cotton clothes, and must have been bitterly cold, as the wind was very high and the dust was flying in clouds. Later on he wrapped himself in blankets, and I saw a good deal of him for some time. He got my shrieking steeds taken out and another pair put in; so quiet a pair that they could not get on at all, and they were always stopping, and I was always hanging out of my vehicle to see what was the matter, and at last I began seriously to consider the question of stopping in peace by the wayside and not going on till the morning. Mr. Gordon, however, suggested sending my maid's carriage on to the next stable to fetch some better horses, and mine were taken out. This was all very well for me, but all my suite were shivering with cold, and they soon offered to drag me themselves. There were some body-guard men and some servants, and Mr. Gordon, and they set to and took me at a rattling pace for about two miles. After this I was fortunate, and had good horses and went very fast, but I never could sleep from anxiety as to the probable character of the next team. One of my nocturnal troubles was that I had lost a shoe, and as I was always expecting to have to take to the road on foot, it was, I felt, a serious loss! This most exciting drive lasted from 10 P.M. till 7 A.M., and you may suppose I was pretty tired of it and very glad to see some of the body-guard in full uniform suddenly appear by my side - a sure sign that I was near my destination.

All night we were passing bullock-carts with quaint figures muffled in white driving them through the dark, and sometimes our way was stopped by the upset of one of these carts in the middle of the road. No; a night in a dak gharry does not suit me at all—of that I am quite convinced.

I found the children asleep, but they soon woke up and came and talked to me till their breakfast-time, when I went to sleep and so recovered from the dreadful night.

Dehra Wednesday, 30th - We have taken a bungalow here from a native lady who married a white man, and who is now enjoying his fortune as a widow. It is a very good house with one long room which runs right through it, and which is divided by a curtain into dining room and drawing room. On either side of it are bed rooms, and upstairs there are two good rooms which have been arranged for the Viceroy's business.

We have two other small bungalows belonging to us, and an army of tents, for of course when the Viceroy appears private life ends, and Foreign Secretaries and A.D.C.s, and business people will swarm.

The country round us is lovely. There are mountains quite close, and all the roads are beautifully wooded, and it does feel like a real country place.

We do lessons a great part of the day, and then we ride. The first time we went to look at the tanks from which our water comes, and yesterday we rode to the Goorkha Lines and came home through an avenue of fine trees, with a stream of water running on one side and nice soft ground for the horses' feet. The children are very happy, and are much occupied in looking after three dogs who are supposed to be learning tricks.

I must now give you another bit of D.'s tiger-shooting experience: 'Till now my reports have not been very satisfactory, for when one is after tiger one thinks very little of slaughtering deer, but to-day we have had a really good day, and have brought home three tigers - one of these a very fine male; but as to whom any of them belong it is difficult to say, for what happens is this: There is a sudden shout, "A tiger!" and presently we see the grass moving and get a glimpse of some creature, upon which everybody fires, and of course everybody imagines he hits. The second beast turned up in the middle of a wood with very high grass. He was close to my elephant, and I fired down upon him, and of course I believe I hit him. Then he bounded about, and dozens of shots were fired in every direction. At last he came out into an open place, and I had the good luck to knock him over with a shot which broke his back. I then gave him the 'coup de grace' in his head, so that, at any rate, I had a large share in his destruction'.

Friday, April 1st - My family remains young enough in mind thoroughly to enjoy the privileges accorded to all on the first of April, nor would they hear of ending the 'April Fool' time at twelve o'clock. One day in the year is little enough, they think,

206

for the diversion of taking everybody in, and their one regret is that their father is not here to be practised upon.

We went to tea with the Muirs, and rode with them afterwards, and in the evening we had the further dissipation of a concert and a small play. There was one rather funny scene during the concert. A gentleman who was going to perform on the flute mounted the stage, but the lady who was to accompany him was amusing herself elsewhere, and while he was looking about for her in every direction, we could see her laughing and talking in the ante-room. There were screens across the back of the stage to hide the preparations for the play, and after the flutist had peered behind each one of these, he at last in despair retired there himself, but his coat-tail had scarcely disappeared when the lady marched on to the front of the stage, and all the audience laughed and applauded - she could not imagine why. The play was 'Cut off with a Shilling'.

Sunday, 3rd, to Wednesday, 6th - D arrived safe and well, and is delighted with this place, with the house and his own cheerful rooms, with the views and the trees and the climate. And we have managed to maintain our privacy and to lead a family life. Not one A.D.C. appears at any meal, and we can almost fancy ourselves at Clandeboye. We have a nice long ride every afternoon, and we enjoy our quiet evenings.

Thursday, 7th - One day here is so like another that I shall miss a few every now and then, but to-day we had special dissipations. Even the weather went on in an unusual way, occasionally emitting a growl from behind banks of black cloud gathered together about the hill-tops, or coming out with a sudden little gust of wind, which made one fear a dust-storm, or shedding a few drops of rain upon us, so that we might expect a deluge. None of these things came off - it was all talk; and we got quite safely through the aforesaid dissipations, which were, first (one of an improving and instructive character) - a visit to the Survey office.

Our second engagement prevented our visiting the observatory properly, so I will say nothing about it, as we mean to go there another day. I felt sure that the children would be in a desperate state of impatience for our return, as we were to have some tilting and tent-pegging at the body-guard lines. We accordingly picked them up and drove there. All the ponies had been sent on, and D., with some gentlemen, tent-pegged on one side of the tea, which was laid under some trees, while the ladies tilted on the other side. The children enjoyed themselves immensely, and were particularly pleased with a tiny ditch between the two grounds, over which they could jump.

Good Friday - We had such a curious experience in church to-day. The clergyman was just beginning his sermon when our carriages drove violently past the door, the body-guard rushed after them, and all the other vehicles set off too; there was a great commotion outside, and all the men in the church got up and began to shut the doors and windows. I could not imagine what was the matter, but the word 'bees' soon began to be whispered about. When we were safely shut up, the service went on. These swarms are very dangerous sometimes, and had they got into the church, the ladies would all have had to put their dresses over their heads, and the gentlemen would have had to protect themselves as best they could with their coat-tails. We walked some way to our carriages, and had to jump in and get off as quickly as possible, for the bees were buzzing about, and all our men were much afraid of them. The children were highly delighted with this piece of excitement.

Saturday, 9th - We made a long and very pleasant expedition to Mussoorie, which is the hill station immediately over this. It is much smaller than Simla, but it has the inestimable advantage of being on an outside spur of the Himalayas, and instead of being buried behind range after range of mountains, it is situated at the extreme edge of them and looks down about the plains as upon a map. It is not cut off from the world, and a person there who might be bored by hill station society could mount his horse and descend in half an hour to the larger world below. You can't imagine what a delightful sense of freedom this gives, because you don't know what it is to be encaged in the very heart of the Himalayas for the greater part of the year.

We left our house soon after ten and drove to Rajpore, a village at the foot of the hills, or rather the place where the ascent begins. There we mounted our horses and sat upon them as upon an inclined plane while they toiled up a very steep road. We carried parasols and had on helmets and sunpads, but it was not disagreeably hot, and with Dehra to look at below and the mountains before us, and a certain amount of pretty wood to pass through, we had a charming ride, and we all enjoyed it much. We went straight to the Himalaya Club, where the committee gave us a very excellent lunch, and then we again mounted our horses to see the place.

Mussoorie bears a strong family likeness to Simla, and its view into the mountains is exactly the same. It has its miniature Annandale, called 'the Happy Valley', dedicated to tennis and Gymkhanas. It has its 'Mall', the fashionable promenade, its club - a very superior place indeed - its assembly-rooms, and its 'Jakko', called the 'Camel's Back'. We were very fortunate in the day, which was clear and warm and pleasant, and we saw Mussoorie looking its brightest. The club gave us tea, and then, some on horses and some in dandies we descended the hill again. The girls and I were carried, and we reached the bottom in about an hour's time. The carriage met us at Rajpore, and we got home about seven o'clock, having had a very nice day.

Lord William brought in one of the native conjurers in the evening. He was rather a good one, and was very clean and very musical. Besides consulting his monkey-skull over every trick, he sang, 'Pop goes the Weazle' and other national English songs, mixed up with Indian tunes, which added greatly to the charms of his performance. One of his tricks was, I suppose, a very silly one, but it was very amusing. He made two eggs fight. Unaided by any visible means they hopped and jumped and knocked each other until one broke.

Monday, 11th - This afternoon we went to see a tea-garden and the machinery for turning green leaves into tea-caddy tea. This process only takes a day in fine weather, and the young shoots, which are pulled in the morning, are black and dry and packed away into chests by night. It should not, however, be drunk for six months or a year. A quantity of women and children are employed in picking the leaves; they bring in their baskets full twice a day, and each time the quantity they have gathered is weighed, and they are paid a pice a pound on the spot. These leaves are then spread out on shelves to wither; after that they are put into a machine which rolls them about for half an hour, and out of this they come in a damp and draggled condition. Left on another shelf for a time they turn brown; then they are passed over a very hot furnace in trays, and this dries them and turns them into 'tea'. The only thing left to be done is to sift it in a series of sieves, which divide the tea into four qualities. The coarsest - Souchong - comes out of one sieve; Pekoe Souchong out of another; Pekoe from a third; and Orange Pekoe, the best tea, from the fourth. Nothing remains to be done now but the packing of it in tin-lined cases. Mr. Rogers told me that about 1,30,000 lbs. are sent out of this garden in a year, that it costs five annas a pound to make, and is sold on an average at eight annas.

He gave us some home made beverage before we left, and we walked all over the gardens, which are very pretty. The tea-bushes are neat-looking shrubs, and there are some good trees in the place, and a lovely view of the mountains from it.

Mr. Rogers has a dog who has adopted a little monkey and this creature always lies on the dog's back as he walks about; and, if pulled away from him, cries, and then rushes after him and jumps up to his place again. The dog defends the monkey from the attacks of all other dogs, and it was most amusing to see the way the two went on together as they accompanied us round the garden.

A telescope was put up close to our house, and before dinner two gentlemen came to show some stars. I wished very much to see them, and was particularly delighted with Saturn, which, to my surprise, was exactly like his pictures, and was much more original than any of the other stars. Venus only looked like the moon seen with the naked eye. We saw 'Rigel', of whom I confess I had not heard before, with his small attendant star, Sirius, Castor, the double star, and the Nebulae near Orion- its golden haze with the bright stars in it was quite plain. The moon, unfortunately, rose too late for us to see it.

The weather is quite warm now, but our house is cool in the day, and the evenings out are very pleasant.

Tuesday, 12th - D. and I started off in a comfortable carriage this morning to drive twenty - four miles to Raiwalla. Our way lay through different kinds of wood and jungle, and in many places the lovely little rose, which is so abundant in Dehra, covered the forest trees, and fell in pink cascades from all the branches. Then we saw the tall grasses which reminded D. of his tiger shooting. Some of them grow twenty feet high, and are yellow and dried up now, with black marks on them, so that D. says it is difficult to distinguish the crouching tiger from the jungle, which is so much the same colour as himself.

When we reached our camp, we found it a very pretty one, situated on a high bank overlooking the Ganges, our tents shaded by groups of fine trees. We were rather hot and tired when we arrived, and were glad of some lunch and a rest, but by four o'clock we were ready to go off fishing. We rode on elephants down to the river, and then we did enjoy ourselves: D. fished diligently, throwing a spoon, and I simply sat on the banks and watched him, and looked at the un-Indian scene. It was just like being in Canada again, and it was possible for the time to forget the Indian Empire with its Burmah, its Afghanistan, its Frontier, its India Office, its Civil Service Commission, and all its other cares. For the first time I really appreciated the Ganges. Hitherto it has never 'babbled to me of green fields', as a river should but has been associated in my mind with miraculous cures, burning ghats, crowds of bathers, insanitation, and towns. Here it does not set up for being better than its neighbours, and its clean green and blue waters flow on in all simplicity through pebbly shores and wooded banks, swallowing up a turbulent little tributary and slipping by the Sawalik Hills. These are a low range of mountains which shut in the Dun, and in them some of the most interesting fossils have been discovered; in fact, at Raiwala the Ganges is quite unsophisticated and countrified in its behaviour, and is just like any other river. Even the fish, unawed by the sacred character of the stream, jumped about in a most tantalising manner, and were in far too frivolous a mood to bite. While D. was trying hard to tempt them, I made an excursion on a wonderful kind of boat. It consists of two bullock-skins filled with air, and across them a small bedstead (charpai) is tied, which is the seat of the boat; on it I sat, while the puffed-up animals, lying on their backs with their toes in the air, floated me. Then two loose skins were thrown in, and two men, lying on their chests across them, seized different sides of my bedsted with their hands and paddled with their feet. You can't think how funny the whole thing looks: the four helpless, fat, seal-like animals lying in a row with a prim expression on their faces from having their eyes and mouths tied up into little buttons as if they had died saying 'Prunes and Prism', a person sitting between their upturned paws, and the two men paddling vigorously with their feet. It is a most comfortable and safe machine, as it draws scarcely any water.

Colonel Lane is the Commissioner who looks after us, and we have only got Lord William and Dr. Findlay with us, so we actually sit down to dinner so small a party as five. We were all very sleepy and tired, and went to bed at nine o'clock.

Wednesday, 13th - We have had a most interesting and delightful day. D. began it early, and went down to the river for a couple of hours fishing before breakfast. I remained quiet and sat under the mango-trees, while my ayah packed up and hurried off to Hurdwar, so that she might have time for a dip in the sacred stream at this most propitious time, before I should arrive there. D. was unsuccessful, but was, I think, quite happy in that hope which 'springs eternal' in the fisherman's breast, and he went on trying his luck all the way down to Hurdwar. We breakfasted first, and then, getting into boats, were rowed to that place. We went down several rapids and enjoyed it immensely; the river looked lovely, and on the water the weather was cool enough to be very pleasant. Hurdwar is a most picturesque and curious-looking place; it consists of a row of various temple- and fort- and palace-like-looking buildings at the very edge of the water, a long narrow bazaar running at the back of these and a good way beyond. Some of these buildings are temples, and others are houses belonging to great Hindu Rajahs who like to have residences at such a sacred place, and who generally allow all the pilgrims from their States to live in these houses when these come to bathe. The fair at Hurdwar used to be enormous, but since the railway has come near to it pilgrims visit it all the year round, and there is not so great a rush of them for this 'Puja' or religious festival. I landed on a sort of wooden bridge or barricade which shuts in the principal bathing place. The stream is so strong, and the crowd so great, that the weak and old would run great risk of being carried away were they not penned in. The buildings form a corner here, and the bridge goes across the base of the triangle, while a great flight of stairs - a ghat - down from the bazaar is the apex of it. The houses, ledges, little cupolas, and windows on either side were filled with people, and a compact crowd covered the steps; there were also smaller winding stairs leading to the water, and gaily dressed figures were always going up and down these.

People from all parts of India come here, and you can't think how interesting and amusing it was to watch the multitude both in and out of the water. I sat there for two hours, and D., who arrived a little later, was equally pleased. Some of the bathers stayed in very long, till they were shivering with cold, but still there was a constant change going on, and always something fresh to look at. There was a man supporting two little girls in his arms, who seemed to enjoy it thoroughly. They splashed everyone who came near, and seemed full of fun. Another father of a family came holding a young baby high above the water, while three women held on behind and crossed the bathing place till they reached some quiet corner, when they all held their noses and jumped up and down seven or eight times without stopping. They had looked fully dressed when they entered the water, but after a dip the cotton sheets which had covered them stuck to them, and expressed much more than they concealed. This happened to all the women, but nobody seemed to mind.

When D. arrived, there was a great shouting, and milk and rose-leaves were thrown into the Ganges in his honour. Trays of the latter are kept there on purpose for the devout to offer, and one man pays Rs. 760/- a year for the privilege of selling rose-leaves there. The Brahmins are very busy all the time, receiving gifts from the pilgrims, and I saw one old gentleman besieged by them as he descended into the water. He produced money from some corner of his limited costume, and gave it into the outstretched hands that were thrust in his way. I was very much interested, too, in watching a woman who had evidently brought some of the ashes of her dead to cast into the water. She poured them into her hand out of a little bag, and after much consultation with a Brahmin, paid him something and cast them into the stream. Many people throw in money and jewels with the ashes, and all over the bathing-place men stand with trays, with which they shovel up pebbles from the bottom and look through them in the hope of recovering treasure.

Fakirs were bathing in numbers, and other holy people from afar were filling vessels with the sacred water to carry home. They say the water keeps good for ever and every one likes to take away bottles full of it. Along the edge of the water, on the wall of a house, were a row of niches in which fakirs and gods sat, and where offerings were made, and opposite them on the other side there was a long ledge on which were perched a number of priest-like men in orange turbans. The highest Brahmins sat opposite us in the crowd on the steps, and were very fine looking men in pink turbans; they afterwards came to be presented to D. There was one fat man, a bather, who would come and seize my foot and talk to me, and I had great difficulty in getting him kept off.

Another excitement was the quantity of large fish in the bathing-place, which, being fed constantly, are quite tame, and are not in the least alarmed by the dipping and splashing that goes on around them.

All the people looked so happy and good-humoured, they seemed thoroughly to enjoy the festival, and, as I said before, we could hardly bear to tear ourselves away from it. When we did go we mounted a big elephant and sat in a splendid houdah, the arms of which were silver tigers clawing silver antelopes. Thus enthroned we rode through the bazzar. This is evidently the way to make a state progress in India. One feels so very grand and so very much better and higher than other people as one looks into the upper chambers and on to the roofs of all the houses and down upon the foot and equestrian passengers and the little shops and the daily street-life of people in less elevated positions. We had a procession of twelve elephants, but ours was the biggest and grandest of all, and had much scarlet and gold embroidery hanging about him. We ought to have been dressed in the same style, but alas! we only appeared in travelling garments with sun hats: a smart unbrella with a silver stick held over us improved our appearance a little, I hope.

As soon as we had lunched, we went to look at the head of the Ganges canal, one of the great engineering works of India. It is carried under rivers and over rivers, and is about 500 miles long. Then we proceeded to a dam which regulates the amount of water in the canal, and there we saw a wonderful sight - thousands and thousands of fish struggling to get up the stream, and jumping in shoals far out of the water in their vain efforts to pass the doors of the dam. It was most curious, and one could not have believed in the quantity of fish without seeing them. D. tried to catch some, but I am sure the water was much too turbulent and the fish far too well occupied with their endeavours to proceed up the river to bite. I wandered about the top of the dam and watched the smaller fish trying to get up at other gates, and the smallest of all making their way up a fish-ladder which has been built on purpose for them, but which none of the big ones condescend to use. At five o'clock we had tea, and then went on by train to Roorki. Colonel and Mrs. Blood met us there and we are their guests. They have such a pretty drawing-room, it made me quite envious. It has a high domed roof, supported by four sets of pillars, which make a round centre to the room with large semicircular bows or recesses beyond each. She seems to have great taste in arranging rooms, and she has done this one up very prettily. We dined along with them, and in the evening there was a party in the garden, and all the station was presented to us.

Thursday, 14th - D. spent the whole morning inspecting hospitals, troops, and workshops, and I was ready to go with him, but he persuaded me to give it up, as it was so very hot, and as we had forty-five miles to drive in the afternoon; so I sat at home and talked to Charlotte Blood, who is Sir Auckland Colvin's daughter, and whom I knew at Cairo. D. came in at one, having been interested in all he saw, and we had lunch, and started directly after. I hate driving, and strange horses, but our own met us twenty miles from Dehra, and took us through the Mohun Pass in the Sawalik Hills, a really lovely bit of road, with immensely high cliffs and queer-shaped pinnacle rocks and beds of rivers, and all the trees coming out into blossoms and fresh green leaves. We got home just in time, as a dust-storm followed by rain came on as we got in. The children were all well, and had been having some fun of their own, tilting and tent-pegging at 7 A.M.

The dinner-table had been decorated in the most elaborate way by our servants with 'Welcome, Earl of Dufferin', and crowns, all done in roses. This decoration is a sort of mania which they have taken up lately; and I believe there is great rivalry between the different men as to whether the Staff bungalow table or ours is the more beautifully arranged. The chief decorators were hidden close by to hear what we said about it, and one wrote an elaborate note to Blackwell to ask her to come and see it.

Saturday, 16th, to Tuesday, 19th - I was rather knocked up after my three long days in the sun and heat, so I have been taking things quietly, and had indeed to remain in bed all Sunday. Friday and Saturday afternoon Mr. Gore and I had our hands full. Four hundred Jubilee collection cards to be signed. It proved to be quite a labour, and we had to get in some help. One servant wetted the receipt stamps with a brush (for who could lick 400 stamps at a sitting?), another put them down on the right place. I then ruled lines across the blank spaces on the card to prevent any further collection being made on it, signed and dated and passed it on to Mr. Gore, who took down the number of it and the name of the collector. This set came from Moradabad, and the sum total amounted to Rs. 6,000/-. Most people there had put down their own names on their cards, with the necessary sum as a donation, and had not asked anybody else for more. This money all goes to the North-West Province's Branch of my fund.

D. had two mornings' quail-shooting, which he enjoyed, and the children have been riding as usual.

We gave our one dinner party here on Saturday night, which was unlucky for me, as I felt much inclined to go to bed, and found it difficult to get through the evening. It went off nicely, however.

Monday I was to have visited a native school, and the Leper Hospital, but Dr. Findlay made me give up the latter. I did do the school. It is an American missionary one for native Christians. They have a fine house and grounds, and seem to give a very good education. The sixty pupils, all boarders, were seated in rows, and all wore plain white saris over their heads. When I was seated they began to sing something a little shrill. Then a child got up and, taking a stick in her hand, advanced to a black-board on which some problems from Euclid were drawn in chalk, and as fast as she could speak and point with her stick she gabbled over the explanation. It had a very funny effect. Three more girls followed suit. Then they did geography in the same way, but as I felt a little more at home on this subject, I could see that they really had learnt the map in a very practical way. There was English reading and more singing, and I toiled all over the house, feeling very weak; I asked for a holiday for the pupils, and refused to make them a speech, and got home as soon as I could.

I missed a little Goorkha Review which D. and the children were at, and they came home delighted with it. The girls rode, and Mrs. Becher, the wife of the Colonel, took them about, and they followed the details of the sham battle and were not the least alarmed by firing which went on, and were much amused by the whole thing, and by the cheery and excited demeanour of the sturdy little Goorkhas. A new battalion of them has just been raised, and they have quite a large establishment here called the 'Goorkha Lines'. These soldiers are never moved, except for war, so they are able to settle down comfortably.

Tuesday was our last day at Dehra, and we had fixed upon it for a garden party as a sort of acknowledgement to all the people who had written their names in the visiting-book. We had it at the body-guard lines, and it was very successful. There were two tennis-courts, and tent-pegging and tilting, and every body seemed amused, and all the ladies wondered why they had not tilted before, and determined to get it up here at once. Basil had been out in the morning to try tent-pegging, and having taken three pegs he was much encouraged, and went on at it the whole afternoon, surviving every body else. He was not quite successful before spectators but he has greatly improved in his riding, and he enjoyed himself immensely. Hermie and Victoria tilted. The Dehra people said they were so sorry we were going, and that 'now the season was over and they would be so dull'. I suppose that our cavalcades on the road and all the bustle connected with such a big establishment did enliven a little place like this.

We have been very sorry to hear of the wreck of the Tasmania, the ship we came out in. The Captain, who was drowned, was such a nice man, and it is a sad ending to his career. He was so anxious to get a shore appointment, poor man, and D. had done what he could for him, without success. We knew many of the people on board of her.

Wednesday, 20th - We left Dehra in the morning and had a long drive to Saharanpore. The wind was very high and very hot, and the dust fearful, but we got through it, and the children seemed, as usual, to enjoy everything. We were glad of tea on our arrival at the station. Then we had an hour and a half in the train, and awoke into Viceregal life again at Umballa, where guards of honour, bands, carriages and four, a salute, and all the signs of it came to remind us of our 'official position' after a month of private life. We put up at the hotel for the night, and sat out all the evening''.

This time the tea garden visited by the Dufferins was Kaulagarh Tea Estate which at that time was owned by the Raja of Sirmur. The Raja after purchasing the property, from the Government of India, appointed Europeans to manage it. Amongst them Mr. Bowman and Mr. Seymour on dismissal, for their mismanagement of the estate, gave the Raja a lot of trouble. Bowman would not leave the charge till he was imprisoned for misappropriation while Seymour vacated his residence only after a notice was served on him by the Superintendent of the Doon (the District Magistrate of Dehra). Mr. Roger, the man mentioned by Lady Dufferin, on the other hand won a suit against the Raja for wrongful termination of his (Roger's) services. The Raja, under orders of the Allahabad High Court paid Rs. 40,000/- by way of damages and compensation.

The Sirmur Raja had also purchased the Annfield Tea Estate in the Western Doon. It was the property of General Sir H. Macpherson a former Commanding Officer of 2nd Gorkha Rifles (Sirmur Battalion), who owned Niranjanpur Tea Estate also. The sale was negotiated for Rs. 1,90,000/- on the assurance by Macpherson that the grant of land was permanent and that the income from the Zamindari, Forest and Tea garden was far more than the interest one could expect by investing the same amount of money in a Bank or any Joint Stock Company. The Raja believing the General gave him a letter to the effect that the estate had been purchased by the Raja for Rs. 1,90,000/-. But it transpired, after an examination of the official records, that the grant was only for a period of 50 years, out of which 28 years had already passed, that the forest was all cut and there was no prospect of any profit out of the estate for 15-20 years to come. On the basis of these facts the Raja held that the sale agreement was null and void whilst the General insisted on its execution. The case was brought to the notice of the Governor of the Province who advised both the parties to refer the dispute to arbitration. As a result of it the sale price was reduced by Rs. 50,000/- and the Raja got the property for Rs. 1,40,000/-.

The property rented by the Dufferin's belonged to Mrs. Wilson (the widow of Pahari Wilson) and was situated on Rajpur Road. The road at the northern end of Astley Hall, connecting Rajpur Road to Subhas Road (old Lytton Road) was named Dufferin Road, after the Viceroy.

Shooting three tigers in one day, in the Shiwaliks points out to the abundance of game those days. To-day there may not be three tigers in the entire Dehra Dun district. Life and action at Haridwar is much the same now as it was hundred years ago.

Those days wild life was available in abundance in spite of wholesale destruction, and apart from the tiger, the other animals found were sloth bears, leopards, hyenas, sambhar, chital, chowsingha, goorul, kakur, parha, pigs, porcupines and all varieties of snakes and birds. Boas twenty feet long were quite common. There are stories that lions existed, on the Saharanpur side of the Shiwaliks, till as late 1820. In Emperor Babar's time rhinoceros was found in the Punjab. The scale of rewards for killing animals in the Doon was: Tiger Rs. 10/-, Panther Rs. 5/-, Panther cub Rs. 2.50, Bears Rs. 5/-and Hyena Rs. 3/- each.

The Shiwalik range is the home of the wild elephants. Before a ban was placed by government they were trapped by driving them into a 'Cul de Sac' (a narrow passage closed at one end), and then noosing them.

In those days the Maharaja of Balrampur, the biggest Zamindar of Uttar Pradesh had organised several "Khedda" operations in the Doon. In 1872 he is reported to have caught a herd of twelve elephants. The indiscriminate destruction of wild life led Williams to make the following remark in 1873:-

"I may here remark that unless government places some restriction on such permissions, not a single head of large game will be left in the Doon before many years, and even small game will become very scarce. I have heard that (Rana) Jung Bahadur (of Nepal) is about to make a raid upon the district similar to that undertaken by the Balrampur Rajah last year, but on a much larger scale ...."

Oudh and Rohilkhand Railway Company had put Haridwar on the Railway map by 1887. It took another thirteen years before Dehra Dun was connected to Haridwar by railway. This branch line from Haridwar to Dehra Dun and Rishikesh, though worked by the above mentioned Company, was not owned by it. It was owned by a Company which belonged wholly to the Prince of Wales (later King Edward VII).

During World War II as a measure of economy and to meet the shortage of steel, the Raiwala-Rishikesh section of this railway was closed. The track was uprooted for use elsewhere. It was reopened when the IDPL complex at Virbhadra was being built. The fare on the Haridwar-Dehra and Rishikesh section per kilometre was higher than that charged by the other railway companies operating beyond Haridwar. It became uniform once the Company was merged with the Northern Railway.

In Mussoorie the Himalaya Club had been instituted in 1841 with 148 members and Col. F. Young was the first President. Civil Servants, Commissioned Officers of His Majesty's or the Viceroy's Indian Commissioned Services, Medical Officers, the Bench, the Bar, the Clergy, and gentlemen not in the Services residing in "Bengal or Agra Presidencies" were eligible for membership. It ceased to function soon after World War I. It was one of those select institutions which was not only the 'White man's Preserve' but distinguished between one who was a merchant and one who was a mere tradesman. While merchants were permitted entry the latter were taboo. Perhaps the distinction was adjudged on whether one sold tin cans or tin cars, although the Box-wallah was generally frowned upon.

The Happy Valley estate belonged to Mr. Vansittart, a former Superintendent of the Doon, where he had tennis courts and held gymkhanas including polo on the estate. In 1904 it was purchased by Mr. V.A. Mackinon, the son of teacher Mackinon, who had left teaching and had gone into the business of brewing beer. By consensus amongst the gentry it was decided to start an amusement club. The Happy Valley Club was formed in 1904 and carried on till 1947. Perhaps the last big event that was held in the Club grounds was a "Pagal Gymkhana" on 19th June, 1943 to collect funds for the Red Cross during World War II. The rulers of Kapurthala, Rampur, Rajpipla, Palanpur, Baoni, Kasmanda, Bansi, Pratapgarh, Nanpara, Bhadri and Sir Padampat Singhania of Kanpur, who had been just knighted for his contribution to the War effort, were amongst the list of patrons of the show.

Dehra got its 'White Man's Preserve' - The Dehra Dun Club Ltd. in 1878. Originally it was housed in Col. Young's bungalow where St. Joseph's Academy now is. The present Club house was built in 1903-04 under the supervision of Col. Philimore of the Survey of India. He and his wife spent their last days residing in the Club and writing the history of his Department. Another Englishman and a colleague of his, Lt. Col. Kenneth Mason, when posted in Dehra in 1931-32 was asked by an Indian doctor who was serving in the Indian Medical Service to put him up for the Club's membership. By then Indianisation of both civil and military services had commenced and racial barriers fell easily. Mason agreed to propose the Doctor and got the I.C.S. Superintendent of the Doon, another Englishman to second.

In those days there were very few Indians who were members of the Club. Amongst them were the Maharaja of Tehri Garhwal and a descendant of Raja Lal Singh the exile from the Punjab, who had settled in the Doon. The members balloted on the proposal. Each one had to write his name in a book and then put a white or a black ball into the ballot box. The ballot was open for a month to enable a member to exercise his vote. A certain number of names were already in the book when Mason invited the Doctor to dine with him at the Club. Every thing went well till the Doctor committed the 'faux pas' of clearing his throat, turning around and spitting on the floor. Mason, knowing that the action had been noticed by others present, deliberately made the ballot void by putting in a handful of balls, both black and white, far more than the number of names likely to appear in the book. The Doctor was politely informed that the ballot was void, but that he could apply again for election after six months. This time he got someone else to propose his name again. He got two white balls and all the rest were black. There was an outcry and the Commander-in-Chief himself castigated the military officers of the station. Fortunately for them it turned out that every Indian who was a member had black balled him. Did the Indians really not want the officer to become a member or were they toadying to the white masters? In 1947 only a handful of Englishmen were left as members of the Club. They decided to liquidate it and share the spoils, since those who had resigned were not entitled to their share. A deal was struck with a local Indian businessman for selling the Club premises to him for Rupees six lakhs. Amongst the Indian members the one who was the biggest stumbling block in taking Indians into the Club, now took upon himself the problem of saving it from liquidation. He was Col. Kunwar Shamsher Bahadur Singh, a grandson of Raja Lal Singh. He took the case to the High Court and had the liquidation proceedings annulled, thus saving the Club for posterity.

In 1884 the Duke and Duchess of Connaught paid a visit to the Doon. Amongst the various places they stayed was the house now called Connaught Castle Hotel in Mussoorie. The Hearseys had opened an amusement park, called Tivoli Gardens on their estate in Barlowganj. It had a dancing pavilion, dressing rooms, a dining saloon, tennis and badminton courts, summer houses, ''bowers'' for lovers and all sorts of luxuries. The Royal couple spent sometime at this spot by doing some shooting, followed by lunch and much merry making. Barlowganj took its name from General Barlow who built the ''Whytbank Castle'' perched on the hill west of St. George's College. The ''Mossy Falls'' are also on Hearsey's estate. This waterfall had long evaded a name till one day the owner's family was picnicking by this waterfall, and had with them Mr. Moss, Manager of the Himalaya Bank, as a guest. He was called ''Mossy'' by his friends. Scrambling over some rocks he slipped and fell, in the middle of the pool at the bottom of the fall, to a chorus of, amidst laughter and shouts of ''Mossy Falls'', thus giving his name to them.

What the social life of Mussoorie was in those days, is best stated in the words of a young bachelor Captain (later Lt. Genl. Sir) Robert Baden-Powell:-

"On one occasion I went to Mussoorie, a straggling station about three miles in length, situated on a woody ridge. The paths were rough with grit and exceedingly dusty; house refuse was chucked about on the slopes; untidy little shanties were all over the place and smells were everywhere. The "Society" was extremely mixed and included many with very foreign sounding names, who adorned themselves with all the finery they could lay their hands on in imitation of fashionable dresses - with a special eye for hats - and their manners were of the highest class. There were comparatively few English people.

On the night of my arrival I found that I was expected to attend a grand Masonic banquet, at which I was called upon to make a speech, and after that to continue being funny until one o'clock in the morning. This was merely the beginning. Invitations floated in upon me for every night of the following week, not to mention the cards and notes reading, ''Mrs. So-and-so wants me to bring you to tea tomorrow, etc.'' They were all very kind and I accepted every one with a grin, in some cases two or three invitations for the same night. One day, according to my diary, I seem to have taken myself to task.

''You have accepted all these festivities'', I told myself ! ''You are engaged for a farewell dinner to Colonel B. to-night, you are asked to come with a good repertoire of songs and musical sketches; to-morrow you are to lunch with Mrs.—, to tea with Mrs.—, to dine at the—. Are you to do all these things?''

''No—'' replied my alter ego.

''Well then, if it is not a rude question, what are you going to do?''

''I am going to make a bolt of it.''

This is exactly what I did.''

What a bold and naughty place was Mussoorie then is illustrated from the following report appearing in ''The Statesman'' dated 22nd October, 1884:-

''Last Sunday a sermon was delivered by the Reverend Mr. Hackett, belonging to the Church Mission Society; he chose for his text Ezekiel 18th and 2nd verse; the latter clause, 'The fathers have eaten sour grapes and set their children's teeth on edge'. The Reverend gentleman discoursed upon the ''highly immoral tone of society up here, that it far surpassed any other hill station in the scale of morals; that ladies and gentlemen after attending church proceeded to a drinking shop, a restaurant adjoining the Library (the old ''Criterion'') and there indulged freely in pegs, not one but many; that at a Fancy Bazaar held this season, a lady stood up on a chair and offered her kisses to gentlemen at Rs. 5/- each. What would they think of such a state of society at home? But this was not all. Married ladies and married gents formed friendships and associations which tended to no good purpose, and set a bad example.''

Rudyard Kipling was one of them. He spent a week in Mussoorie, in June 1888, where his friend Edmonia Hill and her husband were staying.

In spite of the Reverend's admonition, the way of life in Mussoorie did not change. On the other hand the manager of a large hotel felt constrained to employ an old myopic and discreet bearer for the purpose of walking the hotel's dark corridors, ringing a bell, just before sunrise. This gave adequate warning to all concerned to return to their rooms before daylight made a public scandal of some very private flirtations. As late as 1932 at a charity show a lady auctioned a single kiss for which a gentleman paid Rs. 300/-. Perhaps the reason for such a free life was the absence of protocol. This was because unlike some of the other hill stations no Viceroy or Governor ever camped at Mussoorie during the summer.

People usually came to Mussoorie either for business or for a holiday. Amongst those who came on a jaunt, after the railway had come to Dehra, were some of the ''Bhoys'' or the gay blades. They usually came on leave from lonely outposts and their initial thirst was for companionship. Sometimes in the Station Master at Dehra who would either be an European or an Anglo-Indian, probably the latter, they would find a friend, philosopher and guide. For him it was a common place request to direct the "Bhoys" to the right companion in the Hills. As every one of both sexes had to pass his watchful eyes before leaving the railway station, he knew whether Jill had come up the hill or not, and he knew too whether it was politic or not to send Jack up for company. Thus for years, the Station-Master moved the pawns much to his amusement. Then came a day when a particular "Gallant" sought his guidance and was told of the possibilities. Yes the prospects sounded great, and the Gallant went up the hill, had all he wanted and much more. Within four days the Station Master received this laconic but expressive message: "Send second relief"

The picture of Mussoorie of those days, would be incomplete without a mention of the good old "Tommy", or the common British Other Rank (soldier). He too made his contribution in the day to day happenings in the station. There are many ways of repudiating claims to nobility, one of the simplest of which was adopted by a Tommy. He was bound for the Palladium Cinema, situated on the ground floor of Hakman's Hotel, when heavy rain made it necessary for him to engage a rickshaw. "Well" said the spruce soldier at his destination, "Kitna paisa?" (how much money) to which the rickshaw men replied, quite reasonably, "barra anna" (to-days 75 paise). "Darn it!" retorted the wise man "do you think I am a bleeding Rajah? here, Pakro ek rupiya", (take a rupee), and throwing them the rupee he expanded his chest and strutted into the shelter of the cinema, well pleased with the bargain.

During World War II, some American troops were stationed in Dehra Dun. In the beginning when they had just arrived, they would be taken for a ride by the local tonga-drivers, not only literally but figuratively as well. If three or four soldiers shared a tonga and at the destination the fare asked for was Rs. 5/- each one of them paid the amount, which was glibly pocketed. Once they got wise, they got so wise that no tonga was engaged without first haggling over the fare.

The earliest Post Office in the Doon was opened in 1827 at Landhaur for the benefit of the Invalids recuperating there. However around 1850 a district postal system was organised and a service of runners started between Dehra and outlying places like Mussoorie, Rishikesh, Choharpur etc. The cost of the service was defrayed from a cess levied on the land-holders. The service was opened to the public in 1873 and a fee of 2 pice (3 paise) was charged on the delivery of every packet. Official correspondence was, however, delivered through the agency of the police. A major change took place in 1893 when the Imperial Postal System gradually extended its operation and absorbed the district postal lines and offices. By 1900 the District Post was completely abolished and the service was reorganised with headquarters at Dehra Dun. The mail was sent, as it still is, to Saharanpur by road where it was put on and collected from the Mail trains passing through that point, as it is the nearest station on the main railway line.

The Telegraph came to Dehra and Mussoorie in 1865 whilst the Telephone was not installed in the district till the beginning of the present century. In the 1930s the Doon could boast of a Radio broadcasting station of its own at Dehra. It was put up by the efforts of the then District Magistrate B.J.K. Hallows, I.C.S. with monetary contributions made by the local Indian gentry. It was managed by a committee headed by him. It would broadcast Indian musical and other programmes in the evenings, daily, for a couple of hours. The talent was mostly local. It was located in the Tehsil compound, in the building now occupied by the rationing office. On the outbreak of World War II it was closed down as Radio broadcasting had become the State's monopoly.

Mussoorie City Board was the second local body in the country, the first being Bombay, to set up a Hydro-electric supply undertaking. A power house with water turbines was established at Galogi at the base of the Bhatta Falls. At that time it was the highest lift of water in Asia, being 1700 feet. The first electric lights were switched on in Mussoorie on 24th May, 1909. The installed capacity of the power station was 750 kilowatts. Electricity was sold at 4 annas (25 paise) per Board of Trade Unit. With the availability of electric power piped water supply to the town was also laid. Most of Mussoorie was supplied by gravity from Gun Hill, where the reservoir was filled by pumping water by electric pumps placed at various springs in the station. The charges for water were Rs. 2/- per 1000 gallons. The total cost of the two projects came to Rs. 9,72,000/-.

In 1918 the United Provinces Government, at the request of Dehra Dun City Board, allowed the Mussoorie Board to supply electricity to the territory of the former. In 1919 after government had stopped the firing of the noon-day gun, the electric voltage was reduced at 9 P.M., for three minutes every evening. This resulted in the brightness of the lights being dimmed thereby letting the public know it was 9 o'clock. In 1934 the authorities realised that this action was an infringement of the Indian Electricity

Act, and had to obtain special sanction from government to continue the practice.

With the availability of electricity the first movie houses to open were the Olympia, Auroras and Orient in Dehra and the Roxy and Picture Palace in Mussoorie. Of these the Orient and Picture Palace are still functioning. In those days the cinema halls not only showed movie pictures but provided other entertainment and refreshments also. Picture Palace had a tea and refreshment room (Bar) on one side of the hall. One could take alcoholic drink or tea with him inside while watching the cinema and was allowed to smoke. There was a Billiards room and a string band played in the cafe. One cinema hall in Dehra even had a roller skating rink on the first floor.

In addition to the cinemas and clubs the other places of amusement in Mussoorie, for the Europeans, were the Ball-rooms and cafe-restaurants at Stiffles and Hakman's Grand Hotel. These places specialised in daily "Tea" and after dinner dances with a live dance band in attendance during the season. Hakmans was run by a Mrs. Hakman whose husband was a tonsorial artist (a barber) who ran his salon in the same building. Stiffles was closed down after World War II and the building burnt down some years later. Savoy and Charleville hotels also had their own Ball-rooms with live bands which catered to their resident guests.

Dehra Dun apart from the cinemas, theatre and clubs also had Dance Halls cum restaurants. Occasionally there would be concerts in aid of various charities, for which local talent was persuaded to perform. These concerts were quite popular and were held frequently. Special dances in aid of charities were also held. Apart from club-life, which offered tennis, badminton, billiards, cards, there were occasional "At Homes" and social gatherings. These were organised under the auspices of either Anglo-Indian and Domiciled Europeans Association, the Y.W.C.A. or various Church Societies. The Indian gentry started its own Club called the Siwalik Club which is still going strong. The amusements for the native population were restricted to the various local religious fairs with their folk theatres, singers, dancers and other entertainers. The first Ram Lila in Dehra was held in 1863 and it is still organised annually. A peculiarity about it is that its script was written by a local businessman named Bhakta Jamuna Das which is still followed and enjoyed by the people. It is set in a sing-song verse and enacted in "Nautanki" (a form of Indian theatre) style.

Horse-racing in Dehra was popular till the end of World War I. There was a regular race-course, with a pavilion, east of the railway station, off Haridwar Road where there is, now, a residential colony. On certain days, with a good pair of binoculars one could see the horses running from certain points in Mussoorie. Amongst other sports fishing and shooting were popular. As far back as 1867 the Doon Fish Protection Association was formed by some enthusiastic anglers of the district, but it failed to enforce any proper protection. In 1887 the Dehra Dun Fishing Association was formed. It leased certain portions of the Song, Suswa and Asan rivers from the Forest Department for the use of its members as, generally, the rivers were poisoned or dynamited by the general public. Angling with rod and line only was permitted and members were expected to return to the water Mahseer weighing less than 500 grams or Trout weighing less than 200 grams. The Association owned two bungalows, for use by its members, one being at Sat Narain at the Song-Ganga junction and the other at Kulhal near the Asan-Yamuna junction. These are now with the Forest Department.

After the opening of the Hardwar-Dehra railway in 1900 the old route from Saharanpur through the Mohand Pass was used less frequently by people coming to the Doon. "Dolies" and "Dak Gharies" were soon forgotten and were replaced by Tongas, Phaetons and Buggys between Dehra and Rajpur. From Rajpur one still travelled to Mussoorie by "Dandi" or by pony.

Rajpur, which consists really of three villages, viz., -Rajpur, Dhakpatti and Birgirwali, was first in the early days of British occupation, a sanitorium for invalid soldiers. When Landhaur was opened up Rajpur became a staging post on the journey to Mussoorie. At one time it boasted of a club, two hotels (both of which were destroyed by fire), a mule breeding farm, the Sahastradhara Mineral Water Company. Some of the Agencies like Smith Rodwells, Ellenborough, the Prince of Wales (1835) and Chapmans (1860) were established for transporting baggage and attending to the many wants of the traveller passing through. The Himalaya Glass Works Ltd., was established at Rajpur in 1901.

This Company was started by Sir D.P. Masson and Mr. C.H. Ortel, Barrister-at-Law with a paid-up capital of Rupees 1,00,000. It produced all kinds of glassware which found a ready market. The raw material required for glass manufacture was available in abundance on the spot. The reason for its liquidation is not known. At one time sand from Rajpur was sent to the Ambala Glass Factory.

The old "Cart Road" remained in fairly good order from Rajpur to Kolukhet. With the advent of the motor car, Col. E.W. Bell a Tea Planter and a son-in-law of the Swetenhams thought of testing this road by car. He successfully drove a T-model Ford car, in 1920 by this road from Dehra Dun to Kulri in Mussoorie, thus paving the way for motor transport to the hill station. In 1926, the Mussoorie City Board obtained a substantial loan from the State government for the construction of a motor road upto Bhatta which became the terminus. This motor road was gradually extended till in 1930 "Sunny View" four miles beyond Bhatta, became the terminus. Mr. Shiv Darshan Lal, Barrister-at-Law, popularly known as Barrister Darshan Lal, during his tenure as Chairman City Board Mussoorie, had in 1936 another one mile of motorable road built and "Kincraig" became the terminus for cars and buses. To-day cars are plying all over Mussoorie like the rickshaws did in the old days. The Gwalior and Northern India Transport Co. Ltd., a company owned by His Highness Gwalior, plied its buses between Saharanpur and Mussoorie. This company had the contract for carrying the Royal Mail on this route. In those days because of the heavy bullock and horse traffic the roads used to be strewn with the animals' shoes and nails. These punctured a large number of motor vehicle tyres which passed over them. In order to reduce the punctures the transport company had people, on contract, collecting nails and animal shoes from the roads where its buses plied. It was cheaper to employ the labour than buying a set of tyre and tube for the vehicle and the time wasted on the road in replacing them. A toll tax was imposed by Mussoorie City Board on all modes of transport using the motor road, to defray the cost and upkeep of it. Buses took 3 1/2 to 4 hours from Saharanpur to Mussoorie. In 1954 motor traffic went upto the Library and in 1957 upto Picture Palace.

Before motor transport came fully into its own an attempt was made to connect Dehra and Mussoorie by tram-way. In 1919 an Indian Christian entrepreneur from Gujranwala (now in Pakistan) named Gilani, his initials being B.S. (Belti Shah) which people later changed to G.S. (Guilty Shah), floated a public limited Company. It was called the "Dehra Dun-Mussoorie Tramways". A number of people invested their money in this Company. One of the major share-holders was Maharaja Ripudaman Singh, of Nabha, who on the advice of his Accountant General, invested one million rupees. According to a contemporary courtier of the Maharaja the latter could not discern whether the advice tendered to him was sincere or not. The Accountant General, however, took advantage of this investment by getting his semi-educated son a job in the Company. In order to enable the Company to go ahead with the project Rajpur town, which was a Notified area under the Notified Areas Act, was denotified and placed under the Mussoorie Municipal Board. This was done because under the above mentioned Act the laying of a tramway system in the Notified area was prohibited. In spite of all available facilities and finance the bubble burst and no tramway service came into being, and the Company went into liquidation. Gilani was prosecuted and convicted, for misappropriation of the Company's money, and imprisoned. Hence the name "Guilty Shah"!

As there was no Christian grave yard in the Doon till after the annexation of the Valley by the British, General Gillespie had to be buried in Meerut. The present Dehra Dun cemetry was started around 1819 or thereabouts. The oldest marked grave in it is a tombstone bearing the inscription, "Sacred to the memory of John Graves, son of John Graves, Sgt. Major, Sirmur Battalion, who died on 9th April, 1820, aged 25 days". It is in the shape of a toy Noah's Ark on a plinth. Some graves have a large one-roomed mausoleum on a raised plinth. Only one side has a wall, which bears the inscription, and pillars on the remaining three sides to support the dome shaped roof which is surmounted by an urn. The reason for erecting such large mausoleums, the largest being 13 feet by 13 feet and 13 in height and the smallest being 6 feet by 6 feet by 6 feet, over the graves was because of a belief that was prevalent amongst Christians in the first half of the 19th century.

The belief was that after death the spirit, after leaving the body hovered over it for ten days before uniting with God. So, to provide a suitable "Shelter" for the hovering spirit this type of a mausoleum was provided. This belief is identical to the belief amongst the Hindus. In their case since the body is cremated the spirit continues living in the room where the person died, for ten days. In order to keep the spirit company, the chief mourner lives and sleeps in that room and a lamp is kept lighted in it for ten days. On the eleventh day the spirit leaves the place and merges in the Cosmos.

Apart from the styles mentioned above there are tombstones in the Dehra Dun cemetery in the shapes of coffins, urns, pillars, marble slabs with a cross or a scroll, Bible or an angel placed upon them. Some inscriptions are quite interesting. One such inscription on the tomb of a wife reads:-

"Weep not for me my husband dear,
But pray and think of me;
As I am now so you must be,
Prepare yourself to follow me."

From the lychgate register it appears that the oldest person buried in the cemetery was a lady who was 100 years, while amongst the men is one who was 99 years.

With the opening up of Landhaur (Mussoorie) Cantonment the first burial in Mussoorie was that of Captain Sir C. Farrington of the 35th Regiment, who died on 28th March, 1828, aged 35 years. He was buried by the side of the Rajpur-Mussoorie bridle path, to the left of the Halfway House. Perhaps he was too ill to make it to the Invalids Home in Mussoorie and died enroute and buried where he died. His grave was later moved into the Oak Grove School's estate in Jharipani. In Mussoorie proper there are two cemeteries, one at Landhaur and one along the Camel's Back road. The first European buried in Landhaur was Captain George Bolton who died on 13th June, 1838, after some months of painful suffering. His memorial was erected by his affectionate widow. Amongst those buried in Mussoorie is a survivor out of the "six hundred" from the 1854 "Charge of the Light Brigade" in the Crimean war made famous by the poem of that name. The person is John Hindmarsh who died at Landhaur on 16th April, 1890 in his 59th year. Another person is the first Australian born novelist John Lang. Two of his works, "The Weatherbys" and "The Ex-wife", find mention in the Cambridge History of English Literature. He was a Barrister by profession and had come out to India to make a living. In Australia he found it difficult to practice because he was a convict's son. He died in Mussoorie in 1864 at the age of forty-seven, after having retired there from Calcutta.

Similarly with the setting up of Cantonments in Chakrata, Kalsi, Clement Town, Prem Nagar and Rajpur cemeteries were established. The first burial in Chakrata was of Sergeant John Cash, in 1869, of the 55th Regiment, the first lot of troops to occupy the place. One of the persons buried there is a Mrs. E. Reilly wife of the brewer who was employed at the Dyer Meakin Brewery in Chakrata.

Since Muslim graves are usually unmarked there is no record of the oldest among them. Hindus, of course, after cremation of their dead immerse the ashes in the nearest lake or river preferably in the Ganga, at Haridwar, as it is considered the holiest of the holies. Their belief is that as long as a single piece of a dead person's bone lies at the bottom of the Ganga the deceased will not be reborn and thus achieve salvation. Hence there are no tombstones and yet in the pre-vedic times dead were buried in certain parts of India, like the upper reaches of Garhwal. In certain tribes burial of the dead still takes place. Hindus sometimes erect a cenotaph or "Samadhi" at the spot where cremation took place. In Guru Ram Rai's gurudwara precincts there are such "Samadhies" (cenotaphs).

Apart from the coming of the railway to the Doon, the start of the 20th century saw a number of events taking place in the world. Some of these had their impact on the Doon also. One of them was the passing away of Queen Victoria, after a reign of 63 years. She had assumed the title of Empress of India. Like the rest of the country the three Jubilees of her reign - Silver, Golden and Diamond were celebrated in Dehra Dun and Mussoorie by the common man who illuminated his house as did the local institutions. She was succeeded in 1901 by her son Edward VII who was the first King Emperor of India. In celebration of his crowning a Coronation Durbar was held at Delhi in November 1902. The Duke and Duchess of Connaught came out to represent Their Majesties at the Durbar and afterwards visited Mussoorie. His reign was short-lived as he died in 1910.

However during the first decade of the century Dehra Dun and Mussoorie grew tremendously in size. A number of government institutions were established in Dehra Dun. In 1901 the population of Dehra Dun district had grown to 1,78,195 of which that of Dehra Dun was 28,273. It is interesting to note that between 1910 and 1912, at one time, there were five young Indian men of Dehra Dun, of well to do families, all students of Woodside's Mission School, who had gone to England to study law. They were Ugra Sen, Darshan Lal, Ram Chander Kukreti, Uma Prasad and Kishori Lal Shah. Of these the first three came back as qualified Barristers while the remaining two returned with Barmaids for wives instead of a law degree. Unfortunately Kukreti died young. The other two Barristers rose to great heights in the district and played a leading role in its development.

In 1912 the Raja of Tehri Garhwal built a road from Jhalki village, in his territory to Nagal village in district Dehra Dun. This he did in order to get a shorter route, for the produce of his state, to reach Dehra Dun without having to go through Mussoorie.

Lord Curzon, the Viceroy, raised the Imperial Cadet Corps in 1901. The aim of this Corps was to impart military training to young Indian princes, who after their training were allowed to wear Army badges of the rank which was conferred on them by the British Government. For this purpose a College was established at Dehra Dun in the campus now occupied by the Rashtriya Indian Military College. The buildings of the College were designed, by Mr. Ransom, Architect to the Government of India, in the Tudor style, with gabled roofs. Amongst the first batch of cadets was a Col. Sir Pratab Singh, an uncle of the then Maharaja of Jodhpur. He came to attend the College not as a young man but a man ripe in years. He later went to Europe to take part in World War I. While at the Cadet College he was presented an address of welcome by the local Arya Samaj. During her visit to the Doon in 1905 Queen Mary, then Princess of Wales, paid a visit to this College. It had a temple and a mosque on the campus and there were separate messes for the Hindu and Muslim cadets. This College was disbanded at the outbreak of World War I. From 1914 to 1921 the College buildings were occupied by the Mechanical Transport Training School and a convalescent home for the War wounded.

In 1906 Kunwar Balbir Singh, a descendant of Raja Lal Singh, started an industrial complex, in the Pipal Mandi area of Dehra, with machinery imported from England and America. The mills supplied crushed oats, barley, gram, machine polished rice, mustard oil, flour and pure crystal ice. Those days the Civil Surgeon had to certify the purity of the ice sold in the town. In the same year a beginning was made to organise Forest research by establishing an institute at Dehra Dun.

It was housed in the Forest School, in town, and had six research departments. The Inspector General of Forests was the President of the Institute and College. Of the six Research Officers the first and only Indian was Sardar Puran Singh, who was designated Imperial Forest Chemist. He later become a disciple of Swami Ram Tirath and wrote a number of books on religion. The Institute carried on its work in the building in town till 1914 when a part of Kaulagarh Tea Estate, known as Chand Bagh, was acquired and a building was put up to house the offices and laboratories. The new Campus was inaugurated by Lord Curzon, the then Viceroy. By the end of World War I this campus too was found inadequate for the Institute's requirements. Through the efforts of the then Inspector General of Forests, Sir Peter Clutterbuck, the Central Government decided in 1921 to acquire 1300 acres of land where the Institute is now located. Out of the total area acquired a part was given for a Railway Staff College and Training Institute.

The move-over from Chand Bagh was over a period of time as all the buildings were not completed till 1928. However as soon as two houses had been completed the Utilisation Branch moved into one of them, and the other was occupied by its Officer-in-charge Mr. H. Trotter, of the Indian Forest Service. As no electric current was available, light was obtained from a generator driven by a Public Works Department's road roller. The flickering of the lights corresponded rhythmically with the "chug chug" of the roller's engine. The main building of the Institute, an imposing edifice and designed by Luteyns, the architect of New Delhi, is 350 yards long and covers a plinth area of 7 acres. It houses the Administration offices, the Biological branches, the Herbarium, the Museums, the Convocation Hall and the Indian Forest College. The College moved from Chand Bagh in 1933.

The main contractor for the building of this project was Rai Bahadur Sardar Narain Singh who was a hot headed man. His background was dubious. One story was that he was a dacoit in his youth who left his old ways under the influence of some Englishman, and started working as a building contractor in Delhi. The English Engineer, supervising the work of the buildings at the Institute, cast aspersions behind Narain Singh's back on his integrity and honesty. When he heard this, Narain Singh's old instincts were aroused and he vowed to go without food till he had killed the Englishman. The latter having got wind of the former's intention rushed to Delhi and begged the Viceroy to intercede on his behalf. On the Viceroy's request Narain Singh agreed to forgive the engineer provided he left India for good, which he did. The other two partners of Narain Singh in this project were Rai Bahadur Ram Ratan Puri and Lala Mukand Lal.

In those days there were several American and Canadian "Experts" at the Institute. One of them caused continual amusement, by insisting, in true democratic style, on calling his peon "Mister" Ram Parshad.

Dhonda was the head peon in the Forest Products Utilisation branch and was Incharge of the Branch's show-rooms. He knew every exhibit by heart and was prepared to guard them with his life. On one occasion, a walking stick, exhibited in the show-rooms, was lent to a Viceroy who was visiting the place and had come without his stick. Dhonda followed the Viceroy round the Institute, and as he was stepping into his car to leave, still holding the stick, Dhonda stepped forward and said, "My stick, I think Sir," and firmly took possession of it and replaced it in the museum.

Another notable character employed at the Institute was the revolutionary Rash Behari Bose, who was the President's Head Clerk, and lived in Ghosi Gali, off Paltan Bazar. On 22 December, 1912 he took a day's sick leave, caught the night train to Delhi, and threw a bomb at the Viceroy, Lord Hardinge, on the 23rd December while he was going in a procession seated on an elephant. Fortunately he escaped with his life though severely wounded in the neck and left shoulder. Bose came back, collected his pay the next day and disappeared from Dehra, living underground in Varanasi. He got a passport through the efforts of Raja Tagore of Calcutta who had property in Dehra where the Connaught Place complex now stands and was an uncle of the great Rabindra Nath Tagore. Bose left the country and next surfaced in Japan where he took political asylum. There he married a Japanese and along with Raja Mahendra Pratap, another Indian revolutionary and an expatriate, set up a government of Free India in exile. He was also one of the organisers of the Indian National Army and took over from Capt. Mohan Singh in 1943. Bose died in Japan before 15th August, 1947 like his compatriot, Subhas Bose, while Mahendra Pratap came back to India and passed his last days in Dehra, where his son and daughter had already settled.

The Secretary of State for India in 1905 sanctioned the establishment of an X-ray Institute at Dehra. It was set up in the premises on Rajpur Road now occupied by the Controller of Air Force Accounts. It was regarded as a most useful and unique hospital for X-ray treatment. Its chief function was to train government doctors in the various branches of X-ray apparatus and treatment. For this purpose regular courses were held periodically. It ran for the next thirty years when it was closed down as training in X-ray had become common in all medical colleges in the country. On its closure the premises were handed over to the army and were occupied by the headquarters of the Meerut District.

Similarly, by the Leper Act of 1898, a Leper Asylum was started in 1906. It is still functioning near the Dehra Dun railway station and is known as the Mac Laren Leper Asylum in memory of its founder who was the then Civil Surgeon.

In 1905 the two Battalions of the 9th Gorkha Rifles arrived at Dehra Dun on 30th January after a ten-day route march from Lansdowne which had been their Regimental Centre. In the absence of all other accommodation Officers and men were housed in tents on an open space between the lines of the two battalions of the 2nd Gorkha Rifles. After the arrival of the 9th Gorkha's two Mountain Batteries of artillery were also posted at Ganghora, and the Garhwal Brigade Headquarters were also set up. Birpur was eventually selected as the site for the 9th Gorkha's Regimental Centre. At the time the area consisted of a bare stony plateau. The area derived its name from the village which was situated on the site of the present Officers' bungalows. No roads or water supply, other than that in the Tons Nullah (stream), existed nor was there a bridge over it. The troops moved over in May 1905. During the remaining part of the year the men dug and laid foundations for some of the barracks, made sun-dried bricks, collected timber and other building material.

The Garhwal Brigade Commander was made responsible for the troops in Dehra Dun, Landhaur, Chakrata, Roorkee, Almora and Lansdowne. This responsibility was found to be too much for one Commander and in 1910 the area was split into two, the Dehra Dun and the Garhwal Brigades. The former was to look after the first three stations while the latter assumed command of the remainder. The first Dehra Brigade Commander was Major General Browne.

In 1911 both the 2nd Gorkhas and the 9th Gorkhas had the honour of being present in Delhi at the time of the Delhi Darbar at which King George V and Queen Mary were present and where their accession to the throne as Emperor and Empress of India was announced. Another announcement made was that the capital of India was to be transferred from Calcutta to Delhi which would be the winter seat with Simla being the summer headquarters, of the Viceroy and the Government of India. George and Mary had been to India earlier, in 1905, as the Prince and Princess of Wales. On that occasion Queen Mary had visited Dehra Dun and Mussoorie while her husband was on a shoot in Saharanpur.

The 2nd Gorkha Rifles completed their 100 years of existence in 1915. This event was commemorated, among other celebrations, by building a memorial arch at the entrance of the Macpherson Lines. It was designed and executed by the then Assistant Engineer of the Central Public Works Department, Sardar Uttam Singh. As a token of their appreciation for the work done by him, a wall clock was presented to him by the Regiment. This clock still works and adorns his Son's house, 18 Nemi Road, Dehra Dun. This Archway, serves as a reminder of the various battles in which the Regiment took part during those 100 years, and has inscribed on it the names of its dead. A portrait in bronze of King Edward VII the work of Sir G. Frampton, and cast in England, adorned the centre of the arch. Unfortunately this work of art and historical importance was removed, by the powers that be, when the Regiment joined the British army in 1947.

With the outbreak of World War I, in 1914, both the regiments went overseas and saw action in Europe and the Middle East. The 2nd Battalion of the 2nd Gorkhas came back to India in 1916 after eighteen months service overseas. It disembarked at Karachi on 28th February, 1916 and entrained for the Doon. The train made a four hour halt at Lahore where a telegram from the Mahant of Guru Ram Rai's Gurudwara was delivered to the Commanding Officer. It read, "Congratulate you all on your bravery and good service for our government and General Maharaja blessings on the Regiment." Obviously the Mahant was addressing the Commanding Officer as "General Maharaja". The Gorkhas arrived at Dehra Dun on 3rd March.

At the railway station they were greeted by a large number of civil and military officers as well as the local gentry. There was a band playing. Tea and cigarettes were offered to the troops by the citizens of the town. The route from the station to their Lines was decorated and lined by applauding crowds. Garlands and flowers were showered on the men as they marched through Jhanda Bazar and Dandipur Road (now Tilak Road). Welcome arches were put up on the route with words like, "Welcome ye guardians of the Doon" and "you have deserved well of your country," painted on them. The Regimental Truncheon and old retired Gorkha officers led the march. From Bindal bridge to the Centenary Memorial Arch the Mall Road was lined by the new recruits of the Regiment. The Lines were a mass of coloured buntings. Similar receptions were given to the other battalions, of both the Regiments, on their return from overseas duty. Early in 1915 two regiments of the Nepalese army arrived in Dehra Dun as part of that country's assistance to the British, in fighting the war. These troops were under the command of General Tej Shamsher Jung, and were to be used for internal security and for service on the Indo-Afghan frontier. They were located in the Ghangora lines vacated by the Mountain batteries who had gone to war. A similar contingent was sent by Nepal during World War II under the command of General Kiran Shamsher Jang Bahadur Rana, the eldest son of Maharaja Judha Shamsher, the then Prime Minister of Nepal. This contingent was also located in the same lines.

While in Baquba in 1917 the 2nd Gorkha's Band acquired a mascot. After the Band had played one evening for the Brigade Commander's party, the Commander gave the bandsmen some young sheep for their table, one of which the men kept as a pet. In the course of time he grew into a fine large ram, and followed the Battalion all through Persia, and then came to Dehra with the men. He had by then become a Regimental mascot, and had picked up various tricks taught to him. One of these was for the men to tell the ram to go to a spot 50 yards away, where he halted and fronted at the word of command. On the command "charge" he would lower his head and come like a bullet for the men, one of whom would then cry out "Halt" when the animal was within a few yards of them, on which he at once planted his fore-feet and threw up his head. On the occasion of the Duke of Connaught's Darbar in 1920 the ram went to Delhi with the Regiment. There he marched past the Duke at the head of the band—an ornament to the Regiment and living emblem of its badge, a ram's head, a distinction dating from 2nd October, 1824 when under Young the 'Paltan' had stormed the gates of Kalua's Kunja Fort, near Roorkee, with a battering ram.

At the end of 1913 trouble arose in regard to the religious aspect of those Gorkhas returning from overseas duties. Till then the Regimental Pandit (Priest) put the individual through a brief ceremony to regain his caste. This time on the return of a Subedar Major, who had gone to England, as an orderly to the King Emperor, the ceremony he underwent at the hands of the Regimental Pandit was not acceptable to the Nepalese Darbar. After a lot of correspondence between the Governments of India and Nepal it was agreed that the latter government would maintain a specially selected Pandit in India to conduct the required ceremonial, by means of which all could regain their caste when necessary. The Indian Army Chief ordered a ''Paani Patia'' centre, in other words a ''Readmittance to the caste'' Centre at Dehra, in the 2nd Gorkha Lines, known as Patia camp and where this Pandit would reside. Gorkha troops, from all Regiments, who had been overseas would have to come to him for the ceremony. The ceremony took three days to complete, and if any Gorkha Johnny went back home without performing the required ceremonies he was liable to arrest and punishment there for defiling the caste of his people.

Following the passing of the Rowlatt Act in January 1919, disturbances broke out in the country culminating in the ''Jallianwala Bagh'' massacre in Amritsar. In April 1919 a Battalion of the 9th Gorkha Rifles was on its way from Dehra to Peshawar. By the time the special troop train arrived at Amritsar station the riots in the city were at their worst, and the Gorkhas were ordered to detrain to help in restoring order. The Battalion was to be rearmed at this time with a new Rifle, and so the troops had handed in all arms at Dehra prior to their departure. Thus the men had no rifles when they detrained. Fifty men were therefore marched to the Fort and rifles and ammunition were issued from the armoury there. Picquets were then posted at various points in the city and cantonment to assist the police. Brigadier General R.E. Dyer with his staff and reinforcements arrived from Jullundhar and assumed command. Martial Law was then proclaimed. On April 13 (Baisakhi Day) a mob had gathered in Jallianwalabagh in defiance of probihitory orders. General Dyer proceeded to the spot with twenty five riflemen, each from the 9th Gorkhas and 59th Rifles, and fired on the unarmed crowd without warning. The crowd numbered between ten and twenty thousand; the known official casualties were 380 killed and over 1200 wounded. According to the Regimental historian and former Commanding Officer, writing in 1937, ''the men behaved in an exemplary manner in a most trying and distasteful episode''.

Both the 2nd and the 9th Gorkha Regiments were to take part in the third Afghan War in 1919-20 before settling down to peace time duties, till the outbreak of World War II in 1939. One of the annual events that took place, during this period, was a New Year's Day Parade at which all the units in Dehra took part.

After World War I, Field Marshal Lord Rawlinson the then Commander-in-Chief of the Indian Army, pointed out the need for a College to train young Indian boys for eventual absorption in the commissioned ranks of the army. In 1921, it was therefore decided by the Central Legislative Assembly that adequate facilities should be provided in India for imparting preliminary training to boys to make them fit for entry to the Royal Military College, Sandhurst. The Secretary of State for India approved the establishment of such a college by the Government of India, in Dehra, on the Campus of the old Imperial Cadet Corps. On 13th March, 1922 the Prince of Wales (later Edward VIII) who abdicated the throne in order to marry his lady love, an American divorcee, inaugurated the College. It was named the Prince of Wales Royal Indian Military College and its badge consisted of three Ostrich Feathers with the motto ''Ich Dien'' the emblem of the Prince. The words mean ''I Serve.'' On his visit to the Doon for the inauguration, he was accompanied, amongst others, by the Viceroy Lord Reading and Lord Louis Mountbatten, an ADC, who was to later become the last Viceroy and Governor-General of India, in which capacity he again visited the Doon. Amongst the first batch of 37 cadets was a boy named K.S. Thimaya, later to become a General and the Chief of the Indian Army.

Now this institution has become a feeder to the nation's Officer training establishments for the three Services.

The Prince's other engagements, in Dehra, during his visit were to present the King's Commission as Lieutenant to Subedar Major Sarbjit Gurung, M.C., of the 2nd Gorkhas. He also presented the Gorkha Brigade Football Cup to the 9th Gorkhas team which was won by it a few days earlier.

Simultaneously with the building of New Forest as the campus of the Forest Research Institute is called, the Railway Staff College was being laid out on the adjoining land. In 1930 the main building of the College was completed. The Central Hall of this building had a miniature railway system. There were railway stations, marshalling yards and sidings. Across the length and breadth of it were numerous railway lines on which ran miniature trains operated by the trainees. There was a narrow gauge, Victorian era, steam locomotive housed in one of the rooms of the building. This engine was named "Fairy Queen". However this College was closed within two years because of the poor economic condition of the railways.

By now the Officer Cadre of the Indian Army was being Indianised. For training these future officers it was decided to start an Academy, on the lines of the Royal Military Academy, Sandhurst, at Dehra Dun. In those days there was neither an Indian Navy nor an Air Force. The estate of the closed Railway Staff College was taken over for this purpose. On 10th December, 1932 Field Marshal Sir Philip Chetwode, Bt., G.C.B., K.C.M.G., D.S.O. Commander-in-Chief in India inaugurated the Indian Military Academy in the Central Hall where railway personnel were being trained. The Hall and the building were named after him and they still bear the name. During his inaugural speech Chetwode advised Gentlemen Cadets present to always bear in mind the following words:-

"The safety, honour and welfare of your country come first, always and every time.
The honour, welfare and comfort of the men you command come next.
Your own ease, comfort and safety come last, always and every time."

These words have been adopted by the Cadets as their creed to live by as officers. The first Commandant of the Academy was Brigadier L.P. Collins, D.S.O., O.B.E. He had a little over two months with the first batch of forty cadets, who had arrived on 30th September, 1932, to whip them into shape for the Inaugural parade on 10th December. Incidentally his brother was, at that time, commanding the Dehra Brigade. The "Pioneers", as these forty cadets were called, were commissioned into the army in December 1934. Amongst them was Sam Manekshaw, later to become a Field Marshal. Amongst the other cadets who have brought laurels to the Academy were Lt. Gen. P.S. Bhagat, who won the Victoria Cross in World War II, and Maj. Som Nath Sharma who won the Param Vir Chakra posthumously during Kashmir operations in 1947. Both had done their schooling at the Royal Indian Military College, Dehra Dun, before joining the Academy. Melville DeMellow, the famous one time announcer and news reader over All India Radio was also amongst the "Pioneers". He had done his schooling at St. George's College Mussoorie, and had to leave the army for romantic reasons.

The daily needs of the Cadets, like food, clothes etc. were supplied by a civilian contractor. The contract was given to Rai Bahadurs Ram Rattan and Prem Nath Puri who were father and son and were both Rai Bahadurs. The former was earlier a partner in the firm of the New Forest building contractors. In order to execute the contract efficiently the Rai Bahadurs started an establishment of their own, outside the Academy limits. They were able to prevail on the government to establish a Post and Telegraph office within their establishment which included a dairy and an ice factory. They named this little township Prem Nagar after Prem Nath and Prem, a son of Barrister Darshan Lal, who was treated by Ram Rattan as his own grandson.

During World War II the Academy became an Officer's Training School for the training of Emergency Commissioned Officers. The duration of the training period was cut down from two and a half years to one and a half years. In the five years between 1941 and 1945 over a thousand Officers - Indian, British and from other British dominions were commissioned. In early 1946 the Emergency courses were discontinued and the old routine resumed. After 15th August, 1947 the last English Commandant handed over charge to his Indian Deputy, Brigadier Thakur Mahadeo Singh D.S.O., who later became a Major General and has a road named after him near the Academy.

In December 1885 the Indian National Congress was inaugurated at Bombay. Its first President was a retired British Civilian, A.D. Hume (no relation of General Hume). Initially it was a modest body consisting of upper middle class Indians and Englishmen as its members. Even Lord Dufferin the Viceroy, gave his guarded initial approval. However after a decade it had grown into a position of political opposition to government. From the Doon, a descendant of Hyder Hearsey, Capt. A.W. Hearsey who was a Congressman spoke at one of the All-India sessions of the party. An English newspaper, published from Lahore, reporting the meeting's proceedings wrote that a "brown man "who called himself a military Captain" said so-and-so. Being called a "brown man" cut Capt. Hearsey to the quick and arming himself with a horse-whip he caught the first train to Lahore. He asked for the reporter who had written the news. On being told that the concerned person was away on leave, Hearsey stomped into the Editor's room and without much ado whipped him. The court case that followed evoked wide-spread interest. In the cross examinations of various persons there were quite a few verbal duels fought in the court room. One such instance was when the opposing counsel wanted Hearsey to acknowledge the authorship of a doggerel which had appeared in the Mussoorie papers. It was:

"While your fathers were selling caps, coats and breeches, our sons were fighting in trenches and ditches". "Do you mean to say," questioned the lawyer, "that while you were fighting we were selling coats and breeches?" The answer given was: "And caps—oh! and if anything fits you are welcome to wear it!" Obviously the reference was to the Box-wallah (the editor) and the Soldier (Hearsey). This episode was before the Europeans and the Eurasians had changed their views about the Congress party.

The Doon saw a number of activities connected with the freedom struggle launched by the Congress, and a large number of people participated in them. The first district political conference was held in 1920, and amongst others was addressed by Lala Lajpat Rai, Jawahar Lal Nehru, Saifuddin Kitchlu, Stokes and Asif Ali. After attending the conference Nehru took his mother and his wife to Mussoorie as they were both unwell. Indira, his baby daughter, was also with them. In Mussoorie they stayed at the Savoy Hotel. The Afghan delegation, who had come for peace talks with the British, after the 1919-20 Anglo-Afghan War, was also staying in the same hotel. While staying there, one evening, Nehru was visited by the District Superintendent of Police who had been directed by the government to obtain an undertaking from the former that he would not have any dealings or contact with the Afghans. Since he had no contact with them during the month he had been there, and also had no intention of doing so, he refused to give such an undertaking. The result was that an externment order was served on him calling upon him to leave Dehra Dun district within twenty four hours. Nehru left the Doon, leaving the two ladies behind, as he did not want to defy the government order.

Thereafter a correspondence followed between Governor Sir Harcourt Butler and Pandit Moti Lal Nehru, who knew each other well, regarding the externment order. Finally Moti Lal wrote and said that order or no order, if the ladies' health required his son's presence he will go to Mussoorie. In the meantime the senior Mrs. Nehru's (Swarup Rani) condition took a turn for the worse and the father and son rushed to Mussoorie. A telegram rescinding the order was delivered to them just before they left Allahabad. Jawahar Lal had visited Mussoorie for the first time in 1906 summer when he came from England, on a few weeks holiday, to be with his parents at the hill station. He had gone to Harrow in 1905 at the age of 15 years and was in England for seven years. It was in the summer of 1928 when his family was in Mussoorie that Jawahar Lal wrote his famous letters to his daughter Indira (Gandhi). In 1930 he published them in a book form for school children.

In 1921 the Congress launched the non-cooperation movement. The people of Dehra Dun collected Rs. 16,000/- for the Tilak Swaraj Fund and a number of shops, dealing in foreign cloth were picketed because their owners had broken the pledge not to sell such cloth. One of the earliest Congressmen to go to jail for his Congress activities was Nardeo Shastri. As the agitation against the sale of foreign cloth and picketing of liquor shops was going on an ugly incident occurred resulting in violence. On the evening of December 24, (Christmas eve) 1921 an altercation took place at one of the liquor shops between some Congressmen and an English youth, who fired two shots from his revolver wounding one person. By January 1922 over a thousand volunteers had enrolled to carry on the agitation. Meetings were held, processions were taken out and at a meeting in March 1922 it was decided to boycott the visit of the Prince of Wales who was coming to Dehra on the thirteenth of the month. On arrival at the Dehra Dun railway station the Prince was greeted with black flags by some Congress workers, who were promptly arrested. On the other hand, the official reception was a glittering affair. School children from the European Schools lined his route from the station to the Cantonment.

The year 1922 was a momentous one, politically, for the Doon. During the beginning of the year Congress organised a number of meetings. One such meeting was organised at Doiwala which Jawahar Lal Nehru and Swami Shankracharya addressed. Nehru in his speech called upon the people to adopt the use of Swadeshi textiles, eschew violence in the agitation against government, refer their legal disputes to arbitration and work for national unity. At the annual Gang Bhewa fair, in the Western Doon, a congress worker from Gujarat exhorted the people to abstain from using foreign sugar and medicines as bones were used in their manufacture. In those days a lot of sugar was imported from Indonesia. The Khilafat movement of the Muslims led by Maulana Mohammad Ali and Maulana Shaukat Ali, commonly known as the Ali brothers, also found support in the Doon. In the month of July a meeting was addressed by Pandit Madan Mohan Malaviya. In the following October a Provincial Congress Conference was held in Dehra. Over 6000 persons attended it, amongst them were Mrs. Sarojini Naidu, T.A.K. Sherwani, V.J. Patel (Sardar Vallabhbhai Patel's elder brother), Bhai Amman, Begum Mohammad Ali, and was presided over by Moti Lal Nehru. The Provincial Khilafat Conference was also held simultaneously in the town and amongst those who attended it were a number of women and Hindus. In April 1924 Jawahar Lal Nehru visited the Doon and was presented with a purse of Rs. 1900/- for the Tilak Swaraj Fund. In November 1924 an All India Hindi Literary Conference was held in Mussoorie under the auspices of the Tilak School of Politics. Maharaja Ripudaman Singh of Nabha, who was residing in Mussoorie at the time, was invited by Babu Purshottam Das Tandon, who had earlier been the Maharaja's political adviser in Nabha, to address the Conference. The Maharaja who was later deposed for his national outlook, spoke against the British government's policy of repression and exploitation. He also gave a donation towards the setting up of the Tilak Memorial Library in Mussoorie. This action of the Maharaja brought him one step closer to deposition.

During the next two years political/social activity in the Doon was confined to two episodes. The first one was the filing of a case by the local Arya Samaj against the Englishman owning the Herbertpur Tea Estate in the Western Doon. He had prohibited the Harijans of the area from taking water from the well situated in his estate. The Samaj won the case and the Tea Planter had to withdraw his order.

In those days Arya Samaj was known for its zeal in converting people of all faiths to Hinduism. Under this programme the local Arya Samaj authorities were taken for a ride by one Henry John William, a native Christian. He had his family and himself converted to Hinduism. At the time of conversion he was ill, hence he got monetary help from the Samaj to support his family and for his own treatment. As a further help his grown up children were sent to the Samaj's orphanage at Bareilly for education. After a few months, on recovering from his illness, the ungrateful wretch lodged a report with the Police alleging that the Samaj had abducted his children. On investigation the Police found out the truth and the case was filed.

The other activity was the holding of elections to the Provincial legislative council in 1926. Election meetings were held by the Congress throughout the district and they were addressed by Moti Lal Nehru, Hakim Ajmal Khan, Maulana Abul Kalam Azad, Horniman and Mahatma Gandhi's son Dev Das Gandhi. The Congress candidate was Thakur Manjit Singh, son of Thakur Mitrajit Singh a great Arya Samajist and social worker. Manjit Singh had been orphaned in his childhood and was brought up by his widowed sister with help from a friend of their father's Mr. Jyoti Swarup, Advocate, the founder of the local Mahadevi Kanya Pathshala. Manjit had been jailed in the 1921 agitation. In the election he defeated Rai Bahadur Ugra Sen, Barrister, the sitting member.

A public meeting was held and was addressed by a British Labour member of Parliament Mr. Mardy Jones. At this meeting a resolution was passed urging the people to boycott the Simon Commission. A black flag demonstration was held at the railway station on the visit of two members of the Commission to Dehra. Demonstrations were also held on the arrest of Bhagat Singh and Batukeshwar Dutt the persons responsible for throwing a bomb in the Assembly Hall at Delhi and the Lahore conspiracy case. At a public meeting they were praised for their bravery.

On 16th October, 1929 Mahatma Gandhi paid his first visit to Dehra Dun. He came to address a district political conference being held in the town under the Presidentship of Babu Purushottam Das Tandon. Jawahar Lal Nehru also came for this conference.

The same day Gandhiji laid the foundation stone of Swami Shradhanand Anath and Vanita Ashram (an orphanage and rescued women's home) in the presence of Nehru and a large gathering of the town's people. The one acre plot of land and one wing of the buildings, of this institution situated on Dandipur Road (now Tilak Road), were donated by the family of Barrister Darshan Lal. This donation was made to commemorate the memories of his two elder brothers-Dr. Kunj Lal Vaish and Mr. Moti Lal, Advocate, who had both died young and childless. The former who belonged to the Provincial Medical Service was the first lecturer in Surgery at King George's Medical College at Lucknow, while the latter was a noted lawyer of Dehra Dun. The silver trowel and plate used at the ceremony are still preserved in the Ashram's office. That evening Mahatma Gandhi addressed a ladies' meeting at which nearly 4000 of them were present. He exhorted them to wear Khadi (handloom cloth) and ply the spinning wheel regularly. He was given a sum of Rs. 260/- towards the Lajpat Rai Memorial fund for which he had been given Rs. 825/- earlier in the day at the conference. Amongst the resolutions passed at the conference were those regarding removal of untouchability, agitate for reducing the number of Europeans on local self-government bodies like the Municipal Boards, prohibition, and making Hindi the common language of the country. A couple of days later he went to Mussoorie where at a public meeting he was presented with a silver replica of a Dandi (one of the conveyances, like a sedan chair, used at hill stations). This he auctioned on the spot and got Rs. 908/- for it towards his Khadi Development fund.

In September 1930 Moti Lal Nehru, on his release from jail, because of serious illness, came to Mussoorie to recoup his health. He was accompanied by his wife and the two daughters - Mrs. Krishna Hutheesingh and Mrs. Vijaya Lakshmi Pandit (who later lived in Rajpur). Jawahar Lal, and his wife also came up in October, for three days to be with the family. These were to be his last three days with his father before he died. During Moti Lal's stay at Musoorie Reverend Chisholm, the Chaplain of Christ Church there, in one of his Sunday Services prayed to God for Moti Lal's speedy recovery. This act of the padree earned him a severe reprimand from the Government of the day.

On the launching of the Salt Satyagraha by Mahatma Gandhi, by breaking the Salt Act at the end of his Dandi march, the district of Dehra Dun also became involved in it. People made unlawful salt in the compounds of government offices like the District Court, Municipal Office and other public places, and were imprisoned for their action. By this time the people of the Doon had become so politically conscious that anti-British meetings were becoming a common phenomenon and the crowds at these meetings becoming larger and larger. On August 29, 1931 a bomb the size of a cricket ball, was thrown into the house of the city's Kotwal (police chief) injuring a number of people.

The two decades between the two World Wars were the heyday of the Raj in India. The saying that "The Sun never sets on the British Empire" was geographically true. Politically, during this period, apart from the Congressmen who were anti-government, there were the Liberal Indians like Sir Tej Bahadur Sapru and Mr. Jayakar and the complete toadies who would always side with the government. There was a sprinkling of the Liberals amongst the educated in every town in the country which had a sizable European population, whilst the other two categories abounded everywhere. These Liberals mixed with the Europeans, dressed like them and sometimes tried to live like them. Yet when it came to nationalism they were as nationalist as the Congressmen. Some of them surreptitiously gave monetary help to the families of indigent Congressmen when the menfolk went to jail, while others provided shelter to those who went underground. Jai Prakash Narain, Ram Manohar Lohia and Govind Sahai satyed in the basement, in Mussoorie in 1942-43, at the house of one such so called toady. In the Doon, at that time, amongst such Liberals were Rai Bahadur Chowdhary Sher Singh, Rai Bahadur Ugra Sen, and Barrister Darshan Lal. All three had been classmates in the local A.P. Mission school founded by Woodside. After completing their High School the last two went to England to qualify at the Bar while the third looked after his Zamindari. During the 1930s all three were simultaneously presiding over the three local self-government bodies - Sher Singh over the Zila Parishad, (District Board), Ugra Sen over Dehra Dun Municipality and Darshan Lal over Mussoorie City Board. They were considered toadies by the local Congressmen. Yet, if they (the three) played host to Jawahar Lal Nehru or Vijaya Lakshmi Pandit or had Gandhiji lay the foundation stone of the family's gifted orphanage, the Provincial Governor and his underlings were also entertained by them. In that decade these three sons of the Doon contributed a lot towards the development of the district. The present water-works, which supplies the town of Dehra, was the work of Ugra Sen who also built the commercial complex of Astley Hall and Manda House on Rajpur Road. The latter property belongs to a former Prime Minister V.P. Singh. Barrister Darshan Lal extended the motor road to Kincraig, increased the generating capacity of electricity at Galogi power-house and reduced the toll tax on bus passengers travelling to Mussoorie. He was also responsible for the erection of the clock-tower at Landhaur and also later became the first Indian Chairman of the two tea companies in Dehra. Rai Bahadur Sher Singh opened up primary schools in the villages and made roads by which the villages in the interior of the Valley were connected to the nearby townships.

Those days apart from the Congress agitation two events of importance took place. One was the Silver Jubilee celebrations of King George V's reign. The event was celebrated on 6th May, 1935 with the usual army parade, a holiday for every one, sweets for school children, balls, illuminations, fireworks, titles and decorations for the "faithful". Rai Sahibs became Rai Bahadurs and so on. Unfortunately George V died on 20th January 1936 soon after the Jubilee. One year's state mourning was announced throughout the Empire and all the Englishmen in the Doon went about either wearing a black arm band or a black tie. This was their way of showing that they were in mourning. Some Indians also wore black ties or arm bands. He was succeeded by his eldest son Edward who abdicated, before being crowned, for the sake of marrying his lady love, Mrs. Wallis Simpson an American divorcee. They became the famous Duke and Duchess of Windsor and lived in exile. On 12th May, 1937 his younger brother the Duke of York was crowned King as George VI. The celebrations were similar to those of the Silver Jubilee. This time the Proclamations of his crowning were read by the heads of districts at the Army parade. In Mussoorie it was read by Barrister Darshan Lal, as the first citizen, being the Chairman of the City Board, at a parade held at the Library chowk (square). In Dehra the District Magistrate made the announcement. Special Jubilee and Coronation medals were struck and given to the leading citizens throughout the Empire.

In spite of the stronghold of the British over the Indian people the Indians always sided with the Congress party. A good example of this was when in the 1935 Dehra Dun Municipal elections all the seven elected seats went to the Congress nominees. Mr. Khurshid Lal became the first Congress Chairman of the Dehra Dun Municipality replacing Rai Bahadur Ugra Sen.

During his tenure as Chairman Khurshid Lal was able to prevail, on his friend Mr. Nemi Das, Chairman and Managing Director of the oldest Indian Bank in the Doon to make various "Gifts" to the town. These gifts were a sports pavilion on the Parade ground, a town-hall in the Municipal Board's office compound and a Women's Hospital Wing at the Doon (Civil) Hospital. The Bank was the Bhagwan Das Bank Ltd. Later on two of the local Congressmen, Mahabir Tyagi and Khurshid Lal, were to become ministers in Jawahar Lal Nehru's ministry. Likewise, in the 1937 elections to the Provincial Legislature, under the Government of India Act 1935, both the seats (rural and urban) from the Doon went to Congressmen.

In 1932 the Arya Samaj members in Dehra Dun organised a community lunch. At this meal people from all castes and creeds sat and ate together. The food was served by Harijans and eaten by the so called higher castes. For those days it was an unique achievement. The cost of the meal worked out to 3 annas (19 paise) per head and over a thousand people were fed.

In May 1933 a movement for the removal of untouchability was launched in the Doon by Mrs. Swarup Rani Nehru, Kamla Nehru and the wife of Raja Mahendra Pratap. Harijan Day was observed and non-Harijan Hindus cleaned the houses of their Harijan brethren.

Jawahar Lal Nehru came to Dehra Dun again in the summer of 1932, but this time as a prisoner of the Government and was lodged in the district jail where he stayed for fourteen and a half months. Along with Nehru, who had been transferred from Bareilly District Jail, Pandit Govind Ballabh Pant was also sent to Dehra Dun jail. His sentence expired two months later and he was released. While in jail Nehru was allowed to receive food from outside. This was brought to him regularly by Pandit Kashi Narain Tankha and his sons who are a Kashmiri family living in Mohalla (sector) Anand Chowk. In the afternoons Nehru could sometimes be seen taking a walk down Haridwar Road escorted by two Warders, who walked two paces behind him and he was not handcuffed. Sometimes he would be visited by his family members. In his autobiography which he started writing in June 1934 in Dehra Dun, he describes his stay in various jails in the country. It was in the Dehra Dun jail that he saw a Pangolin (ant eater) for the first time. This animal abounds in the Doon. He was allowed to keep a pet dog. On 23rd August, 1933 he was transferred to Naini prison from where he was released on 30th August because of his mother's illness.

Nine months later he was back in Dehra Dun jail. This time he was kept in a different ward which was worse than the previous one. According to him that year when the monsoon broke at the end of June Dehra had twelve inches of rain during the first seven days. He was not allowed out of his enclosure to take his exercise, as he had in the past, and the walls were so high that even the mountains were not visible. This time, because of his wife's illness, he was released on the 12th August, 1934 for a brief period of eleven days, and on being rearrested was sent to Almora. In 1940, on his being sentenced to two years imprisonment for offering individual Satyagrah or civil resistance against India's participation in World War II, Nehru was again lodged in Dehra Dun jail. He was released in December 1941. His next visit to the Doon was as Prime Minister, and he kept coming here for a holiday whenever he could take time off from his work. He was last in the Doon a day before he died.

After his fast, during his incarceration in the Agha Khan's palace in Pune, Mahatma Gandhi's health had been shattered. The British government released him in the middle of 1944. On being released he came to Mussoorie to recuperate and stayed at Birla House in Happy Valley. Every evening he would come to Kulri and hold his prayer meeting on the tennis courts in the compound of Sylverton, opposite Picture Palace. This was his last visit to the Doon.

After having made his peace in 1938 with the Government of India, the revolutionary and one time arch Communist M.N. Roy and his American wife Ellen made Dehra Dun their home. He had established the Communist Party of India in exile while residing in Moscow. It was in Dehra that he later established the Radical Renaissance Institute.

On October 27, 1935 Lord Willingdon, Viceroy and Governor-General of India inaugurated the first Public School of India - The Doon School. It was established at Chand Bagh, the old campus of the Forest Research Institute and College. This estate, which was the property of the Government of India, had been lying unused after the New Forest estate had been established. The government leased this property to the Indian Public Schools Society on a token lease money of Rupees 3000/- per year for the purpose of setting up a Public School. The first Headmaster of the school was selected in England by Willingdon's predecessor Lord Irwin (Halifax) who at that time was President of the British Board of Education. The man selected was A.E. Foot, a science teacher at Eton College in England. The most famous alumnus, so far, of the Doon School is Rajiv Gandhi a former Prime Minister of the country.

In February 1937, on the occasion of Id-ul-Zuha (Bakra Id) the Muslims of Dehra, took out a procession of gaily decorated cows. These were to be ultimately slaughtered to celebrate the festival. The Hindu population of the town took objection to this blatant demonstration, of complete disregard of their religious sentiments, by another community. The situation in the town became so tense that, in an otherwise peaceful town, Hindu-Muslim riots could have been sparked off. In order to defuse the explosive situation a delegation of leading Hindu citizens of the city, including Messrs. Ugra Sen, Khurshid Lal, Nardev Shastri, Triloki Nath Arti, Digamber Prashad, Chaudhary Behari Lal the Harijan leader, Sardar Amar Singh, Thakur Krishna Singh, Rai Bahadur Sher Singh and Mrs. Sharmada Tyagi wife of Mahabir Tyagi and a member of the Provincial

Legislature, headed by Mahant Lakshman Das of Darbar Guru Ram Rai met the District Magistrate. An assurance was obtained from him that in future such mischief will not be allowed to happen. The members of the local Arya Samaj, in 1939, sent four batches of volunteers to Hyderabad Deccan to participate in the All India agitation against the Nizam's order. He had ordered that throughout his state no new Hindu temples could be built and even the existing ones could not be repaired without his permission. Ultimately he had to give in to the agitators and rescind his orders.

The same year in the month of March, Subhas Chandra Bose, came to Dehra Dun after being elected Congress President, and addressed a public meeting at the grounds of the Municipal Office at Faltoo line.

Dehra Dun had come to be recognised as an ideal place for retirement, especially for civil and military officers. Climatically the place was more like England, unlike Bangalore and Pune which have a low rainfall and a warmer winter. The settlers came in large numbers after the opening of the Haridwar-Dehra Dun railway line and built houses, in the English style, in Dalanwala and along the Rajpur road. The areas assumed the appearance of a garden town as each house was situated in one to five acres of land (one acre being the minimum area required in Dalanwala under the Municipal Bye-laws). The spare land, in each compound, was dotted with lichi orchards and enclosed with well trimmed hedges so much so that Dehra came to be called a 'town of grey heads and green hedges'. The period between the two World Wars was placid, everything being cheap and plentiful. Socially 'Elevenses', like the 'Kitty Party' today, was an institution far too important for the lady of the house to omit. Neighbours dropped in and over a cup of coffee discussed the world and his wife. Tennis and Badminton parties were common and held by turns at various people's houses.

The following prices give an idea of the cost of living in those days:-

Houses were always available both for rent and for sale: average rent being Rs. 100/- per month and purchase price Rs. 20,000/-. Land for building varied from Rs. 750/- to Rs. 1000/- for one fifth of an acre. Food wise wheat was 16-17 Kgs to the rupee; lentils (Dal) 3-4 Kgs., sugar 3-31/2 Kgs, ghee 3/4 to 1 Kgm, milk 4-6 Litres, meat 60-80 paise per Kgm, pork (local) 25-35 paise per Kgm; eggs 60-80 paise per dozen, poultry 40 Paise to Rs. 1.50 each, Ducks Rs. 1.50 each and Turkeys Rs. 10 to 15 a pair. Game was available in season, jungle murgi at Re. 1/- to Rs. 1.50 each, pheasant Rs. 1.25 to Rs. 2/- each, peafowl Rs. 2-3 each, pigeon 25-35 paise each while quail were 6-8 for the rupee.

Fruit was available at: apples 35-50 paise, pears 15-30 paise, lichies 30-75 paise, plum 15-30 paise, peaches 25-50 paise and loquats at 25-35 paise per kilogram while mangoes were at 12-14 and desi ones 25-100 for the rupee, bananas being 15-35 paise per dozen. Vegetables varied according to season but were plentiful and cheap.

The cost of a Ford or a Chevrolet car was Rs. 3,000/- to Rs. 3,500/- while that of an Austin 8 Horse Power or Baby Austin as it was called was Rs. 1,800/-. It was the equivalent of the modern Maruti car. The most expensive car - the custom built Rolls Royce was priced from Rs. 50,000/- to Rs. 1,00,000/-, and Dehra could boast of having two of them. A Japanese car was available for Rs. 800/-. There was one such car in town belonging to a lady doctor. The problem with it was the non availability of spare parts - hence it never became popular. A good horse and buggy cost around Rs. 1,000/-while an elephant was double that. A good bicycle cost around Rs. 30/- while the expensive ones were Rs. 100/- with fancy fittings. One could buy a Japanese one for Rs. 10/-.

Domestic servant's wages were, Cooks Rs. 18/- to Rs. 25/-, Bearers Rs. 15 to Rs. 20/-, Malis (gardners) Rs. 12/- to Rs. 15/-, Sweepers Rs. 8-14, Syce or coach man for looking after horses Rs. 15/-, Tailor Rs. 25/- to Rs. 30/-, Car Driver Rs. 25/- to Rs. 60/-, and Motor cleaners Rs. 12/- to Rs. 18/- per month. Dhobi (Washerman) charged Rs. 2/- to Rs. 3/- per person of a family per month irrespective of the number of clothes and linen.

Masons, Carpenters and other skilled workers charged from Rs. 1.25 to Rs. 2/-per day while unskilled labours' wages were 35 paise to 65 paise per day.

Conveyance fares were:- Motor: Dehra Dun to Rajpur 50 paise to Rs. 2/- per seat, Dehra Dun to Saharanpur Rs. 1.50 to Rs. 3/- per seat, Dehra to Bhatta Rs. 5/- per seat while the hire of a full taxi car was 50 paise per mile inclusive of petrol or Rs. 4/- to Rs. 5/- per hour within Municipal limits. Phaeton (Victoria) and Tonga hires for the first hour were Rs. 1.25 and 75 paise and for subsequent hours were 50 paise and 35 paise respectively. Bullock carts could be hired at 50 paise per trip or 1/- per day.

Till the end of the British Raj trade and commerce was carried on by both Indian and European communities. In Dehra the shopping centre for Europeans was Astley Hall and the Natives shopped in Paltan and Peepal Mandi Bazaars. There were Dilman's Stores, General Merchants, Motor Stores and Workshops, Dispensing Chemists, Drapers and Milliners, Furniture Stores, Jewellers, Taxidermists, Tailors, Auctioneers and Photographers. Similar was the situation in Mussoorie with the Library and Kulri areas catering to the Sahib-logs and Landhaur to the Indians. A typical advertisement of a business establishment of those days is reproduced on the next page.

244

During the first year the impact of the War against Germany which was declared on 3rd September 1939, was hardly felt. It was only after the entry of Japan and the United States that activity in the Doon increased in raising men and material for fighting it. A large number of young men joined the Armed Forces. Even women, mostly from the Anglo-Indian community and westernised Indian families, got into uniform as Nurses or in the Women's Auxiliary Corps (India). They helped in handling office jobs previously held by men in uniform, who had now been sent on fighting duties. Two large camps were established in the Valley. One was for Italian Prisoners of War and the other for German, Italian and Japanese civilians who were living in India, Burma, Malay and Ceylon at the outbreak of the War and were interned.

In 1936 an Italian priest, Father Clement, had formed an Anglo-Indians and Domiciled Europeans Cooperative Housing Society. This Society had established a housing colony which was named Clement Town. As this colony was developing, the War started and suddenly something like 80,000 Italians taken prisoner in the African Campaign, had to be housed. As a consequence the Government of India requisitioned a number of houses belonging to the colonists along with a good slice of the Society's land for building a camp. The owners were promised that their properties which were taken on nominal rent, would be returned to them within six months after the end of the war. This was not done. After the prisoners had been repatriated on the conclusion of the War the entire camp was converted into the Joint Services Wing, the forerunner of the National Defence Academy, Pune. Amongst the Italian prisoners there were five Generals who were housed separately in a bungalow in Dilaram Bazar on Rajpur Road.

Similarly a Central Internment Camp was established at Prem Nagar, the township which had come into existence on the establishment of the Indian Military Academy. All the citizens of the Axis Powers, who had been rounded up in the South East Asian part of the British Empire were kept in this place for the duration of the War. It was from this camp that Heinrich Harar escaped into Tibet. There he became a teacher of the Dalai Lama and later wrote his memoir "Seven Years in Tibet". As many as ten Italian and Germans were rounded up in the Doon itself and initially interned in the 9th Gorkha Regiment's lines. One of the ten was Father Clement the Roman Catholic Padree.

Another village which became a township during the War is Raipur. Here an Ordnance Factory was established which manufactures optical instruments for the Services. Nearby an American army camp was established at Sunderwala to house the 653rd Engineer Topographic Battalion. This unit was responsible for surveying and producing maps for the American Forces in the China, Burma India (CBI) theatre of War. It had a compact highly mobile Printing Press with machinery outfit equipped to move cross country right behind the advancing armies and air force. When this unit was assigned to the CBI theatre it was decided that it would work more efficiently by being located in a secluded stationary camp, and Dehra Dun was it. This Battalion formed part of the U.S. Third Army. One of the G.Is (the name given to an American private soldier) described their arrival and stay in India thus:-

"Out of the frying pan into the fire could describe our change from Louisiana, USA to India from the heat, rain, mud and mosquitoes of Camp Claiborne to India, hotter, rainier, thicker mud and bigger mosquitoes, with the longest trip Uncle Sam ever sent any of his Nephews on, thrown in for good measure. Our equipment arrived two months after we did, and then we started supplying the CBI theatre with laundry slips, letter heads and pay roll forms and we wondered if that was our mission in India. One day a very secretive stranger popped into camp, then things started popping for us. We were selected to furnish maps for a raid on Tokyo and Yawata, for the 20th Bomber Command. We had never heard of the 20th before, but were thrilled at the thought of doing a map of Japan. We had a bigger thrill a few days later when we learned that the B-29 Super Fortress's of the 20th Bomber Command, based in India, had made a successful raid on the Japanese mainland. This was our first important assignment, the first of many. From then on it was a steady flow of rush jobs, staying ahead of General Stillwell's troops in Burma and General Cheanault's Air Force in China; terrain maps, Artillery and target charts; Lashio, Bhamo, Myitkyina, Mandalay, Rangoon, Hongkong, Yawata, Kobe, Anshan, Yokohama, Nagasaki and then.... the repeat on Tokyo. Our reputation grew with every map. If a map was needed in four days Headquarters would say "The 653rd can do it in two". Our orders would be to do it in one.

We've never won battle stars for our Asiatic Theatre ribbons, nor made the headlines in the newspapers, but from the men of the 20th Bomber, 14th Air Force, Army Transport Command, Merrill's Marauders, Mars Task Force, the British 14th Army and the Chinese Armies, we've heard the same thing: "You guys have done a PUKKA job". Among Topo Battalions we are rated with the best, but, maybe we are prejudiced."

G.I. in American army parlance is an abbreviation for "Government Issue". The ordinary solider or the equivalent of a Jawan or other Rank, gave this name to himself because once he gets into the army he is issued everything by Government right from his shoe laces to food and housing - hence he considers himself also as issued by government. Likewise the "general purpose" motor vehicle from the war days became the Jeep.

Another G.I., from the same Battalion and a friend of the author, William G. Hudson from Florida, has the following reminiscences of his stay in Dehra.

"....I did not have any background in the printing press business - but had experience with mobile farm machinery equipment so was assigned to one of the 13 large vans as Driver and to set up the large auxiliary power units and furnish electricity for the unit...after we settled in the camp (Sunderwala). My duties were reduced to minor maintenance and motor pool work. I had regular trip assignments delivering maps to Delhi and various airports for plane pick up and making regular runs to New Delhi for collecting Mail and supplies as well as transporting personnel back and forth. You may remember I drove the shuttle back and forth to Dehra Dun and camp a lot. At near the end I was promoted to Company Despatcher for the motor pool, and besides assigning all vehicles out and in, kept records of maintenance, parts, inventories etc.

The most interesting interludes in my tour of duty were the trips to Calcutta, where we picked up our vehicles and drove back to Dehra Dun, our volunteer trip delivering a one hundred vehicle convoy, loaded with munitions, to General Chiang-ki-Shek in Kunming, China - a 13 day rugged trip along the Ledo-Burma road. Some of my off duty hours were spent enjoying trips to Agra to see the Taj Mahal, week-end passes to Mussoorie, Rap sessions with you (the Author), Restaurant meals in town, and the two weeks rest and recreation in Kashmir. Of course I spent one two weeks trip of not too much fun - in a mountain hospital recovering from a bout of Hepatitis (a spoonful of Epsom Salts every morning before breakfast). We had regularly assigned Red Cross workers (Girls) to help plan recreational activities - some of the in town social gatherings did not always go peaceful. There was a U.S.O. (United Services Organisations) club where we intermingled with the British troops, Indian, Burmese, English and Anglo Indian girls. I attended a dance at this club which ended with a general fight between the British (Limeys - as we called them) and our troops. I think the British were jealous of us dancing with some of the Anglo Indian girls. I did not get involved - usually it was between fellows on both sides who had too much to drink. One time I was at a restaurant on Main St. (Rajpur Road) Dehra Dun and it was full of American and British troops - the band played the British anthem and every one stood at attention - then the American anthem was played and some of the British did not stand-a general free for all followed - when the chairs started flying in the air I made a quick exit.

There was no love lost between American and British troops - I think they resented us being over there - but when it came to uniting for the common cause - beating the Japs out of India and Burma, we must have had some excellent leadership that kept the ball rolling in the right direction. I know we had a lot of respect for the varied Indian armies. I especially remember the Gurkhas. They invited us to an "Open House" field day at their camp and served us food and drink. The food was served on a large leaf that substituted for a plate. We saw the Gurkha soldier cut the head off a water buffalo with one whack with his Gurkha knife....we were glad they were on our side. (He is referring to being invited to Dushera celebrations at one of the Gorkha Regimental Centres).

I don't remember the incident where the (British) Governor visited our camp and the fellows failed to salute or pay any attention to him. I may have been away at the time - although I am not too much surprised. Some of the troops didn't have the best of training or manners. Monday morning quarter backing! I think it would have been in the best interest of all concerned if there had been rapport among our Allies...."

The incident regarding the Governor occurred when Sir Maurice Hallet, Governor of United Provinces was visiting the American camp and on the spur of the moment he asked the Commanding Officer to show him one of the barracks in which the men lived. He took him reluctantly inside one where the men were lounging about. Some were playing cards, while others were lying in their underpants trying to get a snooze, and still others were busy with their personal chores. The result was that when the Governor and party walked past none of the men took any notice of him although they knew who he was. At this behaviour the Governor remarked to the Commander that his men were rather indisciplined. The Officer replied that when not on duty the men do not take notice of anyone, more so, when a superior barges in on their privacy without notice. Entertainers from the United States would come out for the benefit of the troops in the various theatres of war. Once the troops in Dehra Dun were entertained by the Hollywood actress Ann Sheriden and her troupe. She was one of the stars who were given major roles in B Grade films and starred with President Ronald Reagan in a couple of them. The troupe performed in the Convocation Hall of the Forest Research Institute. After the Americans left Sunderwala Camp, at the end of the war, the place was occupied by the Technical Instruments and Electronics Development Establishment.

The Forest Research Institute played a major role during the War by supplying the Allied Forces with a number of items developed at the Institute. Laminates were made by using strong and durable species of timbers like Sal *(Shorea robusta)* for the faces and non-durable and non-treatable species like Salai *(Boswellia serrata)* were used for the core. Laminated curved members such as arches, ship members like ribs, knees etc. were made; as also skis, snow shoes and tobaggons were developed for use by the Army and the Air Force. Even aeroplane propellers were made of laminated woods, amongst the most used were the propellers for the Spitfire fighter plane. Cheap preservatives were developed for treating army tent bamboo and wood poles and timbers used in harbours. With the shortage of iron a number of articles like big cans, oil and petrol drums, parachute assemblies were developed by using plywood. The Royal Air Force used the facilities at the Institute for repairing damaged airplane parts. Railway fish plates, machine pulleys and air propellers were manufactured and supplied. A War Technical Training Centre was established in 1941 and was closed in 1945 on the termination of hostilities. Part of the main building was converted into a hospital for British troops. The forests of the Doon were felled far in advance of their working plan to meet the War requirements. This depleted them to a great extent.

As travel to England was not safe and there was lack of shipping, the probationers of the Indian Civil Service (ICS) from 1940 to 1944 (when fresh recruitment was stopped) were trained at the Institute. A training establishment was opened there under the charge of a senior ICS officer as Director. This cadre was later replaced by what is now called the Indian Administrative Service (IAS).

Indians were being recruited into the Armed Forces in a big way. The Indian Army was the largest volunteer army in the world as in other countries conscription had been resorted to. However the Indian government had appointed Honorary Recruiting Officers who were rewarded for motivating youngsters to join the Forces. Some were rewarded with titles or with Honorary ranks in the Armed Forces while some were given gold and silver watches with the Viceroy's or the Governor's crest engraved on them, and yet others were given certificates of commendations for helping in the War effort.

The start of World War II saw the troops stationed in and around Dehra go overseas to fight. The 2nd Gorkhas were sent to the Middle East. As part of the Persia and Iraq force known as the "Paiforce," they landed at Basra and from there marched to Tehran via Baghdad. After a year's stay they left Persia and crossed the desert to go to Cyprus where they had fought earlier in 1878. In Cyprus they formed part of the 4th Indian Division and trained for operations in the African desert. In the desert, west of Cairo, they were thrown into battles against Rommel's Afrika Corps. Rommel's troops had replaced the Italians who had surrendered in hundreds of thousands (80,000 of them being prisoners in Clement Town) to Field Marshall Lord Wavell's army in the early days of the War. Tobruk, El Alamein and Benghazi were taken and lost and retaken in a tug of war between the opposing armies. Every time the British captured any of these towns, a holiday was declared in the schools in the Doon to celebrate these small victories over the Axis powers.

At the battle of El Alamein, the 2nd Gorkhas played their part so well that this battle was also added to their battle honours along with Tunis and Akarit. The last named battle was the most stirring of all. In this battle thirteen Gorkhas were responsible for opening a way for the advance of a Division through enemy occupied territory.

Battalions of the 9th Gorkha Rifles, the other regiment having its home in Dehra, were also sent overseas to fight. A Regimental Centre was formed at Dehra Dun in November 1940. The function of this Centre, apart from training recruits, was to coordinate the work of the different Battalions and act as a base. As transport was becoming more and more mechanised troops were training as drivers. For this purpose the first batch of riflemen were converted to become drivers and were taught on six old lorries hired from a contractor. Six men even volunteered to master a motor-cycle to become Despatch Riders.

The Ist Battalion was sent to Basra in October 1941. It had served there 26 years earlier. While in Africa the Battalion was part of the 4th Indian Division. In June 1944 the Division lined the Tripoli highway in a full ceremonial turn-out, for inspection by King George VI. He stopped at each unit and shook hands with the Commanding Officer and his Subedar Major. The old Gorkha veterans were overwhelmed by the gesture while many of the young men, seeing the King in uniform, remarked, "Oh! He is only another General, after all".

The 2nd Battalion went to the South East Asia Theatre of War where large number of Officers and men were taken prisoners by the Japanese forces. On 8th September 1944 they were released and came back to Dehra Dun on September 22nd. The Viceroy Lord Wavell and his wife as well as the Commander-in-Chief General Auchinleck came to Dehra especially to meet these Officers and Men.

The 3rd Battalion saw action in Malay Peninsula and Indonesia. The 4th and 5th Battalions were busy on the North-West Frontier and were also busy with police duties like meeting Italian prisoners-of-war at Bombay and escorting them to their destinations in India.

In 1946, after the War, a detachment of the 2nd Gorkha Rifles took part in the Victory March in London.

On India becoming independent in 1947, the Indian army was broken up. The Mussalman troops went to Pakistan and in the case of the Gorkhas six regiments were to stay with India while the remaining four, including the 2nd Gorkha Rifles were to go to the British army. These four regiments were to be made up of volunteers from all the ten Gorkha regiments. The 4th Battalion, of the 2nd Gorkha Rifles, as a whole opted for India. It was merged with the 8th Gorkha Rifle Regiment as its 5th Battalion. Those men, from the other Battalions of the 2nd Gorkhas, who also opted for India were absorbed in a newly raised 6th Battalion of the 8th Gorkha Rifle Regiment. In April 1947 the Regimental Centres of the 2nd and 8th Gorkhas were merged. A new centre named the 28th Gorkha Rifles Regimental Centre (later to be called the 58 on 5th Gorkha Rifles Centre being merged with it) was established, at Dehra Dun. It occupied the estate vacated by the Sirmur Gorkhas (the 2nd Gorkhas). The last British Commandant of the 28th Centre was Col. H.F.C. Armstrong of the 2nd Gorkhas. He and his men played a significant role in quelling the communal riots, in the Valley during August 1947.

The 9th Gorkha Rifles Regiment continues to be a part of the Indian army.

Dehra Dun had a Company of the Auxiliary Force, India, a semi-military unit like the present day Territorial Army. Its (A.F.I.) membership was open to European and Anglo-Indian men, resident in Dehra Dun, who were fit for service in the regular army. Formerly this Company was a detachment of the United Provinces Horse, (like the Calcutta Horse, made famous by their raid on German warships in Goa during World War II). The foot volunteers were attached to the Mussoorie Volunteer Corps, known in turn as the M.V. Rifle Corps. It was formed in 1874. In 1889 it was named the M.V. Reserve Corps, which in 1920 was called the Mussoorie Battalion and Indian Defence Force. At different times it amalgamated with different units of the Thomason Engineering College, Roorkee and the Meerut Detachment No. 5 Company, M.G. Corps. The whole lot were amalgamated in 1925 to form the Dehra Dun Contingent Auxiliary Force, India. The Adjutant, Sergeant-Major and Sergeant-Instructors were British soldiers seconded from the regular army while the other officers, including the Commandant, and men were civilians.

It had its annual training programmes and camps and its basic duties were to come to the aid of the local civil police in times of law and order crises. On the outbreak of the War its men were mobilised into the regular army and attached to various British units. The Adjutant who was attached to the Suffolk regiment was kept on in Dehra, throughout the War to look after its affairs. In spite of the fact that he never crossed the Shiwaliks he would start wearing a new ribbon on his chest every now and again. On being asked that how he was wearing the Africa Star, he would reply that he may not have been there but his regiment has been there. The result was that at the end of the conflict he had a chest full of ribbons, without having stepped out of the Doon or firing a shot in battle.

In order to rehabilitate the War blinded troops a centre was started at the Governor-General's Bodyguard estate. It was known as St. Dunstan's Centre for the Blind. Its first Director was Col. Sir Clutha Mackenzie who himself was blinded in World War I. Today this is the Government of India's Training Centre for the Visually Handicapped.

Col. (later General) Wingate had introduced the concept of dropping troops behind enemy lines and frightening the enemy into withdrawal by threat to its rear. This operation under General Wingate was planned to help General Stilwell's advance into Burma in 1943. For this purpose special Jungle Warfare training had to be imparted to infantry soldiers, and a Jungle Warfare School was started in the Shiwaliks between the Yamuna and Khairawanaka stream. The headquarters of the organisation were at Badshahi Bagh. The staff of this establishment was drawn from the officers and men of the 2nd and 9th Gorkha Rifles and were named 29th Gorkha Rifles. During its two years existence 36 British and 2500 Gorkha troops were trained. The emblem, of this special long range Penetration Force, which the men wore on their sleeve was a snarling leopard's head. This head was taken from "Chinthe" the lion headed dragon that sits outside all Burmese Pagodas. It is supposed to be the only living thing, in the Buddhist religion, that is permitted to use force in guarding the sacred pagodas. For some reason people started pronouncing "Chinthe" as "Chindits", and this was the name given to this force. It still forms a part of the Indian army.

This force was to pass through the enemy front, unlike guerrillas, and operate against the less protected lines of communication. They blew up bridges, ambushed road convoys and attacked isolated enemy posts. Their supplies were mostly air-dropped and they were trained to live off the land by even eating snakes if need be. Another job of this establishment in the Shiwaliks was fire fighting in the forest, during summer months. They also replanted, under the orders of General Lentaigne, the hill sides which had been denuded of forest cover, due to the cutting of trees to meet the requirements of War.

During World War II Generalissimo and Madame Chiang Kai Shek came to India to confer with their allies in the war against the Japanese. Madame Chiang took time off from her duties in Delhi and came to Dehra Dun to spend a quiet weekend.

With the failure of the Cripp's Mission the Indian National Congress passed its famous "Quit India" resolution on 7th August, 1942. All Congressmen throughout the country were arrested and imprisoned - Gandhiji his wife Kasturba, and Mrs. Sarojni Naidu were lodged at the Aga Khan's palace in Poona, while the President and members of the Working Committee were kept in the Ahmadnagar Fort. In the Doon the shopkeepers registered their protest against the arrest of the Congress leaders by downing their shops' shutters, and the public held protest meetings, and took out processions in violation of the Prohibitory Orders. More than 300 people were sentenced to various terms and collective fines were levied. A couple of incidents that occurred during these disturbances come to mind. The people of the Doon are by and large peace-loving and law abiding; however the spirit of nationalism amongst them is as strong as in any other Indian.

One day during August 1942, a procession of students started from the D.A.V. College, in support of the Congress agitation. As it was going past St. Joseph's Academy some of the processionists came to the Principal and asked him to close the school in support of the Congress cause. The Principal - an Irishman, whose own country had fought against British rule, instead of closing the school took them around the senior classes and told the students that any one of them who wanted to join the procession was free to do so. He would not take any action against them for being absent from class. A few boys went and joined the procession which was stopped near the railway station by the police. Here they were herded into waiting trucks and buses. As they were entering the vehicles each one's name, name of the school and father's name was being recorded. When the boys from the Academy mentioned the name of their school they were taken out of the crowd and sent home with the admonition that they should not get mixed up in such crowds. The others were formally put under arrest and then driven to the Asarori tunnel where they were let off and had to walk home. This kind of arrest enabled a lot of people, after Independence, to claim the benefits and privileges given by the Indian Government to "Freedom Fighters". The District Magistrate at that time was Hifazat Hussain, I.C.S., and the Superintendent of Police was C.P. Luck, an Englishman.

The second incident was also connected with another procession. As the procession came face to face with the police and the Magistrates present there, the Police Chief wanted to shoot at the crowd to stop them as he felt that his force would be over-powered. For this purpose he asked the District Magistrate to give his permission as without it the firing would be illegal. Permission was refused as the crowd was peaceful. Later the Superintendent of Police made a report to his boss against the Superintendent of the Doon regarding his refusal to give the order to shoot. The Provincial Governor asked for an explanation from Hifazat Hussain. In his explanation he contented that

252

the reasons for his refusal were that: (a) the mob was peaceful (b) had the mob turned violent, on being fired at, and decided to go and free the 80,000 Italian prisoners in Clement Town and the Internees in Prem Nagar, neither the civil nor the military authorities could have prevented them. Those days the War was being fought by the British with their backs against the wall and a very small armed force was available for maintaining law and order. Although no action as such was taken against Hifazat Hussain, he was transferred to the Secretariat in Lucknow. His successor was Johnston an Englishman who, as District Magistrate Fyzabad had suffered a nervous breakdown during the disturbances there. On his return from medical leave he was sent to the Doon which was, comparatively, a peaceful district in the Province. Because of its being an administratively easy district, senior officers who were marking time for the next promotion were posted to the Doon so that they could sit back and do some thinking and planning in the peace of the Valley. It is only after the War that officers with less than ten years service have been sent as District Magistrates.

Amongst the prominent citizens of the Valley who were arrested and sentenced to various terms of imprisonment was the future Mahant of Guru Rai's temple, Mahant Indresh Charan Das. At the time he was studying, at the Allahabad University, when he jumped into the fray, against the declared policy of his Guru Mahant Lachman Das who was a 'Loyalist'. While Indresh was still in jail Mahant Lachman Das died. With a lot of wire pulling and great difficulty Indresh was released by the British, and installed, as the Mahant, by Johnston in his capacity as the Superintendent of the Doon. In recognition of being installed the Mahant, a pair of gold bangles was presented to him by the British Government of India. Indresh, however, continued to be a Congressman and for a while became the first citizen of the town on being elected the Chairman of the City Board. A celibate, his aim in life is dissemination of education to the largest numbers possible. Of the other 300 persons who were arrested some of them were Khurshid Lal, Mahabir and his wife Sharmada Tyagi, Acharya Narendra Dev, Chandramani Vidyalankar, Amar Nath Vaid and Master Ram Swarup.

The same year, on the formation of the Indian National Army by Subhas Chandra Bose, a number of Gorkha soldiers belonging to the Doon joined it. Among them were NCOs Sher Bahadur Bhandari, Durga Mall and Kesri Chand, residents of villages Ballupur, Doiwala and Kailana respectively. Bhandari served as a Captain in the first Bahadur Group in Malaya and died of wounds in a Burmese hospital. Durga Mall and Kesri Chand were court-martialed after the War, for treason. Their court-martial was held in the Red Fort at Delhi. On being convicted they were sentenced to death and executed.

With the end of the War in August 1945 peace returned to the World yet the shortages of essential items of daily use like food, clothing, petrol cement, iron and steel etc. continued. The rationing of these items which had been introduced at the beginning of the war carried on, and unfortunately for the country had given birth to the system called "Black Market". In spite of the prosecutions and punishments under the Defence of India Act the system flourished, and has to-day generated a parallel economy in the country.

In the winter of 1945-46 General Elections were held and Mrs. Sharmada Tyagi was elected to the Assembly from Dehra Dun. On her sudden death, half-way through her term, her husband Mahabir Tyagi filled her seat in a bye-election. The British Cabinet Mission was in India on 23rd March, 1946 to discuss with the representatives of the Indian people the question of Independence for them. Maulana Abul Kalam Azad, the Congress President, took time off from the deliberations with the members of the Mission and came to Mussoorie towards the end of April for a short holiday. While in Mussoorie he met some members of the Muslim League but nothing much came out of these meetings.

In August 1946 an interim government was formed at the Centre with Jawahar Lal Nehru as the Prime Minister. With the arrival of Lord Mountbatten on 22nd March, 1947, the time to reach 15th August was made shorter, and the day dawned in the Doon also, as elsewhere in the country, with jubilation, communal frenzy and blood baths.

From times immemorial a number of people have found shelter in the Doon as ascetics, exiles or refugees. The earliest ascetic referred to is Jahnu who finds mention in the Rig Ved and the Ramayan. He is followed by Ram and Lakshman who came to the Valley to do penance. For the Pandavas of the Mahabharat, the Doon was like a second home. Amongst the notables who came to the Valley and lived and died here, the first documented account is of Guru Ram Rai who sought refuge here at the behest of the Moghul Emperor Aurangzeb.

Guru Ram Rai may be called the founder of the present town of Dehra Dun as it is around his cenotaph that the population initially settled.

Ram Rai was born in 1646 A.D. and was the elder son of the seventh Sikh Guru Har Rai. He was born at Kiratpur and the spot where he was born is still preserved. After having firmly established himself on the throne Aurangzeb summoned Guru Har Rai to his court as he was piqued at Har Rai for having gone to the aid of Dara Shikoh in the Mughal War of succession. Har Rai, instead of going himself, sent Ram Rai who was then a lad of 15 years. At the time of his departure his father enjoined him to fix his thoughts on God and every thing would prove successful. He was also told not to countenence any objection the Emperor might make to the Guru Granth but to reply patiently and to the purpose. Ram Rai who was an intelligent and an ambitious lad, instead of following his father's exhortations began to curry favour with Aurangzeb by acting in a manner which was not in consonance with the teachings of the Gurus. He performed as many as forty miracles according to the book "Sri Gur Pratap Suraj Granth".

The first such miracle was when the Emperor sent him a robe, treated with poison, to wear. Ram Rai uttered the word "Waheguru" and wore it. The poison is supposed to have become ineffective as it touched his body. A daily allowance of Rs. 500/- was sanctioned by the court for meeting Ram Rai's expenses while in Delhi. In addition rations were supplied for his kitchen. One day the Emperor asked Ram Rai, in open court, at the instigation of one of the Mullahs, to produce the slaughtered goat that had been sent to his kitchen the previous day. A three-legged animal appeared on the scene. On being questioned about the fourth leg, Ram Rai replied that it had been kept back by the servant, on instructions of the Mullah who now wanted the animal produced. The Mullah admitted his guilt.

After settling in the Doon, Ram Rai's young wife Punjab Kaur was stung by a scorpion, which abound in the Valley. As she was writhing in pain Ram Rai uttered a curse and since then the scorpions of Dehra, lost the sting in their bite. It has been the author's personal experience that on being stung by a scorpion on the toe, the pain felt was like that felt on being bitten by a red ant. Mahant Indresh Charan Das narrated his experience with a scorpion. He had come to Dehra as a young boy and was living in the Gurudwara. One day he saw his first scorpion scampering on the wall. Being ignorant he caught the insect and placing it on the palm of his hand asked a person nearby what it was. The person got a fright, told him what it was, and asked him to throw it away before he was stung. Sting it did but without much effect.

Guru Nanak, while explaining that there was no difference between Hinduism and Islam, was asked if Hindu cremation and Muslim burial were also the same. Nanak said:-

"The clay from a Mussalman's grave is kneaded and finds its way into the potter's hands, who makes vessels and bricks from it and then fires them in the kiln.

Burning, it wails-helpless clay by cinders engulfed. The Creator, sayeth Nanak, alone knows what befalls the soul which has departed. . . .

Whether cremation is better or the burial."

This verse from the Guru Granth reflects on the essentially conditioned state of man against the mystery and absoluteness of Divine power and on the futility of dividing humanity by the rites of cremation or burial. It criticizes no religion. This passage was considered offensive to the tenets of Islam. Aurangzeb asked Ram Rai to explain it. Ram Rai knew what offended them and very cleverly replied that the text had been corrupted by ignorant persons and the word "Mussalman" inserted in place of "Baiman" (dishonest) or faithless. By doing so he was able to satisfy the Emperor and the Ulemas. Ram Rai had forgotten that being the Guru's son and employed on such a delicate political mission, he had an onerous duty on his shoulders. When this incident was conveyed to Guru Har Rai he declared Ram Rai unfit to become a Guru and excluded him from succession. The younger son Har Kishan was chosen as the next Guru. To Ram Rai he wrote; "I did not like the way you explained Guru Nanak's lines. You go where you want to, but do not show your face to me".

Ram Rai went to Kiratpur and personally begged his father to forgive him. He even asked his uncle Dhir Mal to intercede on his behalf but Har Rai did not relent. Thereupon Ram Rai turned hostile towards the Panth and like his uncle Dhir Mal, set up his own following, and joined hands with the Mughals. In view of the above mentioned fact Williams' assertions in his Memoir of the Doon, that Ram Rai was not made the Guru because he was the son of a hand-maiden or that his legitimacy was questionable are wrong. Obviously Williams did not possess the correct information. Walton in his District Gazetteer repeated the same mistake, probably taking his information from Williams.

Ram Rai stayed on at the Mughal court and became a faithful courtier of the Emperor. On the death of his father in 1661 Ram Rai staked his claim for the Guru's chair against that of his brother Har Kishan.

Although no physical reason has been ascribed for the death of Guru Har Rai, Surjit Singh Gandhi, a Sikh chronicler feels that Har Rai was poisoned at the instance of Aurangzeb. According to Gandhi Ram Rai is suspected of having had a hand in this killing which has no historical or factual evidence to support this theory. Aurangzeb, took advantage of the rift between the two brothers over the claim for the Guru's Gaddi. He was keen to use Ram Rai in wrecking the Sikh movement. Har Kishan was summoned to Delhi to justify his claim to the seat and Mirza Raja Jai Singh was sent to fetch him.

Although Har Kishan's mother was afraid of the Emperor's and Ram Rai's intrigues, she could not stop her son from going. On his arrival in Delhi Har Kishan was put through some tests to satisfy the Emperor's curiosity about the mental capacity of the boy Guru, who was seven years old at the time. Aurangzeb was satisfied that the choice in making the younger son the Guru was not wrong, and dismissed Ram Rai's claim. On 30th March, 1664 Har Kishan died in Delhi as a victim of small pox. While on his death bed he was asked by his followers to name his successor as Ram Rai was plotting at Court, while Dhir Mal and the other clansmen the Sodhis were waiting for his death to put forward their claims. He named Tegh Bahadur as his successor. In spite of their differences it was Ram Rai who brought his brother's ashes from Delhi to Haridwar for immersion in the Ganga.

The institution of Masands and Sants had been founded by Guru Amar Das. Their function was to spread the teachings of the Gurus, to collect offerings from the people on their behalf and act as liaison officers. The office of a Masand was initially filled by men of integrity and piety. With time, like the Guruship, the office became hereditary in the families of the first lot of Masands. The subsequent successors to the office became casual about their religious duties and lacked integrity in respect of financial matters. The succession of Gurus had become hereditary and followed the law of primogeniture from the time Arjan Das became the Guru. After the death of Har Kishan, Dhir Mal the eldest living son of Guru Har Gobind and Ram Rai disputed Teg Bahadur's succession to the "Gaddi" (Pontifical seat). These two turned hostile towards the Panth and formed their own splinter sects with the help of the Masands. Dhir Mal's followers were known as Dhirmalias while the latter's were called Ram Raiyas. The Masands played an important role in siding with one faction or the other in the fights for the gaddi. In Ram Rai's case Masands Tara, Goinda and Gur Das were the prime instigators in his attempts to become the Guru.

Guru Tegh Bahadur was a man of a quiet and retiring disposition. He was harrassed by his rivals, amongst them Ram Rai and Dhir Mal being the main ones. As he was not allowed to remain in peace at any one place for long he was constantly on the move administering to the needs of his disciples. Once while in Delhi, before his martyrdom, Ram Rai had him arrested as an imposter and disturber of the peace. Mirza Raja Jai Singh's son, Raja Ram Singh, intervened on Tegh Bahadur's behalf and had him released on his personal surety for the Guru's good conduct. Thereafter, Tegh Bahadur continued on his travels upto Assam, from where he was urgently summoned to the Punjab. Because of Aurangzeb's reign of religious persecution the non-Muslims were in a state of nervous agitation. Tegh Bahadur's exhortations to the people to stand firm in their belief led to his being arrested and brought to Delhi. After a trial of sorts he was sentenced to death and achieved martyrdom on 11th Nov., 1675. Once again, as in the case of Guru Har Krishan, Ram Rai performed the last rites of Tegh Bahadur's body, the head having been stolen and taken to Anandpur where it was cremated by Govind Singh.

Once again Ram Rai laid claim to the Guru's gaddi, but the undeniable superiority of Govind Singh's right to the gaddi frustrated his attempt. By now Aurangzeb had also got fed up with Ram Rai's machinations. He was given a 'Firman' by Aurangzeb, addressed to the Raja of Garhwal. Ram Rai arrived in the Doon an exile from the Mughal

Court. There is confusion regarding the actual year of his arrival in the Doon. According to Williams he came in 1699 A.D. while as per Walton and Munshi Maiku Lal, a biographer of Ram Rai, the year was 1675. It has to be the latter year as he died in 1687. Ram Rai first pitched his camp at village Kandlee, on the bank of the river Tons, in the Western Doon, before shifting to the present day site at Khurbara. This place got its name because it was here that Ram Rai's horse shed a shoe, and he, while leaving Kandlee, had vowed that he would make his permanent home wherever the horse shed a shoe. "Khur" means hoof and "Bara" means grown. The horse's hoof had grown so much that the shoe dropped off at this spot. This, of course, is one of the folk-lores. Aurangzeb's firman to the Garhwal ruler enjoined upon him to provide Ram Rai with enough monetary help as would keep him comfortable. Thus initially he was given the villages of Khurbara, Rajpur and Chamasari, later followed by Dhamanwala, Dhartawala, Mianwala and Panditwari as revenue free grants. The income from these villages in those days was around 13 to 14 hundred rupees annually. This amount was not enough to meet his personal expenses and that of his entourage. His income was supplemented by the offerings received from his devotees and followers. These followers are known as Ram Raiyas or Rai Sikhs. They do not follow the tenets laid down by Govind Singh for the Khalsa namely, not cutting the hair, not smoking, wearing a comb, kirpan, underpant, and bangle. They do not consider themselves bound not to smoke, cut their hair or wear a comb or a kirpan. According to Macauliffe, Govind Singh specifically prohibited the Sikhs from having social inter-course with the descendants or followers of Ram Rai and others like him, who claimed the Guru's gaddi. After Ram Rai had settled at Khurbara; he soon attracted a number of his devotees and followers and a town grew up around his dwellings. The locality or the town around his settlement came to be called "Dera" Doon ("Dera" meaning abode and "Doon" meaning Valley), and later became Dehra Dun and encompasses the present city. In the early maps of the Doon, drawn by British surveyors in the early 19th century, the town is marked as "Gooroodwara". Raja Fateh Shah became an ardent admirer of Ram Rai, and would often seek his advice and went to the extent of building him a Gurudwara, at Srinagar, where he would often go and live. For its maintenance an endowment of revenue of some villages across the Ganga at Haridwar was made. The revenue from them was Rupees thirty-five annually.

As has been mentioned earlier, Guru Govind Singh was at one time living at Paonta. With the lapse of time both he and Ram Rai wanted to patch up their differences. The former, on sensing this, sent two of his men to the latter at Dehra to re-assure him and asked him to agree to a meeting. On getting this message a meeting between the two was arranged. It took place on a ferry in the middle of the river Yamuna, that being no man's land. According to Macauliffe, Ram Rai touched the other's feet in obeisance and said "I am fortunate to have obtained a sight of thee and when I am gone, protect my family .... my father Guru Har Rai used to say that someone would be born from our family who would restore and refit the vessel for the safe conveyance of souls". Govind Singh, apart from being the anointed Guru, was Ram Rai's uncle also, as Guru Govind Singh and Ram Rai's father were first cousins.

258

Ram Rai had the habit of going into a trance for long periods during meditation. In September 1687 he shut himself up in a room and told his wife Punjab Kaur that on no account was he to be disturbed till he came out himself. The Masands of his entourage after some days started browbeating her, to open the room as no one could still be alive without food and water. Perforce she yielded to their pressure and opened the door. Ram Rai, according to Williams and Walton, was found lying naked on his bed and was taken for dead; he may have actually died from being unable to retrieve himself from the deep trance. In any case he was cremated by the Masands against her entreaties and requests to postpone the cremation. She is reported to have complained to Guru Govind Singh regarding the Masands' action. He responded to her request to rid her of the Masands. The guilty ones were punished and made to leave Dehra. Later some Ram Raiya Masands carried on their activities in the Punjab. As they were bereft of any spiritual motives and their activities sprang from lust for power and greed for wealth, their influence amongst the Sikhs disappeared with time.

After Ram Rai's death his widow managed the affairs of the Gooroodwara with the help of two of his trusted disciples, Avadh Das and Har Sewak. They were ordained as the first and second Mahants of the endowment respectively. Although Ram Rai was a married man, having four wives, he had no children. In order to avoid division and family feuds regarding the vast properties of the endowment he had willed that his successors will be men who will take life long vows of celibacy. Today in the mausoleum are displayed Ram Rai's personal relics including the silver bed on which he is supposed to have died. At the corners of the compound are smaller monuments in memory of his four wives. The entire structure is covered with paintings, some of them depicting the miracles performed by him like the production of the three legged goat. In the compound is a reservoir in which rain water used to be collected for use in cooking lentils for which purpose the canal water was too hard on account of dissolved limestone. To-day neither canal water nor water from this tank is used in the town for cooking because of the piped water supply from the Bandal river and tubewells.

The Mahants (head priests) named their successor from among their "Chelas" (disciples). In the earlier days the selection was guided by the Chiefs of the Sikh states of Punjab. At the time of assuming office by the new Mahant, a 'Nazrana' (present) of Rs. 500/- was made to the British Government by him. The complementary gift in return, as a sign of recognising him as the Mahant, was a pair of gold bangles. These were presented by the Superintendent of the Doon on the occasion. The acknowledgement of Ram Rai's saintship is not confined to the Ram Raiya Sikhs, but practically all Hindu sects furnish devotees, especially in Dehra Dun where his influence was most felt. Owing to the divergence of his doctrines from those of the ten Sikh Gurus, the Akalis do not recognise him, yet, notwithstanding this, it is on record that Maharaja Ranjit Singh, when apprehensive of impending death in the spring of 1826, sent an offering of Rs. 500/- to this Gurudwara.

The annual commemorative festival of Guru Ram Rai, as he is commonly known, is held five days after the Holi festival on his birthday. It is known as Jhande-Ka-Mela or Jhanda fair. On this day the Guru's 'Nishan' (flag) which flies from a huge staff is changed. The flagstaff is shaped from the tallest Sal tree, selected in advance, from amongst those growing in government forests at Doodhli-Lachiwala. The fair lasts ten days and is attended by devotees from all over. Those coming from out of station are housed and fed at the Mahant's expense.

According to a local folk-tale the story of Ram Rai's death is as follows:-

The ship of one of his devotees, who had gone on a voyage, was caught in a storm at sea. The devotee fearing for his life thought of Ram Rai and prayed to him, to come to his aid. Ram Rai, who was in Dehra, dreamt of the devotee's plight. Informing Punjab Kaur that he was going in a trance, and was not to be disturbed under any circumstances, shut himself in his room. After a few days on the persistent demand of the Masands she opened the room and found Ram Rai lying lifeless on his bed. Taking him for dead they cremated him. That night he, in Punjab Kaur's dream, admonished her for disobeying him, and told her the story of how he had gone to the help of his devotee. Now that his physical body had been destroyed his spirit could not become his tangible self again hence it would merge in the Cosmos.

As regards the punishment to the Masands the other story is that at the congregation, on the day of Ram Rai's last rites, his chief Masand Gurbax alias Gurdas tried to sit on the seat where Ram Rai used to sit. On seeing this the other Masands physically pulled him down and he was made to leave the ceremony. After this incident Gurbax left Dehra Dun for good.

On hearing of Ram Rai's death Emperor Aurangzeb sent his representatives with his condolence message to Punjab Kaur. He also ordered the building of the present mausoleum to the memory of Ram Rai based on the architecture of Jehangir's tomb at Lahore. On the top of the South gate to the mausoleum is embedded a large marble slab on which are inscribed 66 verses in Persian. These lines have been there since the beginning and have their own story to tell. Given below is the official translation:-

ENGLISH TRANSLATION OF THE INSCRIPTION IN THE GURDWARA OF DARBAR SHRI GURU RAM RAI SAHIB (VERSE BY VERSE)

1. Praise be to God whose attribute is mercy, and by whose grace man has received life.
2. The powerful group of the faithful make it their principle to worship Him.
3. Truly, he has life who belongs to Him. Woe to the man who neglects to worship Him.
4. Nanak, who understood the mysteries of Godhead, the Prince of the Righteous, and a Guide and Leader of both the Sects (Hindus and Muslims).
5. When he left this world full of changes and revolutions.
6. Guru Hari Rai ascended the throne of Khilafat or religious leadership (Caliphate).
7. At the expiry of the reign of Shah Jehan, the second, who was born at the auspicious moment of the convergence of Venus and Mars (which brings luck).
8. The mighty king Aurangzeb rode to acquire his kingdom.
9. Dara Shikoh (Aurangzeb's elder brother) received a crushing defeat of such a terrible nature, at the hands of Aurangzeb, that the mountains and rivers began to tremble and quake.

10. After lowering his banners all over the kindgóm, he (Dara Shikoh) made it known to the people that he was going in the service of the Guru.

11. Finally the unfortunate Prince (Dara Shikoh) went to Multan where he was utterly ruined.

12. The reigning monarch, after his victory, quickly sent a letter of joyous tidings (to the Guru) saying.

13. "It is only right and proper that an exalted and lofty personality like yourself should be in my court."

14. When the saintly Guru read this letter, he opened his tongue to shed pearls of wisdom.

15. In reply to the command of the enlightened monarch he said "I am confined to the prison of body just for a short period (I have a very short time to live now).

16. For this reason I am not able to come. It is becoming of the Monarch to forgive, under such circumstances, for this refusal.

17. On hearing this reply, the Emperor sent another letter very soon (saying).

18. "Your excellent qualities are known throughout the world; but if it is decreed by God that you are veiled to disappear from this world through death.

19. At which time men cannot be comforted, it is only proper that the hidden mysteries (of life and death) should be explained to them.

20. So please send some one from among your sons or disciples, who is enlightened and understands the mysteries of the facts of life".

21. When the King of the Righteous (i.e. the Saint) heard all this, he for once, plunged into meditation.

22. After much thought and consideration he found Guru Ram Rai the ablest person for this purpose.

23. In reply to the, sincere invitation, the saint respectfully submitted:-Emperor,

24. O, who adorns the throne of the earth, everything from earth to heaven is under thy sway (i.e. I cannot but obey thy command).

25. Men of God have always been treated graciously by the rich".

26. When this news spread among all sects, followers of every belief assembled together.

27. I was not the originator of this assembly. God is a witness to all these happenings.

28. By the Kings favours the holy Guru reached the Palace, after discomforts of travelling.

29. Whatever questions were asked by the illustrious monarch, were satisfactorily answered by the Guru.

30. After questions and answers the King was delighted with all his sayings.

31. With boundless bounty the king granted him one township of 'Khera Chandrawal' for his stay.

32. After a period of time he left the village and the wise Guru with a foresight, requested the King for permission to leave.

33. The Ruler of the Time, gave his permission, and wrote to the holy born saint:-

34. "By the grace of God and with your mercy as our guide, your disciple is being sent safely back to you."

35. After many difficulties (of travelling) Guru Ram Rai presented himself before the saint.

36. When the saint considered all these services (of Guru Ram Rai) he conferred favours on him, more than customary.

37. He did more than what was the tradition of this family since olden times.

38. A short time after these events, the great Teacher and world Protector departed from the world (the saint died).

39. After the saint's death, the King again issued a royal decree requiring the presence of Guru Ram Rai at his court.

40. Guru Ram Rai made up his mind a second time to take up the journey, and entered the town, (Capital),

41. And made his old residence his home.

42. After a short time when the Emperor went to that house.

43. He gave the Guru a house on the bank of a pond.

44. The good Guru lived beside this pond for 20 years.

45. When the cup of his life began to be empty of life, and was getting filled with extinction (when he felt his end drawing nigh).

46. He said to himself, "I should like to live in a place whence I could see everything and where no one could see me".

47. He chose the village Kher Doh among the lofty mountains as a place to spend his last days there.

48. On each side of this place sprung and bubbled the streams of flowing waters, if you would like to see Paradise on earth, see this (this is Paradise on earth).

49. It is bound on one of its sides by mountains, and on the other by thick forests, each tree of which bears the fruits of Paradise.

50. Between the Ganges and the Jamuna is a delightful spot which birds of Paradise have made their home.

51. On every side flow streams of bright sparkling water (incomplete verse).

52. 53 and 54, obliterated.

55. He planted some dry sticks with his miraculous hands, and as they touched the earth they became thousands of flourishing trees.

56. Later, the great Guru himself made two wooden Posts.

57. (First line incomplete), and with another piece of wood he constructed a Tower or Minar (or a pole for flag hoisting).

58. After all these achievements he left for the land of extinction and constructed a home for himself in the land of Inexistence (He died).

59. The learned people quote the date of his death as 1099 (Hejri) by repeating the line "Haihat Guru Ram Rai".
Note - Each letter of alphabet in Urdu has a numerical value. By adding these numbers the total comes to 1099).

60. The learned Monarch honoured the place of the Guru's death like high heavens, and erected a monument to his beloved memory.

61. Obliterated.

62. At the site where the Guru committed his soul to God stands a magnificent building with garden and residence.

63. The altar at which the Guru worshipped, has become a place of worship for kings and the paupers alike.

64. The wealth of that Benefactor is feeding thousands.

65. He truly lives who himself eats, and sows for others to eat. (He lives in a real sense who makes the best use of life, and enriches other lives by what he can impart) woe betide the man who leads a selfish life, and dies with his hoardings.

66. I pen the history of the Benefactor by way of my esteem for him.

(End of the Poem)

Date of death 6th Zikadh 31, in the reign of the Pious King Alamgir in the year 1099 Hijri. By the Hindi Calendar 1744 Sunday in the month of Bhadon Sudi Ashtami.

In these lines ''Khera Chandrawal'' refers to a village, near Majnu-ka-Tila in Delhi and the village ''Khar Doh'' is the locality of Khurbarah in the Doon. The construction of the mousoleum was started in 1689 and completed in 1708 A.D.

After the Anglo-Afghan War of 1839 Shah Shuja-ul-Mulk had retrieved his throne from Dost Mohammed Khan, in Kabul, though not the Koh-i-noor diamond which he had lost to Maharaja Ranjit Singh. Dost Mohammed had escaped from the battlefield and was leading a life of a guerrilla and harrassing the English. One afternoon Sir William Hay Macnaughten, the British envoy at the court of Shah Shuja, was taking a ride on the Kabul plains, when a horseman galloped up to him and announced that the Amir was approaching. "What Amir?" asked Macnaughten. "Dost Mohammed Khan," was the reply. Dismounting, the Afghan prince Dost Mohammed saluted Macnaughten and offered him his sword, which the Envoy declined to take. Dost Mohammed and the Englishman rode into Kabul together, and such was the impression the former made on the latter that Macnaughten, who a month earlier was thinking of putting a price on "the fellows" head, begged of the Governor-General "that the Dost be treated more handsomely than Shah Shuja, who had no claim on us".

Henry Durand, the English Engineer officer, who later became the Governor of Punjab and after whom the famous dividing line between Afghanistan and British India was named, regarded Dost Mohammad's surrender as evincing cowardice. This abusive judgement, according to another Englishman, appeared unjustified. He felt that the action was motivated by higher and purer patriotism that moved Dost Mohammed to cease, by his surrender, from being an obstacle to the tranquilisation of the country of which he had been the ruler.

Dost Mohammed remained for a few days in the British camp on the Kabul plain as an honoured guest rather than a prisoner. In the middle of November 1840 Dost Mohammad began his journey toward British India accompanied by Sir Willoughby Cotton and his troops who had completed their tour of duty in Afghanistan. Dost Mohammad with his son Akbar Khan and their retinue were brought to the Doon to live in exile. In the summer months they were sent to Mussoorie where they were accommodated in a house which till recently was part of Allen Memorial Boys' School, and stood on the hillock above Barlowganj and below Wynberg Girls' School. The building was named "Balla Hissar" after the Amir's palace and fort at Kabul. The place continued to be called by that name even after he went back to his own country.

After the murder of Macnaughten in Kabul in December 1841, and the famous evacuation of British personnel from Kabul and their massacre, Shah Shuja had become shaky on his throne. He was murdered at the beginning of April 1842. His second son Fateh Jung had himself proclaimed as his father's successor. By September Fateh Jung had fled from Kabul and he came to the British Camp at Gundamuk, seeking refuge after ceding his throne, or what was left of it, to another British puppet of his race. The British had decided to restore Kabul to Dost Mohammad and to withdraw the "army of occupation" from there. Thus at the end of 1842 Dost Mohammad left the Doon for Kabul to reoccupy his throne. The famous Basmati rice was introduced to the Doon by Dost Mohammad. He had brought with him the rice seeds from Kunar in Afghanistan. The climate and soil conditions in the Doon suited this strain of rice and its cultivation was taken up by the local farmers. This information is given by one of Amir Yakub Khan's grandsons who lives in Dehra Dun. Similarly the Lichee plant was brought, along with the Tea plant, from China by the English. The word 'Basmati' in the local language means "smell of the earth" (Bans=smell+matti=earth). The best Basmati rice comes from the fields, belonging to the Bharat Mandir, at Tapoban near Rishikesh.

The Balla Hissar estate had a hoodoo about it. After the place had been vacated by the Amir it was occupied by army officers attached to the Landhaur cantonment. One of them, Captain Deane Spread, who was living in the main house was struck by lightning and killed on 3rd September, 1879.

Many years later another building on the estate was struck by lightning and burnt but according to some it was a defective electric wiring in the building that was to blame. Whatever it be, the fact was that Mr. Mackintosh, the Principal of Balla Hissar School at that time was urged, much against his will, to go to a cinema show. He went reluctantly but thanked God for having gone as when he returned in the midst of a storm, he found his room on fire. A few years later yet another fire broke out in the building and this time a Mr. Fitzpatrick was the victim. Perhaps the school authorities got so fed up that they eventually pulled down the old "Balla Hissar" and have now put up a multistoried structure in its place.

The next Afghan ruler to be exiled in the Doon was Amir Yakub Khan, a grandson of Dost Mohammad. His son Sher Ali succeeded him as the Amir in 1863. The relations between Sher Ali and the successive Viceroys of India were friendly although not close. The consistent aim of the British policy towards Afghanistan was to utilise that country as a "Buffer" state between the north western frontier of British India and Russia. Sher Ali was never a very comfortable ally. He was of a staturnine and suspicious nature, and he seems also to have had an overweening sense of value of the position of Afghanistan, interposed between two great powers profoundly jealous of one another. His suspicious nature can be gauged from the fact that on assuming the throne he had imprisoned his son Yakub Khan. Sher Ali had refused to receive a British Embassy at his court while accepting one from Russia. No other course was open to the English than to insist on the reception at Kabul of their mission, by force of arms if necessary. The government in London directed the Viceroy to ask for an apology for the refusal and for the acceptance of a permanent mission. If this was not accepted by a certain time hostilities would immediately commence. No answer to the ultimatum was received from the Amir and on November 21st General Sir Sam Browne (after whom the Sam Browne belt of an officer's dress is named) crossed the Afghan frontier. Thus started the second Anglo-Afghan War. By Janurary 1879 the Russian Embassy had withdrawn from Kabul, and Sher Ali realised that he could not hope for any help from the Russians. Sam Browne had occupied Jallalabad and was moving towards Gundamuk. Sher Ali's chiefs were unanimous in their opinion that further resistance by him was hopeless. As a consequence he released his son Yakub Khan from his long imprisonment, constituted him Regent, and went towards Taskhant. After a painful illness he died on February 21st, 1879.

There had been plenty of verve originally in Yakub Khan, but much of that attribute had withered in him during his imprisonment. Sher Ali's death made him nominal master of Afghanistan. He reigned but did not rule, and how precarious was his position was evidenced by the defection of many leading chiefs who went across to the English camps and were ready to come to terms. The result was that the treaty of Gundamuk was signed on 26th May, 1879 between the Amir and Major Sir Louis Cavagnari acting on behalf of the Viceroy. By this Treaty the Amir, for a time, became virtually a feudatory of the British Crown. Cavagnari was appointed the British Resident at Kabul according to the terms of the treaty and he rode into Balla Hissar on 24th July, 1879. By 5th September, 1879, history had repeated itself and Cavangari like Macnaghten was slaughtered along with his staff. An army of retribution was ordered against the Afghans. This time it was commanded by General Sir Fredrick Roberts V.C. (later Field Marshal Lord Roberts of Kandhar) whose father had taken part in the battle of Kalanga under General Gillespie.

The massacre of the British mission had no sooner been perpetrated than Yakub Khan found himself in a bad way. His Sirdars (chiefs) urged him to raise the banner of "Jehad" or religious war, a measure for which he had no nerve. The result was that he resolved to leave Kabul and commit himself to the protection of Roberts and his army. The Amir arrived at the British camp at Kushi accompanied by his eldest son and some of his Sirdars. The Amir and his entourage accompanied Roberts to Kabul. On 12th October, the day of General Roberts' durbar, in Balla Hissar, which Yakub Khan was also to attend, he told Roberts that he would not go to the durbar. What he specifically apprehended is unknown. He told Roberts that he had decided to abdicate the throne, and begged that he might be allowed to do so at once. Roberts explained that the acceptance of the resignation rested not with him but with the Viceroy, pending whose decision the General desired matters should remain as they were with affairs continuing to be conducted in the Amir's name as before. To this the Amir consented. His tents were moved to the vicinity of Roberts' headquarters and a closer surveillance over him was maintained.

On 28th October the following announcement was made:-

"The Amir has of his own free will abdicated his throne and left Afghanistan without a government. The British government now commands that all Afghan authorities, Chiefs and Sirdars, do continue their functions in maintaining order—till permanent arrangements are made...."

General Roberts became satisfied from the results of the proceedings of the court of inquiry, that the attack on the Residency, if not actually instigated by Yakub Khan might at least have been checked by active exertion on his part. According to another source of information it was found that the Amir was contemplating a flight toward Turkistan, which made it necessary to place him in close confinement. He remained a close prisoner till 1st December, when after taking their leave of Roberts, the Amir and his entourage surrounded by a strong British escort started their journey to India.

Eventually the British placed Dost Mohammad's eldest grandson, Abdur Rehman, on the throne of Kabul. In 1868 Yakub Khan had defeated Abdur Rehman at Bamian and restored his own father Sher Ali on the Kabul throne to the exclusion of Abdur Rehman's father, Afzal Khan.

After the battle of Kandhar in September 1880, in which Roberts defeated Yakub Khan's brother Ayoub Khan, temporary peace reigned in Afghanistan and the British decided to withdraw from that country. The province of Kandhar was also handed over to Abdur Rehman, thus ending the second Anglo-Afghan War. History repeated itself a hundred years later when the Russians occupied the country and placed their puppet as head of Government at Kabul. After a few years of occupation they (the Russians) too decided to withdraw as they could not contain the rebels operating from Pakistan and Iran.

The Doon was selected as a convenient backwater, probably because of its peculiar isolated position and mild climate, in which to confine Yakub Khan on his arrival in India. He was in Dehra in March 1880, and lived first on the estate opposite the present Electric Department's office on East Canal Road. It was he who built the high wall, around the place to obtain the necessary privacy for his harem. Later he built a double storied miniature palace, on the lines of Balla Hissar, lower down along East Canal Road, facing the parade ground. This is where the State Bank of India building now stands. Yakub Khan was accompanied by a large retinue, which included three prominent Sirdars, relatives and staff, some of whom were resident in Dehra and others scattered all over India. Descendants of some of the people of his retinue are still living in Dalanwala and in the original compound. The present Electric Department's old building and compound, referred to above, was occupied and owned by one of his Sirdars, who was the father of General Nadir Khan. Nadir Khan was born in this building in 1883 and brought up and educated in Dehra. After the third Anglo-Afghan War of 1919-1920 he went to Kabul and became the Amir as a result of the parleys at Mussoorie, between the British and the Afghans who were staying at the Savoy Hotel. To commemorate the signing of the Anglo-Afghan treaty King Amanullah had a mosque built in the Library bazar area of Mussoorie. This mosque still stands and is called Masjid-a-Amania or Mosque of Amanullah.

In Mussoorie Yakub Khan was provided a house called Bellvue, by the government, as a summer residence. The house was situated on the southern spur of Vincent's Hill beyond the Library. While in Mussoorie he was escorted by four men of a British Infantry regiment, one of whom was a J.C. Fisher. Fisher's son stayed on in Mussoorie and became an "Undertaker" till he himself was buried in the local cemetry. One of his sons still lives in the Doon and can be sometimes seen roaming around Mussoorie and Dehra collecting scrap to sell and make a living. The Masonic Fraternity also gives him a monthly stipend.

Coming back to Yakub Khan, while in Mussoorie, he had free access to all parts of the town and its surroundings, and frequently took advantage of it by riding around on his horse accompanied by his escort and a British Political Officer attached to him. The Amir however under estimated the extent of his freedom as is seen from the following incident.

The English officer, who accompanied the Amir on his rides, could not understand the prisoner's habit of suddenly spurring his horse into a fast gallop without a word of warning to his companion. These bursts of speed became more and more frequent and the officer put it down to mere whim, till one day the full meaning was brought home to him in a most discomforting manner. The Englishman had stopped to converse with a friend while the rest of the party ambled on till the bifurcation of the road was reached at the Library, whereupon the Amir spurred his pony to dart forward down the road going to Rajpur and perhaps to freedom. That, at least, was what the officer thought the sudden spurt down the Rajpur Road was manouvered for, and his only chance of intercepting the Amir was to get his own pony to leap down the hill side to the road below, which is what he did. The Amir was stopped and made to come back. The whole incident was reported to the Viceroy and orders were sought for future line of action under similar situations. The telegraphic reply was, "Don't hurt one hair of his head".

Initially, as mentioned earlier, a special British Political Officer of the rank of a Deputy Collector was in charge of the colony of Afghans in Dehra and Mussoorie, but in later years he was replaced by a Tehsildar on Special Duty styled Political Tehsildar. The civil war and the tussle for the throne in Afghanistan, after World War I, prompted the British Indian Government to exercise closer surveillance over Yakub Khan's relatives in India, particularly after the escape of one of his sons, Abdul Karim Khan from Dehra Dun. Practically the whole colony of Afghans in Dehra was removed to Burma for safety. A number of them returned after Nadir Khan moved to Kabul, and peace had been restored in Afghanistan.

Yakub Khan died in Dehra in November 1923 and was buried in his family's cemetry on the Raipur Road across the Rispana river.

Yakub Khan's children were living all over India including what is now Pakistan. His eldest son Crown Prince Musa Khan became a Christian and lived in Dehra till 1947 when he migrated to Kabul where he died in 1951. Another of Yakub's sons, Abdul Karim, on escaping from exile made a bid for the Afghan throne during King Amanullah's time. Abdul Karim was able to besiege Kabul but at the eleventh hour was betrayed by one of his commanders. He was later made prisoner by the British and deported to Burma where he died (some say murdered) in exile. One of Yakub's 13 sons Abdul Rahim won recognition as an accomplished calligrapher. He died in the United States. The Amir's second son Mohamad Yunus, was a mystic and he died in Dehra in 1931. Today the only direct descendants of Yakub Khan living in Dehra are his grandson Sardar Azim Khan, son of Nabi Khan and Osman Khan son of Azim Khan. The other descendants of the Amir and his entourage living in the Doon, are well integrated in the Indian mainstream. They have worked or are working in Government departments like the Air Force, Oil and Natural Gas Commission, Police and local organisations like the Society for the Prevention of Cruelty to Animals. One of them has even been elected to Uttar Pradesh's legislature. Sardar Azim Khan for 45 years, till 1947, remained a political prisoner. A pension was given to him by the then Indian Government which is still being paid by the Government of India.

One day a strapping young Brahmin lad named Lal Singh Rohtasya, from Kaithal (in present day Haryana), arrived at the court of Maharaja Ranjit Singh, at Lahore, seeking employment. He was the youngest son of Misr Amir Chand, who was the Head Cashier in Ranjit Singh's treasury. On being employed he inveigled himself into his employer's good books to the extent that he ultimately rose to become the Wazir or Prime Minister, and the unabashed lover of Rani Jindan, the mother of Maharaja Dalip Singh. She was a woman of extraordinary beauty and talent and was the daughter of one of Ranjit Singh's army officers. A year before his death in June 1839 Ranjit Singh had gone through a form of marriage with her. She has been described in various terms by her contemporaries. Lord Ellenbrough said of her, "She seems to be a woman of determined courage, the only person at Lahore apparently who has courage". Her name was linked with many courtiers. At one time she was said to have become pregnant through a liaison with Lal Singh. She became very ill after an abortion and it was said openly that if she died, Lal Singh would be executed. She survived the illness. Through her influence Lal Singh was given the title of Raja and he dropped the name of Rohtasya being known only as Raja Lal Singh.

Lal Singh's influence on Rani Jindan was so strong that at times she had to mediate between him and her brother Jawahar Singh. In 1845 the English envoy Broadfoot reported to his government, the following incident which occurred after the death of Ranjit Singh.

"A quarrel arose between Lal Singh and Jawahar Singh owing to his jealousy over the former's resumption of his visits to the Rani, after his recovery from cholera, of which there was then a serious epidemic in Lahore. Lal Singh aware that the Maharani had a passionate desire for him, tried to undermine Jawahar Singh's standing with his sister by letting her know that he was afraid to visit her because he might be murdered at her brother's behest. She cleverly brought about a reconciliation between the two, and to celebrate it presented each of them with a beautiful slave girl, both of whom she had received from a Sikh chief who knew of her fondness for attractive girls. With the girls went the message that she expected that they would do proper honour to her gift".

Broadfoot described the Rani's appetite for sex thus:

"Messalina picked big men and Catherine liked variety, but what do you think...of four young fellows changed as they cease to give satisfaction passing every night with the Rani...."

In August 1845 Broadfoot complained that he was unable to get a reply to his letters "because the Rani, Jawahar Singh and Raja Lal Singh were all drunk together with the Khalsa Generals. They listen to no business but send for dancing girls, Jawahar Singh dresses himself as one and dances with the rest".

Ranjit Singh had concocted a new drink, which he made popular at court, and which contained orange spirit, crushed emeralds, pearls and brandy. "A horrible spirit, one drop of which actually burnt my lips," confessed Emily Eden, Lord Auckland's sister, on their visit to Lahore.

After the death of Ranjit Singh the struggle for power at Lahore had started between various factions, culminating in the army Panchayat taking over the affairs of State on the assassination of Rani Jindan's brother, Jawahar Singh, in September 1845. It acted in the name of the Khalsa. The British did not like this new form of government. They instructed their envoy Major George Broadfoot to make it clear to the court at Lahore that no other form of government, except a monarchy, would be recognised. The army with its self-constituted Panchayats was seen in no other light than as servants of the government. The Sikh treasury was empty and the rebellious Khalsa army was clamouring for war with the English. Even Rani Jindan and Lal Singh were afraid of the Khalsa. They wanted it destroyed, somehow. Even one of Broadfoot's assistants remarked, "the sooner we put down the rabble army the better. We are too near it for the example not to be detrimental".

The policy of the Rani, Lal Singh and the Chiefs was to establish the army on the Sutlej and bring on a war so that they could get freedom from the Khalsa. Raja Gulab Singh of Jammu also warned the British that the Sikhs intended war, and that he himself would support the British. By 10th December, 1845 the Sikh army was on the move crossing the Sutlej at Harike-Patan, opposite Ferozepur, under Tej Singh and Lal Singh. In spite of the fact that the town of Ferozepur was poorly defended by the British garrison under General Littler, and repeated requests by the Khalsa troops to Lal Singh to lead them against Littler's force Lal Singh refused. His excuse was that he wanted to fight only the Commander-in-Chief and considered anyone else below his notice. It was an excuse for treason.

Lal Singh, the Wazir, and Tej Singh, the Commander-in-Chief of the Lahore Darbar were in the field hoping to see their uncontrollable troops destroyed by the British. The British, as victors, would then keep the two in power as reliable ministers in a dependency of England. According to Nicholson, one of Broadfoot's assistants, Lal Singh had already in a letter requested the English "to consider him and the Bibi Sahiba (Rani Jindan) as their friends and cut up the 'Burchhas' or the uncontrollable Khalsa ruffians on their behalf." Hence there was no point in Lal Singh and Tej Singh compromising themselves by destroying Littler's small force.

Nicholson had also received a letter from Lal Singh, after having crossed the Sutlej, affirming his friendship with the English and asking what he should best do. He was told not to attack Ferozepur, but march towards the Governor General delaying it as much as he could. Lal Singh followed the advice and divided the Lahore army into two. Tej Singh with his troops proceeded towards Ferozepur to threaten but not attack Littler's while Lal Singh led the other part south to Pheru Shahar (later known as Ferozeshahar). Thus, through their treachery, Littler and his troops were saved from a possible massacre. Lal Singh entrenched the larger part of his army at Ferozeshahar and himself went on to intercept Gough and Hardinge. He was surprised to find the enemy at Mudki, and in spite of its superiority in men and arms ordered his own troops to start the fight. Lal Singh himself returned to Ferozeshahar leaving his troops leaderless. They fought a hand to hand battle which continued till the mid-night of 18th December, 1845. After the loss of half the force and a number of heavy guns the Sikhs withdrew from Mudki.

On the morning of 21st December General Gough, the British Commander-in-Chief, and his force came in sight of the Sikh forces at Ferozeshahr. By the afternoon General Littler, who had eluded Tej Singh joined forces with Gough. That afternoon the battle started and carried on late into the evening without any results. The next morning Tej Singh armed with his troops from Ferozepur attacked the English whose morale was low because of paucity of ammunition. Then suddenly as the victory for the Sikhs was in sight Tej Singh ordered his troops to retreat. Gough realised that the Sikh Commanders Lal Singh and Tej Singh had kept their promise and committed treason against the Lahore government.

According to Lt. Col. Gardner, an American in the service of the Lahore Durbar, Lal Singh ran back to Lahore after the first encounter at Mudki, "preferring the embraces of Venus to the triumphs of Mars". At the palace he found that instead of welcoming him to her bed, the Rani jeered at him for running away, and the court followed her example. Soon however, she once again succumbed to his sexual prowess and issued orders that there were to be no more jokes at his expense.

The next example of treachery by Lal Singh was when he posted himself a little up the river to where Tej Singh's forces were stationed at Sobraon, to prevent an attack on Amritsar.

Gough decided to make a frontal attack on Sobraon, which he was to later describe as 'the Waterloo of India' and destroy the Sikh army in one blow. Through inter-mediaries the British were able to get enough information from Lal Singh to enable them to know the position and strength of the Khalsa army at Sobraon. On the morning of 10th February 1846 the battle of Sobraon started, resulting in a shattering defeat of the Lahore troops. Nearly 10,000 Sikh troops lost their lives in the action, while all their guns were either captured or abandoned in the river.

At the end of first Anglo-Sikh war of 1845-46 the following limerick in Punjabi with puns on the names of the two traitors Lal Singh and Tej Singh became popular.

"Laaloo de laali gai, Teju da giya tej, Ran vich peeth dekhai ke modha aaie pher"
Roughly translated it runs:

Laloo lost his blush of shame,

Teju lost his lustre, by turning their backs in the field they turned the tide and lost the war.

By the treaties of Lahore signed in March, 1846 between the victorious British and the government of Dalip Singh, his mother Rani Jindan was to continue as Regent and Lal Singh as Wazir (Prime Minister). The de-facto power was vested in the English Resident who was posted at Lahore.

As the Lahore Durbar was unable to pay the 15 million rupees as indemnity for the expenses of the war, or to give satisfactory security to the British government for its eventual payment, Maharaja Dalip Singh ceded to the East India Company, as an equivalent of ten million, his possessions in the hilly areas between the Beas and Indus rivers, including the provinces of Kashmir and Hazara, and promising to pay the balance on or before the ratification of the treaty dated 9th March, 1846.

By another treaty dated 16th March, 1846 with Raja Gulab Singh, of Jammu, the British government, "transferred and handed over forever, in independent possession, to Maharaja Gulab Singh and the heirs male of his body, all the hilly and mountainous country, with its dependencies, situated to the eastward of the river Indus and westward of the river Ravi, including Chamba and excluding Lahaul, being part of the territories ceded to the British government by the Lahore state." In consideration of this transfer Gulab Singh was to pay the English seventy-five hundred thousand Nanakshahi rupees (the currency of the time) and in recognition of the supremacy of the British government was to present to it annually one horse, twelve perfect shawl-goats of approved breed (six male and six female) and three pairs of Kashmir (Jamawar) shawls.

Although Gulab Singh became the ruler of Kashmir he did not get its actual possession without difficulty. The governor of Kashmir at the time was Shaikh Imamuddin who had received orders from the Lahore Durbar to hand over his charge to Gulab Singh. At the same time he received a secret note from Raja Lal Singh, the Wazir, who had been acutely vexed by the British government's generosity to Gulab Singh. In the note the Shaikh was advised to resist the handing over of the state to Gulab Singh, which would be receipt in full for payment of his Kashmir accounts to the Lahore Durbar. Gulab Singh offered to keep him on as Governor on a salary of one lac rupees per year. Another alternative before him (the Shaikh) was to try and buy over the British and make himself an independent ruler. He chose the first course and took up arms to oppose the entry of Gulab Singh. In this he was successful as Gulab Singh could not himself drive the Shaikh out by force of arms.

The English on getting the information declared "that the British government would give every possible support to Maharaja Gulab Singh in compelling the servant of the Durbar, Shaikh Imamuddin, to evacuate Kashmir, holding the Durbar responsible for the acts of their officer, in this gross violation of the treaty". The Lahore Durbar was asked to place its troops under Gulab Singh and to act on his instructions. The Maharaja was advised to coerce the rebels to surrender and to offer an amnesty for submission upto a certain date. A British force, under Brigadier Wheeler, was ordered to move up while the Sikh troops moved under the command of the British Agent Henry Lawrence. These measures had the desired effect and Imamuddin capitulated throwing Raja Lal Singh over board, and leaving Srinagar on 23rd October, 1846. Gulab Singh entered his new kingdom on 9th November, 1846 accompanied by Lawrence the English Agent. The next thing to be done was to bring Lal Singh to trial and exposure before all the Chiefs of the Lahore Durbar, for secretly instigating Shaikh Imamuddin in opposing Gulab Singh. The Shaikh had turned "King's evidence" or an "Approver" against Lal Singh, by having placed in Lawrence's hands three original documents, purporting to be instructions from Lal Singh to the Shaikh to oppose Gulab Singh, and to the Darbar's Officers and soldiers in Kashmir, to be faithful and obedient to the Shaikh. These papers were put in as evidence at the subsequent trial of Raja Lal Singh for his complicity in the affair.

The Governor General deputed Frederick Currie, Secretary to the Government of India in the Foreign Department, to investigate in conjunction with Lawrence the conduct of the Shaikh in resisting by force of arms the handing over of Kashmir to the British nominee. Currie was further instructed that if it was proved that Raja Lal Singh did encourage the Shaikh to violate the treaty, the consequences of this betrayal of duty to Dalip Singh and of good faith to the British government, were to be the deposition of the Wazir, Raja Lal Singh from the Wazarat and his immediate exile from the Punjab into British territory. If however the authenticity of the documents produced by the Shaikh, was disproved, he was to take the consequences of his own misdeeds. The Governor-General's further instructions to Currie were, "...... it is not my intention to make the Lahore State responsible for the misconduct of one or more individuals when there is every reason to believe that the misconduct is to be attributed to personal hatred of Maharaja Gulab Singh and not to any political combination to violate the treaty with the British Government. The individuals, however, who may be implicated must be held responsible for their conduct in this transaction...."

Currie was further told that there was a probability in the case of Lal Singh's deposition that Rani Jindan may interpose in his favour and that she would not consent to his exile. In such a situation she should be told that her relations with him have rendered her government as Regent odious to the people, and that she would be deprived of her Regency.

On 1st December Currie arrived at Lahore and it was no longer doubted that an inquiry into the causes of Kashmir insurrection was to take place. Lal Singh and Jindan were in great distress; the former holding private interviews from morning till night, the latter consulting astrologers, and offering sacrifices to the Gods in favour of the Raja.

On 2nd December Currie informed the Lahore ministers and the Chiefs that the next day he would hold a Court of Inquiry. The court was to be open to all and the Chiefs of all ranks were invited. The court consisted of Currie as President and Col. Lawrence, General Littler, Col. Goldie and Mr. John Lawrence as Members. The court which opened at the appointed time was attended amongst others by Raja Lal Singh, Diwan Dina Nath, Khalifa Nuruddin, and Sardars Attar Singh Kalehwala, Tej Singh, Sher Singh Attariwala as well as Shaikh Imamuddin and their supporters.

The Shaikh, on being called upon to make his statement, denounced Raja Lal Singh as the sole instigator of the rebellion in Kashmir against Gulab Singh. Three papers signed by the Raja, two addressed to the Shaikh and one to the Darbar's troops, in Kashmir under the Shaikh's command, were produced in evidence. The papers were:-

1. A letter dated 26th July, 1846 said to have been written by Lal Singh to the Shaikh, desiring him to create disturbances in Kashmir and oppose its occupation by Gulab Singh.

2. An "Iqrarnama" or Deed of Promise dated 25th July, 1846 to the Shaikh engaging to maintain him in his jagirs and to intercede with the British for his Jullundhar

property, and promising further reward to him, and to his followers, if he did as directed.

3. A "Parwana", an Order dated 28th July, 1846 in the name of Maharaja Dalip Singh, to the troops in Kashmir exhorting them to exert themselves and do good service at the bidding of the Shaikh, without fear of consequences, and promising that in that case they would be kept in service when they came to Lahore.

In addition there were four witnesses for the prosecution and one for the defence.

The last of the above mentioned papers was acknowledged by Lal Singh, and the other two, though denied were, in the opinion of the court, fully established to be genuine as well. The evidence was most conclusive, the defence miserably "weak", and after two sittings the court, declared Raja Lal Singh guilty.

On 4th December, on termination of the proceedings of the Court of Inquiry, and after the sentence of "Guilty" was pronounced, Henry Lawrence, along with the rest of the Lahore Ministers, went to the palace, and the result of the investigation and the removal of Lal Singh from the Ministry were communicated to Rani Jindan. Meanwhile Lal Singh was conducted by Lieutanant Edwardes from where the court was held to the Raja's house, in the city. After his deposition as the Prime Minister it was decided to remove him from Lahore as well. This was considered necessary because of his intimacy with the Queen-Mother, who, laying aside all appearances of womanly modesty, had abandoned herself to alternate ravings and intrigues—now cursing, now imploring the other Ministers, the British Resident, in fact anybody and everybody to restore her lover.

In the interest of peace it was considered that both the Raja and Rani Jindan could not remain in the Punjab. Therefore Lal Singh was to be banished by the Maharaja and sent to Agra in British India. On 14th December, 1846 Maharaja Dalip Singh wrote to Currie informing him, "....that I have deposed the Wazir, and given pre-emptory orders to him to take his departure for Ferozepur (enroute to Agra), without loss of time; that preparations necessary for his departure have been made, and that carriage etc., have been supplied by this government, for the conveyance of his baggage... He has this day, the 1st of Poh, 1903 (Sammat), taken his departure for his destination ......". Lal Singh was escorted out of Lahore by the Assistant British Agent, and was given a monthly pension of Rs. 2000/- from the Lahore state exchequer.

Lal Singh secretly entered the Punjab in October 1848, raised a force in the west and marched from Wazirabad to Gujranwala a place only 60 odd miles north of Lahore. He joined forces with Sher Singh's army. After the battle of Gujrat in February, 1849 the Khalsa army was finally defeated, by the British, and Lal Singh along with Sher Singh surrendered to General Gilbert. As a consequence of this action of Lal Singh's his pension was reduced to Rs. 1000/- instead of Rs. 2000/- per month. The pension was restored to the original amount after 1857 on a representation made by him to the British. In it he pointed out his services to their government during the mutiny, when he helped in keeping peace in the Doon. He had stayed at Agra till October 1852, when he was allowed by the Governor General to reside at Dehra Dun in the winter and Mussoorie in the summer. After his escape from Agra he was kept under strict surveillance till the annexation of the Punjab.

On his arrival in the Doon the Raja purchased a number of properties in Mussoorie and Dehra, some of which are still owned by one branch of his descendants. Obviously he must have been allowed, through Rani Jindan's good offices, to bring away as much loot as possible on leaving Lahore. In June 1862, he petitioned the British praying to be permitted to return to the Punjab, but the request was turned down. His eldest son Raja Ranbir Singh was allowed, after his father's death, to enter the Punjab in 1867. Lal Singh was survived by three sons namely Ranbir Singh, Balbir Singh and Tegh Bahadur Singh. After Lal Singh's death the British conferred the title of Raja on Ranbir Singh as a personal distinction. Ranbir Singh was survived by Raghu Nath Singh whose progeny moved to Calcutta and are living there. Balbir Singh died childless. He was the person as mentioned earlier who set up the Rice, Flour, Oil and Ice Mills in Dehra in 1906. The youngest Tegh Bahadur had one son Col. Kunwar Shamsher Bahadur Singh, whose children still inhabit the Doon. He was one of the leading social figures of the town, was at one time the Chairman of the District Board (Zila Parishad), and a pillar of the British Raj in the Doon. On the other hand it was he who stopped the British members from liquidating the Dehra Dun Club Limited in 1947.

In 1902 the Doon gave refuge to another potentate, this time from the Himalaya mountains. He was Deb Shamsher, the second son out of the seventeen of Dhir Shamsher the youngest brother of General Sir Jang Bahadur Rana, G.C.B. etc. of Nepal. Jang Bahadur had come to power after the famous ''KOT'' (the quadrangle in the Royal Guard building), massacre and became the Prime Minister and Commander in-Chief of the army, as well as the de facto ruler of Nepal. The Shah king was relegated to being only a titular head of state. These positions were to be held, in this family, for the next hundred odd years, till 1951, when King Tribhuvan Bir Bikram Shah regained his throne after having sought political asylum in India. After Jang Bahadur's death in 1877 the succession to the offices of the Prime Minister and the Commander-in-Chief was from brother to brother rather than from father to son.

In April 1849 Jang Bahadur is reported to have given asylum to Maharani Jindan when she was exiled from Lahore. She had been confined by the British in the fort at Chunar in Uttar Pradesh. She escaped from there by substituting a female slave in her stead. Travelling with a group of pilgrims on their way to the Pashupati Nath temple in Kathmandu she reached Bichhakheri in Nepal. On reaching Nepal she disclosed her identity and was thereafter treated as a state guest. The British asked her extradition but Jang Bahadur refused as it was against the laws governing the granting of political asylum and hospitality. Later she joined her son Dalip Singh in England where she died in 1863.

Succession to the offices held by Jang Bahadur would sometimes come through blood-shed and at others by kidnapping and exiling. Deb Shamsher and his brothers are supposed to have killed their Prime Minister uncle Udip Shamsher as he was showing favour to Jang Bahadur's sons in preference to Dhir Shamsher's the latter being sons of the younger brother. The motive behind this assassination was to pre-empt the bid to wrest succession to the Prime ministership by the cousins, namely Jang Bahadur's sons. This was in 1885. By 1893 Deb Shamsher had been elevated, in the line of succession, to the position of being the nominal Commander-in-Chief of the Nepalese army while his younger brother Chandra Shamsher was the executive chief. It was in these capacites that the two brothers received the British Indian Army Commander-in-Chief, Field Marshal Lord Roberts, when he went to a military review held in his honour, during his visit to Nepal in that year.

In March 1901 Deb became the Prime Minister on the death of his elder brother Bhim Shamsher. His reign was to last for exactly three months before he was kidnaped and sent into exile by his younger brothers. Chandra Shamsher was the chief conspirator and succeeded Deb.

On 26th June Deb along with His Majesty King Prithvi Bir Vikram Shah, who was also a cousin and friend, went to a prize distribution function at the local High School in Kathmandu. After the function the two went to one of the Rana's palaces, a property which was in dispute. Deb was to arbitrate among the parties to the dispute. Once inside the building the king was separated from Deb by his younger brothers and whisked off by a side door. Deb was informed by Dumbar Shamsher, one of the brothers, that "Maharaja Chandra has ordered me to inform your Highness that it is owing to your too much contact with the king....that you have suffered this misfortune". In that brief announcement Chandra Shamsher had, by being addressed as Maharaja, been made the Prime Minister. Deb remonstrated with him but to no avail.

The reasons given by the Viceroy, in his despatch to the Secretary-of-State for India, for the downfall of Deb Shamsher are more appealing: "During his brief term of office, Deb Shamsher is said to have been active in introducing reforms. He had instituted a Nepalese news-paper. His views on education were liberal, and he had taken steps towards the abolition of slavery. It seems not improbable that these progressive measures contributed to his downfall".

All this happend in the late afternoon and Deb was kept in a room till 9 P.M. when curfew used to be clamped in the town. He was then taken out of Kathmandu on his way to exile at Dhankota, a town in Eastern Nepal and twenty days march from the Capital. On the first night stop on the road a letter was delivered to him from Chandra Shamsher telling him that he had been obliged to depose him by order of the King so as to save the Shamsher family. Deb's escort commander, who was one of his nephews, told him that he and other men in the Rana family had been told that Deb was going to expel them from Nepal. It was for fear of this that they (brothers and nephews) had gone to Chandra for protection and the result was this deposition. Deb was outraged for he had no such thought. After his arrival at Dhankota his senior Maharani joined him after a couple of months, and at the end of October she delivered a daughter.

Although he was under surveillance around the clock he was free to move about in the area. On these outings he would be accompanied by a guard under an officer. After his wife's confinement Deb starting formulating plans for his escape to India. Towards this end he wrote to his brother Chandra Shamsher, the new Prime Minister, that he may be allowed to shift his residence for climatic reasons, to a place called Illam. This place is a short distance from the Indo-Nepal frontier near Darjeeling and has a fortress. He was allowed to go and look up the place. From Illam he went to the village called Maipokhri where he apparently knew a man called Agham Singh. With his help Deb worked out his escape route to India and was also given a sword to arm himself with. He rode out on the track that Agham Singh had told him of. Deb, being better mounted than his guards, suddenly spurred his horse into a gallop and left them standing; the only one who managed to keep up with him was the stable-boy who was clinging to the horse's tail.

The boy, who could not keep up for long, implored him to stop for if he let go and left him, he would certainly be hanged. Deb did not stop but swinging round, in his saddle, with a quick back-hand drive chopped off his horse's tail. The boy fell away, still clinging to the severed tail which would explain how he had escaped and the boy could not be held responsible. Deb escaped into India and arrived in Darjeeling. He requested the British Deputy Commissioner of Darjeeling to forward his representation to the Viceroy. In the representation he requested permission to reside at Calcutta and Darjeeling till he could build himself a house at Darbhanga, in Bihar where the Raja was his friend. He was allowed to stay in British India. As for his place of residence, he was told that he would not be allowed to live either at Darjeeling or at Darbhanga as both these places were too near the Nepalese frontier for comfort especially since he had it in mind to stage a comeback. One of the alternatives suggested to him was Mussoorie.

He came to see the place and saw Fairlawn estate sited on the Jharipani ridge. Having taken a liking to it he bought the place, levelled the hill, built a palace in Nepalese style and settled down. He was offered General Dick's Dalanwala Tea Estate for Rs. 75,000/- which he did not buy. It was later purchased by a conglomerate of local Bania Businessmen, who developed it into the present Dalanwala Colony. In due course his family along with its entourage of concubines, "TALIMAS", and a host of male attendants arrived along with the baggage consisting of all their movables, including stocks of rice, pickles and other household items. While most of the wealth had come concealed in waist belts around the women's waists, the family's priceless heirloom, the "NAU LAKHA" necklace, came concealed in a jar of pickle. This ornament had been taken by Jang Bahadur from Nana Sahib when to took refuge with him, on escaping from the British in 1857. The name connotes that at that time it cost rupees nine hundred thousand. This piece of jewellery was later sold by Deb to his friend the Maharaja of Darbhanga. It was probably sold to raise funds when Deb organised a plot to kill Chandra Shamsher during his visit to India to meet the Viceroy. The plot was foiled by the British intelligence in India. Later the two brothers met once in Calcutta. Part of the conversation at this meeting ran as follows:-

Chandra: "So, Your Highness you escaped and tricked me of your person".

Deb, who was also a stickler for protocol, replied: "Your Highness tricked me of my rightful kingdom." The emphasis being on the word kingdom.

This confrontation was witnessed by some of Chandra's sons who for the first time saw and heard their formidable father worsted and flushed red in the face at this sally.

The Rana men, for that matter all Gorkha men, are known for their love of wine, women and song. The Ranas would vie with each other as to the number of women that had been in their beds and had been made love to—Jang Bahadur, being the superman of the clan, is given the credit of having had the largest number of women in bed— over fourteen hundred. He would tell everyone, "Never miss a chance with any woman you can get - any woman". Maharaja Judha Shamsher Jang Bahadur Rana, who came and settled in Dehra fifty years after Deb, had a record of over twelve hundred. Another brother Kaiser Shamsher had nine hundred which was considered a poor record. Even the king had his women and he and Deb would present each other with pretty young girls as if they were chattels. Some of them who are called "TALIMA" are a blend of a concubine and a courtesan. According to a family tale Deb had a couple of concubines sleeping with him even on the night of his deposition. At Fairlawn his four poster bed was like a small room, fitted with mirrors on the sides and the canopy. The reason for the mirrors is obvious. Apart from the favourite woman of the night in his bed, often there would be other women sleeping alongside in the same room. It was rumoured at the time that because he caught his eldest son in bed with one of his Ranis he threw the son out of the house and disinherited him at the same time. The son came down and settled in Dehra, as he like his father could not go back to Nepal.

Before his death Deb had been partially paralysed and the happening of this illness had been dreamt earlier in the night by his Maharani who was in bed with him at the time. After the stroke Deb wrote to Chandra Shamsher saying: "Your Highness, I am growing old and am now a broken man. Pray grant that I may see my country once again before I die".

After a long silence Chandra's reply was, "Just as no forest can contain two tigers, nor one scabbard two swords, so there is no room in Nepal for me and you." On getting this reply Deb burst into a flood of tears. He died, of a broken heart, in 1914 at the age of fifty-two.

When Deb had arrived in Mussoorie his Maharani had borne him a son and three daughters. While in Mussoorie, till her death in 1909, she had another three children - all boys. The boys were named Narendra, Jagat and Bahadur and the youngest was called Mussoorie, all with the surname of Shamsher Jang Bahadur Rana. Of the daughers Madalsa married the Maharaja of Sirmur, and was the mother of Rajendra Prakash the last ruler of Sirmur. His daughter married Maharaj Bhawani Singh of Jaipur. The next one Bhuban was married to an ICS Officer, Raja Pratap Bikram Shah of Singhai—a Zamindari in Oudh. Her daughter Gita married General Raj Kumar Jasbir Singh of Jind. The third daughter was married to the Raja of Pratapgarh and died young. Of Deb's children, the families of Narendra and Bhuban live in Dehra while the son Jagat lives on his estate "Sun Saan" in the Western Doon. Fairlawn, his home in Jharipani, has been sold and Bahadur's as well as Mussoorie's families have gone to Nepal.

Amongst the people, other than those mentioned earlier, there are a large number of families still resident in the Valley whose ancestors came and settled here. Some of them have been here since the Garhwali and Gorkha times, while the majority of them particularly the business families, came after the British occupation.

Apart from the Darbar Sahib (Ram Rai's endowment) being the largest Zamindar (landlord), the other Zamindars of repute in the Valley were Chowdhary Shib Ram of Doonga and Mamraj Singh of Jassowala. Another family was that of Chowdhary Diwan Singh of Sahaspur, one of the earliest Tomars from the plains to settle in the Valley.

The Rawats of Ajabpur village are indigenous Rajputs of hill extraction. The "Kalals" or Kalars or Kalwars (as they are known in the plains) were concentrated mostly in the villages of Seola Kalan, Seola Khurd, Seola Majra, Jogiwala, Badripur and a few other villages around Dehra.

Unlike their namesakes of the plains (who are reputed for their brewing, selling and consuming of liquor) they, the Kalals of Dehra disclaim all connection with the production and consumption of spirits. Their disclaimer in the latter regard is contrary to facts. However they are undoubtedly some of the earliest settlers in the Doon. According to Dampier who did the Revenue Settlement of the Doon in 1907 there was a saying in the Doon that:-

Kaulagir Ka Nauthal

Seola Ka Kalal, aur

Ghate Ka Sal, ek hain — meaning

that the Nautial Brahmins of Kaulagarh, the Kalals of Seola and the Sal trees on the slopes of the Shiwaliks are all coeval. The other ancient settlers were the Banjaras. They were, according to tradition, the earliest colonists and paid homage to the Garhwal Darbar for their land holdings. The village of Banjarawala is named after them. They were of Hindu and Muslim stock.

Subsequent to the British conquest of the valley the Maharaja of Sirmur purchased quite a few properties in the Doon. The families of Lalas Nand Lal, Partap Singh, Mana Ram and Tulsi Ram were prominent among the Bania landlords. One of the best private forests in village Kandhauli, which was valued in 1901 at rupees one lac, was purchased by Partap Singh for a little over one thousand rupees from an impecunious Rawat Zamindar in 1900. The largest among the Gujar community was Chaudhri Ram Singh of Timli.

The two main Brahmin Zamindars were Pandit Fakir Chand of Raipur and Mahant Paras Ram of Rishikesh. They were the head priests of the Shakumbari and Bharat Mandirs (temples) respectively. Another Brahmin who purchased a lot of land in Dehra and Mussoorie was Raja Lal Singh.

The Powells, descendants of one of the earliest British settlers, and the Quarrys, Ouseleys, Raynors, Vansittarts, Rennies, Macphersons, Thatchers and Swetenhams were amongst the European Zamindars.

With the withdrawal of the British Government from India in August 1947, and the resulting Hindu-Muslim riots in the Doon, following the partition of the country, the local Europeans and Anglo-Indians sold their properties and went "Back Home". Some of them left for fear of being murdered in their beds while others because of the change in the political, economic and social conditions. Depending on the size of one's purse and the shade of ones skin "Back Home" could be anywhere from London to Bangalore. However, some diehard India hands like the Quarrys, the Martyns, the Raynors, Sir Edmund Gibson and a few others like them stayed on. They were not sorry for having done so as they continued to live the kind of life they were accustomed to. Those who left were replaced by a new breed of "Brown Sahibs" which had sprung up from amongst the Natives. The Dehra Dun Club became their meeting place before it was taken over by the local Nouveau-riche. There are still a few survivors in the Valley of this breed of Brown Sahibs.

The English came, they saw, they conquered and stayed for a hundred and thirty three years. Then, all of a sudden they left, for "Home", making way for the refugees from Pakistan to establish their new "Home" in 'The Doon', and thereby hangs another tale.

BIBLIOGRAPHY

1. G.R.C. Williams, B.C.S.—Historical and Statistical Memoir of Dehra Dun, Roorkee, 1874.
2. A.L. Basham—The Wonder that was India, Fontana Books, Calcutta, 1971.
3. L.P. Sharma—Ancient History of India, Vikas Publishing House, New Delhi, 1981.
4. Hari Krishan Raturi—Garhwal Ka Ithas, Bhagirathi Publishing House, Tehri Garhwal, 1980 (In Hindi).
5. Col. R.H. Phillimore—Historical Records of the Survey of India, Vols. II and IV, Dehra Dun, 1950 and 1958.
6. A.R. Gill—Valley of the Doon, Doon Printing House, Dehra Dun, 1952.
7. Rogers and Beveridge—The TUZUK-I-Jahangiri or Memoirs of Jahangir, Munshi Ram Manohar Lal, Nai Sarak, Delhi, 1968.
8. Dr. Y.S. Katoch—Archaeology in Mid-Himalaya published by him, Lucknow, 1981 (In Hindi).
9. Romila Thapar—A History of India Vol. I, Penguin Books, England, 1966.
10. Percival Spear—A History of India Vol. II, Penguin Books, England, 1981.
11. Garhwal-Ke-Pramukh Tirath—Garhwal University Srinagar Garhwal, 1981 (In Hindi).
12. Peter Mayne—Friends in High Places, London, 1974.
13. Col. Hugh Pearse—The Herseys, London, 1899.
14. Eliot & Dowson—History of India as told by its own Historians, Kitab Mahal Pvt. Ltd., Allahabad.
15. Sirmur State Gazetteer.
16. Dr. S.P. Dabral—Uttarakhand Ka Ithas - Vir Gatha Prakashan, Doggadda, Garhwal (9 Vols. in Hindi).
17. 100 Years of Forestry in India, Vol. I and II - Government of India, 1978.
18. Forest Research Institute Golden Jubilee Souvenir, Dehra Dun, 1956.
19. Centenary Souvenir of Dehra Dun Arya Samaj (In Hindi) Arya Samaj, Dehra Dun, 1980.
20. Capt O.E.S. Power—Dehra Dun Past and Present, Gorkha Press Co. Ltd., Dehra Dun, 1929.
21. Quarter-Master Sergeant George Noakes - Historical Account of H.M's 34 and 55 Regiments, England, 1875.
22. Sergeant Major T.H. Vickers - 55 Regiment in India during 1863-1869. 55 Regimental Press, Chakrata 1870.
23. Lt. Genl. Sir Robert Baden Powell - Indian Memories. Herbert Jenkins Ltd., London, 1914.

24. Andrew Wilson—The Abode of Snow. William Blackwood and Sons, London, 1875.

25. Harbans Singh—The Heritage of the Sikhs, Manohar Lal Publications, New Delhi, 1983.

26. Hari Ram Gupta—History of Sikh Gurus. U.C. Kapur & Sons, New Delhi, 1973.

27. Surjit Singh Gandhi—History of the Sikh Gurus. Gurdas Kapur and Sons (P) Ltd., Delhi, 1978.

28. D.P. Varun, I.A.S—Gazetteer of Dehra Dun District, U.P. Government Press, Allahabad, 1979.

29. Balgobind—Life of Raja Sir Shamshere Prakash, G.C.S.I. of Sirmur. Thacker, Spink & Co. Calcutta, 1901.

30. Maulana Abul Kalam Azad—India Wins Freedom, Orient Longman Private Ltd., Calcutta, 1959.

31. Eric Wakeham—Bravest Soldier - Life of Major General Sir Hugh Robert Rollo Gillespie, London.

32. R.K. Mookerji—Emperor Ashoka, Allahabad.

33. E.T. Atkinson—The Himalayan Gazetteer of North-West Provinces. Allahabad, 1882.

34. Valmiki-Ramayan. Gita Press Gorakhpur, 1985 (In Hindi).

35. Lt. Col. J.C. Fife-Cookson—Tiger Shooting in the Doon and Ulwar. Chapman & Hall, London, 1887.

36. Lady Emily Eden—Up the Country—Letters from India, London, 1866.

37. H.G. Keene—Hindustan Under Free Lances, London, 1890.

38. Field Marshall Lord Roberts—Forty One Years in India - From Subaltern to Commander-in-Chief. London, 1898.

39. Lady Dufferin—Our Viceregal Life in India, 1884-1888 "Selections from My Journal", London, 1890.

40. Regimental History of 2nd King Edward's Own Gorkhas (The Sirmoor Rifle Regiment). Vol. II. London, 1936.

41. Regimental History of the 9th Gorkha Rifles 1817-1947. New Delhi, 1984.

42. Duncan Forbes—Johnny Gurkha. Robert Hale, London, 1964.

43. The Rambler—A Mussoorie Miscellany. Mafasilite Press, Mussoorie, 1936.

44. F. Bodycot—Guide to Mussoorie. Mafasilite Printing Works Mussoorie, 1907.

45. H.G. Walton, I.C.S.—Dehra Dun a Gazetteer, Government Press, Allahabad, 1911.

46. Archibald Forbes—The Afghan Wars. Seely & Co., London, 1892.

47. Fanny Parks—Wanderings of a Pilgrim in Search of the Picturesque with revelations of life in the Zenana, London 1878.

48. G.R. Dampier, I.C.S.—Final Settlement Report of the Dehra Dun Tehsil, U.P. Government Press, Allahabad, 1907.

49. Kushwant Singh—History of the Sikhs. Oxford University Press, New Delhi, 1970.

50. Lt. Col. H.J. Huxford, O.B.E.—Regimental History of the 8th Gorkha Rifles 1824-1949. Gale and Ploden Ltd., Aldershot, England, 1952.

51. D.N. Wadia—Geology of India, Tata-McGraw Hill Publishing Co., Ltd., New Delhi, 1983.

52. Jawaharlal Nehru—An Autobiography, Allied Publishers Private Ltd., New Delhi, 1962.

53. Nilkanta Sastri & Srinivasachari—Advanced History of India, Allied Publishers, New Delhi, 1971.
54. B.D. Basu—Rise of the Christian Power in India, M.C. Sarkar & Sons, Calcutta, 1923.
55. Thomas Pinney—The Letters of Rudyard Kipling, Vol. I, 1872-89, University of Iowa Press, Iowa City, USA-1990.